Truth and Words

Truth and Words

Gary Ebbs

OXFORD
UNIVERSITY PRESS

OXFORD
UNIVERSITY PRESS

Great Clarendon Street, Oxford OX2 6DP

Oxford University Press is a department of the University of Oxford.
It furthers the University's objective of excellence in research, scholarship,
and education by publishing worldwide in

Oxford New York

Auckland Cape Town Dar es Salaam Hong Kong Karachi
Kuala Lumpur Madrid Melbourne Mexico City Nairobi
New Delhi Shanghai Taipei Toronto

With offices in

Argentina Austria Brazil Chile Czech Republic France Greece
Guatemala Hungary Italy Japan Poland Portugal Singapore
South Korea Switzerland Thailand Turkey Ukraine Vietnam

Oxford is a registered trade mark of Oxford University Press
in the UK and in certain other countries

Published in the United States
by Oxford University Press Inc., New York

British Library Cataloguing in Publication Data

Data available

Library of Congress Cataloging in Publication Data
Ebbs, Gary.
Truth and words / Gary Ebbs.
p. cm.
Includes bibliographical references and index.
ISBN 978-0-19-955793-6
1. Truth. 2. Predicate (Logic) 3. Language and logic. 4. Grammar, Comparative and
general—Sentences. I. Title.
BC171.E23 2009
306.4401—dc22
2008048453

Typeset by Laserwords Private Limited, Chennai, India
Printed in the United Kingdom by
Lightning Source UK Ltd., Milton Keynes

ISBN 978-0-19-955793-6 (Hbk)
ISBN 978-0-19-969226-2 (Pbk)

To Hilary Putnam

Preface

This book is an attempt to fuse together two apparently independent ideas—the idea that truth and satisfaction are disquotational and the idea that unless we see good reason in a given context for not doing so, we are entitled to trust the non-deliberative identifications of sentences and words on which we rely when we take ourselves to agree or disagree with others, to learn from what they say, or to express a new discovery. It is not my first attempt to link these ideas. In *Rule-Following and Realism* (Ebbs 1997), I recommended that we describe what it is to share a language from our perspective as participants in actual linguistic interactions with other speakers, and proposed that we take such descriptions to license us to apply our disquotational definitions of truth and satisfaction directly to other speakers' words and to our own words as we used them in the past. I still think this proposal points in the right direction. But I now think it does not go far enough. If we wish to describe our linguistic practices in a way that fits with a disquotational account of truth and satisfaction, we need a more radical approach.

My approach in this book is shaped at every step by the assumption that we desire to clarify and facilitate our inquiries by regimenting our sentences and formulating logical generalizations. Given this assumption, I ask, "Do we need a truth predicate?" and "If so, what sort of truth predicate do we need?" I answer these questions in a way that clarifies the non-deliberative identifications of words on which we rely when we take ourselves to agree or disagree with others, to learn from what they say, or to express a new discovery. I explain how to resist our tendency to think of words as individuated by their spellings or pronunciations together with facts about how speakers use them, and show how to construct an alternative conception of words that fits with the non-deliberative identifications of words on which we rely in our inquiries. I propose that we combine this alternative conception of words with our disquotational definitions of truth for sentences as we now use them. The result radically transforms our understanding of truth and related topics, including anti-individualism, self-knowledge, and the intersubjectivity of logic.

During the planning and writing of this book I was fortunate to receive excellent advice and criticism from many friends and colleagues. When I started planning the book in 1998, Tom Ricketts warned me, in a tone of voice that he reserves for his most urgent and provocative philosophical remarks, "There will have to be *regimentation*." I knew he was right, but it took me years to figure out exactly how to fit regimentation into my account (see Chapters 1 and 3). Also in 1998, Hilary Putnam convinced me that Tarski's definitions of 'truth-in-*L*' for sentences individuated *orthographically* (as strings of letters and spaces) are at best *incomplete* because they leave us in the dark about the relationship between those definitions and our ordinary non-deliberative applications of truth to other speakers' utterances. Yet another central part of the book started coming into focus in 1997 and 1998 when I first formulated various versions of my gold–platinum thought experiment (see Chapter 6). Conversations with Adrian Cussins, Brian Loar, Tom Ricketts, Mark Wilson, and George Wilson were especially helpful to me at that stage, but I also learned a great deal from discussions at Arizona State University, Florida State University, Grinnell College, UC-San Diego, UC-Irvine, University of Illinois at Urbana-Champaign, and Smith College, where I presented papers that feature the gold–platinum thought experiment. In my 2000 Central APA symposium paper "Denotation and Discovery", I further developed my view of sameness of satisfaction across time. Mark Wilson was the commentator for that paper; his comments prompted me to clarify how my view applies to natural kind terms found in texts written centuries ago. Starting around 2003, I had several helpful conversations with Henry Jackman, whose temporal externalism is in some ways similar to my view of sameness of satisfaction across time, but in other ways fundamentally different from it (see Chapter 8). In my 2004 Eastern APA symposium paper "Truth and Words", I first presented an alternative to the standard conception of words. This time Steven Gross was the commentator; he urged me to clarify my pragmatic grounds for thinking that a disquotational definition of 'true-in-*L*' is satisfactory only if it implies that we are directly licensed to apply 'true-in-*L*' to other speakers' sentences and our own sentences as we used them in the past. Steven later sent me references to a number of articles that I found very helpful when I wrote Chapter 4. From 2003 to 2006, I participated in a reading group on linguistics and philosophy of language with Peter Lasersohn and Lenny Clapp. In bi-weekly discussions with Peter and Lenny I learned a great deal about recent work in formal semantics, and gradually developed my current view (see Chapter 1) that much of this work can be detached from the controversial explanatory ambitions of its various authors and pressed into service as part of a pragmatic account of regimentation. In the spring semesters of 2005 and 2007, I presented drafts of the book in seminars at the University of Illinois at Urbana-Champaign and Indiana University, respectively; the graduate students in these seminars raised many challenging criticisms that helped me to clarify my arguments. In the final stages of the writing I received excellent criticisms and advice from Katy Abramson, Imogen Dickie, Michael Glanzberg, Steven Gross, David Hills, Henry Jackman, John MacFarlane, Joan Wiener, and two anonymous readers for Oxford University Press. Many others also raised objections or gave me advice that helped me to write this book, including Ben Bayer, Stephen Biggs, Susan Blake, Bill Brewer, Kyle Broom, Jessica Brown, Nancy Cartwright, Hugh Chandler, Yajun Chen, Lenny Clapp, Jim Conant, Mike Dunn, Daniel Estrada, Anthony Everett, Kit Fine, David Finkelstein, Brie Gertler, Sandy Goldberg, Warren Goldfarb, Robert Gooding-Williams, Tara Gilligan, Richard Heck, Jon Jarrett, Darryl Jung, Mark Kaplan, John Koethe, Scott Kimbrough, Phil Kitcher, Phil Kremer, Michael Kremer, Wolfgang Künne, Mark Lance, Peter Lasersohn, Michael Liston, Adam Leite, Brian Loar, Pen Maddy, Ruth Barcan Marcus, Patricia Marino, Mohan Matten, Tim McCarthy, David McCarty, Art Melnick, Tom Meyer, Nathalie Morasch, Michael Morgan, Erica Neely, Charles Parsons, Terry Parsons, Oliver Pooley, Michael Resnick, Sam Rickless, Bill Robinson, Joseph Rouse, Dick Schacht, Fred Schmitt, Peter Schwartz, David Shwayder, Sanford Shieh, Barry Smith, Tom Stoneham, Tadeusz Szubka, Alessandra Tanesini, William Taschek, Kevin Toh, Charles Travis, Steve Wagner, and Chuang Ye. Warm thanks to all.

Most of the material in Chapter 5 was previously published under the title "Learning from Others" (Ebbs 2002a), and Chapter 6 draws heavily from my papers "The Very Idea of Sameness of Extension across Time" (Ebbs 2000) and "Denotation and Discovery" (Ebbs 2003). I thank the editors and publishers of these articles for their permission to include large parts of them in this book.

I received a fellowship at the Center for Advanced Studies at the University of Illinois at Urbana-Champaign (UIUC) to write a first draft of this book (2001—2), several travel grants from UIUC that made it possible for me to present some of the central arguments in this book at other institutions, two grants from the Freeman Fellowship Exchange Program to present some of these arguments at universities in China (2002, 2004), and funding from the British Academy that covered the costs of my attendance at Tom Stoneham's workshops on sameness of extension across time (2004, 2005). I am grateful to these institutions and programmes for their support.

I thank Peter Momtchiloff for his early interest in this project and his patience while I worked on it.

Above all, I thank my wife, Martha, for her unfailing support and understanding throughout this long project.

Gary Ebbs

Bloomington, Indiana
23 September 2008

Contents

Introduction

My goal in this book is to develop an account of truth that we can use to clarify and facilitate our inquiries. Unlike most recent accounts of truth, my account does not aim to analyse a concept we express when we use the ordinary English word 'true', to say what 'true' means, or to explain all our uses of it. Instead, my account of truth is addressed to those of us who desire to clarify and facilitate our inquiries by regimenting our sentences so that we can express logical generalizations, such as "Every sentence of the form '$S \vee \sim S$' is true". I ask, "Do we need a truth predicate to express logical generalizations?" and "If so, what sort of truth predicate do we need?" I answer these questions by showing how to reconcile two appealing yet apparently incompatible answers to them.

The Tarski–Quine Thesis

The first answer, due in essentials to Alfred Tarski and W. V. Quine, is that to express logical generalizations we need a disquotational truth predicate—one that entitles us to affirm such sentences as

'Snow is white' is true if and only if snow is white,

which are instances of the disquotational pattern

(T) '_____' is true if and only if _____ .

This answer takes for granted that the regimented part of our language comprises infinitely many sentences, so we cannot express our acceptance of all regimented sentences of a given form, such as '$S \vee \sim S$', by writing out and affirming an infinitely long conjunction of all of the instances of that form. To express our acceptance of all those sentences and thereby affirm a logical generalization we therefore need some practical way to affirm, in effect, an infinite conjunction of sentences. And for this purpose, according to the first answer, we need a truth predicate that entails all and only (non-paradoxical) instances of (T).[1] Following Tarski, we can each satisfy this need by replacing 'true' with 'true-in-L', where L is the regimented part of our language, and defining 'true-in-L' in terms of *satisfaction*. To define 'true-in-L' for quantified sentences, we must define satisfaction in terms of sequences of objects. I shall explain how to define satisfaction in terms of sequences for a regimented fragment of English in Chapter 2. For present purposes, however, it is enough to see that we can each define something *like* satisfaction for our own one-place predicates by accepting such sentences as

x satisfies 'white' if and only if x is white,

which are instances of the disquotational pattern

(S) x satisfies '____' if and only if x is ____ .

When our definitions of satisfaction for predicates are disquotational in this way, I call the resulting Tarski-style definition of 'true-in-L' disquotational.[2]

Without supplementation, a Tarski-style disquotational definition of 'true-in-L' applies *only* to the sentences for which it is disquotationally defined. But this very limitation of a Tarski-style disquotational definition of 'true-in-L' is what guarantees that the definition is clear. As Quine emphasizes, a disquotational definition of 'true-in-L' has "every bit as much clarity, in any particular application, as is enjoyed by the particular expressions... to which we apply it. Attribution of truth in particular to 'Snow is white', is every bit as clear to us as attribution of whiteness to snow" (Quine 1961a: 138). If our goal is conceptual analysis, it may seem that this clarity comes at too high a price—the price of changing the subject from a concept (if there is one) expressed by our ordinary English word 'true' to an ersatz concept expressed by 'true-in-L' that may be

---

[1] One might object that we can express logical generalizations without using a Tarski-style truth predicate. I raise and answer several versions of this objection in Chapter 2.

[2] What I call a Tarski-style disquotational definition of satisfaction also typically includes disquotational satisfaction clauses for two- (and, in general, n-) place predicates, as well as *non*-disquotational clauses for logical constants, such as 'not', 'or', and 'all'. I give the details in Chapter 2.

useful for some purposes, but does not deserve to be called *truth*. If our leading questions are "Do we need a truth predicate?" and "If so, what sort of truth predicate do we need?", however, then the utility and clarity of Tarski-style disquotational definitions of 'true-in-*L*' might motivate us, following Quine, to use them *in place of* our ordinary English word 'true', and thereby to endorse what I call the *Tarski–Quine thesis: there is no more to truth than what is captured by a Tarski-style disquotational truth predicate.*

The Intersubjectivity Constraint

According to the second answer, we need a truth predicate that we are licensed to apply not only to our own sentences, as we now use them, but also *to other speakers' sentences and to our own sentences as we used them in the past*. This answer apparently conflicts with the Tarski–Quine thesis. To see why, note that when we are defining truth for our own sentences as we now use them, we may stipulate that in, for instance,

'Snow is white' is true if and only if snow is white,

the sentence that appears within quotation marks on the left of 'if and only if' is the same (in relevant respects) as the one that appears without quotation marks on the right. In contrast, if another speaker utters 'Snow is white', we cannot stipulate that the sentence she utters is the same (in relevant respects) as our own sentence 'Snow is white', as we now use it, and so we have no formal guarantee that her sentence is true if and only if snow is white (Putnam 1983, Davidson 1994a). For the same reason, we have no formal guarantee that our own sentence 'Snow is white', as we used it in the *past*, is true if and only if snow is white. Hence it seems that a Tarski-style disquotational truth predicate is not defined disquotationally for others' sentences or our own sentences as we used them in the past. As I mentioned above, however, without supplementation, a Tarski-style disquotational definition of 'true-in-*L*' applies *only* to the sentences for which it is defined disquotationally. Hence it seems that without supplementation a Tarski-style disquotational definition of 'true-in-*L*' does not apply to others' sentences or our own sentences as we used them in the past.

If the problem were one of how to analyse the concept of truth, a defender of the Tarski–Quine thesis could simply *deny* that a full account of the concept of truth must include an account of the extension of 'true-in-*L*' for other speakers' words or his own words as he used them in the past. To avoid fruitless disputes about how to capture a supposedly unique concept we express when we use the ordinary English word 'true', however, we should focus instead on the question "Do we need a truth predicate that applies to others' sentences and to our own sentences as we used them in the past?" To *this* question, unlike the one about how to analyse the concept of truth, it is relevant that we typically want to formulate and apply logical generalizations partly because we want to collaborate fruitfully with others. As Gottlob Frege emphasized (Frege 1964: 17), to collaborate fruitfully with others we need to formulate logical laws that can serve as *arbiters* of conflicting beliefs. For this purpose, we need a truth predicate that applies not *only* to our own sentences as we now use them, as the Tarski–Quine thesis suggests, but *also* to other speakers' sentences and our own sentences as we used them in the past.

It might seem that a person who is only interested in her own solitary inquiries and does not desire to collaborate with others need not worry about this pragmatic objection to the Tarski–Quine thesis. But even a person who does not desire to collaborate with others presupposes that she may someday discover that a sentence she previously accepted is false. And to make sense of this presupposition, she needs a truth predicate that she can apply to her own sentences as she used them in the past.

Judged by these pragmatic criteria, it seems that a Tarski-style disquotational truth predicate is not by itself satisfactory. The pragmatic criteria therefore motivate us to adopt what I call *the intersubjectivity constraint: a Tarski-style disquotational truth predicate is satisfactory only if it is supplemented by an account of why it is epistemically reasonable for one to apply it to other speakers' sentences and to one's own sentences as one used them in the past.*

Practical Judgements of Sameness of Satisfaction (PJSSs)

To clarify the intersubjectivity constraint, we need to examine how we identify other speakers' words and ascribe satisfaction conditions to them.

Suppose my friend Alice is telling me about a house she would like to buy. I have not seen the house, and ask her "What colour is it?" She replies, "It's white." In this context, without hesitation or deliberation, I will take her to have said that the house is white, and in so doing, I will take her word 'white' to be the same as my word 'white'—the word I would use to express what I take her to have said. In short, I will accept

(1) Alice's word 'white' is the same as my word 'white'.

If I also accept

(2) x satisfies my word 'white' if and only if x is white,

then I commit myself to

(3) x satisfies Alice's word 'white' if and only if x is white.

And by accepting (2) and (3), I commit myself to accepting their conjunction, namely,

(4) (x satisfies my word 'white' if and only if x is white) and (x satisfies Alice's word 'white' if and only if x is white)

A commitment of this kind is what I call a *practical judgement of sameness of satisfaction* (or a PJSS, for short). I call such judgements *practical* because they are exercises of a learned yet typically non-deliberative ability that is acquired over a period of years. I call an exercise of this ability a *judgement* because we will reject it if we come to think it is wrong. I will reject (4), for instance, if I come to make other PJSSs for Alice's word 'white' that conflict with and discredit (4).

As this example suggests, we regard our PJSSs as true or false, and we assume it is epistemically reasonable for us to trust sentences that express our PJSSs unless we have particular, local reasons in a given context for not doing so. In short, we regard our PJSSs as both *factual* and *trustworthy*. In so doing, we take them to license our applications of our own Tarski-style disquotational truth predicates to other speakers' sentences and to our own sentences as we used them in the past. We may therefore reformulate the intersubjectivity constraint as follows: *a Tarski-style disquotational truth predicate is satisfactory only if it is supplemented by an account of why it is epistemically reasonable for one to regard one's PJSSs as both factual and trustworthy.*

The Token-and-Ex-Use Conception of Words

The intersubjectivity constraint appears incompatible with the Tarski–Quine thesis, for reasons I sketched above: it seems that without supplementation, a Tarski-style disquotational definition of 'is true' applies *only* to our own sentences, as we now use them. Hence it seems that to supplement a Tarski-style disquotational truth predicate with an account of why it is epistemically reasonable for one to regard one's PJSSs as both factual and trustworthy would be to commit ourselves to the thesis that there is *more* to truth than what is captured by a Tarski-style disquotational truth predicate, and thereby to abandon the Tarski–Quine thesis. In my view, however, to understand why we feel so sure that the constraint is incompatible with the Tarski–Quine thesis, we must reflect on how we conceive of words.

When we first ask ourselves what words are, we are strongly inclined to start with an orthographic conception of word types, according to which the ink marks 'white, white', for example, comprise two tokens of the same word type w-h-i-t-e, and the word tokens themselves are strings of tokens of letter or sound types. But from this perspective, word tokens appear lifeless and insignificant. How do they come to have meanings and satisfaction conditions? The only answer, it seems, is that there are facts about the word tokens—facts that are additional to and independent of the tokens' spellings or pronunciations—that determine whatever meanings and satisfaction conditions they have.

Facts about a word token that are supposed to determine whatever meanings and satisfaction conditions it has are facts about what I shall call the token's *explanatory-use* (*ex-use*, for short). Every substantive theory of meaning and reference includes an account of ex-use. According to some of these theories, for instance, the meaning and satisfaction conditions of a given word token are determined by facts about why the word token was uttered, together with facts about the speaker's mental states and causal-historical relations between the word token, objects in the speaker's environment, and other speakers' word tokens. Such theories appeal to us because we presuppose

> *The token-and-ex-use conception of words.* Two word tokens are of the same word type if and only if

(a) they are spelled or pronounced in the same way, and

(b) facts about the ex-uses of the word tokens determine that they have meanings and satisfaction conditions and that their meanings and satisfaction conditions are the same.

A crucial consequence of the token-and-ex-use conception of words is

(P) Sentences that express our PJSSs are factual (true or false) only if they have truth values that are determined by facts about the ex-uses of the word tokens they contain.

For instance, recall (4), the sentence that expresses my PJSS for Alice's word 'white':

(4) (x satisfies my word 'white' if and only if x is white) and (x satisfies Alice's word 'white' if and only if x is white)

The token-and-ex-use conception of words implies that (4) is factual only if it has a truth value that is determined by facts about the ex-uses of Alice's and my tokens of the orthographic word type w-h-i-t-e.

This consequence of the token-and-ex-use conception of words explains why we feel so sure that the Tarski–Quine thesis and the intersubjectivity constraint are incompatible. We see that a Tarski-style definition of truth for one's own sentences tells us nothing about how another speaker ex-uses a given string of letters or sounds. From this we infer there is no way to explain why it is epistemically reasonable to regard one's PJSSs as both factual and trustworthy without concluding that there is more to truth than what is captured by a Tarski-style disquotational truth predicate defined for one's own regimented sentences. In short, we feel sure that the Tarski–Quine thesis and the intersubjectivity constraint are incompatible because we presuppose the token-and-ex-use conception of words, which *implies* that the thesis and the constraint are incompatible.

The PJSS-Based Conception of Words

A central goal of this book is to develop an alternative conception of words that does *not* imply that the Tarski–Quine thesis and the intersubjectivity constraint are incompatible. I start this task by showing that the type–token distinction presupposed by the orthographic conception of words is not as straightforward as it initially appears. To see why, consider letter types and their tokens. We may suppose that all letter tokens are particulars, or what I shall call *marks*—inscriptions in ink, pencil, chalk, grooves in wood, stone, or plastic, electronic events on a computer screen, uttered sounds, and so on.[3] But what are letter *types*? It is tempting to think of them as context-independent patterns, or sign designs.[4] But a careful look at how we actually identify marks as letters suggests that there is no single, context-independent pattern that settles when a given mark counts as a token of some given letter type. We ordinarily have no difficulty identifying handwritten tokens of the letter type w, for instance, yet each person has his own unique way of writing such tokens.

I propose that we try to accommodate these context-sensitive aspects of our practice of identifying letters by using 'replica' in place of 'token', taking 'is a replica of' to express an equivalence relation on replicas,[5] and identifying the letter type w with {x: x is a replica of the mark **w**}, where the mark in boldface is used as a sample replica of the letter type w.[6] The plausibility of the proposal depends on how we explain what is meant by the phrase 'is a replica of'. I propose that we explain this by looking at our actual practices of classifying marks for various purposes. For instance, we will not count **w** a replica of *w* if we are sorting the two marks by font, but we will do so if we are sorting them by letter type. Now suppose, as suggested above, that our established practical criteria for sorting replicas by letter type, including our criteria for identifying handwritten tokens of letter types, cannot be replaced by context-independent definitions. Then when we use such phrases as '{x: x is a replica of the mark **w**}' to refer to the sets that explicate our ordinary notion of letter types, we can provide

---

[3] The term 'mark' is from Goodman 1976: 131.

[4] The term 'sign design' is from Carnap 1942: §3.

[5] See Goodman 1966: 361–2, and 1976: 138–43. The term "replica", but not Goodman's nominalistic use of it, is due to Charles Sanders Peirce, who writes, "Every legisign signifies through an instance of its application, which may be termed a *Replica* of it" (Peirce 1933: 143).

[6] Since by supposition we use '*x* is a replica of *y*' to express a reflexive relation, the boldface mark in '{x: x is a replica of the mark **w**}' is a replica of itself, and is therefore a member of the set that is the letter type w. See Goodman 1966: 361–2.

at most an *elucidation* of the relation we express by using the phrase 'is a replica of' on that occasion.

Similar observations hold for our explications of *word* types. Here we may draw on the fact that a single orthographic type may have different satisfaction conditions. For instance, the British word 'robin' and the American word 'robin' are spelled in the same way, but a bird that satisfies the British word 'robin' does not satisfy the American word 'robin', and vice versa—British robins and American robins are birds of different species. Now suppose that in the following sentence

(*) A **robin** is not a **robin**.

the first boldface mark **robin** is a token of the British word 'robin' and the second boldface mark **robin** is a token of the American word 'robin'. Then (*) is true, but we will not see this if we take *both* boldface marks to be tokens of either the British word 'robin' or the American word 'robin'. For some purposes, such as copy editing, we group the first boldface mark in (*) with the second, but for others, such as applying a truth predicate to another's words, we do not. Corresponding with these different purposes are different "is a replica of" relations. There are many different "is a replica of" relations, each of which can be used to specify a different class of letter or word replicas. Some of these relations can be defined in more primitive terms. But it seems that many of the relations that are most valuable to us cannot be defined in more primitive terms. As I noted earlier, for instance, it may be that even the simple letter types that we use in everyday linguistic interactions must be elucidated by careful investigations of our actual identifications of letter replicas.

To elucidate the "is a replica of" relation that is relevant to our applications of Tarski-style definitions of satisfaction and truth to others' sentences and to our own sentences as we used them in the past, we must examine our ordinary criteria for identifying words. One might think, following David Kaplan (in Kaplan 1990), that the relevant criteria are the ones we rely on when we judge whether one speaker has *repeated* a word uttered by another speaker. But a conception of words rooted in such criteria would not by itself license us to make PJSSs. If I utter an ambiguous word, such as 'bank', just to provide you with a word to repeat, you may repeat the word, but you will not make a PJSS for my token of it, since you will see that I did not use that token to say anything, and hence that I did not disambiguate it.

To elucidate an "is a replica of" relation in a way that fits with the intersubjectivity constraint, I propose that we adopt

> *The context principle: never ask for the word type of a word token in isolation, but only in the context of one's PJSSs for that word token.*

The context principle amounts to a constraint on one's explication of what I call *PJSS-based* word types, which license our intersubjective applications of Tarski-style disquotational definitions of satisfaction and truth. The idea behind the principle is that my PJSS for Alice's word 'white', for instance, is simultaneously (i) *licensed by* my unhesitating judgement that Alice's word token 'white' is of the same type as my word token 'white' and (ii) *a constraint on* my understanding of the word types of which I take Alice's word token 'white' and my word token 'white' to be members. Hence to obey the context principle is to conceive of words in such a way that we each accept

(1) Alice's word 'white' is the same as my word 'white',

if and only if we take it to license a corresponding PJSS, namely,

(4) (x satisfies my word 'white' if and only if x is white) and (x satisfies Alice's word 'white' if and only if x is white).

In the midst of our inquiries we are always committed to some PJSSs or other. To obey the context principle is to seek a reflective equilibrium between our specification of word types and our PJSSs—an account of word types that fits with all and only the PJSSs we see no reason to reject.[7] The context principle thereby disciplines our understanding of the "is a replica of" relation that we can use to group word tokens into PJSS-based word types. To group word types in a way that obeys

---

[7] The reflective equilibrium I have in mind is modelled on Nelson Goodman's classic account of the justification of deductive inferences: "How do we justify a deduction? . . . *A rule is amended if it yields an inference we are unwilling to accept; an inference is rejected if it violates a rule we are unwilling to amend.* The process of justification is the delicate one of making mutual adjustments between rules and accepted inferences; and in the agreement achieved lies the only justification needed for either" (Goodman 1983: 63–4).

the context principle is to adopt what I call the *PJSS-based conception of words*.

Why the Tarski–Quine Thesis is Compatible with the Intersubjectivity Constraint

If we adopt the PJSS-based conception of words, we can see that the Tarski–Quine thesis and intersubjectivity constraint are compatible. There are two crucial considerations.

First, if we adopt the PJSS-based conception, we will regard any criterion for sameness of word types that violates the context principle as irrelevant to truth and satisfaction. Any criterion for sameness of word types that implies (P) violates the context principle, because it presupposes that there are criteria for sameness and difference of word types that can be stated without using any sentences that express our PJSSs. Hence if we adopt the PJSS-based conception of words, we will reject (P), and thereby discredit the reasoning that initially led us to think the Tarski–Quine thesis and intersubjectivity constraint are incompatible.

Second, if we adopt the PJSS-based conception, we will recognize no legitimate perspective independent of all of our PJSSs from which to question them, and so we will be entitled to regard them as factual and trustworthy. We will be entitled to regard them as factual because we will take ourselves to have no grip on sameness of satisfaction apart from them, and we will therefore be entitled to trust them unless we see special reason in a given context for not doing so.

I propose that we adopt the PJSS-based conception of words. By doing so, we transform our understanding of the word types to which our Tarski-style disquotational definitions of satisfaction and truth apply: we come to see our PJSSs as integral to our grasp of our Tarski-style disquotational truth predicates. Hence if we adopt the PJSS-based conception of words, we supplement our understanding of our own Tarski-style disquotational truth predicates with an account of why it is epistemically reasonable for us to regard our PJSSs as both factual and trustworthy *without* undermining the Tarski–Quine thesis that there is no more to truth than what is captured by a Tarski-style disquotational truth predicate defined for one's own sentences. We thereby come to see that the Tarski–Quine thesis and the intersubjectivity constraint are compatible.

Costs and Consequences

The compatibility comes at a cost. If we adopt the account of truth that I propose, we will commit ourselves to the context principle. We will therefore be unable to explain what *makes it the case* that our PJSSs are true—that particular word tokens have the satisfaction conditions we take them to have. Why should we be willing to pay this price? Why not stick with the token-and-ex-use conception of words, reject both the Tarski–Quine thesis and the PJSS-based conception of words, and try to show that facts about ex-use make it the case, or determine, that particular word tokens have the satisfaction conditions we take them to have?

The answer, I shall argue, is that for any substantive theory of what determines the satisfaction conditions of word tokens—any theory that presupposes the token-and-ex-use conception of words—there are cases in which speakers rely on PJSSs that conflict with the theory but that we cannot reject without giving up the intersubjectivity constraint. I shall examine several of the most influential and initially promising substantive theories of what determines the satisfaction conditions of word tokens, and present examples and thought experiments in which speakers rely on PJSSs that conflict with these theories. I shall argue that we can make sense of these PJSSs, and thereby satisfy the intersubjectivity constraint, *only if* we adopt the PJSS-based conception of words. I conclude that if we want to clarify and facilitate our inquiries by formulating logical generalizations, we need a truth predicate, and the truth predicate we need is one that results when we combine Tarski-style disquotational definitions of truth with the PJSS-based conception of words.

The resulting account of truth transforms our understanding of a number of central topics in the philosophy of language. It fits with and makes sense of the observations that motivate many philosophers to embrace the causal theory of reference for predicates. It enables us to eliminate names in favour of descriptions whose denotations remain the same despite the sorts of radical changes in belief that led Kripke and others to abandon Russellian and Fregean accounts of names. It enables us to understand anti-individualism without positing or presupposing social norms for language use or explicit identity conditions for linguistic communities. Finally, and perhaps most important of all, given the pragmatic considerations that motivate the account, it enables us to formulate and affirm logical laws that we can apply intersubjectively, without embracing a substantive theory of meaning or reference.

1

Regimentation

1.1. Regimentation as Linguistic Policy

As I emphasized in the introduction, my account of truth begins with the assumption that we want to clarify and facilitate our inquiries by regimenting our sentences so that we can formulate and apply logical generalizations. My goal in this opening chapter is to sketch a pragmatic account of regimentation that I will presuppose in the rest of the book. The basic idea is that to *regiment* a given natural language sentence S, as one used it on a particular occasion O, is to adopt a certain kind of *linguistic policy*—to decide to use a sentence S' with a perspicuous logical grammar *in place of* S, as one used it on occasion O—for the purpose of clarifying and facilitating one's inquiries. One's desire to show, for instance, that

(1) If there is a sea in which every ship sails, then every ship sails in some sea or other.

is logically valid might motivate one to replace (1) with a sentence in artificial notation, such as,

(2) $\exists x((x$ is a sea) $\land \forall y((y$ is a ship) $\to (y$ sails in $x))) \to \forall y((y$ is a ship) $\to \exists x((x$ is a sea) $\land (y$ sails in $x)))$,

and hence to regard (2) as a *paraphrase* of (1).

To use (2) in place of (1), however, one must be able to explain the artificial notations that appear in (2). As W. V. Quine observes, our explanations of these notations "amount to the implicit specification of simple mechanical operations whereby any sentence in the logical notation can be directly expanded, if not into quite ordinary language, at least into semi-ordinary language" (Quine 1960: 159). For instance, when we learn first-order logic we are taught to expand (2) into

(3) If (for something x such that x is a sea and for all things y (if y is a ship, then y sails in x)) then for all things y (if y is a ship then there is something x such that x is a sea and y sails in x).

This sentence contains ordinary words whose use is disciplined by the insertion of parentheses, variables, quantifiers, and the decision to take 'and' and 'if…then ____' to conform to the standard truth tables for '∧' and '→', respectively. By opting to use ordinary words in such artificially circumscribed ways, we in effect extend ordinary language so that it includes semi-ordinary words and the sentences we can construct with them. Once we extend our language in this way, our decision to use (2) in place of (1) looks similar to "what we all do every day in paraphrasing sentences to avoid ambiguity" (Quine 1960: 159).

When a speaker decides to use a sentence S' of an artificial first-order language in place of a sentence S of his ordinary language, the relation of S' to S "is just that the particular business that the speaker was on that occasion trying to get on with, with the help of S among other things, can be managed well enough to suit him by using S' instead of S" (Quine 1960: 160). We generally defer to a speaker's judgements about what his goals are and whether a given paraphrase will help him to achieve his goals. If he judges that by using a regimented sentence S' in place of an ordinary language sentence S, he can more easily achieve his goals, then we grant that he is entitled to use S' in place of S. I shall call this the pragmatic account of regimentation.

One might think we should add the further constraint that a speaker's decision to use S' in place of S, as he used S on some previous occasion O, is satisfactory only if as the speaker now uses S', it expresses the same statement that S did when he used it on O, where the 'same-statement' relation is assumed to be objective and context independent. For suppose a speaker's goal is to determine whether or not S, a sentence he used yesterday, is logically valid, and to do so he uses sentence S' in place of S as he used it yesterday. If S' as he now uses it does not express the same statement as S did yesterday, where "same-statement" is assumed to be objective and context independent, then his present evaluation of S' is not guaranteed to achieve his goal.[1]

---

[1] Some philosophers, such as Emma Borg, in Borg 2004: 72, are apparently inclined to assume that the *only* legitimate purpose of regimentation is to figure in an explanatory semantic theory for

This reasoning overlooks the fact that our ordinary standards for "same statement" are shaped by our goals, and our goals may shift from context to context. If the speaker aims to evaluate S, as used on occasion O, and does so by evaluating S', then given his present goals, he takes his use of S' to express the same statement that S expressed when it was used on O. One might think that there is some standard for sameness of statement independent of such context-sensitive goals. But even if there is such a standard, and we know that there is, it is too strong to say that a speaker is entitled to use S' in place of S, as used on O, only if, according to the supposed standard, his present use of S' expresses the same statement that S expressed when it was used on O. For if the speaker's goal is not to find an S' that expresses the same statement that S expressed when it was used on O according to the supposed standard, but simply to paraphrase S, as used on O, relative to his present purposes, then if using S' in place of S serves those purposes, he is entitled to use S' in place of S, even if, according to the supposed standard, S' does not express the same statement that S expressed when it was used on O. And even if the speaker's goal *is* to find an S' that, according to the supposed standard, expresses the same statement that S expressed when it was used on O, the most we can say is that he is entitled to use S' in place of S only if he *believes* that S' satisfies that goal. But this truism is a consequence of more general deliberative norms, and should not be built into one's account of regimentation.

You may therefore accept the pragmatic account of regimentation, provisionally at least, even if you believe that there is a standard for sameness of statement that is independent of individual speakers' decisions about how to paraphrase their sentences. In later chapters I will argue that the relevant standards for sameness of statement are not as independent

---

a natural language, and hence that the logical form of a natural language sentence is an objective, context-independent property of it. But sometimes we just want to evaluate an argument we've made by using a given natural language sentence, without theorizing about which descriptions of logical form best explain the structure of natural language. In such contexts, we use the methods of modern logic to regiment arguments expressed in natural language without committing ourselves to claims that could conflict with current linguistic theory. In any case, there is at present no agreement among linguistic theorists about the logical forms of natural language sentences. A person who wishes to regiment her sentences today could not defer to linguistic theory generally for an account of logical form, but would have to choose from among a variety of such accounts, all more or less incomplete. This is at best impractical. To avoid these problems, I recommend that we embrace the pragmatic account of regimentation.

of our context-sensitive judgements about how to paraphrase sentences as some philosophers believe, and that, properly viewed, the pragmatic account of regimentation is of a piece with a satisfactory account of truth. Between now and then I ask only that you be willing to investigate some of its consequences.

To begin with, given the pragmatic account of regimentation, we may define a *regimented language* as an artificial language whose sentences a person has decided to use for various purposes *in place of* his or her natural language sentences. Suppose one's regimented language L comprises all and only sentences constructed in the usual way from a finite list of basic predicates, such as 'robin' and 'is smaller than', the truth-functional symbols '$\sim$' and '$\lor$', the quantifier symbol '$\forall$', and an unlimited stock of variables 'x_1', 'x_2', ...[2] Then L contains no proper names or indexicals, and its predicates, we suppose, are neither ambiguous nor vague. L is too austere and inflexible to serve many of our everyday and scientific purposes, but it is ideal for formulating logical laws. I assume that to formulate logical laws, we will each be willing to restrict ourselves to the vocabulary of an artificial language like L: we will each be willing to use unambiguous predicates with the grammar of first-order logic in place of ambiguous or vague predicates, and to replace proper names and indexicals, as applied on particular occasions, with definite descriptions that contain regimented predicates specially introduced for the purpose.

My goal in this chapter is to explain what this assumption comes to. For this purpose I review and amend a few well-known methods for regimenting ambiguous or vague words, quantifications, definite descriptions, proper names, pronouns, and demonstratives. I emphasize that if we wish to use these methods to clarify and facilitate our inquiries, we cannot dispense entirely with ordinary (or, at least, semi-ordinary) language.

1.2. Ambiguity

Suppose that on one occasion I utter the sentence 'Riverside is a bank', taking this utterance to be interchangeable on that occasion with an utterance of 'Riverside is a river bank', but that on another occasion I utter

---

[2] L does not contain the symbols for '$\exists$', '$\rightarrow$', or '$\land$', but '$\exists$' may be expressed in terms of '$\sim$' and '$\forall$'; '$\rightarrow$' and '$\land$' may expressed in terms of '$\sim$' and '$\lor$'.

the sentence 'Riverside is not a bank', taking this second utterance to be interchangeable on that (second) occasion with an utterance of 'Riverside is not a money bank.' If I overlook the ambiguity in my word 'bank', I may be in danger of reasoning as follows:

(P1) Riverside is a bank.
(P2) Riverside is not a bank
 (C) Riverside is a bank and Riverside is not a bank.

The conclusion looks contradictory, hence unacceptable, and so it may appear that I must reject either (P1) or (P2). I am rarely tempted to make such simple errors in reasoning, but sometimes I want to take extra steps to guard against making them. At such times, in place of (P1), (P2), and (C), I may write

(P1′) Riverside is a river bank.
(P2′) Riverside is not a money bank.
 (C′) Riverside is a river bank and Riverside is not a money bank.

There is no temptation to regard (C′) as contradictory, hence no reason to take this inference to raise doubts about (P1′) or (P2′).

One may introduce paraphrases like this to avoid drawing bad inferences, whenever one notices the ambiguities that may tempt one to draw them. As an extra precaution, one may decide to use (what one takes to be) unambiguous regimented predicates in place of ordinary ambiguous predicates, such as 'bank', as used on particular occasions. To avoid drawing bad inferences that turn on the ambiguity of one's ordinary word 'bank', for instance, one may decide to use 'bank$_1$' in place of uses of 'bank' that one would paraphrase by 'river bank', and 'bank$_2$' in place of uses of 'bank' that one would paraphrase by 'money bank'.[3]

When I regiment my uses of 'bank', I select from what I take to be a finite number of standard ways of paraphrasing 'bank', including 'money bank' and 'river bank'. This suggests that the English word 'bank' is *lexically ambiguous*, in the sense that any given utterance of a

---

[3] This way of handling ambiguity is sketched by Scott Soames: "Ambiguity can...be treated as a case of homonomy. For example, instead of thinking that English contains a single (ambiguous) word type 'bank', one can take English to contain two different words, 'bank$_1$' and 'bank$_2$', whose tokens are phonologically identical...contextual factors...can then be thought of as determining whether particular utterances are tokens of the type 'bank$_1$' or the type 'bank$_2$'" (Soames 1984: 427 n. 26).

sentence containing it may be paraphrased in one of several standard ways. In contrast, some words seem to be ambiguous in ways that cannot be resolved by selecting from an established list of standard paraphrases. Consider, for instance, the following two contexts in which I use the word 'green':[4]

(1) The leaves on my Japanese maple are reddish-brown. I want the leaves to be green, so I paint them. When I am finished, I say to you, "The leaves are green."

(2) A few minutes later, a botanist friend phones me to ask if she can use the leaves on my Japanese maple for her study of green-leaf chemistry. I reply, "No, the leaves are not green." Neither you nor I take my new utterance to conflict with my previous utterance of 'The leaves are green'.

In addition to these two uses of 'The leaves are green', and 'The leaves are not green', there are many other possible uses of these sentences. Here, for instance, are two more:

(3) You and I notice that the leaves on my Japanese maple, which were reddish-brown a week ago, are now covered with a green mould. I say to you, "The leaves are green." A few minutes later, a botanist friend phones me to ask if she can use the leaves on my Japanese maple for her study of green-leaf chemistry. I reply, "No, the leaves are not green."

(4) I want the reddish-brown leaves on my Japanese maple to be green. Our friend Ali paints them in pointillist style. When Ali is finished, I say to you, "The leaves are green." You reply, "The leaves may *look* green, but only from a distance; up close one can see they are still not green."

These several uses of 'green' suggest that the number of different ways in which one might paraphrases sentences containing 'green' is not fixed in advance of particular contexts in which one uses that word.[5] Words that

---

[4] The following four cases are due in essentials to Travis 1997. Travis's cases, in turn, are inspired by similar ones in Austin 1962.

[5] Charles Travis writes that "There is no reason to think that there is any limit to possible understandings of [what it would be for leaves to be green], each of which might be invoked by some words which spoke on that topic" (Travis 1997: 90).

have this feature are not *lexically ambiguous*, but (as I shall say) *contextually ambiguous*.[6]

Like particular uses of lexically ambiguous words, however, particular uses of *contextually* ambiguous words may sometimes make it difficult to avoid drawing mistaken inferences from premises that we accept. If I do not pay attention to the different contexts of utterance in (1) and (2), for instance, I might be tempted to think my utterance of 'The leaves are green' in (1) conflicts with my utterance of 'The leaves are not green' in (2). While this appearance is not due to my use of a lexically ambiguous word, as in the case involving the word 'bank' described above, the practical remedy for it is the same: to replace the two uses of 'green' with the ordinary English phrases 'looks green from close up under normal lighting conditions' and 'is naturally green', respectively, and introduce regimented words 'green$_1$' and 'green$_2$' that I may use in place of these phrases.

Such efforts to avoid ambiguity by regimentation are not *guaranteed* to succeed: it is always possible that we will need to disambiguate one of our own regimented predicates, such as 'green$_1$', to accommodate new uses of the word that we had not anticipated. As Geach once wrote, "the price of freedom from fallacy is eternal vigilance" (Geach 1962: 71). We are nevertheless guided by a *regulative ideal: adopt a regimentation only if it doesn't leave unresolved ambiguities that prevent us from keeping track of the inferences and logical laws on which we rely.*

1.3. Is Regimentation Possible?

Examples (1)–(4) of the previous section are due in essentials to Charles Travis. For reasons explained above, the examples convince me that 'is green' is contextually ambiguous. Similar examples could be found to show that many other natural language predicates are also contextually ambiguous. But Travis goes further: he takes his examples to show that *no* predicate, on *any* particular use of it, has an extension.[7] This radical claim

---

[6] Many of the English predicates that Charles Travis uses in Travis 2000 to illustrate what he calls *occasion sensitivity* are contextually ambiguous.

[7] Travis writes that "No understanding *we* could have of being green, so none that might attach to a particular use of 'is green', would be one on which 'is green' spoke of a property, if a property must

may look plausible if we focus on occasions in which a speaker applies a given natural language predicate to an object that she sees, touches, or feels on that occasion. For in such cases one might think that to take what is expressed to be true it is enough to settle which objects in the immediate context are supposed to satisfy the predicate in the contextually relevant sense. This apparently leaves it open whether the predicate, as it is used (understood) on that occasion, applies to any object that is *not* present on the occasion. In such cases, then, it is tempting to *equate* the particular use (understanding) of the predicate with our conscious (or, at least, semi-conscious) *beliefs* about what satisfies the predicate on that occasion.

This way of thinking about predicates is much less tempting, however, when we are evaluating arguments involving premises that contain universal quantifiers. For instance, consider the following argument

(P1) All dolphins are mammals.
(P2) Some dolphins live in the sea.
(C) Therefore, some mammals live in the sea.

A standard paraphrase of the first premise, (P1), is

$$\forall y((y \text{ is a dolphin}) \rightarrow (y \text{ is a mammal}))$$

where '$\forall y$' is understood to range over *everything* (in the relevant domain). If we understand the symbol '$\rightarrow$' in the usual truth-functional way, then this paraphrase of (P1) commits us to supposing that the predicate 'is a dolphin' is true or false of every individual (in the relevant domain). More generally, regimented predicates are true or not true (on the understanding assumed by that regimentation) of *every* individual (in the relevant domain), and therefore also have *extensions*—associated sets of objects (from the relevant domain) of which the predicates are true.

If, as Travis claims, no predicate, on any particular use of it, has an extension, then regimentation in the sense just described is not possible. Travis's radical claim will look appealing if we conflate our *beliefs* about how to apply our predicates on particular occasions, on the one hand, with

have an extension . . . . Where 'is green' has made different contributions to different wholes, we may identify different things for it to have spoken of each time—being green on this understanding, and being green on that one. So we may see the predicate as varying its reference across speakings of it. But we must not mistake these different things for properties [or predicates] with extensions" (Travis 1997: 99–100).

the *satisfaction conditions* for our predicates—the conditions that must be satisfied for our predicates to be true of or not true of particular objects—on the other. The conflation is even more tempting if, following Travis, we describe a particular use of a natural language predicate as a particular "understanding" of that predicate on that occasion. For it is natural to understand "understanding" in a way that is closely connected with our current beliefs. If we are to make sense of regimentation, however, we must not conflate the satisfaction conditions for a natural language predicate, as used on a particular occasion O, with our *beliefs* about the conditions under which objects in the intended domain of discourse satisfy that predicate, as used on O. We must distinguish between our beliefs about those conditions, and the conditions themselves. Starting in Chapter 3, I shall highlight and elucidate aspects of our inquiries that commit us to drawing this distinction. In the meantime I shall take the distinction for granted, and assume that regimented predicates have extensions.

1.4. Vagueness

Suppose that Herbert has a full head of hair on Monday, and shaves it all off on Tuesday. Seeing the result on Wednesday, but knowing that Herbert had a full head of hair two days before, you say, "Herbert is bald, like a skinhead." A few moments later, while discussing the kind of baldness that results from a natural and irreversible ageing process, you say, "Herbert is not bald, he just shaved his head." You do not take your utterances of 'Herbert is bald' and 'Herbert is not bald' to conflict.

Now suppose you want to avoid any appearance of conflict between your utterances of 'Herbert is bald' and 'Herbert is not bald.' For this purpose, you introduce the predicate 'bald$_1$' as a paraphrase of 'bald' as you used it when you uttered 'Herbert is bald', and 'bald$_2$' as a paraphrase of 'bald' as you used it when you uttered 'Herbert is not bald.' After the regimentation, you use 'Herbert is bald$_1$' in place of your utterance of 'Herbert is bald', and 'Herbert is not bald$_2$' in place of your utterance of 'Herbert is not bald', and thereby remove the appearance of conflict between the two utterances.

In this case, let's suppose, the goal of your regimentation is to resolve a contextual ambiguity, not to remove the vagueness of your particular uses of your unregimented word 'bald'. You take your regimented words 'bald$_1$' and 'bald$_2$' to *inherit* the vagueness of the two applications of 'bald' that 'bald$_1$' and 'bald$_2$', respectively, replace. The sense in which the predicates 'bald$_1$' and 'bald$_2$' are vague can be explained by examples. If it takes fifteen minutes for Herbert to shave off his hair, for instance, there will be times during the fifteen-minute interval when Herbert is neither clearly bald$_1$ nor clearly not bald$_1$. And if it takes Herbert twenty years to lose his hair by a natural ageing process, there will be times, such as 5 p.m. GMT on 28 March 1985, when Herbert is neither clearly bald$_2$ nor clearly not bald$_2$. A predicate is vague if and only if its application can be unclear in the ways just exemplified.[8]

Many philosophers accept theories of vagueness that imply that a vague sentence such as 'At 5 p.m. GMT on 28 March 1985, Herbert is bald$_2$' is neither true nor false.[9] In contrast, I propose that we take that sentence to have a truth value (true or false) even though no one knows its truth value.[10] To accept this proposal is to accept a theory of vagueness that goes beyond the pragmatic decision to use regimented predicates, such as 'bald$_1$' and 'bald$_2$', in place of ordinary English predicates, as used on particular occasions. But there is no reason we cannot combine such pragmatic decisions with other pragmatic decisions, such as the decision to adopt the theory that our vague sentences are true or false. The advantages are clear: if one adopts the theory, one can introduce vague predicates into one's regimented languages without giving up classical logic, hence without falling prey to sorites paradoxes, such as the following:[11]

(P1) Every person with 0 hairs growing naturally on his head is bald$_2$.

(P2) For any *n*, if every person with *n* hairs growing naturally on his head is bald$_2$, then every person with $n + 1$ hairs growing naturally on his head is bald$_2$.

---

[8] Here I follow Timothy Williamson; see Williamson 1994: 2. However, I do not endorse Williamson's view that we can in principle never know the precise boundaries of a predicate we now regard as vague. In my view, to call a predicate vague is to say something about our *current* epistemological position: there are cases we regard as clear, and others we regard as borderline, and we see no likely prospect of settling the borderline cases. It is not to say that nothing that would settle those cases *could* be discovered.

[9] According to Fine 1975, for example, vagueness is a deficiency of meaning.

[10] Horwich 1998a, Sorenson 2001, and Williamson 1994 each present versions of this view.

[11] This particular sorites paradox is modelled on Paul Horwich's formulation of a sorites paradox about heaps. See Horwich 1998a: 81.

(C) Therefore, for any n, every person with n hairs growing naturally on his head is bald$_2$.

This argument seems to establish the obviously unacceptable conclusion that everyone is bald$_2$. We find (P1) undeniable. We also find it difficult to reject (P2), because we are strongly inclined to suppose that due to the vagueness of 'bald$_2$', there is no number n of hairs such that every person with n hairs growing naturally on his head is bald$_2$, but some person with $n + 1$ hairs growing naturally on his head is not bald$_2$. If we accept bivalence for sentences containing 'bald$_2$', however, we can reject premise (P2), and affirm that for some n, every person with n hairs growing naturally on his head is bald$_2$, but some person with $n + 1$ hairs growing naturally on his head is not bald$_2$, without being able to identify such an n.[12]

Many will be inclined to *insist* without argument that sentences such as 'At 5 p.m. GMT on 28 March 1985, Herbert is bald$_2$' are neither true nor false. This reaction is partly sustained, I believe, by our tendency to conflate our beliefs about how to apply our predicates, on the one hand, with the satisfaction conditions for our predicates, on the other. The reaction also overlooks our desire to avoid paradoxical inferences. By accepting the principle of bivalence for sentences that contain 'bald$_2$', for instance, we can reject premise (P2) of the above sorites argument and bypass the sorites paradox without giving up the deeply entrenched laws of classical logic. This is a good pragmatic reason for accepting the principle of bivalence for regimented sentences that contain vague predicates. If we view regimentation as the adoption of a linguistic policy that furthers our goals, including our goal of avoiding the sorites paradox, we should not be swayed by the feeling that sentences such as 'At 5 p.m. GMT on 28 March 1985, Herbert is bald$_2$' are neither true nor false.[13]

---

[12] For reasons I explain in Ebbs 2001, this does not imply that baldness supervenes on the number of hairs on a person's head. Other factors, such as the thickness and distribution of the hair may be relevant as well.

[13] Quine 1981 offers a pragmatic motivation for accepting bivalence across the board, although, unlike me, he proposes that we actually *specify* particular sharp boundaries for vague predicates. In contrast, the view I advocate is more like what Roy Sorenson calls *epistemicism*. Sorenson writes that "A few trivial inference rules can derive the heart of epistemicism from the empty set of premises. Consequently, the right attitude to epistemicism is to presuppose it. The philosophical problem is to explain why the previous assertion seems so dogmatic and question-begging" (Sorenson 2001: 184). I agree with Sorenson that we need an explanation of the widespread rejection of bivalence for sentences

1.5. Quantifier Domains, Tense, and Time

Suppose that on one occasion I utter the sentence 'All are enrolled in P505,' taking this utterance to be interchangeable on that occasion with an utterance of 'All first-year Indiana University philosophy graduate students in Fall 2006 are enrolled in P505,' but that on another occasion, even though no student has dropped P505, I utter the sentence 'Not all are enrolled in P505', taking this second utterance to be interchangeable on that (second) occasion with an utterance of 'Not all philosophy graduate students at Indiana University in Fall 2006 are enrolled in P505.' If I overlook the implicit domains associated with these two uses of the phrase 'All', I may be in danger of reasoning as follows:

(P1) All are enrolled in P505.
(P2) Not all are enrolled in P505.
(C) All are enrolled in P505 and not all are enrolled in P505.

Since (C) looks contradictory, I may be tempted to reject (P1) or (P2). This would be a mistake, because they are not incompatible. Again, I am rarely tempted to make such simple errors in reasoning, but sometimes I want to regiment my sentences in a way that guards against them. At such times, I may use the symbol '∀', understood as ranging over a fixed domain, and replace (P1) and (P2) by

(P1′) $\forall x((x$ is a first-year Indiana University philosophy graduate student in Fall 2006) $\rightarrow$ (x is enrolled in P505 in Fall 2006)).
(P2′) $\sim\forall x((x$ is an Indiana University philosophy graduate student in Fall 2006) $\rightarrow$ (x is enrolled in P505 in Fall 2006)).
(C′) $\forall x((x$ is a first-year Indiana University philosophy graduate student in Fall 2006) $\rightarrow$ (x is enrolled in P505 in Fall 2006)) $\wedge$ $\sim\forall x((x$ is an Indiana University philosophy graduate student in Fall 2006) $\rightarrow$ (x is enrolled in P505 in Fall 2006)).

Unlike (C), (C′) does not look like a contradiction. Hence if we regiment (C) as (C′), we can guard against the mistake of taking (C)—the conjunction

containing vague terms. My explanation is that we are tempted to reject bivalence for vague predicates because we are tempted by misguided intuitions about meaning to conflate our beliefs about when a given predicate applies to an object, on the one hand, with the satisfaction conditions for that predicate, on the other.

of (P1) and (P2), as uttered on the two occasions described above—to be a contradiction. More generally, to avoid mistakes in reasoning due to the context sensitivity of quantifier domains, we may use the symbol '∀' in place of ordinary occurrences of 'All' or 'Every', where '∀' is understood as ranging over a fixed domain, and the different domains over which the ordinary occurrences of 'All' or 'Every' may seem to range are specified by the antecedents of conditionals bound by '∀'. Similarly, the different domains over which the ordinary occurrences of 'Some' or 'there are' may seem to range can be specified by adding conjuncts to the matrixes bound by '∼∀x∼'.[14]

Here it is important to note that '∀' should be read as timeless—as ranging over all objects, past, present, and future. This reading goes hand in hand with the fact that sentences of regimented English are tenseless; or, to be more precise, they are all in the present tense, understood as timeless. Some, but not all, English sentences are in the present tense, and we sometimes, but not always, take such sentences as timeless: when we say, "All dolphins are mammals," for instance, we typically take ourselves to be generalizing over everything, past, present, and future.[15] In contrast, every regimented English sentence has the surface grammatical form of the present tense, and we must always take such sentences as timeless. In regimented English, to make distinctions indicated in English by tense, we treat time as just another dimension, like space. We regard times as objects and add regimented predicates, such as 'x is before y', that are true or false of ordered pairs of objects, including times. This treatment of time is presupposed by all standard paraphrases of ordinary language sentences into sentences with the grammar of first-order logic.[16] Surprisingly, however, it often goes without saying, even in elementary logic texts. Perhaps the

[14] The phenomenon of the context-sensitivity of quantifier domains is not restricted to utterances of quantifier words in ordinary language. For instance, the sentence '∀x∃y($y^2 = x$)' might appear on two occasions in a mathematics lecture, on the first of which it is paraphrased as '∀x((x is a natural number) → ∃y((y is a natural number) ∧ ($y^2 = x$))', and on the second of which it is paraphrased as '∀x((x is a real number) → ∃y((y is a real number) ∧ ($y^2 = x$))'. For a similar example, see McGee 2004.

[15] Does this imply that we can generalize over "absolutely everything"? For two classic discussions of this issue, Dummett 1981 and Cartwright 1994. For more recent discussions of it, see Williamson 2003 and Rayo and Uzquiano 2006. I have sympathies with both sides of the debate about whether one can generalize over absolutely everything, and will not try to adjudicate it in this book.

[16] For summaries of this standard treatment of time, see Quine 1960: 170–6, Quine 1982: 195, and Barwise and Etchemendy 2002: 398.

main reason is that most competent English-speakers pick it up readily, with little or no explicit instruction.[17]

1.6. Descriptions and Proper Names

Indefinite descriptions such as 'Some sea' and 'Every ship' do not correspond to logically significant parts of the regimented sentences that paraphrase ordinary English sentences in which they occur. For instance,

(1) Every ship sails in some sea or other.

is usually regimented by a sentence such as

(2) $\forall y((y$ is a ship$) \rightarrow \exists x((x$ is a sea$) \wedge (y$ sails in $x)))$.

Such phrases as 'Some sea' and 'Every ship' therefore disappear under regimentation into quantifications.

Definite descriptions of ordinary language can also be eliminated by paraphrase. Consider the sentence

(3) The author of *The Principles of Mathematics* won a Nobel Prize for literature.

Let's say that a *singular term* is a term that can coherently be replaced by a variable of the sort that could be bound by an objectual quantifier.[18] It seems coherent to put such a variable in the place of 'The author of *The Principles of Mathematics*' in (3) to yield the open sentence

(4) x won a Nobel Prize for literature.

Thus it seems as though 'The author of *The Principles of Mathematics*' is a singular term. To regiment sentences that contain such singular terms, we can use Russell's method of paraphrasing definite descriptions. We can first introduce a description operator symbolized by 'the x:' (read as 'the x such that'), which we can prefix to a predicate in regimented notation to create

---

[17] As any experienced logic instructor knows, it is much *more* difficult to explain to the beginner such comparatively trivial points as that the English phrase 'only if' should be paraphrased by '$\rightarrow$'.

[18] This criterion of singular termhood is due to Quine. For his own summary of it, see Quine 1982: 260.

a definite description. Prefixing 'the x:' to the predicate 'x is an author of *The Principles of Mathematics*', for instance, yields 'the x: x is an author of *The Principles of Mathematics*'. Putting this description in place of 'x' in (4) yields

(5) (The x: x is an author of *The Principles of Mathematics*) won a Nobel Prize for literature.[19]

To regiment this into the austere language sketched above, we paraphrase (5) as

(6) $\exists x$ ((x is an author of *The Principles of Mathematics*) $\wedge$ $\forall y$ ((y is an author of *The Principles of Mathematics*) $\rightarrow$ $x = y$) $\wedge$ (x won a Nobel Prize for literature)),

in which the definite description no longer appears as a singular term.

We may also choose to regiment ordinary proper names as definite descriptions. Consider any ordinary sentence containing a proper name, such as

(7) Bertrand Russell won a Nobel Prize for literature.

Quine points out that a sentence of the form (7) is equivalent in truth value to

(8) $\exists w$((w = Bertrand Russell) $\wedge$ (w won a Nobel Prize for literature)).

Quine suggests that we replace the predicate '= Bertrand Russell' with a simple, unstructured, one-place predicate specially introduced to be satisfied only by Bertrand Russell.[20] For this purpose, following Quine 1982: 278–83, we may use the predicate 'is-Russell'. In place of (8), we can then write

(9) $\exists w$((w is-Russell) $\wedge$ (w won a Nobel Prize for literature)).

[19] According to Russell's theory of descriptions, a description of the form 'the x: Fx' is not a singular term, but a sentence in disguise. Nevertheless, Russell proved that in extensional contexts we are licensed to treat a description of the form 'the x: Fx' *as if* it were a singular term that can be substituted for positions in which it makes sense to put a variable of the sort that could be bound by an objectual quantifier. See Neale 1990: 131.

[20] It is not widely known that Tarski anticipated this key move of Quine's treatment of names as descriptions in 1936: "To say that the name x denotes a given object a is the same as to stipulate that the object a (or every sequence of which a is the corresponding term) satisfies a sentential function of a particular type. In colloquial language it would be a function which consists of three parts in the following order: a variable, the word 'is' and the given name x." (Tarski 1936: 194 n. 1)

If we regiment (7) in this way, then the name 'Bertrand Russell' no longer appears in the position of a singular term. On the other hand, (9) is logically compatible with the claim that there is more than one Bertrand Russell. To express our belief that there is only one thing that is-Russell, we can add a clause to our regimentation, as follows

(10) $\exists w((w$ is-Russell$) \wedge \forall z((z$ is-Russell$) \rightarrow z = w) \wedge (w$ won a Nobel Prize for literature$))$.

Thus regimented, the proper name 'Bertrand Russell' becomes, in effect, a sentence unto itself, namely,

(11) $\exists w((w$ is-Russell$) \wedge \forall z((z$ is-Russell$) \rightarrow z = w))$.

If we like, we can abbreviate the description so that it *looks* like a singular term, rewriting (11) as 'The w: w is-Russell' and (10) as:

(12) (The w: w is-Russell) won a Nobel Prize for literature.

But this would be a mere abbreviation for (10), in which the definite description is not a singular term.

To replace a predicate of the form '$= n$' with an unstructured predicate 'is-n', we don't need to make any assumptions about how we came to be able to use the predicate '$= n$' that we rely on to introduce 'is-n'. Quine's method of regimenting sentences that contain proper names is therefore compatible with just about any account of how we came to be able to use '$= n$'. In particular, to apply Quine's method, we need not accept Russell's theory of how we understand sentences that contain proper names (Quine 1982: 276–7). In addition, as I'll argue in Chapter 9, Quine's method is not vulnerable to the semantical arguments that Kripke and others have used against the classical description theory of proper names.[21]

---

[21] First-order logic does not have modal operators, but we can still ask how Quine's method of paraphrasing names would fare if we were to add modal operators. If we prefix the right sort of rigidifying operator R to a definite description d that results when we apply Quine's method to regiment a name n, the resulting rigidified description, Rd, will behave like n in modal contexts. The operator I favour for this purpose is Tyler Burge's @-operator, which *rigidifies* a predicate 'F' in such a way that in all worlds, actual or counterfactual, a use of 'the @ F' denotes the *actual F* (Burge 2005: 229–30). Burge points out (at Burge 2005: 240) that his @-operator escapes a problem Soames 1998 raises for the superficially similar proposal that we use "actually" to rigidify definite descriptions.

1.7. Pronouns and Demonstratives

The pronoun 'he' in

(1) Maurizio broke the bank in Monte Carlo and he admires Tarski

is what Geach calls a pronoun of laziness, because we can eliminate it by paraphrasing (1) as

(2) Maurizio broke the bank in Monte Carlo and Maurizio admires Tarski.

No pronouns occur in (2), and so we can use the methods already introduced to regiment (2), putting regimented definite descriptions in place of the proper names of (2) and regimented predicates in place of the ordinary predicates of (2). In contrast, however, most of us would not be willing to paraphrase

(3) Just one man broke the bank in Monte Carlo and he admires Tarski

as

(4) Just one man broke the bank in Monte Carlo and just one man admires Tarski.

Instead, we see the pronoun in (3) as bound by an implicit quantifier in 'Just one man broke the bank in Monte Carlo.' We see (3) as equivalent to

(5) The man who broke the bank in Monte Carlo admires Tarski.

And if we regiment (5) by using descriptions in place of the proper names and descriptions in (5), we will view the pronoun in (3) as in effect bound by an initial existential quantifier.[22]

In addition to pronouns of laziness and bound pronouns, there are also indexical pronouns, which do not simply stand in for singular terms that have appeared earlier in the same sentence or some relevant previous discourse, and are not usually seen as playing a role similar to bound variables in first-order logic. For instance, suppose that you and I are in a

---

[22] Sentences (1) and (3) are modifications of examples (20) and (21) on page 125 of Geach 1962. The terminology "pronouns of laziness" is introduced on page 124 of Geach 1962.

room filled with people unknown to you, and, while pointing at one of these people, I turn to you and utter the sentence

(6) He admires Tarski.

In these circumstances, you and I might both be willing to paraphrase (6) by

(7) That man over there admires Tarski

thereby replacing the indexical use of the pronoun 'he' by the description 'that man over there', which contains the demonstrative 'that man' and the demonstrative 'there', both of which we understand as supplemented, in the circumstances described, by my pointing gesture.

We may paraphrase sentences such as (6) and (7) into an artificial first-order language that contains no demonstratives, but only if we introduce new regimented predicates that take the place of particular applications of demonstratives. To paraphrase (6), for instance, we may first paraphrase it as (7), and replace the occurrence of 'That man over there' in (7) by 'The x: x is a man and x is over there.' We can then introduce a new regimented predicate to replace our particular application of 'is over there', which we take to express a condition that is uniquely satisfied by one person to whom I pointed when I uttered (6). Finally, we may replace 'The x: x is a man and x is over there' by a definite description that contains only our regimented predicate for 'man' and a newly introduced predicate that expresses a contextually salient condition that we take to be uniquely satisfied by one man to whom I pointed.

The contextually salient conditions on which we rely when we refer to a particular person or object by using indexical pronouns or demonstratives in the way just exemplified always involve our conscious *perceptual* attention to the relevant person or object, and often involve our conscious *visual* attention to it. But this is not to say that conscious perceptual attention, understood as independent of demonstrative or indexical reference, *explains* or *grounds* such reference relations, as Evans 1982 and Campbell 2002 argue. One need not endorse this philosophical thesis to paraphrase sentences such as (6) and (7) in the way just sketched.[23]

---

[23] There is much more to be said about how to paraphrase sentences containing demonstratives and pronouns, in particular, and about regimentation more generally. The vast literature about

1.8. Why Ordinary Language is Indispensable

The methods of regimentation I have canvassed tell us nothing about the context-invariant meanings of contextually ambiguous predicates, proper names, and indexical pronouns and demonstratives. They provide no account, for instance, of how the English word 'green' enables us to introduce and explain an indefinite number of regimented predicates, or of "the rules by which [indexical pronouns and demonstratives] adjust their reference to circumstances" (Davidson 1984: 35). As I have stressed, however, I assume that our primary motivation for regimenting our sentences is to clarify and facilitate our inquiries. For this purpose, we do not need a theory of the context-invariant meanings of contextually ambiguous predicates, proper names, and indexical pronouns and demonstratives. We need, instead, a method for *introducing* and *explaining* regimented sentences that we can use *in place of* particular utterances of ordinary English sentences that contain such expressions.

The methods I have sketched satisfy this need. If we choose to use them, we should find no insurmountable obstacle to paraphrasing many of our ordinary language sentences into an artificial language L that comprises all and only sentences constructed in the usual way from a finite list of basic predicates, truth-functional symbols '$\sim$', '$\vee$', quantifier symbol '$\forall$', and an unlimited stock of variables 'x_1', 'x_2', ... No matter how many utterances of ordinary language sentences we have regimented, however, we may need to introduce and explain new regimented predicates that we can use in place of new applications of contextually ambiguous words. We may also need to introduce and explain new regimented predicates in order to construct definite descriptions that we can use in place of new uses of indexical pronouns or demonstratives. And to introduce and explain new regimented predicates we need to use ordinary language. In short, if we wish to use the methods of regimentation that I have sketched, we

---

demonstratives and pronouns is filled with ingenious proposals, any of which one might adopt in particular contexts for particular purposes. For instance, some would follow Gareth Evans, who argued trenchantly in Evans 1985 that in addition to pronouns of laziness and bound pronouns, we must acknowledge what he called E-type pronouns. For useful bibliographies and detailed discussions of many other important views of demonstratives, pronouns, and descriptions, see Neale 1990 and Bezuidenhout and Reimer 2004. For treatments of pronouns and descriptions within a first-order logical framework associated with Donald Davidson's theory of interpretation, see Larson and Segal 1995 and Lepore and Ludwig 2007.

will always need to use ordinary language to introduce and explain new regimented predicates.

1.9. Limitations of First-Order Logic

At the start of this chapter I assumed that to formulate logical laws, we will each be willing to restrict ourselves to the grammar of an artificial first-order language. This may seem too restrictive, since there are many English sentences that it is either difficult or impossible to paraphrase by structured sentences of a first-order language. The qualification 'structured' is crucial here: trivially, any sentence that one can understand can be paraphrased into an *un*structured sentence of a first-order language, if, as is usual, we suppose that first-order logic includes simple sentential logic as a part. Hence the worry is not that we cannot paraphrase any given English sentence *S*, as used on a given occasion *O*, into a sentence of a first-order language. The worry is that we cannot always do so in a way that by itself makes plain the logical relations that *S*, as used on *O*, bears to other sentences. We can of course always mimic those logical relations case by case, adding premises that, together with *S*, imply the sentences that we take *S*, as used on *O*, to imply. But we may also seek a deeper, more systematic understanding of the logical grammar of such sentences. And this desire may lead us beyond first-order logic. Let us look at some examples.

The Geach–Kaplan sentence

David Kaplan proved that the sentence:

   (a) Some people admire only one another

cannot be paraphrased by any structured sentence of a first-order language (Quine 1982: 293, Boolos 1984: 432–3). One might try to paraphrase (a) as

   (b) There are at least two people who admire only one another.

But unlike (b), (a) "might hold because of some irreducible group of say eleven mutual admirers" (Quine 1982: 293). It is agreed that (a) can be paraphrased by a *second*-order sentence that is not equivalent to any structured first-order sentence (Boolos 1984: 432). This does not mean that to paraphrase (a) with a structured sentence we must use second-order quantification, however, because we can also paraphrase (a) by means of first-order logic and set theory, as follows (Quine 1982: 293):

(c) $\exists z[\exists x(x \in z) \land \forall x\{(x \in z) \rightarrow (\exists y(x$ admires $y) \land \forall y((x$ admires $y) \rightarrow (x \neq y \land y \in z)))\}]$.

More generally, by allowing first-order variables to range over classes, and using '∈' for 'is a member of', we can increase the expressive power of a first-order grammar without using second-order quantification. To paraphrase sentences such as (a), as well as sentences that explicate the ancestral relation (Quine 1982: 292–3) and other complex mathematical notions, a first-order logical language conjoined with set theory is enough.

But why *not* use second-order logic, as some authors (Boolos 1984, Shapiro 1991) urge? My answer mixes pragmatic with theoretical considerations. Classical first-order logic with identity became dominant in the mid-twentieth century, after years of dispute among leading logicians, including David Hilbert, Ernst Zermelo, Leopold Löwenheim, Thoralf Skolem, Kurt Gödel, Alfred Tarski, Rudolf Carnap, and W. V. Quine.[24] Unlike its main rivals, first-order logic is compact and complete, and has a finite proof procedure.[25] It is the logic most widely used in set theory. It is also deeply entrenched in mathematics, linguistics, and philosophy curricula.[26] If we desire to clarify and facilitate our inquiries, as I assume, then the historical pedigree, entrenchment, theoretical appeal, and convenience of first-order logic are good pragmatic reasons for restricting ourselves, as far as possible, to generalizations we can express in a first-order language.[27]

Binary quantification: 'most'

As we've seen, to paraphrase a sentence such as 'All dolphins live in the sea' it is enough to prefix the *unary* quantifier '$\forall x$' to the matrix '(x is a

[24] For detailed accounts of this history, see Moore 1980 and 1988; for a summary of the history, see Shapiro 1991: chapter 7. For a dissenting view, see Eklund 1996.

[25] For proofs of these basic results for first-order logic, and of their failures for one of its main rivals, namely second-order logic, see Boolos, Burgess, and Jeffery 2002.

[26] This is not to say that only first-order logic deserves to be called logic, or that it is 'the' right logic. For a stimulating discussion of what these claims might mean and why it would be so difficult to establish them, see Tharp 1975.

[27] My account of truth could perhaps be extended to define disquotational Tarski-style truth predicates that we could use to express higher-order logical generalizations, but I do not try to extend it in that way here.

dolphin) → (*x* lives in the sea)'. It is therefore natural to expect that in
sentences such as

(d) Most dolphins live in the sea

'most' can also be paraphrased by a unary quantifier 'Most (*x*)', which,
when prefixed to a matrix *A* in which there are free occurrences of '*x*', is
understood to mean that most of the members of the relevant domain of
discourse satisfy *A*. To treat (d) on analogy with 'All dolphins live in the
sea,' however, one would have to find a truth-functional connective ∗ that
could yield a satisfactory paraphrase of (d) of the form:

(e) Most (*x*) ((*x* is a dolphin) ∗ (*x* lives in the sea)).

The problem is that there is no such connective (Rescher 1962, Wiggins
1980: 326, Davies 1981: 123–4, Barwise and Cooper 1981, Neale 1990:
40–1). Those who wish to provide a systematic, compositional theory of
meaning for English must therefore find some other way to understand the
contribution of 'most' to natural language sentences in which it occurs.[28]
This is not the most pressing aspect of the problem for us, however, since
by assumption our goal is not to construct a theory of meaning for natural
language, but to express logical generalizations that we can use to clarify
and facilitate our inquiries. Given this goal, for instance, we could try
directly paraphrasing (d), as used on a particular occasion, with

(f) More than half of the members of the set of all and only dolphins
     live in the sea.

which does not contain the word 'most', thereby (for the moment, at least)
avoiding the problem of providing a systematic account of the contribution
of 'most' to natural language sentences in which it occurs. To paraphrase
(f) into a sentence with a first-order grammar, however, we would again
need to add some set theory to our first-order language. Moreover, we may
want some assurance that we will always be able to come up with adequate
paraphrases of sentences that contain 'most'. If so, we could adopt one of
several strategies for systematically specifying truth conditions for natural

[28] Such a desire leads Martin Davies, for example, to seek a systematic compositional account of the
contribution of 'most' and other quantifier words to the truth conditions of natural language sentences
in which they occur—an account that fits as closely as possible with the surface grammatical structure
of natural language sentences (Davies 1981: 123–4).

language sentences that contain 'most' (see, for instance, Neale 1990: 41–2, Glanzberg 2006, and Lepore and Ludwig 2007: 62–3), provided we keep in mind that, insofar as our project is to clarify and facilitate our inquiries, our *motivation* for adopting one of the standard strategies is *not* that we wish to construct a systematic theory of meaning for natural language.

Relativity of adjectives: 'short'

Consider the sentence

    (g) John is a short basketball player.

One might at first be tempted to paraphrase this in first-order grammar as follows:

    (h) (John is a basketball player) ∧ (John is short).

But this paraphrase misses the relativity of the attribution of shortness in (g) to *basketball players*. A better paraphrase of (g) would express the idea that there is at least one person who is *short for a basketball player*. One way to express this idea would be to paraphrase (g) as

    (i) (John is a basketball player) ∧ (John is shorter than most basketball
        players).

where the 'most' that occurs in 'John is shorter than most basketball players' is paraphrased in one of the several ways mentioned above.[29] There is apparently no general obstacle to producing paraphrases, case by case, that respect this kind of relativity of adjectives to particular nouns they modify.

Belief sentences

The difficulty of paraphrasing sentences such as

    (j) Frege believes that Mont Blanc is in France.

into first-order logical notation is well known. The context following 'that' in (j) is opaque, in the sense that not all substitutions of coextensive terms

---

[29] For details, see, for instance, Heim and Kratzer 1998: 68–73 and Lepore and Ludwig 2007: 162–73. A number of other approaches could also work. There is no need to settle between them here.

for terms that follow 'that' in (j) and not all substitutions of coextensive sentences for the sentence that follows 'that' in (j) preserve the truth value of (j). But first-order logic is extensional: in a language with a first-order logical grammar, substitutions of coextensive terms and sentences always preserve truth value. How then can one paraphrase belief sentences by sentences with a first-order logical grammar? Given the pragmatic purposes that I have described, this question, though serious, is less problematic than it may at first appear, for two main reasons.

First, there is no obstacle to accepting Quine's proposal that we regiment '*x* believes that Mont Blanc is in France' with a one-place fused predicate '*x* believes-that-Mont-Blanc-is-in-France' (Quine 1960: 216). Donald Davidson objects that Quine's proposal would prevent us from providing a theory of meaning for English, because it would entail that English has infinitely many semantical primitives—one for each predicate constructed by concatenating 'believes that' with an English sentence (Davidson 1984: 13–14). If our goal is not to construct a theory of meaning for natural language, however, but, as I have assumed, to regiment our sentences, then in principle we are free to adopt Quine's proposal, or any other proposal that yields a distinct regimented predicate for each new occasion on which we ascribe a belief by using a natural language sentence.

Second, if we want a general method of paraphrasing belief sentences into a language with a first-order logical grammar, one that also illuminates the logical structure of belief sentences, we may adopt some version of Davidson's *paratactic* account of the logical form of belief sentences (Davidson 1984: 93–108). There are several apparently powerful objections to Davidson's original proposal. Most of the objections presuppose that an account of how to paraphrase belief sentences into first-order logic is satisfactory only if it is faithful to all aspects of our ordinary concept of belief, as revealed by our intuitions about which belief reports to accept in various circumstances and what those belief reports imply. Since our present project of regimenting our sentences to clarify and facilitate our inquiries does not require us to be faithful to all aspects of our ordinary concept of belief, or to preserve all of the intuitions that are usually associated with it, however, many of the standard objections to Davidson's proposal will not count against our using it, at least on some occasions, to further our goal of clarifying and facilitating our inquiries. I conjecture that the remaining objections could be addressed by modifications of Davidson's original proposal, but I will not try to establish this here.[30]

Necessity and possibility

It is now widely accepted that the expressions 'necessarily', 'possibly', 'it is necessary that', and 'it is possible that' are typically used in English to express notions that cannot be paraphrased by sentences of an extensional first-order language. Thus, consider the sentence

(k) Necessarily, $9 > 7$.

Perhaps in some special contexts one might use this sentence in a way that could be replaced by a metalinguistic sentence, such as

(l) '$9 > 7$' is analytic,

where 'is analytic' is understood to mean 'x follows from the semantical rules for the language of which x is a part'. To make sense of such a paraphrase, however, we would need to make use of the notion of semantical rule—a notion that cannot be explained in purely extensional terms. In addition, however, there are other uses of (k) that we would not be willing to paraphrase by (l). The most important challenges to paraphrases such as (l) are those in which (k) is used on a particular occasion in such a way that it is taken to imply

(m) There is something x such that necessarily, $x > 7$.

A sentence such as (m), while not strictly speaking part of ordinary language, makes explicit use of a notion of *de re* necessity that many philosophers take to be expressed by some uses of modal adverbs and corresponding phrases in ordinary language. How are we to paraphrase such sentences?

There are two main strategies. The first is to add modal operators to a regimented first-order language, taking the operators as primitives synonymous with the ordinary language modal adverbs 'necessarily' and

---

[30] For a list of the main objections to Davidson's proposal, plausible replies to these objections, and a new proposal inspired by Davidson, see Lepore and Ludwig 2007: chapter 11. Since Lepore and Ludwig share Davidson's assumption that an account of belief sentences is satisfactory only if it can be part of a finitely stated compositional theory of meaning—an assumption to which the project of this book does not commit us—some of their replies concede to the objections more than is necessary for my purposes.

'possibly', or 'it is necessary that' and 'it is possible that' (Peacocke 1978, Davies 1981: 187–93). The second is to paraphrase sentences that contain ordinary language modal operators by regimented sentences that quantify over possible worlds (Lewis 1968, Davies 1981: 193–201, Larson and Segal 1995: 426–9). I find the second strategy more appealing than the first, mainly because it is analogous to paraphrasing sentences that contain second-order quantifiers by a first-order language with set theory added.[31] The idea is to start with a regimented first-order language and add a theory of possible worlds over which the quantifiers of that language range, and then to explain necessity and possibility in terms of quantification over possible worlds. It is a huge task to work out the details of either of these strategies. In this book I shall remain officially agnostic about how to handle ordinary language sentences that contain modal operators, and focus on those aspects of ordinary language that can be paraphrased into a first-order language without modal operators and without quantifying over possible worlds. This attitude is justified, if at all, by the fact that it is difficult enough to reconcile the Tarski–Quine thesis with the intersubjectivity constraint even if we restrict ourselves to the extensional fragments of ordinary language. I conjecture that any adequate treatment of the modal sentences will be an extension of the treatment I offer for the non-modal ones. Unfortunately, however, in this book I shall have to leave this as a conjecture, since I have not yet worked out an adequate treatment of modal sentences. In any case, as I shall try to show, the account of truth that I shall propose solves a pressing pragmatic problem that arises if we restrict our attention to sentences of ordinary language that can be paraphrased by structured sentences with a first-order logical grammar.

---

[31] Another reason is that unlike the first strategy (see Peacocke 1978: §III), the second strategy does not require that we employ infinite conjunctions.

2

The Tarski–Quine Thesis

2.1. The Indispensability Argument

Regimentation is not an end in itself. We regiment our sentences in order to clarify and facilitate our inquiries by formulating and applying logical generalizations such as "Every regimented sentence of the form '$S \lor \sim S$' is true."[1] As I explained briefly in the Introduction, however, we cannot actually write out all of the sentences of any given logical form, and so we cannot express logical generalizations by writing out and affirming conjunctions of all of their instances. We therefore need some way to express such conjunctions *without* actually writing them out. Let us now consider in more detail how this need may motivate us to use a truth predicate, and, ultimately, to embrace the Tarski–Quine thesis that there is no more to truth than what is captured by a Tarski-style disquotational truth predicate defined for one's own sentences.

To begin with, consider Quine's classic account of why we need a truth predicate to express logical generalizations:

We can generalize on 'Tom is mortal', 'Dick is mortal', and so on, without talking of truth or of sentences; we can say 'All men are mortal'. . . . When we want to generalize on 'Tom is mortal or Tom is not mortal', 'snow is white or snow is not white', and so on, we ascend to talk of truth and of sentences, saying 'every sentence of the form 'p or not p' is true', or 'every alternation of a sentence with its negation is true'. What prompts this semantic ascent is not that 'Tom is mortal or Tom is not mortal' is somehow about sentences while 'Tom is mortal' and 'Tom is Tom' are about Tom. All three are about Tom. We ascend only because

---

[1] Such generalizations are among the truths that we take to be worth formulating if we participate in rational inquiry. By formulating logical generalizations, we can also clarify corresponding *logical consequence* relations on which we may then choose to rely.

of the oblique way in which the instances over which we are generalizing are related to one another.   (Quine 1986: 11)

In this passage Quine does not explicitly limit his reasoning to logical generalizations on sentences in a regimented language. But if we are to be clear about the logical generalizations that we aim to express, we must first regiment our sentences. I shall therefore assume that Quine's reasoning applies in the first instance to logical generalizations on sentences of one's own regimented first-order language, and that by combining a recursive grammar of our regimented language L with standard syntactic criteria for substitution of regimented predicates or sentences for schematic term and sentence letters, we can specify the set of all and only the regimented sentences of L with a given form, such as 'p or not p'.[2] Given these assumptions, it would be needlessly indirect to define truth first for propositions, and then to extend that definition of truth to sentences, as Horwich 1998a and Soames 1999 propose. To use a truth predicate defined for sentences is *also* indirect, but not needlessly so. When we wish to generalize on sentences such as 'Tom is mortal or Tom is not mortal', 'snow is white or snow is not white', and so on, our primary goal is not to say anything about such sentences, but to affirm that Tom is mortal or Tom is not mortal, snow is white or snow is not white, and so on. Nevertheless, according to Quine, due to "the oblique way in which the instances over which we are generalizing are related to one another", to affirm that Tom is mortal or Tom is not mortal, snow is white or snow is not white, and so on, we must use a truth predicate that applies to sentences.

Brian Loar rejects Quine's argument that a truth predicate is indispensable for generalizing on sentences. Loar writes:

As an explanation of the *point* of 'true', [the Quine passage cited above] leaves me puzzled. Evidently 'when we want to *generalize...*' does not bear its meaning on its face. One way of generalizing with regard to sentences of the form 'p or not p' is to say we would *accept* all instances; but that does not require 'true'. No, 'we want to generalize' must mean 'with regard to their *truth*'. But how does that tell us what is important about truth? Why do we *want* to generalize in terms of T and not some other T'? Why *any* truth predicate?   (Loar 1981: 171–2)

---

[2] For syntactical criteria for substituting regimented predicates or sentences for schematic term and sentence letters, see Quine 1982: chapters 26 and 28.

But these questions reveal a misunderstanding. To say that we would accept all sentences of the form '$S \lor \sim S$' is one way of *saying something general about* sentences of the form '$S \lor \sim S$', but it is not to *generalize on* sentences of that form, in the sense of 'generalize on' that is relevant to Quine's reasoning. Quine notes that "we can generalize on 'Tom is mortal', 'Dick is mortal', and so on, without talking of truth or of sentences; we can say 'All men are mortal'."[3] The crucial consideration is that the generalization 'All men are mortal' *implies* each of 'Tom is mortal', 'Dick is mortal', and so on, given the corresponding tacit premises 'Tom is a man', 'Dick is a man', and so on. These elementary implications serve as Quine's model for what it takes to generalize on sentences, and are therefore worth examining in detail. The generalization 'All men are mortal' may be paraphrased as 'For all x, if x is a man, then x is mortal', which, like any universal generalization, implies each of its instances. In particular, 'For all x, if x is a man, then x is mortal' implies 'if Tom is a man, then Tom is mortal'. Finally, 'if Tom is a man, then Tom is mortal' and the tacit premise 'Tom is a man' together truth-functionally imply 'Tom is mortal.' In the same way, we can derive any sentence of the form 'N is mortal', where the position marked by 'N' is filled by a proper name, if we accept a corresponding premise of the form 'N is a man.' This example suggests that to generalize on 'Tom is mortal', 'Dick is mortal', and so on, is to write or utter a (non-contradictory) generalization that, together with some independently plausible auxiliary premises that are not identical to the sentences that we wish to generalize on, *implies* all those sentences. Similarly, I suggest, to generalize on regimented L-sentences of a given form is to write or utter a (non-contradictory) generalization that, together with some independently plausible auxiliary premises that are not identical to any of the L-sentences of that form, implies them all.[4] For instance, to generalize on L-sentences of the form '$S \lor \sim S$', such as

(Tom is mortal) $\lor \sim$(Tom is mortal)
(Snow is white) $\lor \sim$(Snow is white)

---

[3] Quine 1986: 11. Loar does not quote this sentence; perhaps he just overlooked it.

[4] It is likely that Quine's use of the phrase 'generalizes on' is not taken from ordinary language, but from the natural deduction rule known as universal generalization (UG). In standard systems of natural deduction, one 'generalizes on' sentences in Quine's sense when one applies the rule UG, which allows one to infer '$\forall x(x = x)$', for instance, from '$z = z$'.

and so on, is to write a (non-contradictory) generalization that, together with auxiliary premises that are not identical to any of those sentences, implies them all.

Do Loar's proposed alternatives generalize on sentences in this sense? Consider Loar's generalization, "We would accept all sentences of the form '$S \vee \sim S$'," which we may rephrase as "We would accept any given sentence of the form '$S \vee \sim S$'." This generalizes on such sentences as "we accept the sentence '(Tom is mortal) $\vee \sim$(Tom is mortal)'" and "we accept the sentence '(Snow is white) $\vee \sim$(Snow is white)'". Hence Loar's generalization does not imply '(Tom is mortal) $\vee \sim$(Tom is mortal)', for instance, unless we *also* accept the conditional

(a) If we accept the sentence '(Tom is mortal) $\vee \sim$(Tom is mortal)', then (Tom is mortal) $\vee \sim$(Tom is mortal).

Granted, (a) is true, because its consequent is (logically) true. But to generalize on sentences by using Loar's method, we would need to suppose that it is epistemically reasonable to accept *any* given instance of the pattern

(A) If we accept the sentence '____', then ____.

To see what is attractive, yet misleading about (A), consider the corresponding first-person singular version:

(A′) If I accept the sentence '____', then ____.

If it were epistemically reasonable to accept every instance of (A′), it would be epistemically reasonable to accept

(b) If I accept the sentence 'There are black holes', then there are black holes.

It would then be epistemically reasonable to *infer* that there are black holes from (b) and 'I accept the sentence 'There are black holes'.' Why would anyone be tempted to trust such an inference? One possible explanation is that after reflection, no one can accept the sentence

(c) I accept the sentence 'There are black holes', but there are no black holes.

The problem is that to accept (c) is to suppose that one accepts the sentence 'There are black holes', and thereby to suppose that one believes that there are black holes; yet to accept (c) is also to assert that there are no black holes, and thereby to express one's belief that there are no black holes. To accept (c), then, is to express, and thereby commit oneself to, beliefs that one knows to be incompatible. Hence anyone who utters (c) expresses incompatible beliefs.[5] An analogous problem affects some statements made by using the first person plural pronoun 'we', such as

> (d) We accept the sentence 'There are black holes', but there are no black holes.

But if anyone who utters (d) expresses incompatible beliefs, and any reflective person can come to see this by going through the reasoning just sketched, then one might think that those who go through this reasoning are entitled to accept

> (e) If we accept the sentence 'There are black holes', then there are black holes.

Since this reasoning applies to any sentence, it may *seem* that anyone who goes through the above reasoning is entitled to accept all instances of the form (A), just as Loar's objection suggests.

But this appearance is illusory. To see why, consider a sentence, such as 'The Earth is flat', that we do not actually accept. By asserting either

> (f) John accepts the sentence 'The Earth is flat', but the Earth is not flat.

or

> (g) They accept the sentence 'The Earth is flat', but the Earth is not flat.

we do not commit ourselves to incompatible beliefs. Moreover, we take for granted that *no one's* acceptance of 'The Earth is flat' implies that the Earth is flat. Granted, we can't *simultaneously* express a belief and assert that what we believe is not so. But the intelligibility of assertions of (f) and (g), together with our understanding of acceptance of sentences and the beliefs such acceptances express, show that sentences of the form (A) are not generally acceptable, despite the problems with asserting (d) and (e).

---

[5] This is a metalinguistic analogue of G. E. Moore's paradox about belief.

Hence the auxiliary premises on which we would have to rely to derive the sentences that interest us from Loar's generalization are not generally acceptable. I conclude that while Loar's generalization *says something general about* all sentences of the form '$S \lor \sim S$', it does not *generalize on* them in the sense relevant to Quine's reasoning.

In contrast, if we assume standard syntactic criteria for substitution of regimented predicates or sentences for schematic term and sentence letters, then from the sentence 'Every regimented sentence of the form '$S \lor \sim S$' is true' we may infer

'(Tom is mortal) $\lor \sim$(Tom is mortal)' is true
'(Snow is white) $\lor \sim$(Snow is white)' is true

and so on. To get from these sentences to

(Tom is mortal) $\lor \sim$(Tom is mortal)
(Snow is white) $\lor \sim$(Snow is white)

and so on, we need to accept conditionals of the form

'___' is true $\rightarrow$ ___.

Together with these conditionals, we can derive every sentence of the form '$S \lor \sim S$' from 'Every regimented sentence of the form '$S \lor \sim S$' is true'. And to get from sentences in the second list to sentences in the first list we need to accept conditionals of the form

___ $\rightarrow$ '___' is true.[6]

Hence it seems that to generalize on sentences by using a predicate 'is true' we need to accept T-sentences such as

'(Snow is white) $\lor \sim$(Snow is white)' is true $\leftrightarrow$ ((Snow is white) $\lor \sim$(Snow is white)),

---

[6] If we assume that our metalanguage *ML* is consistent and contains an ω-rule that would license us to derive 'Every regimented sentence of the form '$S \lor \sim S$' is true' from the set of all and only regimented sentences of the form '$S \lor \sim S$', we can conclude that the set of all and only regimented sentences of the form '$S \lor \sim S$' and 'Every regimented sentence of the form '$S \lor \sim S$' is true' are interderivable in *ML*. As Volker Halbach points out, however, if we add such an ω-rule, we would have in effect a definition of 'is true' for sentences of *L* (see Halbach 1999: 11–12). Those who want to add a truth predicate without defining it will therefore not want to accept the ω-rule. They will prefer simply to add all the T-sentences to *L*. For a clarification of the sense in which, given the T-sentences, the sentence 'Every regimented *L*-sentence of the form '$S \lor \sim S$' is true,' for instance, is 'equivalent' to the set of all and only regimented *L*-sentences of the form '$S \lor \sim S$', see Halbach 1999: 12–15.

which are of the form

(T) '___' is true ↔ ___.

with the blanks uniformly filled by sentences of our regimented language.[7]

We may summarize this reasoning as follows. Suppose we wish to generalize on sentences of the form '$S \lor \sim S$'. The recursive grammar of our regimented language generates infinitely many such sentences. We cannot actually write out all of those sentences, and so we cannot directly affirm the conjunction of all of those sentences. We therefore need some way to affirm all of those sentences *without* actually writing them out. We can generalize on the regimented sentences of the form '$S \lor \sim S$', if we assert 'Every regimented sentence of the form '$S \lor \sim S$' is true,' provided that we accept any given sentence that results from the pattern (T) when its blanks are uniformly filled by a given sentence of our regimented language. Moreover, we know of no way of generalizing on all sentences of a given form without using a truth predicate. (I will consider two serious challenges to this claim in §2.3.) Hence to generalize on all sentences of a given form, a truth predicate is indispensable. I shall call this the *indispensability argument*.

Let me digress briefly to highlight an assumption of the indispensability argument that usually goes without saying, but that I will scrutinize, reject, and modify in Chapters 3 and 4. The assumption is that *when we generalize on sentences of a given logical form, such as '$S \lor \sim S$', we identify those sentences solely by their syntactical shapes.* We accept this assumption, in effect, if we restrict ourselves to the standard syntactic criteria for substitution of regimented predicates or sentences for schematic term and sentence letters that occur in our generalizations on sentences. As I noted above, it is by relying on such accounts of substitution that we can infer, for example, that

---

[7] To draw the distinction between saying something general about sentences, on the one hand, and generalizing on them, on the other, we need at least a working grasp of logical implication for sentences of our language. I assume we grasp the notion of logical implication simply in virtue of following deductive inference rules for the sentences of our language, and, in particular, for the language in which we express the T-sentences. We could define a truth predicate for those sentences, and then define implication in terms of the preservation of truth (or the logical truth of certain conditionals). But I assume that we need not define implication in terms of truth for sentences of our metalanguage in order to distinguish between saying something general about sentences of a given object language L, on the one hand, and generalizing on sentences of L, on the other.

'(Tom is mortal) ∨ ∼(Tom is mortal)' is true

and

'(Snow is white) ∨ ∼(Snow is white)' is true

are both *instances* of the generalization "Every sentence of the form 'S ∨ ∼S' is true."[8] For reasons I previewed in the Introduction, I shall propose in Chapter 4 that we conceive of words in a way that licenses us to apply our own disquotational truth predicate to sentences that we do not identify *solely* by their syntactical shapes. If we adopt my proposed alternative conception of words, then we can each still identify sentences of our own regimented language solely by their syntactical shapes, but we can no longer claim that the italicized assumption holds for *all* sentences to which our own disquotational truth predicate applies. In particular, if we adopt my proposed alternative conception of words, there are some instances of the generalization "Every sentence of the form 'S ∨ ∼S' is true" that do not count as instances of that generalization given the italicized assumption. In this Chapter I shall nevertheless provisionally accept that the italicized assumption holds for all sentences to which our own disquotational truth predicate applies.

I return now to my clarification and evaluation of the indispensability argument. If the argument is correct, then to generalize on sentences of a given form, we need to accept every T-sentence. Since there are infinitely many T-sentences, however, we cannot express our acceptance of every one of them by writing them out. How then do we express our acceptance of the T-sentences themselves? We cannot do so by affirming 'Every T-sentence is true,' since this generalization presupposes that we have *already* accepted T-sentences for the T-sentences themselves, and would therefore either be viciously circular, or start us on an infinite regress of generalizations and corresponding T-sentences.[9] Hence the indispensability

---

[8] To handle other generalizations, such as "Every regimented sentence of the form '∀x(Fx ∨ ∼Fx)' is true", we will of course also need a purely syntactical (orthographic) account of substitution of regimented predicates for schematic predicate letters, such as 'F', 'G', 'H', and so on. Because of the relationship between free and bound variables, the rules for substituting predicates for schematic predicate letters are trickier to state than the rules for substituting closed sentences for schematic sentence letters, but such rules are nevertheless widely known and can be found in any good text on first-order logic, such as Quine 1982.

[9] In Putnam 1983, Hilary Putnam raises a related concern about circularity. Unlike my concern in the text, however, his is not directed at the indispensability argument, but instead presupposes that the goal of an account of truth is to capture the meaning of the ordinary word 'true'.

argument presupposes that if we can use a truth predicate to generalize on infinitely many sentences, there must be a way for us to affirm every T-sentence *without* using a truth predicate. But now it may seem that the argument faces another version of Loar's objection. For if we can affirm every T-sentence *without* using a truth predicate, then we should also be able to affirm every sentence of the form '$S \lor {\sim}S$' without using a truth predicate, just as Loar suggests.

This objection rests on a subtle but crucial conflation of (a) *generalizing on infinitely many sentences of a given form* with (b) *committing oneself to affirming any sentence of a given form*. To see the difference between (a) and (b), recall that in first-order predicate logic, the logic of identity is completely captured by accepting '$\forall x(x = x)$' and any sentence of the form '$\forall x \forall y((Fx \land x = y) \to Fy)$' as axioms, together with any legitimate reletterings of the bound variables in either of these axioms. We may regard the relettering rules as *additional* to '$\forall x(x = x)$', in which case it is not schematic, but directly *generalizes on* the infinitely many regimented sentences '$x = x$', '$y = y$', '$z = z$', and so on, that it implies. When the axiom '$\forall x(x = x)$' is viewed in this way, to accept it is to state, in effect, that *everything is self-identical*. In contrast, the second of these axioms is *schematic*; by accepting it we do not *state* anything at all, but instead *commit ourselves to affirming* any regimented sentence of the form '$\forall x \forall y((Fx \land x = y) \to Fy)$'. To adopt the axiom schema '$\forall x \forall y((Fx \land x = y) \to Fy)$' is therefore not to *generalize on* all sentences of that form, but only to *commit ourselves to affirming* any sentence of that form. Similarly, contrary to the objection sketched in the previous paragraph, to regard the schema (T) as an axiom schema is not to *generalize on* all T-sentences, but only to *commit ourselves to affirming* any T-sentence. I conclude that to characterize a truth predicate that we can use to generalize on infinitely many sentences of a given form, it is enough to commit ourselves to affirming any T-sentence.

2.2. Why Generalize on Valid Sentences?

One might be convinced that to generalize on infinitely many sentences of a given form, we need to use a truth predicate, but wonder why we *need* to generalize on sentences of a given form, instead of just committing ourselves to affirming each of the sentences. To generalize on sentences of the form

'$S \lor \sim S$', for instance, we would need to affirm a non-contradictory generalization that *implies* all of them, and for this, according to the indispensability argument, we would need a truth predicate. But if we treat '$S \lor \sim S$' as an axiom schema, we commit ourselves to affirming each regimented sentence of the form '$S \lor \sim S$' without generalizing on all those sentences. Hence if we treat '$S \lor \sim S$' and other valid logical schemata as axiom schemata, we can accept the indispensability argument without concluding that we need to use a truth predicate. What then motivates us to generalize on the instances of such schemata?

I assume that our desire to clarify and facilitate inquiry brings with it a desire to classify particular regimented sentences as valid (logically true). Given this desire, we can begin to answer the question just posed by asking how generalizing on sentences is related to classifying particular regimented sentences as valid. An answer is suggested by the following observation:

> If one's first-order regimented language L includes the identity sign and predicates that express addition and multiplication, then to classify one's L-sentences as valid is equivalent to generalizing on them.

This observation is a consequence of standard definitions of validity and a theorem in recursion theory. The definitions are as follows (note the subscripts):

(D1) A first-order logical *schema* is valid$_1$ if and only if it is true for all interpretations.

(D2) A regimented sentence is valid$_2$ if and only if (a) there is a first-order logical schema S from which the regimented sentence results by substitution of regimented sentences or predicates for sentence or term letters, and (b) schema S is valid$_1$.

From (D1) and (D2) we may infer that a particular sentence is valid$_2$ if and only if it results by substitution from a schema that is true for all interpretations. The sentence '$\forall x((x \text{ is white}) \lor \sim(x \text{ is white}))$', for instance, is valid$_2$, since it results by substitution from the schema '$\forall x(Fx \lor \sim Fx)$', which is true for all interpretations.

An interpretation of a closed first-order schema S is usually taken to be an ordered pair of a non-empty domain of discourse D and an assignment A of objects in D to the extensions of the predicates in S, where it is assumed that A may be specified without substituting regimented predicates for term letters in S. When A is specified without substituting regimented predicates for term letters in S, truth-relative-to-an-interpretation is not the same as disquotational truth, as characterized by T-sentences. Nevertheless, a theorem in recursion theory relates the two. The Löwenheim–Hilbert–Bernays theorem, due to David Hilbert and Paul Bernays, extends results of Leopold Löwenheim. It establishes that if one's first-order regimented language L includes the identity sign and predicates that express addition and multiplication, then a schema S of L is true for all interpretations in all non-empty domains of discourse if and only if every L-sentence that results by substitution from schema S is true.[10] The L-sentence '$\forall x((x$ is white$) \lor \sim(x$ is white$))$', for instance, is valid$_2$ if and only the schema '$\forall x(Fx \lor \sim Fx)$' is valid$_1$; and the schema '$\forall x(Fx \lor \sim Fx)$' is valid$_1$ if and only if every L-sentence of the form '$\forall x(Fx \lor \sim Fx)$' is true. Hence if one's first-order regimented language L includes the identity sign and predicates that express addition and multiplication, then *one* way to classify particular L-sentences of a given schematic form S as valid$_2$ is to classify S as valid$_1$ by using a disquotational truth predicate.[11]

---

[10] According to Quine, the Löwenheim–Hilbert–Bernays theorem was first proved in Hilbert and Bernays 1939: 234–53, and later strengthened, as Theorem 35, in Kleene 1953. Quine explains one of the central ideas behind the theorem in Quine 1995a. In Quine 1982, ch. 33, Quine writes that Hilbert and Bernays give "a general rule for writing out, for *any* schema, an arithmetical interpretation which can be depended upon to come out true in case the schema does happen to be consistent" (Quine 1982: 211). As Carl Jockusch (a recursion theorist at the University of Illinois-Urbana) explained to me, the Hilbert–Bernays rule for writing out an arithmetical interpretation of a schema depends on treating a *non-constructive* assignment of truth values to simple sentences as an "oracle". For any schema S, we can apply the Hilbert–Bernays rule to write out an arithmetical sentence s that is true just in case S is consistent, but we do not thereby know whether or not s is true. The dependence in the general case of the arithmetical interpretation on a non-constructive assignment of truth values to simple sentences is reflected in George Boolos's formulation of what Hilbert and Bernays proved: "any satisfiable schema is satisfied by a model whose domain is the set of natural numbers and whose predicates are assigned relations on natural numbers *that can be defined in arithmetic*" (Boolos 1975: 525, emphasis in original).

[11] Strictly speaking, by this criterion of validity, sentences and schemata that can only be proved from the identity axioms noted in §2.1 do not count as valid. As Quine points out, however, there are at least two reasons for counting such sentences and schemata as valid: first, complete proof procedures are available for quantification theory supplemented with the identity axioms, which together constitute the standard logical identity theory; second, this identity theory, like quantification theory, "treats all objects impartially" (Quine 1986: 62). To count schemata that can be proved only from the identity axioms as valid by generalizing on sentences, however, the best we can do is to show that particular *explications* of them are valid. To construct the relevant explications for a given regimented language L, it is enough to define '$x_i = x_j$' as a mere *definitional abbreviation* for an open sentence of L that contains no occurrences of '$=$' but is nevertheless satisfied by a sequence s if and only if $s_i = s_j$. A recipe for

But there are *also* ways of classifying a particular *L*-sentence *s* of a given schematic form *S* as valid₁ *without* using a truth predicate at all. For instance, a given schema *S* is valid₁ if and only if its negation generates a contradiction by a standard method of proof for first-order logic. By definition (D2), then, *s* is valid₂ if and only if the negation of *S* generates a contradiction by a standard method of proof for first-order logic. Why then should we use a truth predicate to classify schematic form *S* as valid₁?

The answer is that we cannot simply take for granted that standard methods of proof for first-order logic are sound and complete. To prove that they are sound and complete, however, we need an independent characterization of what it is to be valid₁. And for this we need a truth predicate.

Given (D1), however, why not just classify a schema as valid₁ if and only if it is true under all interpretations, and leave it at that? One reason is that this preliminary characterization of when a schema is valid₁ does not tell us how the notion of truth that we need to classify a schema as valid₁ is related to the T-sentences that we need to generalize on sentences. If an interpretation *I* of *S* is given by substituting regimented predicates $P_1, \ldots, P_n$ for term letters in *S*, then *S* is true relative to *I* if and only if the regimented English sentence that results from substituting $P_1, \ldots, P_n$ for term letters in *S* is disquotationally true. In such cases, we can explain the two-place relation '*S* is true relative to *I*' in terms of a one-place predicate 'true' characterized by T-sentences, which are as clear to us as the regimented sentences they contain. If we had no general guarantee that an interpretation *I* of *S* can be given by substituting regimented predicates for term letters in *S*, however, then we would have no guarantee that we could explain '*S* is true relative to *I*' in terms of a one-place predicate 'true' characterized by T-sentences. Lacking such a guarantee, we might conclude that the notion of truth that we need if we are to classify schemata as valid₁ cannot be explained disquotationally, hence cannot be shown to

---

constructing such an open sentence is given on page 63 of Quine 1986. By using Quine's recipe, we can define '$x_i = x_i$', in particular, as a definitional abbreviation for an open sentence *q* of *L* that contains no occurrences of '=' but is nevertheless satisfied by a sequence *s* if and only if $s_i = s_i$. Given this definition, '$\forall x_i(x_i = x_i)$' is a definitional abbreviation for '$\forall x_i q$', which "is a truth purely of the logic of quantification and truth functions" (Quine 1986: 63), which is to say that (a) there is a first-order logical schema *S* from which '$\forall x_i q$' results by substitution of regimented sentences or predicates for sentence or term letters and (b) every *L*-sentence of the form *S* is true.

be as clear to us as our own regimented sentences. Fortunately, however, to classify schemata as valid₁ we do not need to make use of a notion of truth that cannot be explained disquotationally. For we can easily include in our regimented languages the identity sign and predicates that express addition and multiplication. The Löwenheim–Hilbert–Bernays theorem then ensures that we can identify interpretations with particular sentences of our regimented language, and classify schemata as valid₁ by generalizing on regimented L-sentences using a disquotational truth predicate.[12]

2.3. Three Attempts to Generalize on Sentences without Using a Truth Predicate

Let us now return to the indispensability argument. Is our confidence in it due to our failure to think of another way of generalizing on sentences? To address this question, I shall now examine three ways of generalizing on sentences without using a truth predicate.

To begin with, one might try to generalize on sentences by using first-order quantification. Instead of affirming 'Every regimented sentence of the form '$S \vee \sim S$' is true,' and 'Every regimented sentence of the form '$\forall x(Fx \vee \sim Fx)$' is true,' for instance, one might try

(D) $\forall x(x \vee \sim x)$

and

(E) $\forall x \forall y(xy \vee \sim xy)$

A superficial problem with this attempt is that the standard rules for constructing sentences of L do not yield either (D) or (E). A deep problem with the attempt is that even if we adopt new grammatical rules that imply that (D) and (E) are sentences, if we take '$\forall x$' to be a first-order quantifier that ranges over objects, we will not be able to make sense of (D) or (E).[13]

---

[12] Quine emphasizes that, unlike (D1), as it is usually understood, a definition of validity in terms of disquotational truth "renders the notions of validity and logical truth independent of all but a modest bit of set theory; independent of the higher flights" (Quine 1986: 56). This is an important consideration, but not, I think, as important as the fact that a definition of validity in terms of disquotational truth is as clear to us as the sentences for which our disquotational truth predicate is defined.

[13] For reasons that Joan Weiner explains in Weiner 2005, we can make sense of something like (D) if, following Frege, (a) we accept that among the objects in the domain of discourse for L are the

A more promising strategy is to use second-order quantification into predicate and sentence positions. Instead of affirming 'Every regimented sentence of the form '$S \lor \sim S$' is true,' and 'Every regimented sentence of the form '$\forall x(Fx \lor \sim Fx)$' is true,' one might affirm such sentences as

(F) $\forall p(p \lor \sim p)$

and

(G) $\forall F \forall \gamma(F\gamma \lor \sim F\gamma)$

where the quantifiers '$\forall F$' and '$\forall p$' are understood as second order, and so the variables 'F' and 'p' occur in positions in a sentence where it would not make sense to place a first-order variable or a singular term.

Most discussions of second-order quantification focus on quantification into n-place predicate positions, where $n \geq 1$. According to the standard semantics for second-order languages, a variable assignment s is a function that assigns a member of a given domain of discourse D to each first-order variable and a subset of D^n to each n-place relation variable. If we accept this semantics, then we will take (G) to be true relative to a given domain D if and only if for every variable assignment s, either $s(\gamma)$ is an element of $s(F)$ or $s(\gamma)$ is not an element of $s(F)$ (Shapiro 1991: 72). The standard semantics treats 1-place predicates as of the form 'is an element of S' for some set S of elements of D; predicates are therefore viewed *extensionally*: their meanings—the properties or attributes, if any, that they express—are irrelevant to the truth or falsity of second-order quantifications.

We can see (F) as a special case of quantification into predicate positions if we see sentences as 0-place predicates. To extend the standard semantics to apply to 0-place predicates, we must assign extensions, namely, true or false, to them. But if this is the proper semantics for a sentence such as (F), then

true and the false, (b) we treat sentences as proper names of the true or the false, (c) we add Frege's horizontal (symbolized by '—'), defined as '= the true', to our language, and (d) we rewrite (D) as

(D$_F$) $\forall x(-x \lor \sim-x)$

(To make sense of (D$_F$), we must also regard the logical connectives '$\lor$' and '$\sim$' not as symbols for operations, in Wittgenstein's sense, but as names of Fregean functions from truth values to truth values.) Even if we are willing to recast (D) as (D$_F$), however, this will not help us to make sense of (E). To generalize on sentences of the form '$\forall x(Fx \lor \sim Fx)$' in the way that Frege did, one must add second-order quantifiers to one's language. I discuss this strategy in the next two paragraphs. For a model-theoretical interpretation of the first-order part of Frege's logic, including definitions of the true and the false, see Parsons 1987.

second-order quantification over sentences can be simulated in our first-order language L. Since L is extensional, we can simply choose an arbitrary closed sentence of L, say '$\forall x_1 (x_1$ is mortal)', and define '$\forall p(\ldots p \ldots)$' as '$(\ldots \forall x_1 (x_1$ is mortal) $\ldots) \wedge (\ldots \sim \forall x_1 (x_1$ is mortal) $\ldots)$'.[14] There is no extensional difference between any two true sentences or any two false ones, so this definition is guaranteed to yield, for each second-order universal quantification over sentences, an L-sentence that has the same truth value as that quantification.

Such simulations of second-order quantification do not *generalize on* sentences, however. If we wish to use (F) to generalize on sentences, we should not presuppose the standard semantics for second-order quantification. Instead, we should try to regard second-order quantification as primitive. We will still need to explain the notations we use to express it, but for this purpose it may be enough to elucidate the inference rules and axioms for a particular artificial language that allows second-order quantification. We may also be able to appeal to second-order quantifications in ordinary language.[15]

It is an open question whether we can give elucidations or explanations of second-order quantification that satisfy us. But suppose we can. The strategy for generalizing on sentences by using second-order quantification still faces two closely related problems. First, unlike first-order logic, second-order logic is incomplete—there are complete proof procedures for validity in first-order languages, such as L, but no complete proof procedures for validity in second-order languages. If we wish to state logical generalizations for a first-order language, such as L, for which there are complete proof procedures, we should not do so by adding second-order quantifiers and variables. Second, '$\forall p(p \vee \sim p)$' does not generalize *exclusively* on sentences of L.[16] To see why, consider again the first-order quantification, '$\forall x(x = x)$'. This implies '$w = w$' for any free variable 'w' in L. We might not have a first-order name or description to put in place of the variable 'w', yet we can still regard the open sentence as true

---

[14] See Quine 1986: 74–5. For a similar simulation of second-order quantification, see Hilbert and Ackerman 1950: 127–8. The significance of Quine's simulation for our understanding of whether we can use second-order quantification to generalize on sentences without using a truth predicate is noted in Forbes 1986.

[15] For one interesting attempt to show that ordinary language makes use of second-order quantification, see Boolos 1984.

[16] As Mike Dunn pointed out to me.

relative to an assignment of some object from our domain of discourse to 'w'. Analogously, if we accept second-order quantification as primitive, we commit ourselves to inferences from '$\forall p(p \lor \sim p)$' to '$p \lor \sim p$', even when we do not put a sentence in place of the free variable 'p'. Hence if we wish to generalize *exclusively* on sentences of L, perhaps for the reasons explained in the previous section, we should not use second-order quantification into sentence positions.[17]

The most promising way to generalize exclusively on sentences of L without using a truth predicate is to use substitutional quantification. By hypothesis, L has the grammar of first-order predicate logic, so we can exploit the grammatical structure of L to specify all (and only) the sentences of L recursively. We can think of the set thus specified as the domain of a universal substitutional quantifier 'Π' which binds an expression-variable 'S' that marks places in a sentence of L for which we may substitute any sentence of L. Now consider

(H) $\Pi S(S \lor \sim S)$

Can we use (H) *in place of* the generalization 'Every regimented sentence of the form '$S \lor \sim S$' is true'? We cannot do so unless we can understand the universal substitutional quantifier that occurs in (H). One might first try to explain the contribution of the universal substitutional quantifier as follows:

(E1)   '$\Pi S(\dots S \dots)$' is true if and only if, for every sentence s of L, the sentence that results from replacing the free occurrences of 'S' in '$(\dots S \dots)$' by s is true.[18]

One might object that this explanation makes use of a truth predicate, and therefore does not help us to understand how we can use substitutional quantification to express logical generalizations *without* using a truth predicate. But (E1) should not be understood as an account of the *meaning* of 'ΠS': a sentence of the form '$\Pi S(\dots S \dots)$' does not *mention* (refer to) any of the sentences over which the quantifier ranges (Soames 1999: 91–2). A proponent of (E1) might therefore claim that once we understand

---

[17] Some philosophers think we want and need to be able to make sense of an open second-order sentence, such as '$p \lor \sim p$', even when we do not put sentences of L in place of the free variable 'p'. I shall examine one version of this view in the next section.

[18] This formulation is due in essentials to David 1994: 86.

substitutional qualification by means of (E1), we can simply use a sentence such as (H) to express generalizations without using a truth predicate. But this reply just presupposes that we can use and understand (H) *without* using a truth predicate. We are so far at a loss to understand (H) without relying on (E1), which contains a truth predicate.[19]

To avoid this problem, we need to provide a different explanation of the universal substitutional quantifier. One might try:

(E2) The notation '$\Pi S(\ldots S \ldots)$' encodes the conjunction of the open or closed sentences that result from replacing the free occurrences 'S' in '$(\ldots S \ldots)$' by sentences of L.[20]

If we explain the notation '$\Pi S(\ldots S \ldots)$' in this way, then we must concede that no finite, first-order sentence of English or Regimented English paraphrases (H), which we must therefore regard as an *abbreviation* for the infinitely long conjunction of all and only the sentences of the form '$S \vee {\sim}S$'. Similarly, suppose we try to use a substitutional quantifier on *predicate-variables* to generalize on sentences of the form '$\forall x(Fx \vee {\sim}Fx)$' without using a truth predicate. For instance, we may write

(I) $\Pi F\forall x(Fx \vee {\sim}Fx)$

where

(E3) The notation '$\Pi F(\ldots F \ldots)$' encodes the conjunction of the open or closed sentences that result from replacing the free occurrences 'F' in '$(\ldots F \ldots)$' by predicates of L. (David 1994: 99)

If we explain the notation '$\Pi F(\ldots F \ldots)$' in this way, then we must concede that no finite, first-order sentence of English or Regimented English paraphrases (I), which we must therefore regard as an *abbreviation* for the infinitely long conjunction of all and only L sentences of the form '$\forall x(Fx \vee {\sim}Fx)$'.[21] In general, for each logical law that we can state by using

[19] This criticism of (E1) is adapted from David 1994: 86, where it is used to reject substitutional definitions of 'true-in-L'. For a lucid investigation of some of the issues at stake here, see Kripke 1976.

[20] See David 1994: 99. Van Inwagen 2002 traces the idea back to a book review by Hartry Field in the 1980s. Before that, however, the idea was already suggested in footnote 9 of Leeds 1978.

[21] This substitutional approach only works if the resulting conjunctions contain no free variables. This is not a serious limitation, however, because an open sentence is logically true if and only if its corresponding universal closure is logically true. Thus we can say that an open sentence is logically true if and only if the appropriate substitutional generalization on its universal closure is true.

a truth predicate, there is a corresponding substitutional generalization like (H) or (I) that contains no truth predicate, but abbreviates the corresponding infinite conjunction of sentences we wish to affirm.

Does this show that we can generalize on sentences without using a truth predicate? The answer depends on whether we can understand explanations such as (E2) and (E3) without relying on a truth predicate. We can understand such explanations only if (a) the language that we use to paraphrase the substitutional quantifications *contains* the infinitely long sentences for which the substitutional generalizations are to be regarded as abbreviations, and (b) we *understand* those infinitely long sentences. But it is unclear whether English or Regimented English contains infinitely long sentences.[22] And even if the grammar of English or Regimented English recursively generates such sentences, it is unclear whether we can understand those sentences directly, without relying on a truth predicate.[23] One might try to lay down inference rules, on analogy with the standard instantiation and generalization rules for objectual quantifiers, in the hope of explaining our understanding of substitutional quantifications *without* presupposing a direct grasp of infinite conjunctions or disjunctions.[24] But to stipulate that such rules together implicitly define the quantifications *is*, in effect, to regard the quantifications as infinite conjunctions or disjunctions. The two strategies are at root one, and hence leave it equally unclear whether we can make sense of the substitutional quantifications without using a truth predicate. A corollary of this conclusion is that if we are unclear about whether we understand infinitely long sentences, it will not help us to use a truth predicate defined by the axiom

(ΠS)   ('S' is true if and only if S)

as Hartry Field proposes (Field 1994: 259). I shall henceforth assume that to generalize on sentences, we need to use a truth predicate that is not itself defined in terms of substitutional quantification.

---

[22] Speaking about an infinitely long sentence "generated" from a multiply substitutionally quantified generalization, Peter Van Inwagen writes that "It is really very hard to believe that there are such sentences as these" (Van Inwagen 2002: 215).
[23] For instance, Van Inwagen says he cannot even understand very long sentences, such as those that contain 3,999 words (Van Inwagen 2002: 216).
[24] As suggested in Hill 2002: 17–22.

2.4. Horwich's Minimal Theory

Even if one grants that to generalize on sentences of our own regimented language L we need to use a truth predicate, one might still ask why we should define our truth predicates so that they apply in the first instance to sentences of L, not to the propositions expressed by those sentences. Paul Horwich observes that we typically apply our ordinary English word 'true' to propositions expressed (*what is said*) by particular utterances of English sentences (Horwich 1998a: 16, 35). When 'true' is applied to propositions expressed by particular utterances of English sentences, however, it might just as well be applied to the sentences directly, for reasons I will explain below. There is significant difference between a disquotational definition of 'true' for sentences we can use, on the one hand, and a definition of 'true' for the propositions expressed by sentences we can use, on the other, only if the latter definition is *also* intended to yield a definition of 'true' for propositions that we cannot express. A central task of Horwich's Minimal Theory is to yield such a definition. I shall argue that the Minimal Theory fails in this task, so we should not prefer it to a definition of truth for sentences we can use.

Suppose that if we put a declarative sentence between the brackets '<' and '>', we form a singular term that denotes the proposition, if any, expressed by (a particular utterance of) that sentence. Then we can express Horwich's Minimal Theory as follows: the meaning of 'true' in English is constituted by our disposition to accept any given instance of the schema

(MT)   <p> is true if and only p. (Horwich 1998a: 128)

If we are disposed to affirm any given instance of (MT), as Horwich claims, then it seems we can rely on instances of (MT) to express generalizations, such as the logical generalization

(i) Every proposition of the form <p or not p> is true.

The basic idea—an extension, to generalizations on propositions, of an idea originally due to Tarski—is that for a given proposition, such as <Snow is white>,

(ii) <Snow is white or not Snow is white> is a proposition of the form
      <p or not p>

and hence

(iii) <Snow is white or not Snow is white> is true

follows by modus ponens from (ii) and a universal instantiation of (i), namely,

(iv) If <Snow is white or not Snow is white> is a proposition of the form <p or not p>, then <Snow is white or not Snow is white> is true.

Since by assumption we are disposed to accept

(v) <Snow is white or not Snow is white> is true if and only Snow is white or not Snow is white,

we can infer (from (iii) and (v)) that

(vi) Snow is white or not Snow is white.

According to Horwich, the Minimal Theory guarantees that a derivation of this kind is in principle available even for propositions we cannot express. As I shall now try to show, however, the Minimal Theory does not explain how we make sense of there being such derivations for propositions we cannot express, because the Minimal Theory does not explain how we can make sense of there being instances of (MT) that explain the meaning of 'true' when it is applied to propositions that we cannot express.

To see why, one must first clear away a grammatical confusion that undermines Horwich's official statement of the Minimal Theory. According to the Minimal Theory, as we've seen, the meaning of 'true' in English is constituted by our disposition to accept any given instances of the schema (MT). On the official statement of the theory, one of its axioms is

(1) <<Snow is white> is true iff snow is white>

Horwich says this is a proposition whose structure is

(E*) << p > is true iff p>,

which he takes to denote a function (Horwich 1998a: 17). How should we think of this function? What are its arguments and values? Horwich takes (E*) to be a function from propositions to propositions: he writes that "the axiom (1) is the result of applying the propositional structure (E*) to the proposition

(3*) <Snow is white>." (Horwich 1998a: 18)

But this cannot be correct. To see why, suppose that (E*) denotes a function whose argument places are marked by the propositional variable 'p'. Then if we apply the function to (3*), namely, <Snow is white>, the result is not (1), but

(1*) <<<Snow is white>> is true iff <snow is white>>.

This is nonsense, as we can see when we try to express it in English: "the proposition that the proposition that the proposition that snow is white is true iff the proposition that snow is white." The problem is that the singular term '<snow is white>' occurs in positions (one within the singular-term forming operator '<>', and another directly to the right of the biconditional) that can only be meaningfully filled by a sentence. More generally, to make sense of (E*), we must view the variable 'p' that occurs in it as a second-order variable. We therefore cannot take (E*) to denote a *first*-order function that takes objects (propositions) as arguments and yields objects (propositions) as values. Horwich nevertheless asserts that the axioms of his Minimal Theory "are given by the principle

(5) For any object *x*: *x* is an axiom of the minimal theory if and only if, for some [object] *y*, when the function E* is applied to *y*, its value is *x*" (Horwich 1998a: 19)

where the quantifiers in (5) range over objects. If we accept (5), then (1*) refers to an axiom of the minimal theory. But, as we have seen, (1*) is nonsense. Hence we cannot accept (5).

How then should we try to make sense of the minimal theory? The best way, I think, is to reject Horwich's official explanation of the axioms of the minimal theory, and adopt an alternative explanation that he offers in a footnote. We should "characterize the axioms of the minimal theory as anything that is expressed by instances of the sentence schema

(E) '<p> is true iff p'." (Horwich 1998a: 19 n. 3)

Can we make sense of this formulation of the minimal theory? The answer depends on whether we can understand Horwich's further stipulation that "the theory cannot be restricted to instantiations of (E) by *English* sentences; for presumably there are propositions that are not expressible in current English, and the question of their truth must also be covered. So further 'equivalence axioms' are needed, one for each unformulatable proposition" (Horwich 1998a: 18–19 n. 3). To understand this aspect of the minimal theory, we must somehow grasp the idea of an unformulatable value for the second-order free variable 'p'. The idea is at best elusive. Since the variable is second order, and we wish to make sense of the resulting instance of schema (E), in which the variable 'p' occurs in positions where it only makes sense to put a sentence, we cannot think of the values that can be assigned to the variable 'p' as *objects*. This makes it difficult to understand how there *could* be unformulatable values for the second-order free variable 'p'. To see why, consider instances of (E) that we *can* formulate, such as

<Snow is white> is true iff snow is white.

Here the 'value' assigned to 'p' is not an object, but a sentence-in-use, which does not refer to an object or a proposition, even if it may express one. For such cases, it would be clearer to write

The proposition expressed by 'Snow is white' (as used in English) is true iff snow is white.

This formulation enables us to exploit the logician's use-mention distinction, putting the sentence in quotation marks on the left-hand side of the biconditional and simply *using* it as a sentence on the right-hand side. As long as we have sentences to fill the positions marked by the variable, we need not ask what 'values' we thereby assign to it. Hence we can avoid the awkward question of whether we are assigning *objects* to the variable 'p'. If we regard formulatable instances of (E) in this way, however, the reference to propositions on the left-hand side can be eliminated. For example, given that

The proposition expressed by 'Snow is white' (as used in English) is true iff 'Snow is white' is true in English,

we can derive

'Snow is white' is true in English iff snow is white.[25]

---

[25] This derivation is suggested in Davidson 1996: 32.

The problem for Horwich is that the use-mention distinction is only defined for sentences that one can actually formulate and use. We understand the positions marked by the variable 'p' as places where we can write such sentences. There is no use-mention distinction for propositions, so we cannot rely on the use-mention distinction to make sense for the supposed instances of (E) that we cannot formulate. It is unclear whether we can make sense of there being such instances at all.

Let us waive this worry, however, and suppose we *can* somehow make sense of there being unformulatable values for the second-order free variable 'p'. Can we then make sense of there being unformulatable instances of schema (E)? In other words, can we understand what contribution the word 'true' makes to such instances? It is difficult to see how. According to Horwich, "the minimalist thesis is that the meaning of 'true' is constituted by our disposition to accept those instances of the truth schemata that we *can* formulate. In that way, the word is provided with the constant meaning wherever it appears—even when ascribed to untranslatable statements" (Horwich 1998a: 128). But if, as Horwich claims (see Horwich 1998a: 1–2), the concept expressed by uses of 'true' in English has no hidden structure—no nature beyond what is settled by our disposition to accept any given instance of the schema (E)—then it seems that our understanding of what it means to apply 'true' to a given proposition must be *exhausted* by our understanding of the corresponding instance of (E). If we cannot express the proposition p that yields a given instance of (E), we cannot state conditions under which 'true' applies to p. Hence even if we suppose we can somehow make sense of the idea that there are unformulatable values for the second-order free variable 'p', the Minimal Theory does not explain what it means to apply 'true' to a proposition that we cannot formulate.[26] On the other hand, as we've seen, if we can use some sentence S to express the supposed proposition p that yields a given instance of (E), we don't need to ascribe truth to propositions at all, but can define truth directly for S.

[26] Field 1992 raises a similar criticism of Horwich's Minimal Theory, but without remarking on the grammatical problems with and limitations of the Minimal Theory that I explain above. It was only after I saw these problems and limitations that I was able to formulate Field's criticism in a way that I find persuasive. My version of the criticism applies also to the following attempt to define truth for propositions: "For all propositions x [x is true iff ($\exists P$)(x = the proposition that P & P)]" (Soames 1999: 48). Here there is explicit second-order quantification over propositions. 'True' is given no independent explanation, so we are left to rely on an instance-by-instance understanding of the matrix 'x = the proposition that P & P'. The trouble, again, is that we have no understanding of a given value for the free variable 'P' if we cannot formulate and *use* a sentence that expresses that value.

I began this section by asking why we should define our truth predicates so that they apply in the first instance to sentences we can use, and not to the propositions expressed by those sentences, as Horwich's Minimal Theory implies. I have argued that the Minimal Theory fails at precisely the point where it *departs* from a disquotational definition of truth for sentences we can use. I conclude that for our purposes in this book, we have no reason to adopt Horwich's Minimal Theory.

2.5. A Naive Theory of Why it is Epistemically Reasonable for us to Accept T-Sentences

Recall that according to the indispensability argument (§2.1), to generalize on all sentences of a given form, we must commit ourselves to affirming any given T-sentence without *generalizing* on all T-sentences. Let us now consider whether, and, if so, why, it is epistemically reasonable for a person to affirm any given T-sentence. One preliminary answer is that we have decided to adopt a schema that licenses us to affirm any given T-sentence. But why is it reasonable to adopt the T-schema as an axiom schema? Before we try to answer this question, let us first consider the analogous question for the axioms of identity. Why does it seem reasonable for us to adopt these axioms? An initially appealing answer is that *the axioms of identity capture the core meaning of '='*, and hence *anyone who both grasps the meaning of '=' and understands the axioms is epistemically justified in accepting them*. Similarly, an initially appealing answer to the question, "Why it is reasonable to adopt the T-schema as an axiom schema?" is that *T-sentences together capture the core meaning of the English word 'true'*, and hence *anyone who grasps the meaning of the English word 'true' and understands the T-schema is epistemically justified in affirming every T-sentence*. This answer to the question, "Why it is reasonable to adopt the T-schema as an axiom schema?" relies heavily on naive, pre-theoretical intuitions about the meaning of 'true'. I shall therefore call it *the naive theory of why it is epistemically reasonable for us to accept T-sentences*, or *the naive theory*, for short.

Given our pragmatic goals in this book, the naive theory is unacceptable. The main problem with the naive theory is that it rests on the notion of meaning. To clarify and defend the naive theory, one would have to provide an account of the meaning of the English word 'true' and explain why that account shows that anyone who grasps the meaning of the English word 'true' is thereby epistemically justified in accepting any given T-sentence. But we are much more likely to agree that it is epistemically reasonable for us to accept T-sentences than we are to agree on how to explain the meaning of the English word 'true'. For any given explanation of this kind, there is likely to be only a minority of inquirers who find it convincing; the rest will not regard the proposed explanation as adequate justification for their assumption that it is epistemically reasonable for them to accept T-sentences. Partisans of particular theories of the meaning of the English word 'true' may of course accept those theories despite the fact that they are controversial. But if we seek a truth predicate that we can use for the purposes of clarifying and facilitating our inquiries, we must avoid partisan debates about the meaning of the English word 'true'. We must seek a truth predicate that we can agree to use for generalizing on our sentences, not a correct theory of the *meaning* of the English word 'true', even if we are confident that there is such a theory.

A related problem with the naive theory is that it apparently implies that we are epistemically justified in accepting paradoxical sentences. Suppose, for instance, that one of the sentences of our regimented language is

(1) The sentence that occurs on lines 45–6 of §2.5 of *Truth and Words* is not true.

According to the naive theory, we are each entitled to accept

(2) 'The sentence that occurs on lines 45–6 of §2.5 of *Truth and Words* is not true' is true if and only if the sentence that occurs on lines 45–6 of §2.5 of *Truth and Words* is not true.

As a matter of fact,

(3) 'The sentence that occurs on lines 45–6 of §2.5 of *Truth and Words* is not true' = The sentence that occurs on lines 45–6 of §2.5 of *Truth and Words*.

But (2) and (3) commit us to

(4) The sentence that occurs on lines 45–6 of §2.5 of *Truth and Words* is true if and only if the sentence that occurs on lines 45–6 of §2.5 of *Truth and Words* is not true.

This is a contradiction.[27] The problem apparently lies with (2). Yet it seems that according to the naive theory we are epistemically justified in accepting (2).

One might try to defend the naive theory by amending it so that it prevents us from inferring (2). But there is apparently nothing about the ordinary use of the English word 'true' that rules out our acceptance of (2). We find the reasoning of the sort just sketched paradoxical precisely because we do not see what is wrong with any of the steps. To defend the naive theory, one would have to develop an account of the meaning of the English word 'true' that rules out our acceptance of sentences such as (2). Theories of this kind are vulnerable to the charge that they do not capture the meaning of the English word 'true'.[28] Partisans will naturally try to defend their favourite theories of the meaning of 'true'. Given our pragmatic goals in this book, however, we must do our best to avoid such partisan debates.[29] We therefore need a different approach.

2.6. Surrogate T-Sentences and Explication

Let us say that a *surrogate* T-sentence, or an ST-sentence, for short, is one that results when we write sentences of our own regimented language *L* uniformly in the blanks of the pattern

(ST) '_____' is true-in-*L* ↔ _____.

---

[27] This version of the liar paradox, due in essentials to J. Lukasiewicz, is based on Alfred Tarski's presentation in Tarski 1936: §7.

[28] For a similar observation about attempts to dissolve the paradox of scepticism about empirical knowledge by appealing to a theory of the meaning of 'know', see Schiffer 1996. For Tarski's argument that the meaningfulness of unrestricted applications of the word 'true' in English leads to the liar paradox, see Tarski 1936: §1. See also Heck 2004. Some authors who are more optimistic about the prospects for solving the liar paradox by developing a theory of the meaning of the English word 'true' nevertheless also reject the naive theory. For a sophisticated recent example of such a view, see Glanzberg 2005.

[29] Although my argument here is officially agnostic about the existence of a correct and consistent theory of the meaning of 'true', I agree with Chihara 1979 that the prospects for preventing the derivation of the liar paradox by 'analysing' the meaning of the English word 'true' are dim. Even Saul Kripke, whose theory of truth is still one of the main contenders today, writes that "I do not regard any proposal...as definitive in the sense that it gives *the* interpretation of the ordinary use of 'true', or *the* solution to the semantic paradoxes" (Kripke 1975: 699). For a sampling of other views of the roots of the liar paradox, including less pessimistic ones, see the classic essays reprinted in Martin 1984.

(The semi-ordinary word 'true-in-L' that occurs in ST-sentences should not be identified with the ordinary English word 'true' that occurs in T-sentences. ST-sentences are so named because they are at best surrogates for T-sentences.) I propose that we replace the question, "Is it epistemically reasonable for us to accept all the non-paradoxical T-sentences, and no paradoxical ones?" with the more tractable question, "Is there a predicate 'true-in-L' from whose definition we can derive all the non-paradoxical ST-sentences we need, and no paradoxical ones, and, if so, can we use this predicate in place of the English word 'true'?"

My answer to this question is an application of the pragmatic methodology of *explication*. To *explicate* a linguistic expression e that one finds useful in some ways yet problematic in others is to decide to use, *in place of e*, a different linguistic expression e' that preserves and clarifies what one takes to be useful about e, yet avoids what one takes to be the problems with e.[30] When one regiments an ordinary English statement S by deciding to use a partly artificial sentence S' in its place, one thereby also typically *explicates* some of the linguistic expressions that occur in S. When one regiments

(1) Every ship sails in some sea or other.

as

(2) $\forall y((y$ is a ship$) \rightarrow \exists x((x$ is a sea$) \land (y$ sails in $x)))$,

for instance, one thereby also chooses to use '$\exists$' and '$\forall$' in place of the occurrences of 'some' and 'every,' respectively, in (1). Just as one's goal in regimenting a given natural language sentence is not to capture its meaning, but to clarify and facilitate one's inquiries, so one's goal in explicating a given linguistic expression is not to capture its meaning, but to fill those of its functions that one finds useful. Hence just as we are entitled to regiment (1), as used on a given occasion, by (2), if we judge (as Quine would say) that the particular business that we were on that occasion trying to get on with, with the help of (1) among other things, can be managed well enough to suit us by using (2) instead of (1), so we are entitled to explicate

---

[30] This account of explication is essentially the same as Quine's (see Quine 1960: §53), which is a modification of Carnap's (see Carnap 1956: 8). Unlike Carnap's account of explication, Quine's makes no mention of concepts.

'some' as '∃', if we judge that '∃' fills those functions of 'some' that we find useful.

I assume that we desire to express logical generalizations on the sentences of a given regimented language L that does not contain its own truth predicate or any predicate coextensive with its own truth predicate. For this purpose, the useful ST-sentences are those sentences which result from substituting L-sentences for the blanks in (ST), where the L-sentences themselves contain no occurrences of the predicate 'true-in-L' or any predicate coextensive with it. In the same pragmatic sense in which we may choose to explicate 'some' and 'there is' as '∃', we may choose to explicate 'true' by a predicate 'true-in-L' that is defined expressly so that from its definition and the logical principles to which we are independently committed we may derive any given ST-sentence of the kind just described and no paradoxical ones.

One way to achieve this goal is to adopt (ST) as an axiom schema, subject to the restriction that the L-sentences that we substitute for the blanks in (ST) contain no occurrences of the predicate 'true-in-L' or any predicate coextensive with it. But there is a better way to achieve this goal. In the next three sections (§§2.7–2.9) I explain how we can use Tarski's methods to define 'true-in-L' for sentences of our own regimented language without presupposing a substantive relation of sameness of meaning or translation. I then argue (in §2.10) that there are reasons to prefer a Tarski-style disquotational definition of 'true-in-L' to a schematic definition of 'true-in-L'.

2.7. Tarski's Convention T

Alfred Tarski developed a method we can use to *explicate* the English word 'true' by defining a truth predicate 'true-in-L' that entails only non-paradoxical ST sentences. His method presupposes that the *object language*—the language L *for* which we define 'true-in-L'—is distinct from the *metalanguage*—the language ML *in* which we define 'true-in-L'. Truth predicates constructed by using Tarski's method are part of ML, but not of L, so the liar paradox cannot be formulated in L.[31]

---

[31] Kripke 1975 outlines a method for defining a truth predicate that applies to some sentences that contain it. Call this predicate 'K-true-in-L'. The basic rule for it is that "we are entitled to assert (or

As we've seen, we need a non-paradoxical truth predicate that we can use to generalize on sentences. It turns out that to satisfy this need it is enough to define 'true-in-L' in a way that satisfies Tarski's Convention T:

> Convention T. A formally correct definition of the symbol 'true-in-L', formulated in the metalanguage, will be called an adequate definition of truth if and only if it implies all sentences which are obtained from the expression 'X is true-in-L if and only if S' by substituting for the symbol 'X' a structural-descriptive name of any sentence of the object language and for the symbol 'S' the expression which forms the translation of this sentence into the metalanguage.[32]

Tarski does not say exactly what he means here by 'formally correct'.[33] He does emphasize, however, that

The question how a certain concept is to be defined is correctly formulated only if a list is given of the terms by means of which the required definition is to be constructed. If the definition is to fulfill its proper task, the sense of the terms in this list must admit of no doubt.   (Tarski 1936: 152–3)

deny) of any sentence that it is K-true-in-L precisely under the circumstances when we can assert (or deny) the sentence itself" (Kripke 1975: 701, with 'K-true-in-L' in place of Kripke's 'true'). By using Kripke's method, we can define 'K-true-in-L' for a language L in L itself without paradox. To apply the method, however, we must leave some predicates of L undefined for some of the objects over which L's variables range, and allow that not all sentences of L "make a statement" or "express a proposition" (Kripke 1975: 699). An apparent advantage of Kripke's method of defining truth is that it mirrors some uses of the English word 'true' that we cannot mirror if we use Tarski's method of defining truth (Kripke 1975: 694–8). If our goal is not to be faithful to our intuitions about the English word 'true', but to define a clear and consistent predicate we can use to generalize on sentences of our own regimented language, however, then I believe that Tarski's method of defining truth is preferable to Kripke's. Tarski's method requires that all predicates of L be defined for all the objects over which L's variables range; if we use Tarski's method, we have no need for a distinction between meaningful sentences of L and sentences of L that "make a statement" or "express a proposition". Hence Tarski-style definitions of 'true-in-L' conform to the lucid disquotational paradigm for defining truth better than Kripke's definitions of 'K-true-in-L' do. I believe this advantage of Tarski's approach outweighs the limitations of it that Kripke identifies, given the goals I have assumed in this book. Unfortunately, however, I do not have the space to justify this claim here.

[32] This version of Convention T is adapted from Tarski 1936: 187–8. I leave out part (b) of Tarski's version of Convention T, and use 'true-in-L' in place of his term 'Tr', which denotes the set of sentences that are true-in-L. More important, I replace Tarski's 'if' with 'if and only if'. Against this, Patterson 2002 argues that Tarski's Convention T should not be taken to state a necessary condition on defining 'true-in-L'. I see this as a dispute about how best to explicate 'true', and hence as a question of policy, not fact. I return to this point below.

[33] We should not assume that Tarski means by 'formally correct' what others mean by it. Two standard requirements for the formal correctness of a definition are *eliminability* and *non-creativity* (see Suppes 1957: 154). But Tarski-style implicit definitions of 'true-in-L' are not *eliminable* from all contexts, as the indispensability argument shows. And, as Michael Glanzberg pointed out to me, they are not *non-creative* (in the sense defined by Suppes 1957: 154), either.

This condition is not formal, but (as one might say) pragmatic: if our goal is to define a truth predicate 'true-in-L' that we can use to formulate logical generalizations, then we will take a definition of 'true-in-L' to satisfy Convention T only if we understand and have no doubts about the clarity of the terms in which it is expressed. That Tarski's method of defining 'true-in-L' satisfies this vague yet intuitive requirement will become clear when we examine a particular application of the method below. Before we get into these details, however, let us now briefly address two other questions that are relevant to applying Convention T: "What is a *structural-descriptive name* of a sentence of the object language?" and "When does a sentence of the metalanguage *translate* a sentence of the object language?" I shall address these in order.

A *structural-descriptive* name of a sentence of the object language is one that names the sentence by describing its syntactical structure. To form a structural-descriptive name of a sentence, we must use names in the metalanguage of the letters of the object language, and describe sentences of the object language as strings of letters and spaces. By this method, the object language sentence 'Snow is white' might be named as follows: "The L-sentence consisting of ess, en, oh, doubleyu, space, eye, ess, space, doubleyu, aiche, eye, tee, ee, in that order." Such structural-descriptive names may be conveniently abbreviated by treating letters and spaces as names of themselves and a hyphen as a sign of concatenation, as follows: S-n-o-w i-s w-h-i-t-e. One can also form structural-descriptive names of object-language sentences by means of Gödel numbering. It is much easier to form a *quotation-mark* name of a given sentence, however—all one has to do is write single quotation marks on the left and right of it. This method is illustrated by the left-hand sides of ST-sentences. To save space, I shall often use quotation-mark names instead of structural-descriptive names, and when I use the latter, especially in later chapters, I shall usually abbreviate them as strings of letters, spaces, and hyphens.

It is not as easy to interpret the term 'translation' as it occurs in Convention T. We may assume that the meta-language contains the object language, and it is therefore tempting to explicate 'translation' as syntactical identity, using ST-sentences as a model. The idea would be that each sentence translates itself, and that no other notion of translation is needed for Convention T. But Convention T does not require that the sentence that replaces 'S' be identical to the sentence named by X. Hence we cannot avoid saying something about how to explicate the term 'translation,' as it occurs in Convention T.

The term is often taken to stand for a fine-grained relation of equivalence in meaning between different natural language expressions, a kind of equivalence that cannot be completely characterized in syntactical terms, and to which our own explanations of the vocabulary of our own regimented languages—what Quine describes as the "simple mechanical operations whereby any sentence in the logical notation can be directly expanded, if not into quite ordinary language, at least into semi-ordinary language" (Quine 1960: 159)—are irrelevant. But this understanding of the term 'translation', as it occurs in Convention T, overlooks two crucial points. First, to apply Convention T, we do not need a fully general account of translation; an account of the "translation" relation between sentences of L and sentences of the metalanguage in which we define 'truth-in-L' is enough. Second, when we define 'truth-in-L' in terms of satisfaction, we thereby *codify* our semi-ordinary-language-explanations of the vocabulary of L—explanations whose indispensability I stressed in §1.7. These two points suggest that we may take our Tarski-style definitions of 'true-in-L' in terms of satisfaction to *define* syntactically the relation of 'translation' relevant to Convention T.[34] To explain this suggestion, I will explain how we may each construct, for our own regimented language L, a Tarski-style disquotational definition of 'true-in-L' in terms of satisfaction.

2.8. 'True-in-L' Defined in Terms of Satisfaction

By design our regimented languages have a very simple structure: they comprise all and only sentences constructed in the usual way from a finite list of basic predicates, such as 'mortal' and 'loves', variables 'x_1', 'x_2', . . . ,

---

[34] Saul Kripke suggests that if we seek an implicit Tarski-style definition of 'true-in-L' that satisfies Convention T of the sort Davidson recommends, we can "let the truth theory itself determine the translation of the object language into the metalanguage" (Kripke 1976: 338). Kripke notes, however, that "the truth theory doesn't really determine a translation of the object language into the metalanguage, since in general for a given ϕ, there is more than one formula ϕ', satisfying all the given criteria, such that $T(\phi) \equiv \phi'$ is provable" (Kripke 1976: 338 n. 14). The approach I shall recommend is based in the observation that we may use a truth theory to *codify* our decisions about how to explain the artificial notations of the regimented object language sentences in semi-ordinary language.

truth-functional symbols '∼' and '∨', and a quantifier symbol '∀'. To define a predicate 'true-in-L' for one's own regimented language L by using Tarski's method, one needs to be able to name each element of L's vocabulary. As I noted earlier, to form names of predicates and constants, one may simply put single quotation marks around them. To form names of variables, let us stipulate that the ith variable in the sequence 'x_1', 'x_2',..., is var(i). One also needs sequences of objects in the intended domain of discourse for L. (These need not be infinite sequences, but I will assume they are.) To form names of the objects in the intended domain of discourse, one can stipulate that the ith object in an infinite sequence s of those objects is s_i.

By using these resources, I can specify, for instance, that

(r) For every sequence s, s satisfies my predicate one place 'robin' followed by var(i) if and only if s_i is a robin.

This fits the disquotational pattern:

(Sat1) For every sequence s, s satisfies my one-place predicate '___' followed by var(i) if and only if s_i is ___.

Similarly, for the two place predicate 'is smaller than', for instance, I can specify that

(s) For every sequence s, s satisfies my two-place predicate 'is smaller than' followed by var(i) and var(j) if and only if s_i is smaller than s_j.

If one abbreviates 's_i is smaller than s_j' as 'is smaller than $s_i s_j$', (s) fits the disquotational pattern

(Sat2) For every sequence s, s satisfies my two-place predicate '___' followed by var(i) and var(j) if and only if ___$s_i s_j$.

In general, for any n-place predicate one can specify satisfaction conditions that fit corresponding disquotational patterns for n-place predicates.

Suppose I have specified the satisfaction conditions for each of the n basic predicates of L in the way just described. Then I can complete my definition of satisfaction for L by adding the following clauses:

(Neg) For all sequences s and sentences S: s satisfies $\ulcorner \sim S \urcorner$ (the negation of S) if and only if s does not satisfy S.

(Disj) For all sequences s and sentences S and S': s satisfies $\ulcorner S \vee S' \urcorner$ (the disjunction of S with S') if and only if either s satisfies S or s satisfies S'.

(All) For all sequences s, sentences S, and numbers i: s satisfies $\ulcorner \forall x_i S \urcorner$ (the universal quantification of S with respect to var(i)) if and only if every sequence s' that differs from s in at most the ith place satisfies S.

Clauses (Neg) and (Disj) are straightforward. The key to understanding clause (All) is to see that if s is any sequence of objects from the domain of discourse D for the universal quantifier of the object language, then *the set of all and only the ith things of any sequence s' that differs from s in at most the ith place* is identical with D.[35]

Together with the disquotational satisfaction clauses for the simple predicates of my language L, clauses (Neg), (Disj), and (All) define satisfaction for all sentences of L.[36] Using this definition of satisfaction, I can then define 'true-in-L' as follows:

(Tr) A sentence S of L is true-in-L if and only if S is satisfied by all sequences.[37]

2.9. How (Tr) Satisfies Convention T and Enables us to Derive ST-Sentences

I propose that we take (Tr) to settle the translation-relation that is relevant to Convention T. When translation is understood in this way, (Tr) is guaranteed to satisfy Convention T. Consider, for instance, the following derivation of a statement of conditions under which the sentence '$\forall x_1 ((x_1$ is mortal) $\vee \sim(x_1$ is mortal$))$' of L is true-in-L:

[35] One need not think of D as a *set*. The question of whether D is a set is important if one wishes to make sense of the idea that sentences of the object language can generalize over absolutely everything. See Dummett 1981, Cartwright 1994, Williamson 2003, and Rayo and Uzquiano 2006. As I noted in Chapter 1, n. 15, I have sympathies with both sides of the debate about whether one can generalize over absolutely everything, and will not try to adjudicate it in this book.

[36] This sketch of Tarski's method of defining satisfaction is modelled on Quine 1986, chapter 3.

[37] The definition of satisfaction is inductive, not explicit. It can be converted into an explicit definition if there is enough set theory in the metalanguage. For details, see Quine 1986: chapter 3. For present purposes, the inductive definition is sufficient.

(1) '$\forall x_1((x_1$ is mortal) $\vee \sim(x_1$ is mortal))' is true-in-L if and only if '$\forall x_1((x_1$ is mortal) $\vee \sim(x_1$ is mortal))' is satisfied by every sequence. [By (Tr)]

(2) '$\forall x_1((x_1$ is mortal) $\vee \sim(x_1$ is mortal))' is satisfied by every sequence if and only if for every sequence s, every sequence s' that differs from s in at most the 1st place satisfies '$(x_1$ is mortal) $\vee \sim(x_1$ is mortal)'. [By (All)]

(3) For every sequence s, s satisfies '$(x_1$ is mortal) $\vee \sim(x_1$ is mortal)' if and only if s satisfies '$(x_1$ is mortal)' or s satisfies '$\sim(x_1$ is mortal)'. [By (Disj)]

(4) For every sequence s, s satisfies '$\sim(x_1$ is mortal)' if and only if s does not satisfy '$(x_1$ is mortal)'. [By (Neg)]

(5) For every sequence s, s satisfies 'x_1 is mortal' if and only if s_1 is mortal. [By the satisfaction clause for 'mortal']

(6) For every sequence s, s satisfies '$(x_1$ is mortal) $\vee \sim(x_1$ is mortal)' if and only if s_1 is mortal or s_1 is not mortal. [By (3)–(5)]

(7) For every sequence s, every sequence s' that differs from s in at most the 1st place satisfies '$(x_1$ is mortal) $\vee \sim(x_1$ is mortal)' if and only if everything (in D) is mortal or not mortal. [From (6) and the fact that the set of all and only the 1st objects of any sequence s' that differs from any sequence s in at most the 1st place is identical with D.]

(8) '$\forall x_1((x_1$ is mortal) $\vee \sim(x_1$ is mortal))' is true-in-L if and only if everything (in D) is mortal or not mortal. [From (2) and (7)]

Note that the sentence on the right-hand side of (8), namely, 'everything (in D) is mortal or not mortal,' is not identical to the sentence on the left-hand side of (2), namely, '$\forall x_1((x_1$ is mortal) $\vee \sim(x_1$ is mortal))'.[38] Hence if 'translation' as it occurs in Convention T is restricted to the relation of syntactical identity, (Tr) does not satisfy Convention T. But if I take (Tr) to settle a translation of sentences of L into the metalanguage in which I state (Tr), then (Tr) settles, for instance, that 'everything (in D) is mortal or not mortal' translates '$\forall x_1((x_1$ is mortal) $\vee \sim(x_1$ is mortal))'. Thus viewed, (8) is of the form X is true-in-L if and only if S, where X stands in for '$\forall x_1((x_1$ is mortal) $\vee \sim(x_1$ is mortal))' and S stands in for 'everything (in D) is mortal

---

[38] As Quine notes, "What we usually come out with under Tarski's truth definition is not literally the sentence to whose quotation the truth predicate had been attached, but another sentence that is equivalent to it under the logical laws of quantification and identity" (Quine 1976a: 313).

or not mortal', which (by stipulation) translates X. More generally, if we may each take our own Tarski-style definitions of true-in-L to settle a translation of sentences of L by sentences of our metalanguage, then for each sentence s of L, we may derive a biconditional of the form X is true-in-L if and only if S, where the symbol 'X' is replaced by a name of s, and the symbol 'S' is replaced by a sentence s' that (by stipulation) translates s. If we understand 'translation' in the way that I propose, therefore, we can see that our own applications of (Tr) to sentences of our own regimented languages satisfy Convention T.

We need now to convince ourselves that from a definition of 'true-in-L' that satisfies Convention T, we may infer ST-sentences, such as

(9) '$\forall x_1((x_1$ is mortal$) \lor \sim(x_1$ is mortal$))$' is true-in-L if and only if $\forall x_1((x_1$ is mortal$) \lor \sim(x_1$ is mortal$))$.

To make this final step, we need only make use of our assumption that our metalanguage *contains* the sentences of the object language. For the translation relation settled by (Tr) is symmetrical. Hence if our metalanguage *contains* the sentences of the object language, we can use sentences of the object language interchangeably with those sentences of the metalanguage that translate them in the sense of 'translate' stipulated above. The disquotational definitions of satisfaction for our basic predicates, together with the satisfaction clauses for the logical words, amount to our decision to expand '$\forall x_1((x_1$ is mortal$) \lor \sim(x_1$ is mortal$))$' into the semi-ordinary language sentence 'Everything is either mortal or not mortal.' Given this decision and the symmetry of the translation relation, from (8) we may infer (9). More generally, for any given sentence S of L, we can derive all the ST-sentences—those sentences of the form 'X is true-in-L if and only if S', where 'X' is replaced by a quotation-mark name of S. In this way, (Tr) enables us to derive ST-sentences, and thereby to state logical laws for sentences of L.

2.10. Schematic Definitions of 'True-in-L' Rejected

We are now in a position to evaluate the suggestion, mentioned briefly above, that we take (ST) as an axiom schema, understood so that the L-sentences that one is permitted to substitute for the blanks in (ST) contain no occurrences of the predicate 'true-in-*L*' or any predicate coextensive with it. When (ST) is taken as an axiom schema, understood in this way, I shall call it the *ST-schema*. From the ST-schema we can derive only non-paradoxical ST-sentences and thereby satisfy Convention T, where translation is understood as syntactical type-identity. Hence to take (ST) as an axiom schema is to define 'true-in-*L*' schematically. The ST-schema is more economical than a definition of 'true-in-*L*' in terms of satisfaction. Should we then prefer the ST-schema, viewed as a definition of 'true-in-*L*', to (Tr)?

On the contrary, for three main reasons, I think we should prefer (Tr) to the ST-schema, viewed as a definition of 'true-in-*L*'. First, the ST-schema does not enable us to explain the contributions of the logical constants to *L*-sentences in which they occur *inside* the scope of an objectual quantifier. To see why, note first that from the ST-schema we can deduce the contributions of the logical connectives '∼' and '∨' to any *L*-sentence in which they occur *outside* the scope of an objectual quantifier.

For instance, suppose that 'snow is white' is a sentence in *L*. Then we can argue as follows:

(1) '∼(snow is white)' is true-in-*L* if and only if ∼(snow is white).
(2) 'snow is white' is true-in-*L* if and only if snow is white.
(3) '∼(snow is white)' is true-in-*L* if and only if ∼('snow is white' is true-in-*L*).

Premises (1) and (2) can be obtained by substituting *L*-sentences for the blanks in the ST-axiom-schema; the conclusion, (3), results from (1), (2), and the standard laws of truth-functional interchange.

In the same way, we can deduce the contribution of '∨' to any sentence in *L* in which '∨' occurs outside the scope of a quantifier. For instance, if that 'grass is green' is also a sentence in *L*, we can reason as follows:

(4) 'snow is white ∨ grass is green' is true-in-*L* if and only if snow is white ∨ grass is green.
(5) 'snow is white' is true-in-*L* if and only if snow is white.
(6) 'grass is green' is true-in-*L* if and only if grass is green.
(7) 'snow is white ∨ grass is green' is true-in-*L* if and only if 'snow is white' is true-in-*L* ∨ 'grass is green' is true-in-*L*.

The premises (4), (5), and (6) can be obtained by substituting L-sentences for the blanks in the ST-axiom-schema; the conclusion, (7), results from (4), (5), (6), and the standard laws of truth-functional interchange.[39]

We can use the ST-schema in this way to derive the contributions of '$\sim$' and '$\vee$' to the truth conditions of sentences in which '$\sim$' and '$\vee$' occur *outside* the scope of a quantifier. But the ST-axiom-schema sheds no light on the contributions of '$\sim$' and '$\vee$' to the truth or falsity of sentences in which '$\sim$' and '$\vee$' occur *within* the scope of an objectual quantifier. Consider again, for instance, the logical truth

(L) $\forall x_1((x_1$ is mortal$) \vee \sim(x_1$ is mortal$))$

We can use the ST-axiom-schema to derive

(M) '$\forall x_1((x_1$ is mortal$) \vee \sim(x_1$ is mortal$))$' is true-in-L if and only if $\forall x_1((x_1$ is mortal$) \vee \sim(x_1$ is mortal$))$.

By the usual laws of interchange, we can replace any of the components in the matrix of the sentence '$\forall x_1((x_1$ is mortal$) \vee \sim(x_1$ is mortal$))$' with their truth-functional equivalents. But such replacements occur within the scope of the universal objectual quantifier '$\forall x_1$', and do not by themselves elucidate the contribution of the connectives '$\sim$' and '$\vee$' to the truth of the whole sentence. Moreover, we cannot use the ST-schema to explain why we accept the laws of interchange. If the universal quantifier '$\forall x_1$' were substitutional, then the sentence would be equivalent to '$\Pi n\,((n$ is mortal$) \vee \sim(n$ is mortal$))$', which is an abbreviation of the conjunction of all the results of replacing the occurrences of 'n' in the matrix with names in the language; given the ST-schema, this conjunction is truth-functionally equivalent to the result of replacing all occurrences in it of sentences of the form 'n is mortal', where 'n' is replaced by a name, by ''n is mortal' is true'. Hence we could use the ST-schema in the way illustrated above to derive an explanation of the contribution of '$\sim$' and '$\vee$' to the truth value of the whole sentence '$\Pi n\,((n$ is mortal$) \vee \sim(n$ is mortal$))$'. If the universal quantifier '$\forall x_1$' is *objectual*, however, as we suppose, we cannot take for granted that there are enough names to yield a conjunction that has the same truth value as the universal quantification '$\forall x_1((x_1$ is mortal$) \vee \sim(x_1$ is mortal$))$'. As a result, the

---

[39] For a similar derivation, see Field 1994: 258–9.

contribution of the connectives '$\sim$' and '$\vee$' to the truth value of the whole sentence '$\forall x_1((x_1$ is mortal) $\vee \sim(x_1$ is mortal))' cannot be derived solely from the ST-axiom-schema. Similar reasoning shows that neither the contribution of the open sentence 'x is mortal' nor the contribution of the corresponding predicate 'mortal' to the truth value of the whole sentence '$\forall x_1((x_1$ is mortal) $\vee \sim(x_1$ is mortal))' can be derived solely from the ST-schema.

A second reason for preferring (Tr) to the ST-schema, viewed as a definition of 'true-in-L', is that to regiment our sentences is to decide how to replace ordinary sentences with regimented sentences. If there are infinitely many sentences in the regimented language, our decisions cannot consist in an infinite number of separate decisions, one for each sentence. The only clear and uncontroversial way to codify these decisions is to adopt a Tarski-style disquotational definition of 'truth-in-L' in terms of satisfaction.[40]

Third, as I emphasized in §1.7, to clarify and facilitate our inquiries we need to be able to introduce and explain *new* regimented predicates for our regimented language while leaving many of our previous explanations of basic vocabulary of L unchanged. As we have seen, from the ST-schema we cannot explain the contributions of our basic predicates to the truth values of all sentences in which they occur, and hence we cannot use the ST-schema to introduce and explain *new* regimented predicates for our regimented language.[41]

These reasons for preferring (Tr) to the ST-schema are not decisive. One's choice between (Tr) or the ST-schema must be made on pragmatic grounds, and can therefore always be resisted by a person who does not share one's goals. I will nevertheless assume from here on that despite its greater complexity, (Tr) is preferable to the ST-schema for the reasons just sketched.

---

[40] Donald Davidson's use of Tarski is incompatible with the one I recommend, since Davidson aims to clarify meaning by assuming a primitive notion of truth. But Davidson also emphasizes that the recursive structure of a Tarski-style theory of truth enables us to encode infinitary consequences.

[41] This is a pragmatic argument based in our need to be able to add new regimented predicates to an already existing regimented language. It makes no assumptions about how we actually learn new vocabulary in a natural language, or about whether it is possible for a person to understand a sentence containing a given predicate without understanding other sentences in which that predicate occurs. The pragmatic argument does not support or presuppose, for instance, that an adequate theory of meaning for a natural language "represents the structure of the ability to speak [the] language" (Lepore and Ludwig 2005: 124).

2.11. Adopting the Tarski—Quine Thesis

Let me summarize the steps I have taken so far. I began by asking "Why do we need a truth predicate?" and "What sort of truth predicate do we need?" and took for granted that our answer to these questions should be shaped by our desire to clarify and facilitate our rational inquiries. This desire motivates us to regiment our words so that we can formulate logical laws in the notation of first-order logic.

I reviewed and modified (§§1.2–1.7) some well-known methods by which we may each regiment our own ambiguous and vague words, quantifications, definite descriptions and proper names, and pronouns and demonstratives, and emphasized (§1.8) that to regiment one's sentences by using the methods I describe, one must use ordinary (or, at least, semi-ordinary) language. I then argued (§§2.1–2.9) that if we use the methods of regimentation that I sketched, and we wish to formulate logical generalizations on sentences of the resulting regimented language L, we will need to define a truth predicate for sentences of L that incorporates and codifies our ordinary and semi-ordinary language explanations of the vocabulary of L. My first step was to emphasize (§§2.1–2.4) that our desire to clarify and facilitate our rational inquiries motivates us to express logical generalizations on sentences of our regimented language L, but that we can express such generalizations only if it is epistemically reasonable for us to affirm any given T-sentence. I argued (§2.5) we cannot explain why it is epistemically reasonable for us to affirm any given T-sentence by appealing to the naive theory that our acceptance of such sentences is justified by our grasp of the meaning of the English word 'true'. I then sketched (§2.6) a better strategy: the strategy of defining 'true-in-L' in a way that enables us to derive non-paradoxical *surrogate* T-sentences (ST-sentences) that mirror the useful functions of the English word 'true.' I proposed (§2.7) that we adopt Tarski's Convention T, where we stipulate that the translation relation is settled by a recursive definition of 'true-in-L' in terms of satisfaction. I explained (§2.8) how to construct such a definition, and showed (§2.9) that from it we may derive, for every sentence s of L, a biconditional of the form X is true-in-L if and only if S, where the symbol 'X' is replaced by a name of s, and the symbol 'S' is replaced by a sentence s' that (by stipulation) translates s. I also showed (§2.9) that we are then licensed to derive ST-sentences by replacing *s'* by *s*. Finally, I argued (§2.10) that even though we could derive the purely disquotational ST-sentences directly by adopting (ST) as an axiom schema, we should nevertheless prefer (Tr), from which we can derive systematic, semi-ordinary language explanations of the basic vocabulary of *L*.

This reasoning shows how our desire to express logical generalizations on sentences of our own regimented language *L* may motivate us to explicate the ordinary English word 'true' by using a Tarski-style disquotational definition of 'true-in-*L*' in its place, and thereby to adopt the *Tarski–Quine thesis* that *there is no more to truth than what is captured by a Tarski-style disquotational truth predicate defined for one's own sentences.*[42]

2.12. Two Objections

This completes my account of what I regard as our strongest pragmatic motivation for embracing the Tarski–Quine thesis. I will end this chapter by considering two objections to the thesis. The first objection begins with the observation that we typically do not apply our ordinary English word 'true' to sentences. If Alice says, "He admires Tarski," pointing at a contextually salient man, and Zed says, "That's true," Zed does not apply his predicate 'true' to the sentence 'He admires Tarski', a different utterance of which, on a different occasion, might have prompted Zed to say, "That's not true." Instead, it is natural to say, Zed applies his predicate 'true' to Alice's *utterance* of 'He admires Tarski', as accompanied by her pointing gesture, and perhaps also to *what Alice said*—the *proposition* she expressed—when she uttered 'He admires Tarski.'[43] We therefore cannot in general assume that a given declarative sentence of English is true or false independent of any particular occasion on which it is used.[44] In contrast, our own Tarski-style disquotational definitions of 'true-in-*L*' are supposed to apply *directly* to the declarative sentences of our regimented language *L*. Such predicates are not directly defined for utterances or propositions, and

---

[42] To adopt the Tarski–Quine thesis for the reasons just given is to accept that in this case, anyway, explication is elimination. See Quine 1960: 260.

[43] Donald Davidson prefers the first option, whereas Paul Horwich and Scott Soames prefer the second. See Davidson 1984: essay 2, Horwich 1998a and Soames 1999.

[44] For an argument to this effect, see Soames 1999: chapter 1.

without further stipulations cannot be meaningfully applied to them. It may therefore seem that 'true in L' is a poor substitute for the English word 'true,' and that, contrary to the thesis, we should not use a disquotational definition of 'true in L' in place of our English word 'true'.

The convictions behind this objection run deep, and cannot be adequately articulated, much less evaluated, without an investigation of the sort I will begin in the next chapter. But the objection itself is based on a misunderstanding of the thesis, which does not aim to mirror all our uses of the ordinary English word 'true' or to analyse a concept we express when we use that word.[45] According to the pragmatic reasoning I have sketched, we need a truth predicate to express logical generalizations formulated in a regimented language devoid of sentences like 'He admires Tarski' to which we cannot apply a truth predicate independent of particular occasions of utterance. To express logical generalizations formulated in such a regimented language L, we need to commit ourselves to affirming non-paradoxical ST-sentences. A Tarski-style disquotational predicate 'true-in-L' enables us to commit ourselves to affirming all the non-paradoxical ST-sentences that we need to commit ourselves to affirming if we are to generalize on our own regimented sentences. This leaves it open, for now, how we are to understand the relationship between 'true-in-L' and utterances of ordinary language sentences like 'He admires Tarski', or the propositions, if any, that such utterances express. One possibility is that our utterance of an ordinary language sentence s on a particular occasion is true-in-L if and only if (a) there is some sentence s' of L that we decide to use *in place of* our utterance of s on that occasion, and (b) s' is true-in-L. To challenge, not just dismiss, the Tarski–Quine thesis, one would have to challenge this and other possible ways of relating the Tarski–Quine thesis to ordinary language. I shall examine and ultimately reject one such challenge—the most powerful one I can formulate—in Chapters 3 and 4.

A second, related objection is that even if all of our declarative sentences are properly regimented, 'true-in-L' must be understood to apply primarily to utterances or propositions, not sentence types, because, as Tarski himself pointed out, "the same expression which is a true sentence of one language can be false or meaningless in another" (Tarski 1944: 342). That there are

---

[45] In this respect, the thesis is different from what David (1994) calls disquotationalism, which is supposed to capture the meaning and use of the ordinary English word 'true'.

possible languages in which a given meaningful sentence of our regimented language is false or meaningless may seem to be enough to show that 'true-in-*L*' does not apply directly to *L*-sentences themselves, considered as strings of letters and spaces, but only to our *utterances* of *L*-sentences, which express just those meanings or propositions that we decided to use the *L*-sentences to express.[46]

This objection is based in misunderstanding the role of sentence types in a Tarski-style disquotational definition of 'true-in-*L*' for one's own regimented language *L*. As I explained briefly in the Introduction, the question whether another speaker is actually using one or more of the sentence types of our own regimented language cannot be answered by formal considerations alone.[47] It does not follow, however, as the objection assumes, that one cannot rely on sameness and difference of spelling to identify and distinguish between the sentence types and ST-sentences of one's own regimented language. To draw this mistaken inference is to overlook the fact that one can disquotationally define a predicate 'true-in-*L*' for sentences of one's own regimented language *L*—regimented sentences that one can actually use. One's disquotational definitions of 'true-in-*L*' apply *directly* to one's own sentence types under the conditions one specifies by *using* those very sentences. The formal (recursive) structure of one's disquotational definition of 'true-in-*L*' licenses one to derive all of the ST-sentences one needs to express logical generalizations on one's own regimented sentences, considered as types. Contrary to the objection, any assumptions about 'meaning' that one needs to license the formal derivations of one's ST-sentences are built into the recursive, disquotational definitions of satisfaction. Hence at any time *t*, one's disquotational definition of 'true-in-*L*' presupposes that one can identify and distinguish *intrasubjectively* between the sentence types of one's own regimented language *L*, as one uses it at *t*, by their spelling alone.[48]

---

[46] For related objections, see Putnam 1983, and David 1994: chapter 5, §6, §9.

[47] The same reasoning is responsible for what Marian David calls the problem of foreign intruders—the problem that our definition of 'true-in-*L*' applies to sentence tokens solely on the basis of their orthographic type, whether or not they mean the same. See David 1994: 159–60. I shall examine the assumption and sketch an alternative to it in Chapter 4.

[48] Quine 1961a: 135 makes a similar point, though only in passing and in much less detail.

3

The Intersubjectivity Constraint

3.1. A Preliminary Formulation
of the Intersubjectivity Constraint

We saw in Chapters 1 and 2 that our desire to clarify and facilitate our inquiries motivates us to regiment our sentences and define a Tarski-style disquotational predicate 'true-in-L' that we can use to formulate logical generalizations on sentences of our regimented language L. If we assume on pragmatic grounds that there is no more to truth than what we need to clarify and facilitate our inquiries, we may each be tempted to endorse the Tarski–Quine thesis that there is no more to truth than what is captured by such a Tarski-style disquotational predicate defined for sentences of our own regimented language.

As I explained in the introduction, however, if we are motivated to adopt a Tarski-style truth predicate by our desire to express logical generalizations, as proponents of the Tarski–Quine thesis claim, then it should occur to us to ask why we want to express logical generalizations in the first place. A complete answer to this question should mention our desire to collaborate fruitfully with other inquirers—a desire that motivates us to regiment our words and sentences so that we can state logical generalizations that clarify our agreements and disagreements. For this purpose, we need to be able to generalize not only over our own sentences as we now use them, as the Tarski–Quine thesis suggests, but also over other speakers' sentences. As Gottlob Frege emphasized, we regard logical generalizations as *arbiters* of collaborative inquiry.[1] But we cannot regard

---

[1] Against the idea that words stand for private psychological items, Frege writes that "if we could not grasp anything but what was within our own selves, then a conflict of opinions based on a mutual understanding would be impossible, because a common ground would be lacking. ... There would be no logic to be appointed arbiter in the conflict of opinions." (Frege 1964: xix).

logical generalizations as arbiters of collaborative inquiry unless we believe it is epistemically reasonable for us to apply logical generalizations to other speakers' sentences. Our relationship to other speakers' sentences is not in this respect different from our relationship to sentences we used in the past. For the same reasons, then, we cannot regard logical generalizations as arbiters of inquiry unless we believe it is epistemically reasonable for us to apply logical generalizations to our own sentences as we used them in the past. But it is at best unclear how one can use a truth predicate that is only defined for one's own sentences *as one now uses them* to express logical generalizations that one also takes to apply to *other speakers'* sentences and to one's own sentences as one used them in the past.[2]

I emphasize our desire to *collaborate* with other inquirers not because it is essential to this criticism of the Tarski–Quine thesis, but because it makes the criticism seem especially pressing. At its most general, the criticism applies even if we do not desire to collaborate with other inquirers. To see why, suppose that out of choice or necessity we desire to engage in *solitary* inquiries only, and hence do not actually need to generalize over other speakers' sentences. We will nevertheless presuppose that our inquiries may lead us to reject (disagree with) some sentences that we previously accepted. If we wish to clarify and facilitate our inquiries, then, we will need a truth predicate that we can use to express logical generalizations that apply not only to our sentences as we now use them, but also to our sentences as we used them in the past. But, again, it is unclear how one can use a truth predicate that is only defined for one's own sentences *as one now uses them* to express logical generalizations that one also takes to apply to one's own sentences *as one used them in the past*.

In short, to regard logical generalizations as arbiters of inquiry, whether collaborative or solitary, we need a truth predicate that we are licensed to apply to other speakers' sentences and to our own sentences as we used them in the past. As we've seen, however, without supplementation, a Tarski-style disquotational truth predicate is not defined for other speakers' sentences or for our own sentences as we used them in the past. The problem is

---

[2] This unclarity is just a symptom of a much deeper problem, if, as Hilary Putnam argues, the Tarski–Quine thesis is compatible with psychologistic accounts of assertion that, if adopted, would prevent us from making sense of agreement or disagreement between speakers, and hence prevent us from regarding logical generalizations as arbiters of collaborative inquiry. See Putnam 1983. I evaluate Putnam's argument, as directed against Quine, in Ebbs 2002b.

not conceptual, but pragmatic—it is not that a Tarski-style disquotational truth predicate fails to capture the concept (if there is one) expressed by the English word 'true', but that it fails to provide an adequate *explication* of 'true' (in the sense of 'explication' defined in §2.6), because it does not capture and clarify some central uses of 'true' on which we rely in our inquiries. This pragmatic criticism of the Tarski–Quine thesis motivates what I call the *intersubjectivity constraint: a Tarski-style disquotational truth predicate defined for one's own sentences is satisfactory only if it is supplemented by an account of why it is epistemically reasonable for one to use it to generalize over other speakers' sentences and one's own sentences as one used them in the past.*

My goal in this chapter is to present in more detail the pragmatic motivation for adopting the intersubjectivity constraint. I shall (first) describe how we actually apply logical generalizations to other speakers' sentences when we take ourselves to share words with them, (second) reformulate the intersubjectivity constraint in light of these descriptions of how we apply logical generalizations, and (third) consider two objections to the reformulated intersubjectivity constraint.

3.2. Practical Identifications of Words (PIWs)

To begin with, let us look at a few simple examples of how we unreflectively identify words when we take ourselves to understand what a person says. Suppose I am on a walk with Alice, a bird lands on a branch in front of us, and Alice says, "That is a robin," pointing to the bird on the branch. Then without hesitation or deliberation, I will take her to say that the bird is a robin, and, in so doing, I will take Alice's word 'robin' to be the same as my word 'robin'—the word that I would use to express what I take her to have said.[3] The sense of "same word" in question here is bound up with my commitment to use my word 'robin' to express what I take Alice to have said: if I later discover that Alice did not say that the bird is a robin, I will regard as false and try to revise my initial, immediate identification

---

[3] This unhesitating response to Alice's utterance illustrates a deep and widespread phenomenon that others have noted before, though for different reasons. For instance, Jerry Fodor observes that "You can't help hearing an utterance of a sentence (in a language you understand) as an utterance of a sentence ... You can't hear speech as noise *even if you would prefer to*" and "It's what's said that one can't help hearing, not just what is uttered" (Fodor 1983: 55, cited in Borg 2004: 91).

of her word 'robin'. In short, when I take Alice to have said that the bird is a robin, there is a sense of "same word"—a sense that I shall investigate and explicate more fully in Chapter 4—in which I accept

> (1) The word 'robin' that Alice used when she said, "That is a robin," is the same as the word 'robin' that I now use to express what I take Alice to have said—namely, that the bird is a robin.

To accept (1) in the context described above is to make what I call a *practical identification of a word* (or a PIW, for short). I call such identifications *practical* because they are exercises of a learned yet non-deliberative ability that is acquired over a period of years. An ability of this sort is more or less refined according as the person whose ability it is acquires it in more or less varied circumstances and is responsive to more or less subtle features of those circumstances. I call an exercise of this ability a practical *identification* of a word because we will *revise* it if we come to think it is wrong. We will revise (1), for instance, if we come to think that it prevents us from being able to state in our own words what Alice's utterance of 'That is a robin' expressed on the occasion described above.

We typically rely on such practical identifications of words when we state what we take ourselves to have said in the recent past. For instance, suppose that a few moments after Alice spoke, I said, "Yes, that is a robin," pointing to the bird on the branch. Then without hesitation or reflection, I will take myself to have said that the bird is a robin, and, in so doing, I will accept

> (2) The word 'robin' that I used when I said, "Yes, that is a robin," is the same as the word 'robin' that I now use to express what I take myself to have said—namely, that the bird is a robin.

This is what I call a *practical identification of a word* **across time** (or a PIW across time, for short). It is not essential to a PIW across time that it be made for one of my own previous utterances. If I reaffirm (1), for instance, several minutes after Alice said, "That is a robin," I thereby make a PIW *across time* for the word 'robin' that Alice used when she said, "That is a robin." By contrast, when I first accept (1)—roughly simultaneously with Alice's utterance of "That is a robin"—I thereby make what I call a *practical identification of a word* **at a given time** (or a PIW at a given time, for short).

In some contexts we will take two or more PIWs to form a chain of PIWs that commits us to making additional PIWs. For instance, suppose that a few moments after Alice says, "That is a robin," indicating the contextually salient bird in the story above, Hermione says, "That is not a robin," indicating the same bird. Suppose also that I don't hear Hermione say this, but Alice does. Then without hesitation or reflection, *Alice* will take Hermione to have said that the bird is not a robin, and, in so doing, *Alice* will take Hermione's word 'robin' to be the same as her word 'robin'—the word that she would use to express what she takes Hermione to have said. Finally, suppose I later learn from Alice that Hermione said, "That is not a robin," while pointing to the same bird that Alice pointed at in the first story above. In this context, if I continue to accept (1) and I suppose that Alice accepts (2) for her own previous use of 'robin', then if I have no reason to question Alice's way of taking Hermione's word 'robin', I will accept

> (3) The word 'robin' that Hermione used when she said, "That is not a robin," is the same as the word 'robin' that I now use to express what I take Hermione to have said—namely, that the bird is not a robin.

In the circumstances just described, however, I accept (3) because I accept that there is an independently existing chain of PIWs that implies (3). Since the PIWs in the chain are revisable, so is (3). For instance, if I come to reject Alice's PIW for the word 'robin' that Hermione used when she said, "That is not a robin," and infer that there is no chain of PIWs from my word 'robin' to Hermione's, I will come to reject (3).

One might think that if a speaker has not regimented her words, one should not identify any of her words (as used on particular occasions) with words of one's own regimented language. As I stressed in Chapters 1 and 2, however, we introduce and explain the words of our regimented language by using words of ordinary language. Just as we use ordinary language to express what another speaker says on a particular occasion, so we can use a regimented language, whose words are explained by particular uses of ordinary language, to express what another speaker says on a particular occasion. Hence we can and often do make a PIW that identifies a particular use of an unregimented word w with a word w' of our own regimented language.

If one makes a PIW of the sort just described for words $w_1, \ldots, w_n$ that occur in an utterance of a (regimented or unregimented) sentence s on a given occasion O, thereby identifying those occurrences of words $w_1, \ldots, w_n$ with occurrences of words $w_1', \ldots, w_n'$, respectively, of one's own regimented language L, then one commits oneself to identifying s, as used on O, with the sentence s' of L (if there is one) that results from combining $w_1', \ldots, w_n'$, in the order in which one takes them to occur in s, according to the standard rules for constructing sentences of L from words (predicates, connectives, and quantifiers) of L. This is what I shall call a *PIW-based identification of s with s'*.

3.3. Practical Judgements of Sameness of Satisfaction (PJSSs)

If we accept Tarski-style disquotational definitions of satisfaction for our own regimented words as we now use them, then our PIWs commit us to applying these disquotational definitions of satisfaction to other speakers' words, and to our own words, as we used them in the past. Our PIW-based identifications of sentences, in turn, commit us to applying our disquotational definitions of truth-in-L to other speakers' sentences. Let us now examine these commitments in detail.

To begin with, consider how a PIW commits us to applying disquotational definitions of satisfaction to other speakers' words. Suppose that I accept Tarski-style disquotational definitions of satisfaction for my own regimented words. Strictly speaking, only *sequences* of objects, not objects themselves, satisfy words of my regimented language L. Nevertheless, to simplify my exposition I will use in place of (Sat) the pattern

(Sats) x satisfies my word '____' if and only if x is ____.[4]

Thus suppose that I accept the following application of (Sats) to my predicate 'robin':

(4) x satisfies my word 'robin' if and only if x is a robin.

---

[4] Read 'x' as bound by a universal objectual quantifier that ranges over the objects in the intended domain of discourse for L.

Now recall the situation described above, in which I commit myself without deliberation or hesitation to (1) and thereby make a PIW for the word 'robin' that Alice used when she said, "That is a robin":

(1) The word 'robin' that Alice used when she said, "That is a robin," is the same as the word 'robin' that I now use to express what I take Alice to have said—namely, that the bird is a robin.

Putting 'Alice's word 'robin'' in place of 'the word 'robin' that Alice used when she said, "That is a robin"', and 'my word 'robin'' in place of 'the word 'robin' that I now use to express what I take Alice to have said, namely, that the bird is a robin', we can rewrite (1) as

(1') Alice's word 'robin' is the same as my word 'robin'.

Together with (4), my unhesitating acceptance of (1') will commit me to

(5) x satisfies Alice's word 'robin' if and only if x is a robin.

By accepting (4) and (5), I commit myself to accepting their conjunction, namely,

(6) (x satisfies my word 'robin' if and only if x is a robin) and (x satisfies Alice's word 'robin' if and only if x is a robin)

In this way, my unhesitating commitment to (1') and my explicit commitment to (4), together with the inference from (1') and (4) to (5), commit me to (6). A commitment of this kind, incurred and sustained in the way just described, is what I call a *practical judgement of sameness of satisfaction* (or a PJSS, for short).

Note that if I'm committed to (6), I am also committed to

(7) x satisfies my word 'robin' if and only if x satisfies Alice's word 'robin'.

This commitment might *also* reasonably be described as a "practical judgement of sameness of satisfaction". As I use this phrase, however, my commitment to (7) is an immediate *consequence* of my practical judgement of sameness of satisfaction for Alice's word 'robin'; the practical judgement itself is my commitment to (6) given my unhesitating commitment to (1'), my explicit commitment to (4), and the inference from (1') and (4) to (5).

Recall that one can make a PIW that identifies a particular use of an unregimented word w with a word w' of one's own regimented language. When one combines such a PIW with an application of (Sats) to w', the result is a PJSS for w. Hence one can make a PJSS for a particular use of an unregimented word.

Let's say that a *licensing PIW for a given PJSS* is a PIW the expression of which figures in an explicit account of what incurs and sustains that PJSS. For instance, my commitment to $(1')$ in the above story expresses a licensing PIW for my commitment to (6)—one of my PJSSs for Alice's word 'robin'. A PJSS whose licensing PIW is a PIW at a given time may be called a PJSS at a given time, and a PJSS at least one of whose licensing PIWs is a PIW across time may be called a PJSS across time. Recall, for instance, that when I *first* accept (1), which we now write as $(1')$, I make a PIW *at a given time* for Alice's word 'robin'. Together with (4), this PIW commits me to (6), which, accordingly, amounts to a PJSS *at a given time* for Alice's word 'robin'. If I later reaffirm $(1')$ I thereby make a PIW *across time* for the word 'robin' that Alice used when she said, "That is a robin." Together with (4), this PIW *across time* commits me to (6), which, accordingly, amounts to a PJSS *across time* for Alice's word 'robin'.

If we make a PJSS for words $w_1, \ldots, w_n$ that occur in an utterance of a (regimented or unregimented) sentence s on a given occasion, by combining our PIWs for $w_1, \ldots, w_n$ with applications of (Sats) to $w_1', \ldots, w_n'$, respectively, of our own regimented language L, then, as we saw above, our PIWs commit us to making a PIW-based identification of s with s', the sentence of L (if there is one) that results from combining $w_1', \ldots, w_n'$, in the order in which we take them to occur in s, according to the standard rules for constructing sentences of L from words (predicates, connectives, and quantifiers) of L. This PIW-based identification of s with s' then commits us to judging that s is true-in-L if and only if s' is true-in-L. And since we have a Tarski-style disquotational definition of true-in-L in terms of words of L, we can derive a biconditional that specifies the conditions under which both s and s' are true-in-L. This is what I shall call a *PJSS-based judgement of sameness of truth value*. Like the PIWs and PJSSs on which they are based, a *PJSS-based judgement of sameness of truth value* may be classified as a judgement of sameness of truth value *at a given time*, or *across time*, according as the utterances or inscriptions of the sentences in question are contemporaneous or separated by some period of time.

3.4. Agreement and Disagreement

To see how our PIWs and PJSSs, hence also PJSS-based judgements of sameness of truth value, are relevant to our understanding of agreement and disagreement, let us revise the robin story slightly. Suppose as before that Alice says, "That is a robin," and I accept (1′) and (4), thereby making a PJSS for her word 'robin'. In this revised version of the story, however, I believe that all robins have yellow beaks, but the bird on the branch does not have a yellow beak, and I see this, so I say, "That is a not a robin," thereby expressing my belief that the bird to which Alice pointed is not a robin. Then Alice will make a PIW for my word 'robin': she will take my word 'robin' to be the same as her word 'robin', in the sense that she will take me to have said what she expresses by affirming her sentence 'The bird is not a robin'. If she also accepts applications of (Sats) to her own words, then she will make a PJSS for my word 'robin'. Suppose, in addition, that Alice and I each introduce a predicate—I will abbreviate it as 'salient bird'—that expresses the contextually salient features and causal connections that uniquely identify the bird in question, and we construct a definite description—I will abbreviate it as 'the salient bird'—that uniquely denotes the bird at which I pointed. (I explained in Chapter 1 why we cannot do without such context-sensitive additions to the vocabulary of our regimented language.) Then if she and I take our respective utterances to be sincere, we will each make PJSS-based judgements of sameness of truth value for our respective utterances. She will take her sentence 'The salient bird is not a robin' to have the same truth value as my sentence 'The salient bird is not a robin', and so will I. We will thereby take ourselves to *disagree* about whether the salient bird is a robin.[5] In this context, we will not take ourselves to disagree about whether the salient bird is a robin if we

---

[5] This account of why Alice and I will take ourselves to disagree relies on an inference from *sincere assertion* to *belief* that accords with Saul Kripke's simple disquotational principle, which Kripke states as follows:

If a normal English-speaker, on reflection, sincerely assents to 'p', then he believes that p. The sentence replacing 'p' is to lack indexical or pronominal devices or ambiguities, that would ruin the intuitive sense of the principle... (Kripke 1979: 248–9)

Kripke adds that

When we suppose we are dealing with a normal speaker of English, we mean that he uses all words in the sentence in a standard way, combines them according to the appropriate syntax, etc.: in short he uses the sentence to mean what a normal speaker should mean by it. (Kripke 1979: 249)

do not trust our PJSSs for one another's words, including our respective tokens of 'robin'.

To understand this observation it helps to consider a context in which Alice may take herself to disagree with me even though she makes no PJSSs for any of my words. For instance, suppose we alter the context described in the last two paragraphs so that Alice does *not* regiment her words or apply (Sats) to them, but everything else that is unaffected by this change remains the same. In the new context, when I say, "That is not a robin," it is still natural to suppose that Alice will nevertheless make a PIW for my word 'robin' and take me to have said something that conflicts with what she said. Moreover, in the new context I will still take Alice's word 'robin' to be the same as my word 'robin'. And since I regiment my words and apply (Sats) to them, I will still make a PJSS for Alice's word 'robin'. (Recall that one can make a PJSS for a particular use of an unregimented word.) I will therefore take myself to disagree with Alice about whether the bird is a robin only if I trust my PJSSs for her tokens of 'robin', even though in this new context *she* need not make any PJSSs for my word 'robin' in order to take herself to disagree with *me*. The crucial point, however, is that if *both* Alice and I regiment our words and apply (Sats) to them, then we will take ourselves to disagree about whether the bird is a robin only if we both trust our PJSSs for one another's tokens of 'robin'.

We must also trust these judgements if we want to formulate logical laws that show that we cannot both be right. Suppose that Alice and I each use '∼' in place of 'not', '∧' in place of 'and', and, as before, we construct the description 'the salient bird' to pick out the bird at which we both pointed. Then I will take Alice to have claimed that the salient bird is a robin, and she will take me to have claimed that ∼(the salient bird is a robin). We will see immediately that the conjunction '(the salient bird is a robin) ∧ ∼(the salient bird is a robin)' is inconsistent. For reasons I sketched in §2.2, the clearest way to articulate the sense in which the conjunction is inconsistent is to formulate the law that every sentence of the form '∼(S ∧ ∼S)' is true, or, equivalently, that every sentence of the form 'S ∧ ∼S' is not true. And to state this law and apply it to the

---

I can agree with this only if it is understood in a pre-theoretical way, so that it does not imply that there is an account of what normal speakers mean by their words that is independent of their PJSSs. The reasons for this qualification will become clear in Chapter 4.

sentences 'the salient bird is a robin' and '∼(the salient bird is a robin)', we may each use Tarski-style disquotational truth predicates defined for our own sentences in terms of satisfaction clauses for our symbols '∼' and '∧'. Alice and I will not be able to use our respective formulations of that law to clarify the sense in which our respective claims about the bird are inconsistent, however, if we do not also trust our PJSSs for one another's tokens of 'robin'. Our judgement that we disagree about whether the bird is a robin rests on the PJSS-based judgements of sameness of truth value for our respective uses of the sentences 'the salient bird is a robin' and '∼(the salient bird is a robin)'.

Although we typically trust these judgements, we also sometimes revise them. Suppose I know Alice is British, but I nevertheless unreflectively accept (1′), thereby making a PIW for her word 'robin'. If I later learn that her word 'robin'—the British word 'robin'—is not true of robins, but of birds of a different species, I will no longer take her word 'robin' to be the same as mine, and so I will no longer take her to have disagreed with me about whether the bird is a robin. I will revise the PIW that I took to license my PJSS for her word 'robin' and regard both the PIW and the PJSS as false. For different reasons I may also revise a PJSS for one of my own previous uses of a given word, and thereby revise my own current evaluations of beliefs I expressed by using that word.

These preliminary observations remind us that when we identify and clarify our agreements and disagreements with others by applying logical laws that we express for sentences of our own language by using a Tarski-style disquotational truth predicate, we make PJSS-based judgements of sameness of truth value. We regard the PJSSs on which these judgements of sameness of truth value are based as themselves true or false, and we assume it is epistemically reasonable for us to trust sentences that express our PJSSs unless we have particular, local reasons in a given context for not doing so. In short, we regard our PJSSs as both *factual* and *trustworthy*. For reasons I shall sketch in the next two sections, we also regard our PJSSs as both factual and trustworthy when we take ourselves to learn from what others tell us and when we take ourselves to be using an old familiar term to express a new discovery.

3.5. Learning from Others

Suppose, as before, that there is a bird on the branch in front of Alice and me, and Alice says "That is a robin." Trusting my practical identification of her word 'robin' with mine, I take her to have said that the bird is a robin; and given my disquotational definitions of satisfaction for my own words, I take my practical identifications of her words to license corresponding PJSSs for her words. In this revised version of the story, however, I believe that all robins have yellow beaks. The bird on the branch does not have a yellow beak, and I see this, so I say, "That is a not a robin," thereby expressing my belief that the bird is not a robin. Finally, suppose again that in this situation Alice and I trust our respective PJSSs for one another's words, and take our respective utterances to be sincere, so that we make PJSS-based judgements of sameness of truth value for the sentences we uttered, and thereby take ourselves to *disagree* about whether the bird is a robin.

Now suppose that when I say to Alice, "All robins have yellow beaks, but the bird on the branch does not have a yellow beak, so it is not a robin," she relies, "No, as Hermione told me yesterday, not all robins have yellow beaks." Suppose, finally, that I take myself to have *learned* from Alice (and indirectly, from Hermione) that not all robins have yellow beaks, and I agree with Alice that the bird looks in all other ways like a robin. Then I will naturally defer to Alice (and, indirectly, to Hermione), and say, "Okay, perhaps I was wrong—the bird we just saw may be a robin, after all."

To arrive at these conclusions I rely on my PJSS-based judgements of sameness of truth value for Alice's sentences, and thereby also on my PJSSs *at a given time* for Alice's words. When I conclude that my previous utterance of "That is not a robin" is false, however, I also rely on my PJSSs for the words in that previous utterance, including my PJSS that

(6) (x satisfies 'robin', as I used it yesterday, if and only if x is a robin)
$\land$ (x satisfies my word 'robin', as I use it now, if and only if x is a robin)

This is a PJSS *across time*, because it relates my current disquotational account of satisfaction for my words as I use them *now*, to my words as I used them in the *past*.[6] If I trust my PJSSs at a given time for Alice's word 'robin' and my PJSSs across time for my word 'robin' PJSSs, then, given my PJSSs for 'the salient bird', I am committed to a corresponding PJSS-based judgement of sameness of truth value for Alice's claim. Hence I am committed either to rejecting Alice's claim, or revising my own previous belief, and taking myself to have learned from Alice that the salient bird is a robin. In short, my trust in my PJSSs yields a contextually fixed framework for evaluating my own belief that the bird is not a robin: if I continue to trust these PJSSs, and *also* accept Alice's claim, I will revise my belief and take myself to have learned from Alice that the bird is a robin.

The situation in which I learn from Alice that the bird may be a robin is typical of situations in which we learn from others by accepting what they tell us and revising our beliefs accordingly. When we learn from others in this way, we regard our PJSSs as true or false, and we assume it is epistemically reasonable for us to trust sentences that express our PJSSs unless we have particular, local reasons in a given context for not doing so.

3.6. Discoveries

Chains of PIWs extend across time, from moment to moment, and, in some cases, for centuries. For instance, if I learn that in 1820, John Audubon pointed to a bird and said, "That is a robin," I will take for granted that there is a chain of practical identifications of words (PIWs) that can be traced from my word 'robin' all the way back to Audubon's unregimented word 'robin'. I will therefore make a practical identification of Audubon's word 'robin' with my word 'robin', and take him to have asserted that the bird was a robin. This practical identification of Audubon's word 'robin' with mine will commit me to a corresponding PJSS for his word 'robin'. Together with PJSSs for some of his other words, my PJSS for his word

---

[6] It may seem odd to qualify "my word" by the time at which I use it. It will become clear in Chapter 4 that this oddity is a consequence of the standard way of individuating words, not of the idea of a PJSS.

'robin' will commit me to PJSS-based judgements of sameness of truth value for those sentences of his in which tokens of 'robin' occur.

We also rely on our PIWs and PJSSs when we take ourselves to have made a discovery, and not simply stipulated a new use for an old term. For instance, John Locke believed that pure gold is yellow. It was later discovered that pure gold is white. The scientists who made this discovery took themselves not to have *changed the topic*, but to have *discovered* that gold is white. To accept this description of the case, we must trust the later scientists' practical identifications of the word 'gold' more than we trust any previous judgement that gold is yellow. The later scientists might be wrong. But we accept their practical identifications of 'gold'. These practical identifications are embodied in their use of that word to express what they take to be *discoveries* about gold. Their use of that word links it to earlier uses of the word, and those earlier uses of the word are linked to even earlier uses of it. Taken together, these uses of 'gold' constitute a trans-temporal chain of practical identifications of the word 'gold' that support our current practical identifications of Locke's use of 'gold' with our word 'gold'. And our current practical identifications of Locke's use of 'gold' with our word 'gold', in turn, license corresponding PJSSs for Locke's word 'gold'. Together with PJSSs for some of Locke's other words, our PJSSs for his word 'gold' commit us to PJSS-based judgements of sameness of truth value *across time* for those sentences of his in which tokens of 'gold' occur.

In a similar way, every inquiry brings with it some PIWs, PJSSs, and PJSS-based judgements of sameness of truth value across time. When we take ourselves to have made a discovery, and not just to have stipulated a new use for an old term, we regard our PJSSs as true or false and we assume it is epistemically reasonable for us to trust sentences that express our PJSSs unless we have particular, local reasons in a given context for not doing so.

3.7. A Reformulation of the Intersubjectivity Constraint

As I explained earlier (§3.1), our desire to collaborate fruitfully with others motivates us to adopt the *intersubjectivity constraint: a Tarski-style disquotational truth predicate defined for one's own sentences is satisfactory only if it is supplemented by an account of why it is epistemically reasonable for one to use it to generalize over other speakers' sentences and one's own sentences as one used them in the past.* We have now seen that when one generalizes over other speakers' sentences and one's own sentences as one used them in the past, one makes PJSS-based judgements of sameness of truth value, and thereby regards one's PJSSs as true or false. One assumes it is epistemically reasonable for one to trust sentences that express one's PJSSs unless one has particular, local reasons in a given context for not doing so. In short, one regards one's PJSSs as both factual and trustworthy. This suggests the following reformulation of the intersubjectivity constraint: *a Tarski-style disquotational truth predicate defined for one's own regimented sentences is satisfactory only if it is supplemented by an account of why it is epistemically reasonable for one to regard one's PJSSs as both factual and trustworthy.*[7] I shall henceforth use this formulation in place of the previous one. In the rest of this chapter I shall consider whether we have good pragmatic grounds for adopting it.

Recall that I do not seek a conceptual analysis of the English word 'true', but pragmatic answers to the questions "Do we need a truth predicate?" and "If so, what sort of truth predicate do we need?" In this context it is not helpful to ask whether the intersubjectivity constraint captures something essential to the concept of truth. Instead, the intersubjectivity constraint should be viewed as a proposed constraint on a satisfactory *explication* of 'true', where the purpose of the explication is to fill the functions of 'true' that we find useful for clarifying and facilitating our inquiries. We saw above (§§2.6–2.9) that a Tarski-style disquotational truth predicate fills some of the functions of 'true' that we find useful for clarifying and facilitating our inquiries. From this pragmatic perspective, the question whether we have good grounds to embrace the reformulated intersubjectivity constraint amounts to the question whether a Tarski-style disquotational truth predicate that does not satisfy the reformulated

---

[7] I assume that to use one's own Tarski-style truth predicates to generalize over other speakers' sentences and over one's own sentences as one used them in the past one must make practical judgements of sameness of satisfaction for other speakers' words and for one's own words as one used them in the past. Some may have intuitions about truth that conflict with this assumption, but it is not part of my pragmatic project to accommodate such intuitions. As I see it, the intersubjectivity constraint is motivated by our desire to use logical generalizations to clarify agreements and disagreements with other speakers in contexts in which our *identifications* of such agreements and disagreements rest on PJSSs for each other's words, and for our own words as we used them in the past.

intersubjectivity constraint fills all the functions of 'true' that we need to fill in order to clarify and facilitate our inquiries.

One's Tarski-style disquotational truth predicate might fail to satisfy the intersubjectivity constraint in either (or both) of two ways: (first) it might not be supplemented by an account of why it is epistemically reasonable for one to regard one's PJSSs as *trustworthy* and (second) it might not be supplemented by an account of why it is epistemically reasonable for one to regard one's PJSSs as *factual*. To clarify the pragmatic grounds for adopting intersubjectivity constraint, I examine these two ways in which one's Tarski-style disquotational truth predicate might fail to satisfy the intersubjectivity constraint, presenting versions of each as *objections* to that constraint.

3.8. Trust without Trustworthiness?

One might object to the intersubjectivity constraint because one thinks that to satisfy our need to generalize on other speakers' sentences by using one's own Tarski-style disquotational truth predicate, it is enough to suppose that it is epistemically reasonable to *trust* one's PJSSs unless one has particular, local reasons in a given context for not doing so; one need not *also* provide an account of *why* it is epistemically reasonable to suppose this, as the intersubjectivity constraint requires. We typically regard our PJSSs as trustworthy—we assume it is epistemically reasonable to trust our PJSSs unless we have particular, local reasons in a given context for not doing so—without even considering the question whether this attitude towards our PJSSs is itself epistemically reasonable. As theorists, however, we cannot be completely comfortable with this unreflective attitude towards our PJSSs. We know that to satisfy our desire to clarify and facilitate our inquiries, we need to explicate 'true' in a way that fills and clarifies the functions of 'true' that we find useful. One of the most useful functions of the word 'true' is that it enables us to express logical generalizations on other speakers' sentences and on our own sentences, as we used them in the past. To make the case that a proposed explication of 'true' is satisfactory, then, we need to make the case that it fills the useful function just described. But if we do not understand *how* it *could* fill that function, then we do not understand how the proposed explication could be satisfactory. Hence we don't understand how a Tarski-style disquotational truth predicate defined for our own sentences could be satisfactory unless we supplement it with an account of why it is epistemically reasonable for one to trust one's PJSSs unless one has particular, local reasons in a given context for not doing so. Contrary to the objection, to establish that a Tarski-style disquotational truth predicate defined for one's own sentences is satisfactory we must supplement it with an account of why it is epistemically reasonable for one to trust one's PJSSs unless one has particular, local reasons in a given context for not doing so. The account need not be one that every inquirer is required to be able to offer in support of her own trust in her PJSSs; instead, it must be one that we *theorists* could use to explain why a given speaker's trust in her PJSSs is epistemically reasonable.

3.9. A Quinean Objection: PJSSs are not Factual

One might grant that a Tarski-style disquotational truth predicate is satisfactory only if it is supplemented by an account of why it is epistemically reasonable for one to regard one's PJSSs as *trustworthy*, yet doubt that such a truth predicate is satisfactory only if it is *also* supplemented by an account of why it is epistemically reasonable for one to regard one's PJSSs as *factual*. This is not just a logically possible doubt: for reasons I will rehearse below, Quine's empirical theory of translation implies that our PJSSs are trustworthy but not factual. If one were to combine one's own Tarski-style disquotational truth predicate with Quine's empirical theory of translation, it would be epistemically reasonable for one to regard one's PJSSs as trustworthy, but it would not be epistemically reasonable for one to regard them as factual. The resulting combination is therefore compatible with the conclusion of the previous section, yet challenges the second part of the intersubjectivity constraint, according to which a Tarski-style disquotational truth predicate defined for one's own sentences is satisfactory only if it is supplemented by an account of why it is epistemically reasonable for one to regard one's PJSSs as factual.[8]

---

[8] The idea that a disquotational account of truth is satisfactory only if it is supplemented with an account of why it is reasonable for one to regard one's PJSSs as trustworthy is compatible with Quine's commitments, but as far as I know Quine himself never explicitly endorsed it.

Before I can review the reasons why Quine's empirical theory of translation implies that our PJSSs are trustworthy but not factual, I must explain in more detail what I mean when I say that PJSSs are factual. I emphasized above that one's PJSSs are factual if and only if they are true or false. The explication of 'factual' that I recommend rejects the traditional idea that a sentence is true or false according as it "corresponds" or fails to "correspond" with facts construed as special kinds of things in the world. Following Quine, I assume that there are no fact-things to which our declarative sentences must "correspond" if they are to be true, and no indispensable uses of the word "fact". ("It is a fact that snow is white," for instance, is equivalent to, and can be replaced, by "Snow is white.") In this Quinean spirit, I propose that we explicate 'factual' as follows:

(F) If S is a sentence we can use, then S (as used on occasion O) is *factual* if and only if either

    (i) we can construct a Tarski-style disquotational definition of 'true-in-L' for some language L that contains S (as used on O), or

    (ii) there is a sentence S′ such that (a) we can construct a Tarski-style disquotational definition of 'true-in-L' for some language L that contains S′, and (b) we take S′ to paraphrase S (as used on O).

We saw in Chapter 2 that

(G) We can each construct a Tarski-style disquotational definition of 'true-in-L' for some language L that contains a given sentence S if and only if S is a regimented declarative sentence S that we can use.

(F) and (G) imply

(H) If S is a sentence we can use, then S (as used on occasion O) is *factual* if and only if either

    (i) S is a regimented declarative sentence, or

    (ii) there is a regimented declarative sentence S′ that we can use and that we take to paraphrase S (as used on O).

It is crucial to see that we cannot determine whether or not one of our sentences is factual according to (H) on *formal* grounds alone. Sentences of ours that *look* like regimented declarative sentences may seem unclear to us in ways that prevent us from regarding them as factual.[9] For instance, sentences that express our practical judgements of sameness of satisfaction *look* like regimented declarative sentences; hence one might think that if we accept (H) we are thereby committed to saying that such sentences are factual. But we may accept (H) without thereby deciding how we will regiment sentences that express our practical judgements of sameness of satisfaction, hence without thereby deciding whether to regard them as factual or as non-factual.

Quine himself is committed to regarding them as non-factual. His theory of empirical translation implies his indeterminacy thesis, according to which a speaker's language can be mapped onto itself (and any other language that it translates can be mapped onto it) in a variety of inequivalent ways, each of which preserves the net behaviouristic association of sentences with sensory stimulation. He explicates 'empirical content' in such a way that the empirical content of any given sentence is exhausted by the behavioural dispositions that link it to sensory stimulation, and hence that the behaviouristic association of sentences with sensory stimulation is all that matters to empirical translation. A translation, or mapping of words to words, preserves the behaviouristic association of sentences with sensory stimulation, according to Quine, just in case the mapping allows for "fluency of dialogue", described behaviouristically. Our linguistic dispositions do not uniquely determine translation, either of full sentences or of the predicates they contain, Quine argues, because countless radically different translations would each pass his behaviouristic test for "fluency of dialogue". He concludes that translation is not settled by all the facts relevant to it, and is therefore objectively indeterminate.[10]

A corollary of his conclusion is that it is not epistemically reasonable for us to regard sentences that presuppose particular mappings between one's own words and another speaker's words as part of an object language for which we can define a Tarski-style disquotational truth predicate. But sentences that we use to express our PJSSs presuppose such mappings. In the robin case described above, for instance, when I affirm

---

[9] Boghossian 1990 argues that if we accept a disquotational deflationism about truth then we are committed to saying that all apparently meaningful sentences are factual. I believe this conclusion is undermined by Quine's sophisticated disquotational deflationism about truth and factuality. For a criticism of Boghossian from a broadly Quinean point of view, see Kraut 1993.

[10] I present a more complete account of Quine's argument for his indeterminacy thesis in Chapter 2 of Ebbs 1997.

(6) (x satisfies my word 'robin' if and only if x is a robin) and (x satisfies
Alice's word 'robin' if and only if x is a robin),

I presuppose, in effect, what Quine calls a homophonic translation manual
between Alice's word 'robin' and my word 'robin'. According to Quine,
translation is objectively indeterminate, and so we should not regard such
sentences, or the PJSSs we use them to express, as factual in the sense
defined by (H).

Nevertheless, if we accept Quine's account of translation it is epistemically reasonable for us to regard the sentences that we use to express our
PJSSs, and, indirectly, our PJSSs themselves, as *trustworthy*, in the pragmatic
sense that we can count on them to facilitate communication with other
inquirers. Quine emphasizes that

Different persons growing up in the same language are like different bushes
trimmed and trained to take the shape of identical elephants. The anatomical
details of twigs and branches will fulfill the elephantine form differently from bush
to bush, but the overall outward results are alike.   (Quine 1960: 8)

Similarly, when a person learns a foreign language, her dispositions to relate
sentences of that language with sensory stimulation come to match the
dispositions of native speakers of the language well enough to facilitate
communication. In both contexts, according to Quine, our behavioural
conditioning ensures that the sentences that we use to express our PJSSs
preserve all the relevant speech dispositions and are therefore *trustworthy*, in
one good pragmatic sense of that word.[11]

If we combine these consequences of Quine's view of translation with
Tarski-style disquotational definitions of truth, we may be tempted to
conclude that even though it is epistemically reasonable for us to regard
our PJSSs as trustworthy, because our homophonic and homographic
translations usually pass the fluency test, it is not epistemically reasonable for
us to regard our PJSSs as factual, because there are countless other equally
acceptable translations of others' words into our own, and of our own
words into themselves. The resulting Quinean explication of truth implies
that a Tarski-style disquotational definition of truth is satisfactory if it is

---

[11] For Quine there is no sharp distinction between epistemological and pragmatic considerations:
"Each man is given a scientific heritage plus a continuing barrage of sensory stimulation; and the
considerations which guide him in warping his scientific heritage to fit his continuing sensory
prompting are, where rational, pragmatic" (Quine 1961b: 46).

supplemented by an account of why it is not epistemically reasonable for one to regard one's PJSSs as factual, and hence (assuming it is consistent) even if it is *not* supplemented by an account of why it is epistemically reasonable for one to regard one's PJSSs as factual. In this way, the Quinean explication of truth yields a powerful objection to the intersubjectivity constraint.

3.10. Realism as Integral to the Semantics of the Predicate 'True'

To evaluate the objection, we must ask whether the proposed Quinean explication of truth is satisfactory. Does it fill the functions of 'true' that we find useful for clarifying and facilitating our inquiries? We stand the best chance of reaching agreement about this if we focus on central aspects of our inquiries. I propose that we focus on Frege's observation that we rely on logic to arbitrate between conflicting opinions. For reasons I explained above (§§3.4–3.6), to take ourselves to be able to apply logical generalizations to arbitrate conflicting opinions, to learn from others by trusting what they say, or to use an old familiar term to report a discovery that conflicts with claims we or others had previously made by using that term, we need to regard our PJSSs as factual. Quine himself emphasizes that

> We should and do currently accept the firmest scientific conclusions as true, but when one of these is dislodged by further research we do not say that it had been true but became false. We say that to our surprise it was not true after all. Science is seen as pursuing and discovering truth rather than as decreeing it. Such is the idiom of realism, and it is integral to the semantics of the predicate 'true'.   (Quine 1995b: 67)

In this passage Quine is in effect drawing our attention to the fact that our scientific re-evaluations of past conclusions typically presuppose PIWs and PJSSs across time. A related, more general, point is that to regard truth as independent of our own current beliefs we need to rely on our PIWs and corresponding PJSSs, both at a given time and across time. This is especially salient when we apply logic to arbitrate disagreements, for to do so we must concede that an interlocutor with whom we take ourselves to disagree may be right, despite our confidence that she is not. The question is whether the proposed Quinean explication of truth does justice to these important aspects of our inquiries.

The answer is that it does not. As I explained above, Quine's indeterminacy thesis implies that PIWs on which our PJSSs rely are not factual: they merely express our immediate, unhesitating *subjective* preference for one kind of translation manual over another. This in turn implies that whether or not we take ourselves to have been wrong or to agree or disagree with other speakers ultimately rests on our subjective preference for some translations (of our own words as used as some previous time, or of the other speakers' words) over other quite different translations (of our own words as used as some previous time, or of the other speakers' words) that are equally correct according to Quine's empirical theory of translation. Suppose we take ourselves to disagree with a particular speaker, making PIWs for her word, and thereby, in effect, "translating" her words. Quine's indeterminacy thesis implies that we could have chosen to translate her words in many other equally acceptable but radically different ways. Relative to some of the acceptable alternative translations of her words, we will not take ourselves to disagree with her. Our identifications of agreements and disagreements are therefore not objective; they reflect our PIWs, which amount to *subjective preferences* about how to translate another's words. Similarly, when we take ourselves to have been wrong, we presuppose PIWs and PJSSs across time for our words. But Quine's account of translation implies there are other acceptable translations of our past utterances relative to which we would not take ourselves to have been wrong. And if the relationship between earlier and later uses of the term is always mediated by subjective preference for one manual of translation over other equally acceptable ones, then so is our understanding of the claim that what we accept now may not be true.

With this in mind, consider again Quine's observation that the idiom of realism—the independence of truth and belief—"is integral to the semantics of the predicate 'true' ". We cannot do justice to this observation unless we regard sentences such as (6) that express our PJSSs as declarative regimented sentences for which we can define truth disquotationally, and hence, as factual, in the sense defined by (H). But the Quinean proposal sketched in §3.9 combines a Tarski-style disquotational definition of 'true-in-L' with Quine's empirical theory of translation, which implies that sentences that express our PJSSs are not factual. Hence the Quinean explication of truth described in the previous section fails to preserve the minimal sort of realism that, as Quine himself observes, is "integral to the semantics of the predicate 'true'".

A principled Quinean should insist that despite Quine's own claim to the contrary, the idiom of realism is *not* integral to the semantics of the predicate 'true'—our strong feeling that our PJSSs are integral to the semantics of the predicate 'true' is just a psychological accompaniment of our habitual applications of 'true'. If we accept this Quinean account, we can at best *simulate* the role of our PJSSs in collaborative inquiries by highlighting the psychological fact that we typically prefer homophonic "translations" of our fellow inquirers' words and of our own words as we used them in the past. There may be long-term stability in our subjective preferences about how to "translate" our fellow inquirers' words and our own words as we used them in the past, but the principled Quinean will insist that this is a merely psychological stability that will end as soon as a number of inquirers choose to adopt radically different (yet, by Quine's standards, equally correct) "translations" of their fellow inquirers' words or of their own words as they used them in the past.

The problem for the principled Quinean is that we take our PJSSs to be trustworthy *and* factual. To accept the Quinean explication of truth would be to discredit our ordinary practice of taking our PJSSs to be factual, and thereby to discredit an attitude towards our PJSSs that partly constitutes our commitment to the stability of our inquiries. My criticism of the Quinean explication is not that our ordinary practice of taking our PJSSs to be factual is part of the *concept* (if there is one) expressed by the English word 'true', but that it is a *useful* feature of our inquiries that we should seek to preserve in our explication of 'true'. I conclude that a Tarski-style disquotational truth predicate defined for one's own sentences is satisfactory only if it is supplemented by an account of why it is reasonable for one to regard one's PJSSs as factual.

4

How to Think about Words

4.1. Is the Tarski–Quine Thesis Incompatible with the Intersubjectivity Constraint?

We have now seen how our initial pragmatic reasons for adopting

The Tarski–Quine thesis: there is no more to truth than what is captured by a Tarski-style disquotational truth predicate defined for one's own sentences

may, after further reflection, lead us to conclude that we also have pragmatic reasons for adopting

The Intersubjectivity Constraint: a Tarski-style disquotational truth predicate defined for one's own sentences is satisfactory only if it is supplemented by an account of why it is reasonable for one to regard one's PJSSs as both factual and trustworthy.

The intersubjectivity constraint is not equivalent to the negation of the Tarski–Quine thesis. Yet we feel confident that the constraint and the thesis are incompatible. They are incompatible if and only if

(C) There is no way of explaining why it is epistemically reasonable for one to regard one's practical judgements of sameness of satisfaction as both factual and trustworthy *without* claiming that there is more to truth than what is captured by a Tarski-style disquotational truth predicate defined for one's own regimented sentences.

We are strongly inclined to accept (C), and hence to conclude that the intersubjectivity constraint is incompatible with the Tarski–Quine thesis. But why are we so strongly inclined to accept (C)?

The answer, as I shall now try to show, is that we tend to conceive of words in a way that *implies* (C). It turns out, however, that this tendency, while strong, is resistible. I shall sketch an alternative conception of words that implies that we have no grip on sameness of satisfaction apart from our PJSSs. If we adopt this alternative, as I recommend, we can simultaneously embrace the Tarski–Quine thesis and show that it is epistemically reasonable for us to regard our PJSSs as both factual and trustworthy.

4.2. Use versus Mention (Transparent Use)

When we are doing logic and semantics, our theorizing about words starts with the unimpeachable logical distinction between *use* and *mention*. Standard expositions of the *use-mention* distinction (starting with Quine 1940: §4) typically focus on the difference between using and mentioning proper names. For instance, if I affirm the sentence

Chicago is a populous city.

I use the name 'Chicago' to *mention* (refer to) Chicago, but do not thereby mention (refer to) 'Chicago'. In the sense of 'language use' that logicians contrast with 'language mention', to use 'Chicago' is to refer to Chicago, not to describe the reference relation between 'Chicago' and Chicago, or to explain how it is possible for one to use 'Chicago' to refer to Chicago.[1]

The use-mention distinction also holds for predicates and logical constants for which we have defined a Tarski-style truth predicate in the way I explained in Chapter 2. For instance, when I entertain, assume, or affirm a sentence such as

$$\forall x_1((x_1 \text{ is mortal}) \lor \sim(x_1 \text{ is mortal}))$$

in which the predicate 'mortal' occurs, I thereby *use* that predicate in such a way that it is satisfied by all and only mortal things, but do not thereby

---

[1] It is not difficult to construct a sentence any utterance of which both uses and mentions a word that occurs in the sentence only once. For instance, there is only one occurrence of 'Chicago' in

(c) The last word in this sentence is causally related to Chicago.

But when I affirm (c) I both *use* the word 'Chicago' to refer to Chicago and *mention* the word 'Chicago', saying that it is causally related to Chicago. Nevertheless, when I affirm (c), I use the word 'Chicago' to refer to Chicago, not to the word 'Chicago'; I use a *different* singular term, namely, 'The last word of this sentence', to refer to 'Chicago'.

mention the word 'mortal'. And when I entertain, assume, or affirm the sentence just displayed, I thereby *use* it in such a way that it is true-in-*L* if and only if everything is mortal or not mortal, but I do not thereby *mention* the sentence itself.

Insofar as one is *using* one's regimented predicates, logical constants, and closed sentences, one does not refer to them or consciously attend to them as linguistic items—they are, one might say, *transparent*.[2] This metaphor allows for a convenient shorthand. In place of the phrase, "language use of the sort that contrasts with mention", we can write, "transparent use". And instead of saying that a person "is using her words in the sense that contrast with mentioning them" we can say she is using her words "transparently". One should resist any temptation to take the shorter, metaphorical phrases to have special explanatory content of their own. I shall use them *only* as a convenient shorthand for the longer phrases they replace.

Despite the practical indispensability of our transparent uses of words, the logician's use-mention distinction leads in three apparently irresistible steps to the conclusion that our transparent uses of words are not fundamental to our conception of the word types relevant to truth and logic. In the first step we group word tokens into types by their spelling or pronunciation alone; in the second step we conjecture that the meanings and satisfaction conditions of word tokens are determined by facts about the tokens; and in the third step we conjecture that two word tokens are of the same type if and only if they are spelled or pronounced in the same way and facts about them determine that they have the same meanings and satisfaction conditions. Let us examine these three steps in detail.

4.3. The Orthographic Conception of Words

The first step is an immediate consequence of the standard way of drawing the use-mention distinction. When logicians draw that distinction for a regimented language, they identify words by their spelling alone, and regard them as strings of tokens of letter types. According to this *orthographic* conception, the ink marks 'Chicago, Chicago', for example, instantiate two

---

[2] It is for this reason, I think, that Quine calls disquotational truth transparent (Quine 1992: 82).

tokens of the same word type C-h-i-c-a-g-o.[3] The orthographic conception of word types provides explicit criteria of sameness and difference of word types that we exploit *intra*subjectively when we apply Tarski's method of defining truth and satisfaction for our own regimented sentences and words. Recall that Tarski's method requires (as a regulative ideal) that one be able to identify and distinguish between the words and sentences of one's own regimented language by spelling alone. For instance, we are each in a position to affirm

(4) *x* satisfies my word 'robin' if and only if *x* is a robin

taking for granted (as a regulative ideal) that we can identify our own regimented word 'robin' from all other words of our current regimented language by spelling alone. When we affirm (4), we mention (refer) to our word 'robin' on the left side of the biconditional in (4), and use it on the right side. If we start with an orthographic conception of words, it is also natural to add a corresponding phonetic conception of words, according to which we map uttered sounds to spellings and spellings to words when we identify words in speech.[4] Given such a mapping, when we each affirm (4) we each thereby specify conditions under which a given object satisfies our own current written or spoken tokens of the orthographic type: r-o-b-i-n.

4.4. Explanatory Use (Ex-Use)

In the second step of the reasoning previewed above, we ask how word tokens individuated orthographically or phonetically come to have meanings and satisfaction conditions. Once we adopt both the orthographic and phonetic conceptions of words, we are inclined to infer that (i) any inscription or utterance can be viewed as an inscription or utterance of tokens of

---

[3] Peirce 1933: iv. 423 is the classic source of the distinction between a type and its tokens. I get the term "orthographic" from Kaplan 1990.

[4] For languages that have no orthography, the closest analogue to sameness of spelling is sameness of the *sounds* or *gestures* that speakers of the language use to communicate. Those who are attracted to the orthographic conception may want to extend their account of words to encompass languages without orthography by specifying analogous criteria for sameness and difference of words in terms of sounds or gestures. I will not try to do this here, since I am primarily interested in how we identify the words of regimented languages.

word types, considered as strings of letters and spaces. We then notice that (ii) tokens of a given string of letters and spaces, such as r-o-b-i-n, may have different satisfaction conditions depending on where, when, and by whom they are inscribed or uttered. And (i) and (ii) naturally lead us to ask, "How do such tokens, which appear lifeless and insignificant, come to have the meanings and satisfaction conditions we ordinarily take them to have?"

The only plausible answer, it seems, is that there are facts about our word tokens that determine their meanings and satisfaction conditions, to the extent that their meanings and satisfaction conditions are determined at all. But what sorts of facts? And do such facts uniquely determine the meanings and satisfaction conditions of our word tokens? Every substantive theory of linguistic meaning offers its own distinctive answers to these questions. W. V. Quine's theory of linguistic meaning focuses on facts about how impacts at a speaker's nerve endings prompt her to assent to sentence tokens that contain her word tokens, and implies that the totality of such facts about word tokens does not uniquely determine meanings and satisfaction conditions for the word tokens. Similarly, Donald Davidson's theory of linguistic meaning focuses on facts about how observable circumstances in a speaker's surrounding environment prompt her to *hold-true* sentence tokens that contain her word tokens, and implies that the totality of such facts does not uniquely determine meanings and satisfaction conditions of the word tokens. H. P. Grice's theory of linguistic meaning focuses on facts about speakers' intentions to convey their beliefs to others by instituting and exploiting linguistic conventions. Unlike Quine and Davidson, Grice assumes that such facts uniquely determine the meanings and satisfaction conditions of a speaker's word tokens. The causal-historical theories of linguistic meaning inspired by the work of Saul Kripke and Hilary Putnam focus on facts about causal-historical relations between a speaker's word tokens, other objects, and word tokens uttered by other speakers. There are many other substantive theories of meaning, each of which implies its own distinctive account of which facts about word tokens, if any, determine their meanings and satisfaction conditions.

The facts about word tokens that figure in such theories are supposed to describe or explain linguistic events that occur simultaneously with speakers' own transparent uses of their words. When I say, "That is a robin," while pointing at a particular robin, thereby using tokens of my words 'That', 'is', 'a', and 'robin' to say that the bird is a robin, there are simultaneous linguistic events of my uttering or inscribing tokens of these words. An event of uttering or inscribing a word token *t* that is simultaneous with a particular transparent use of *t* is what I call an *explanatory use* (or *ex-use*) of *t*. An *account of ex-use* is a theory of linguistic meaning that specifies which linguistic events count as ex-uses of word tokens, and which facts about the ex-use of a given word token determine whatever meanings or satisfaction conditions the word tokens have.

There are as many different accounts of ex-use as there are substantive theories of linguistic meaning. According to Quine's theory of linguistic meaning, for instance, a speaker's ex-use of a word token *t* is an uttering of sounds or a writing of marks, and the facts that determine the meaning and satisfaction conditions of *t*, to the extent that these are determined at all, are facts about which patterns of impacts at the speaker's nerve endings trigger her dispositions to assent to her sentence tokens, including the particular sentence token in which *t* occurs (Quine 1960). Similarly, according to Davidson's theory, an ex-use of a word token *t* is an uttering of sounds or a writing of marks, and the facts that determine the meaning and satisfaction conditions of *t*, to the extent that these are determined at all, are facts about the observable circumstances in which the speaker *holds-true* her sentence tokens, including the particular sentence token in which *t* occurs (Davidson 1984). In contrast, according to Grice's account, a particular ex-use of a word token *t* is not (or not only) the result of a triggering of linguistic dispositions, or the *holding-true* of particular sentences under particular circumstances, but (also) the result of a speaker's *intention* to utter a sentence token that contains *t* in order to convey one of her beliefs to someone else, and the meaning and satisfaction conditions of *t* are determined by the facts about the particular intention with which the speaker utters *t* (Grice 1957). Kripke's and Putnam's causal-historical accounts of linguistic meaning also characterize ex-use partly in terms of speakers' intentions, but stress that what is expressed by an ex-use of a word token *t* is determined in part by facts about how *t* is causally related to word tokens uttered by other speakers on previous occasions, as well as to objects in the speaker's environment, and objects in the environment of speakers who lived long ago (Kripke 1980, Putnam 1975).[5]

---

[5] In later chapters I shall discuss several of these examples in much more detail. There are many other substantive theories of linguistic meaning currently available in the literature, but I assume that

Accounts of ex-use disagree about how to describe the relationship between a transparent use of a word token *t* and an ex-use of *t* with which it is simultaneous. According to Davidson's account of ex-use, for example, each transparent use of a word token *t* is *identical to* an ex-use of *t*. To describe a transparent use of *t* as an ex-use of *t*, or to describe an ex-use of *t* as a transparent use of *t*, is, according to Davidson's account, to *re*describe one and the same action event.[6] According to some other accounts of ex-use, in contrast, each transparent use of a word token *t* is *expressed by*, but *not identical to*, an ex-use of *t*.[7]

Despite such differences of detail, however, *every account of ex-use implies that when I use a word token transparently, I do not thereby characterize its ex-use.* For instance, when I affirm

(4) *x* satisfies my word 'robin' if and only if *x* is a robin.

I do not thereby say anything about the ex-use of my word 'robin'. Similarly, when I affirm

(6) (*x* satisfies my word 'robin' if and only if *x* is a robin) and (*x* satisfies Alice's word 'robin' if and only if *x* is a robin).

I express a practical judgement of sameness of satisfaction (PJSS) for Alice's word 'robin', but I do not thereby state facts about the ex-uses of tokens of *Alice's* word 'robin' that together *determine* that tokens of Alice's word 'robin' are satisfied by an object *x* if and only if *x* is a robin. In general, to make a PJSS for a word token *w* is not to say anything about the ex-use of *w*, but to specify satisfaction conditions for *w* by *transparently* using a word token *w'* that one takes to be of the same word type as *w*. To state facts about a word token's ex-use one must affirm some sentences that do *not* express PJSSs for it.

one does not need a complete list of such theories to understand what I mean by "an account of ex-use".

[6] Hence Davidson writes that: "We interpret a bit of linguistic behavior when we say what a speaker's words mean on an occasion of use. The task may be seen as one of redescription. We know that the words 'Es schneit' have been uttered on a particular occasion and we want to redescribe this uttering as an act of saying that it is snowing" (Davidson 1984: 141). The same contrast can be drawn for one of our *own* current utterances of 'It is snowing': viewed transparently, it is an act of saying that it is snowing; viewed as an ex-use of 'It is snowing', it is "a bit of linguistic behavior".

[7] These other accounts presuppose accounts of act individuation similar to the one presented in Goldman 1970.

4.5. The Token-and-Ex-Use Model of Words

If we accept the reasoning of the last two sections, we will be strongly inclined to take the third and final step in the reasoning previewed above—to conjecture that two word tokens are of the same semantic type if and only if they are spelled or pronounced in the same way and facts about them determine that they have the same meanings and satisfaction conditions. In other words, we will be strongly inclined to think of the word types that are relevant to satisfaction and truth in the following way:

(U) Two word tokens t and t' are of the same word type if and only if
    (i) t and t' are each tokens of the same orthographic or phonetic type, and
    (ii) facts about the ex-uses of t and t' determine that they each have semantic values and that their semantic values are the same.

This is what I shall call a *token-and-ex-use conception of words*. There is a family of such conceptions, each member of which defines the word types relevant to satisfaction and truth in terms of word tokens and facts about their ex-uses, where the facts about the ex-uses of two word tokens are supposed to determine whether the tokens each have semantic values, and, if so, whether they have the *same* semantic values. To conceive of the word types relevant to satisfaction and truth in this way is to accept what I shall call the *token-and-ex-use model* of words.

Although some token-and-ex-use conceptions of words, such as Quine's, presuppose that the ex-uses of word tokens can in principle be completely specified in non-intentional, scientific terms, other token-and-ex-use conceptions of words require only that the ex-uses of word tokens can in principle be specified without using any sentences that express our practical identifications of words (PIWs) or practical judgements of sameness of satisfaction (PJSSs) for the word tokens.[8] To fix ideas, I shall take (U) as a representative of the token-and-ex-use conceptions of words that make only this minimal demand on our specifications of ex-uses of word tokens. We can therefore adopt (U) without committing ourselves

---

[8] And without using any sentences whose content depends anaphorically on a sentence that expresses a practical identification of a word or a corresponding PJSS for that word token. Thanks to Steven Gross for pointing out that I need to close this legalistic loophole.

to reductionism about meaning, hence without ruling out that among the facts about the ex-uses of word tokens are irreducible facts about what the word tokens mean. For instance, we can adopt (U) without rejecting the anti-reductionist views of meaning that Boghossian 1989, Horwich 1995, McGinn 1984, and Wright 1984 defend in response to Kripke's Wittgenstein-inspired scepticism about meaning in Kripke 1982. We can also adopt (U) without rejecting that the ex-use of a word token t is fixed by the dispositions and functional states, if any, that are causally responsible for a speaker's applications of t and facts about causal relations that exist between t, other speakers, objects, and events in the social and physical environment in which t is uttered. Hence we can adopt (U) without thereby rejecting any of the standard projects of explaining meaning in naturalistic terms, including projects of this kind that are inspired by Grice 1957, Putnam 1975, and Kripke 1980. One can even adopt (U) without ruling out the possibility that no two word tokens are tokens of the same word type, in the sense of "word type" specified by (U), as Quine is compelled to conclude by his argument for indeterminacy of translation.

Regardless of our particular views about meaning, we are all strongly inclined to accept some token-and-ex-use conception of words or other, for reasons I sketched above. The diagnostic significance of this fact is that all token-and-ex-use conceptions of words, including (U), imply

(P) Sentences that express our PJSSs are factual only if they have truth values that are determined by facts about the ex-uses of the word tokens they contain.

Since we each tend to theorize about words in a way that supports some token-and-ex-use conception of words or other, such as (U), we are each tacitly committed to (P), and this explains why we feel so sure that the Tarski–Quine thesis and the intersubjectivity constraint are incompatible. We see that a Tarski-style definition of truth for one's own sentences does not settle the question whether truth values of sentences that express our PJSSs are determined by facts about the ex-uses of the word tokens they contain. From this observation and our tacit commitment to (P), we infer that a Tarski-style definition of truth for one's own sentences leaves open the possibility that our PJSSs are not both factual and trustworthy, and hence that (C) is true—there is no way of explaining why it is epistemically reasonable for one to regard one's PJSSs as both factual and trustworthy *without* claiming that there is more to truth than what is captured by a Tarski-style disquotational truth predicate defined for one's own regimented sentences.[9]

4.6. Types and Tokens

My first step towards developing an alternative to the token-and-ex-use conception of words is to show that the orthographic conception of word types is not as straightforward as it initially appears. Here, again, my approach is pragmatic. I ask, "Do we need a type–token distinction," and "If so, what sort of type–token distinction do we need?"

To begin with, recall that according to the orthographic conception of word types, the ink marks 'Chicago, Chicago', for example, instantiate two tokens of the same word type C-h-i-c-a-g-o, and each token of the type C-h-i-c-a-g-o is a string of tokens of letter types. Let us focus first on the relationship between letter types and their tokens. We may suppose that all letter *tokens* are concrete particulars, or what I shall call *marks*—inscriptions in ink, pencil, chalk, grooves in wood, stone, or plastic, electronic events on a computer screen, utterances, such as "Tee," "Double-yu," and so on.[10] But what are letter *types*? It is tempting to think of them as abstract patterns or forms. If we think of letter types in this way, we will think that what counts as a token of a letter type is somehow settled by the type's abstract pattern or form. I shall call this the naive theory of letter types.

There are two related problems with the naive theory of letter types. First, it is unclear how *any* object—abstract or not—could settle whether or not a given mark is a token of some specified letter type. It is not enough to say that the pattern or form that (for now) we assume to be identical

---

[9] In the philosophical literature today there are two entrenched but opposing attitudes towards sentences like (6), both of which presuppose (P). The first attitude is exemplified by Quine's indeterminacy thesis, according to which sentences like (4), and any sentences that contain them, such as (6), have no determinate truth values, and hence cannot be regarded as factual. If we accept (H) of §3.9, and Quine's indeterminacy thesis, then we will not regard such sentences as among our regimented declarative sentences. The opposing view, held by a majority of philosophers today, is that sentences that express our PJSSs have truth values that are settled by the truth values of other sentences, including sentences that describe how the relevant speakers use their words. If we accept (H) and this majority view, we will regard sentences like (6) as declarative sentences of our regimented language, and hence as factual.

[10] I take this use of the term "mark" from Goodman 1976: 131.

with the letter type is *similar* to the mark. Any two marks are similar in some respect or other. One might hope to avoid this problem by appealing to similarity in the *relevant* respects. But how could a pattern or form settle which respects are relevant? The idea of an abstract form or pattern that somehow by itself singles out its tokens is puzzling, at best.[11]

Second, even if we could solve the first problem, the naive theory of letter types would not fit with our actual practice of classifying marks. A careful look at how we actually identify marks as letters suggests that there is no single, context-independent pattern or form that settles when a given mark counts as a token of some given letter type, such as A. Is 'a' a token of the letter type A? That partly depends on whether we want to take the letter type A to encompass both upper and lower case tokens. Even when we distinguish between upper and lower case letter types, however, questions remain. Are the marks a, *a*, and a, for instance, all tokens of the lower case letter type a? One might hope to make a list of all context-independent patterns instances of which count as tokens of the upper or lower case letter types A and a. But we have no reason to think that such a list could ever be completed. We ordinarily have no difficulty identifying handwritten tokens of the letter types A or a, for instance, yet each person writes letter tokens in a slightly different way. As Nelson Goodman points out, "it may happen that one of two marks that looks in isolation more like an 'a' may count as a 'd' while the one that looks more like a 'd' counts as an 'a'" (Goodman 1976: 138). Goodman illustrates this possibility with tokens of "bad" and "man" written roughly as follows:

baɑ

maɳ

(Goodman 1976: 138).[12] No context-independent criterion for being a letter token could match our actual classifications of letter tokens into types.

---

[11] These doubts about the naive theory of types are similar to doubts that Ludwig Wittgenstein raises about the idea that a picture that comes to mind when we use a word somehow guides our application of the word. See Wittgenstein 2001: §§138–42. For a more dogmatic dismissal of the role that similarity is supposed to play in the naive theory of types, see Goodman 1972.

[12] The same sort of problem arises for a naive theory of phones (i.e. those aspects of an acoustic stream produced by a given speaker that count in context as the speaker's utterance of particular letters).

Despite these problems with the naive theory of letter types, it is difficult to imagine how we could communicate in writing or speech if we could not in practice distinguish between types and tokens. Our practical ability to distinguish between letter types and letter tokens is indispensable to our system of writing, which depends on our recognition of a fixed alphabet, tokens of which can be combined into words that themselves can be classified into types. The type–token distinction is therefore worth preserving, despite the problems just described.

A first step towards preserving and clarifying the distinction is to explicate types as classes of all and only their tokens.[13] Consider the letter type A, where this is understood to encompass all As, whether upper or lower case, italicized, large, small, handwritten, electronic, and so on. We may identify the letter type A with the set $\{x: x$ is of the same letter type as the mark **a**$\}$, where the mark in boldface is used as a sample token of the letter type A. When we explicate a letter type in this way, we suppose that the phrase 'is of the same letter type as' expresses an *equivalence* (reflexive, symmetric, and transitive) relation. By identifying the letter type A with the set $\{x: x$ is of the same letter type as the mark **a**$\}$, we do not state explicit criteria for membership in the set, so we are still left with the problem of clarifying what it is for a mark x to be of the same letter type as the mark **a**. Clearly, we cannot take '$\{x: x$ is of the same letter type as the mark **a**$\}$' to signify the set $\{x: x$ is of the same letter type as the mark **a**$\}$, reading 'x is of the same letter type as the mark **a**' as 'for some letter type y, x is a member of y and **a** is a member of y', on pain of circularity. Still, we are now in a position to see how to say what a letter type is without committing ourselves to the existence of a pattern or form that somehow by itself settles what counts as one of its tokens: we must view 'x is of the same letter type as the mark

---

Linguists noticed long ago that among American English-speakers, in any two utterances of 'writer' and 'rider', for instance, the part of an acoustic stream that counts in context as an utterance of the *t* in 'writer' may be indistinguishable when heard out of context from the part of an acoustic stream that counts in context as an utterance of the *d* in 'rider' (Rey 2006: 247). If we suppose that phone *types* are context-independent sound patterns, and we see no alternative to that supposition, then, like Rey, we will take the data to imply that no phone *tokens* are produced in ordinary speech. For reasons I'll explain soon, however, there is an alternative to the supposition that phone types are context-independent sound patterns. I propose that we continue to believe that phone tokens are produced in ordinary speech, and take the data to undermine the supposition that phone types are context-independent sound patterns.

[13] In Carnap 1942: §3, Rudolf Carnap distinguishes between sign-designs and sign-events, and proposes that we view sign-designs as classes of sign-events. He proposes that we group the sign-events together into classes by their design. As I explained above, however, for many of our purposes, it is not helpful to classify sign-events by their design.

a' as of the form '*Rxa*', where *R* is logically simple. It would help to find some way of replacing the phrase 'is of the same letter type as' by another expression that does not contain the words 'letter type' at all. Following Nelson Goodman, I propose that we replace the phrase 'is of the same letter type as' by 'is a replica of', and stipulate that a replica is what we misleadingly call a token, and 'is a replica of' expresses an equivalence relation between replicas.[14] With this new terminology, we can rewrite '{*x*: *x* is of the same letter type as the mark **a**}' as '{*x*: *x* is a replica of the mark **a**}' and identify the letter type A with {*x*: *x* is a replica of the mark **a**}.[15]

We introduce sets such as {*x*: *x* is a replica of the mark **a**} to solve or dissolve the problems with the naive theory of types, not to provide rules for deciding when two marks are replicas of each other. Nevertheless, we must now face the question "What counts as a replica of a given mark?" We cannot answer this question by examining how speakers use the phrase 'is a replica of', since few speakers, if any, use that phrase at all. Moreover, if we wish to use the phrase 'is a replica of' to specify sets that explicate (replace) the naive theory of types, then, for reasons noted above, we should not equate 'is a replica of' with 'is physically similar in shape to' (as Hugly and Sayward (1981) suggest). If we wish to use 'is a replica of' to solve or dissolve the problems with the naive theory of types, we need a different approach. I propose that we look at our actual practices of distinguishing between and classifying marks for various purposes.

Still sticking to letters, then, let us consider how we might elucidate such sentences as '**a** is a replica of **a**'. We will not count the first of these boldface marks as a replica of the second if we are sorting them by font, but we will count the first as a replica of the second if we are sorting them by letter type. Hence we can rely to some degree on our established practice of distinguishing between letter types to elucidate the relation that is expressed by a particular use of 'is a replica of' in such phrases as '{*x*: *x* is a replica of the mark **a**}'. The alternative of classifying the two marks by font type shows that the phrase 'is a replica of' is contextually ambiguous in the sense explained in §1.2; we need to introduce regimentations of

---

[14] See Goodman 1966: 361–2 and 1976: 138–43. The term "replica", but not Goodman's nominalistic use of it, is due to Charles Sanders Peirce, who writes, "Every legisign signifies through an instance of its application, which may be termed a *Replica* of it" (Peirce 1933: ii. 143).

[15] Since "*x* is a replica of *y*" is reflexive, the boldface mark in "{*x*: *x* is a replica of the mark **a**}" is a replica of itself, and is therefore a member of the set that is the letter type A. See Goodman 1966: 361–2.

the phrase before we can use such phrases as '$\{x: x$ is a replica of the mark $\mathbf{a}\}$'. In some cases we will be able to define the regimented relation explicitly, and in other cases, we will not. As Nelson Goodman observes, for instance, "The letter-classes of our alphabet . . . are established by tradition and habit; . . . defining them would be as hard as defining such ordinary terms as 'desk' and 'table'" (Goodman 1976: 138). Hence when we use such phrases as '$\{x: x$ is a replica of the mark $\mathbf{a}\}$' to refer to the sets that explicate our ordinary notion of letter types, we can provide at most an *elucidation* of the relation we express by using the phrase 'is a replica of' on that occasion; we cannot explicitly define that phrase.[16]

New replicas of $\mathbf{a}$ are produced each day. Hence if we suppose that a use of '$\{x: x$ is a replica of the mark $\mathbf{a}\}$' at a given time t specifies the set of all and only the replicas of $\mathbf{a}$ that have been produced at t, then the set specified by a use of '$\{x: x$ is a replica of the mark $\mathbf{a}\}$' on one day may differ from the set specified by a use of that expression on the next day. This consequence does not fit with our pretheoretical view that letter types are timeless. We should therefore reject the supposition that a use of '$\{x: x$ is a replica of the mark $\mathbf{a}\}$' at a given time t specifies the set of all and only the replicas of $\mathbf{a}$ that have been produced at t. But we in effect *already* rejected it when we decided (see §1.5) to take first-order variables to range over all objects, past, present, and future. Hence just as the quantified variable in '$\forall x_1 ((x_1$ is mortal) $\vee \sim(x_1$ is mortal))$' ranges over all objects, past, present, and future,

---

[16] Goodman notes a complication with this strategy: there may be "a mark that, equivocally, reads as different letters when placed in different contexts at different times" (Goodman 1976: 139). For instance, in a crossword-puzzle configuration of marks, a single, enduring, mark may count as a "d" when read horizontally from left to right, as part of a token of "bad", but as an "a" when read vertically from top to bottom, as part of a token of "man". One could construct such an example by rearranging the handwritten letters displayed on page 115 above, using just *one* token of the enduring mark that ambiguously reads as an "a" or a "d" according as it is read in the left-to-right context or the top-to-bottom context. To handle such cases, Goodman proposes that "not such enduring marks but, rather, unequivocal time-slices of them must be taken as . . . inscriptions of letters" (Goodman 1976: 139). This proposal does not handle all unequivocal cases, however. Dilworth 2003 points out that even a *time-slice* of a mark may count as a "d" for a person reading it from one point of view, and a "b" for a person simultaneously reading it from a different point of view. He imagines a transparent plastic sign with the letters "din" painted on it; a person reading this sign from one point of view will read the marks as spelling the word "din", a person simultaneously reading it from the other side will read the marks as spelling the word "nib". Dilworth takes this to undermine Goodman's strategy of explicating letter types as sets of equivalence classes of particulars. But we could amend Goodman's account to accommodate Dilworth's transparent sign by taking inscriptions of letters to be *ordered pairs of time-slices of marks* and *space-time points*, where the points represent spatio-temporal locations of persons reading or writing those time-slices of marks. This is highly artificial, but that by itself is no objection, given that our aim is explication (see §2.6), not conceptual analysis.

and hence each use of '$\{x: x$ is mortal$\}$' refers to the same set—the set of all and only the past, present, or future mortal things, so the variable in '$\{x: x$ is a replica of the mark $\mathbf{a}\}$' ranges over all objects, past, present, and future, and hence each use of '$\{x: x$ is a replica of the mark $\mathbf{a}\}$' refers to the same set—the set of all and only the past, present, or future replicas of the mark $\mathbf{a}$.

Similar observations hold for our explications of *word* types. Here we may draw on the fact that a single orthographic type may have different satisfaction conditions. For instance, the British word 'robin' and the American word 'robin' are spelled in the same way, but a bird that satisfies the British word 'robin' does not satisfy the American word 'robin', and vice versa—British robins and American robins are birds of different species. Now suppose that in the following sentence

(*) A **robin** is not a **robin**

the first boldface mark **robin** is a token of the British word 'robin' and the second boldfaced mark **robin** is a token of the American word 'robin'. Then (*) is true, but we will not see this if we take *both* boldface marks to be tokens of either the British word 'robin' or the American word 'robin'. For some purposes, such as copy editing, we group the first boldface mark in (*) with the second, but for others, such as applying a truth predicate to another's words, we do not. Corresponding with these different purposes are different "is a replica of" relations. For purposes of copy editing, we may be able to define the relevant replica relation orthographically (or phonetically), in terms of strings of classes of letter replicas. But some of the word types that matter to us cannot be defined in this way. When we explicate these word types, we can reasonably require at most an *elucidation* of the phrase 'is a replica of' that we use in such terms as '$\{x: x$ is a replica of the mark **robin**$\}$' to refer to the relevant equivalence classes of marks.

The method just sketched requires that letter and word classes be classes of marks, defined in relation to particular letter or word tokens (marks) that occur in the definitions themselves. Hence it cannot be applied to define classes of strings of letters or words, including sentences, that no one has yet identified, displayed, or used.[17] Yet in logic we are committed to the existence of strings of letters or words that no one has yet identified,

---

[17] In Wetzel 2006: §4.1, Linda Wetzel calls this one of the two main problems with explicating types as sets. She does not mention Quine's proposed solution to it.

displayed, or used. As Quine points out, for instance, "fruitful work in the mathematical theory of proof... hinges on the existence and distinctiveness of strings of signs of all finite lengths" (Quine 1987: 217; see also Quine 1960: 194–5). We therefore need a way of extending our explication of letter and word classes to encompass strings of letter and word classes of all finite lengths.[18] For this reason, following Quine, I propose that we explicate strings of letter and word classes as finite *sequences* of letter and word classes (Quine 1987: 218).

One may choose the method just sketched to explicate the type–token distinction while simultaneously affirming a token-and-explanatory-use conception of word types, such as (U) of §4.5, and thereby committing oneself to accepting (P) of §4.5, where 'token' is understood as 'mark' and 'type' as an equivalence class of marks defined by some regimented relation expressed by a particular use of the phrase 'is a replica of'. Nevertheless, for reasons I shall explain in the next three sections, the method just sketched also enables one to explicate the word types relevant to satisfaction and truth in a way that does *not* commit one to accepting (P).

4.7. Kaplan's Common Currency Conception of Words

In a seminal paper titled "Words" (Kaplan 1990), David Kaplan articulates a conception of words that can help us to take another step towards developing an alternative to the token-and-explanatory-use model of words. To begin with, he highlights aspects of our actual practice of individuating words that should lead us to reject (U), the token-and-explanatory-use conception of words that I specified above:

(U) Two word tokens *t* and *t′* are of the same word type if and only if
    (i) *t* and *t′* are each tokens of the same orthographic or phonetic type, and

---

[18] Georges Rey claims that standard linguistic entities (SLEs), such as word tokens, sentence tokens, and phone tokens, are *unlike* abstract objects, such as numbers, because "our best theories of the nonpsychological world seem to be committed to numbers," whereas *in linguistic theorizing*, SLEs "have no role to play independently of our representations of them" (Rey 2006: 250). What Rey apparently overlooks is that our best theories of some non-psychological topics (e.g. mathematic proofs) are committed to SLEs.

(ii) the explanatory uses of *t* and *t'* determine that they each have semantic values and that their semantic values are the same.

Although Kaplan does not explicitly state (U), he in effect challenges condition (i) of (U) by elucidating what he calls the *common currency* conception of words, which is rooted in our ordinary criteria for judging when a speaker has *repeated* a word. To highlight these ordinary criteria he describes the following thought experiment: "I say the name of an individual, possibly a name known to the person to whom I'm speaking. The subject is to wait for a count of five, and then repeat the name..." (Kaplan 1990: 102). Kaplan remarks that in these circumstances, "we are very strongly inclined to say that when this person speaks, he is repeating the very name that he heard.... it's clear that we would agree to describe his output as a *repetition* of *that* name" (Kaplan 1990: 102–3). He emphasizes that if repetition of the sort he describes is central to our understanding of the same-word relation, then a speaker's output could be a repetition of a word even if it sounds very different from the input she heard: "In view of the fact that individual differences in psychological processing... may affect the resemblance of output to input, ... we [can] get differences in sound *just about as great as we would like* between what comes in and what goes out" (Kaplan 1990: 105). Similar thought experiments support the conclusion that one could get differences in *spelling* between what comes in and what goes out. Such thought experiments therefore conflict with clause (i) of (U).[19] Kaplan concludes that

The identification of a word uttered or inscribed with one heard or read is not a matter of resemblance between the two physical embodiments (the two utterances, the two inscriptions, or the one utterance and one inscription). Rather it is a matter of [intrapersonal and] interpersonal continuity, a matter of intention: Was it *repetition*? We depend heavily on resemblance between utterances and inscriptions... in order to devine these critical intentions. If it sounds like "duck", it probably is "duck". But we also take account of accent and idiolect and all

---

[19] Linda Wetzel emphasizes that "there is an important and very common use of the word 'word' that lexicographers and the rest of us use frequently. It is, roughly, *the sort of thing that merits a dictionary entry*" (Wetzel 2006: §4.2.1). She concludes that "the final nail in the coffin for the suggestion [that] all tokens of the same word have the same sound is that words can be mispronounced" (Wetzel 2006: §4.2.4); in support of this conclusion she cites David Kaplan's word-repetition thought experiment.

the usual clues to intention. It is the latter that decides the matter. (Kaplan 1990: 104)

In this last sentence, I take 'the latter' to be short not for 'intention', but for 'accent and idiolect and all the usual clues to intention', and infer that word repetition on Kaplan's understanding is not settled by a speaker's intention *unless* the intention is of the appropriate sort—the sort that others can identify by taking account of 'the usual clues to intention'. I shall return to this point below.

To accommodate his observations about word repetition, Kaplan proposes that we think of words not as abstract types that classify their tokens by their resemblance to each other in certain respects, but as "trees...stemming out from their creations, with physical and mental segments..." (Kaplan 1990: 117). These are what I shall call *repetition trees*. Kaplan's fundamental idea is that *common currency words are repetition trees generated by actual, not merely possible, acts of repeating words, as these acts are understood and elucidated by our ordinary criteria for word repetition.* Our ordinary criteria for word repetition allow for the possibility of mistakes: we distinguish between our *belief* that x is a repetition of y, on the one hand, and x's *being* a repetition of y, on the other. Hence Kaplan's fundamental idea is that common currency words are repetition trees generated from an original mark or marks by chains of actual word repetitions, understood as logically independent of our beliefs.

Kaplan suggests that if words are not abstract types that classify their tokens by their resemblance to each other in certain respects, then they are not *types* at all, but "natural objects," or "continuants"—particular *repetition trees* whose *nodes* are utterances or inscriptions (marks) (Kaplan 1990: 98, 116–17). This is, at best, misleading. For if we are willing to accept certain constraints on what counts as a repetition tree, it is not difficult to explicate word types in a way that fits with Kaplan's observations about our ordinary criteria for word repetition. To do so, we can apply the strategy for explicating types that I introduced above (§4.6). Starting with the relation expressed by 'is a repetition of', we can explicate a common currency word as a certain sort of equivalence class of marks (word replicas). We are assuming that the relation expressed by 'is a repetition of' is asymmetric, irreflexive, and intransitive, so we cannot use this phrase directly to define an equivalence class of word replicas. But if we stipulate that as we shall use the term 'repetition tree', every word replica is a node of one and only one repetition tree, it follows that 'for some repetition tree z, x is a node of z and y is a node of z' is an equivalence relation.[20] We can then identify the common currency word 'robin', for instance, with $\{x: x$ and **robin** are nodes of the same repetition tree$\}$. If we introduce a new phrase 'x is a repetition replica of y', defined as follows:

x is a repetition replica of y if and only if for some repetition tree z, x is a node of z and y is a node of z

we can rewrite '$\{x:$ for some repetition tree z, x is a node of z and **robin** is a node of $z\}$' as '$\{x: x$ is a repetition replica of **robin**$\}$' and identify $\{x:$ for some repetition tree z, x is a node of z and **robin** is a node of $z\}$ with $\{x: x$ is a repetition replica of **robin**$\}$.

To elucidate '$\{x:$ for some repetition tree z, x is a node of z and **robin** is a node of $z\}$' as '$\{x: x$ is a repetition replica of **robin**$\}$' we must elucidate the phrase 'is a repetition replica of' by investigating our actual context-sensitive practices of identifying repetitions of words.[21] We can survey some of the issues that we would have to settle in order to elucidate 'is a repetition replica of' by considering two objections to Kaplan's conception of words. Both objections focus on a consequence of my explication of Kaplan's proposal—the consequence that an object is a word replica if and only if it is produced with an appropriate kind of intention.

[20] This stipulation may seem too artificial, since our ordinary criteria for word repetition might sometimes seem to commit us to count a single mark as a member of two different words. But we should judge the stipulation by its fruits: the question is whether it yields a satisfactory *explication* of words as equivalence classes of marks, not whether it captures *all* our pre-theoretical judgements about when a person repeats a given word.

[21] If we explicate Kaplan's common currency conception of words in the way I propose, it is a type–token conception of words, where 'token' is understood as 'mark' and 'type' as an equivalence class of 'marks' defined by some regimented relation of the form 'x is a replica of y'. Does the explication then undermine Kaplan's claim to be offering an alternative to what he calls the type–token model of words? That depends on how one understands the main target of his criticisms. One might take Kaplan to be trying to discredit every conception of words that could plausibly be called a type–token conception. Gregory McCulloch apparently reads Kaplan in this way, and emphasizes that "Kaplan's point is that token word-occurrences are bound together into word types by criteria which are neither geometrical nor phonological [an observation that] . . . leaves the type/token vocabulary, apparently without strain, in place . . ." (McCulloch 1991: 74–5). McCulloch does not actually provide an explication of Kaplan's conception that shows it to be a type–token view, but I assume that he would accept my explication, and see it as a vindication of his criticism of Kaplan. Perhaps Kaplan was confused about this point, but in any case, as I shall try to show at the end of this section, his common currency conception of words is incompatible with the token-and-explanatory-use model of words.

Consider first the "only if" part of the claim. One might think that there can be word replicas that are not produced with any intention at all. Suppose, for instance, that you and I see ripples in a sand dune caused by the wind, and that the ripples seem to spell out the English sentence, "We are lost." I point to the ripples and say to you, "I believe that," and you take me to have thereby expressed my belief that we are lost. One might think that in this context the ripples in the sand count as words of English even before I or anyone else even notices their similarity with words of English. One might therefore take the example to undermine the consequence that it is necessary for an object to be a word that the object be produced with an appropriate kind of intention.[22]

There are two main problems with this first objection. First, even if it were generally accepted and uncontroversial that the ripples in the dunes were words of English before I or anyone else noticed, the objection wrongly presupposes that the goal of Kaplan's (or any other) explication of words is to capture *all* generally accepted and uncontroversial beliefs about words. The objection overlooks the possibility that to explicate words in a way that we find fruitful, we may have to accept some counter-intuitive consequences. Second, one might agree with Peter Alward that "in our speech acts, we do not use preexisting tokens; we produce new ones" (Alward 2005: 183). On this view, when I say "I believe that," gesturing at the ripples in the dunes, I thereby intentionally produce contemporary tokens of the English words 'We are lost' by my gesture towards the ripples that only seem to spell out those words; it is the new tokens I thereby produce, not the ripples themselves, that count as nodes of repetition trees.

A second objection to Kaplan's conception of words begins with the observation that according to it, an object is a word replica—a node of a repetition tree—if it is produced with an appropriate kind of intention. One might think that if we were to accept this consequence, we would be committed to the conclusion that a speaker could count as having uttered a word even if no other speaker could identify what word she uttered. This conclusion does not fit with our public, intersubjective practice of identifying words. One might therefore object that contrary to Kaplan's

---

[22] For a similar objection that I used as a model for this one, see Cappelen 1999: 95.

proposal, it is not sufficient for a mark to be a word replica that it be produced with an appropriate kind of intention.[23]

The problem with this objection is that it rests on a dubious and uncharitable understanding of the role of intentions in Kaplan's account. As I noted above, word repetition on Kaplan's understanding is not settled by a speaker's intention *unless* the intention is of the appropriate sort—the sort that others can identify by taking account of "the usual clues to intention". More important, we have no grip on the idea that a speaker's output is the repetition of a word apart from our ordinary *public* criteria for taking it to be the repetition of a word, criteria that are bound up with our ordinary public criteria for identifying a speaker's intentions to use the same words that other speakers use. Hence we must rely solely on these ordinary public criteria if we are to make sense of Kaplan's proposal.

As I see it, the underlying target of Kaplan's criticisms is the token-and-explanatory-use model of words. His emphasis on word repetition discredits (i) of (U). For instance, suppose that in one of Kaplan's experimental situations, I say, "dolphin," and a test subject, Alice, is supposed to count to five and then repeat the word I uttered. If Alice follows the instructions, and says something that sounds like DULL-FIN, she will count as having repeated the word I uttered, even if I pronounced it DAWL-FIN not DULL-FIN. Thus her performance counts as a repetition despite a significant difference in pronunciation. This discredits the phonetic part of (i). Similarly, suppose I *write* a token of the English word 'dolphin' and ask Alice to write another token of the same word. If Alice, intending to follow my instructions, writes a token of d-o-l-f-i-n, she will nevertheless by our ordinary standards count as having *rewritten* (but misspelled) the English word 'dolphin'. This application of the common currency conception of words discredits the ortho*graphic* part of (i).

A proponent of (U) could try to accommodate this criticism by changing clause (i) to allow for alternative spellings and pronunciations. To remain in the spirit of (U), a clause that replaces (i) must include a fixed and finite list of admissible spellings or pronunciations for each word type. But for any such list, one could likely generate a new alternative spelling or pronunciation that is acceptable by ordinary criteria, but is not on the list. Anticipating this, a proponent of (U) might be inclined to dismiss Kaplan's criteria

---

[23] For a similar objection, see Cappelen 1999: 94–5.

for word repetition. But Kaplan's criteria for word repetition are just our own ordinary criteria for word repetition. We cannot simply dismiss these criteria. Hence his common currency conception convincingly discredits both (U) and any modifications of (U) whose first clauses include a fixed and finite list of admissible spellings or pronunciations for each word type.

One might still think one can still salvage the token-and-ex-use *model* of words if one builds Kaplan's common currency conception of words into a token-and-explanatory-use conception of words, as follows:

(U′) Two word tokens (marks) t and t' are of the same word type (in the sense relevant to truth and logic) if and only if
  (i) t and t' are members of the same common currency word (t and t' are nodes of the same repetition tree), and
  (ii) facts about the ex-uses of t and t' determine that they each have semantic values and that their semantic values are the same.

To make sense of (U′), however, we must suppose that the question whether two word tokens (marks) t and t' are members of the same common currency word is independent of the questions whether they each have semantic values and, if so, whether their semantic values are the same. But Kaplan seems to understand word repetition in such a way that we cannot settle whether two word tokens (marks) t and t' are members of the same common currency word without thereby also settling that they each have semantic values and, if so, whether their semantic values are the same. Kaplan emphasizes, for instance, that two marks count as the same common currency name only if they name the same individual.[24] This treatment of names suggests that he would also endorse the more general conclusion that two marks count as the same common currency *word* only if they each have semantic values and their semantic values are the same.[25] If we understand Kaplan's criteria for word repetition in this way, we cannot accept *any* token-and-explanatory-use conception of words, for all of them require that we be able in principle to identify word tokens *prior to and independently*

[24] See Kaplan 1990: 110–11, where Kaplan emphasizes that his common currency name "David" is different from David Israel's common currency name "David".

[25] This interpretation of Kaplan's common currency conception of words fits with what Kaplan elsewhere calls *consumerist semantics*, according to which "we are, for the most part, language *consumers*. And words come to us prepackaged with a semantic value. If we are to use *those words*, the words we have received, the words of our linguistic community, then we must defer to *their* meaning" (Kaplan 1989b: 602).

of settling that they do or do not each have semantic values and, if they do, whether their semantic values are the same. Hence Kaplan's remarks about how we keep track of words suggest that his common currency conception of words is incompatible with any token-and-ex-use conception of words.

4.8. The Context Principle and the PJSS-Based Conception of Words

From the pragmatic perspective that motivates the intersubjecivity constraint, the central problem with Kaplan's common currency conception of words is that it does not actually keep track of the word types relevant to generalizing on other speakers' sentences. If Kaplan's test subject does not know English and is asked to repeat an English word, she will repeat that word without having any idea what one might use it to say, or even whether it is a predicate or a logical constant, and hence without being in a position to make a PJSS for it.[26] But, as I argued above, if we are to generalize on other speakers' sentences, we need to rely on our PJSSs for their words. The problem is that Kaplan's common currency conception of words does not license us to apply our own disquotational truth predicates to other speakers' sentences.

One might try to avoid this problem by restricting Kaplan's repetition test to subjects who know, or are competent in the use of, the natural language of which the test word is a part.[27] But if one accepts the common currency conception of words, then to regard a speaker as competent in the use of a natural language is just to count some of her utterances as repetitions of words of the language. Hence the proposed restriction is circular. Even if we were to adopt the restriction, however, we would still have a problem with ambiguity. If you ask me to repeat the English word

---

[26] Adèle Mercier also objects to Kaplan's conception of words. She claims that "you have not repeated my word, indeed that you cannot be said to have repeated any word, unless you can make a mental commitment as to the sort of word you are repeating (proper name, common noun, verb, and the like). For without this committing yourself syntactically, you will not be able to use the word productively yourself, to generate sentences using it" (Mercier 1999: 93; see also Cappelen 1999: 97). Mercier's objection is similar in spirit to the one I raise in the text, but there is a fundamental difference between them: my objection is not that Kaplan's conception of words fails to fit with our intuitions about what it is to *repeat* a word, but that it yields a conception of words that does not license our PJSSs, and hence does not show us how to satisfy the intersubjectivity constraint.

[27] This is how Peter Alward proposes that we deal with the problem. See Alward 2005: 183.

"bank", for instance, I will do so without being able to make a PJSS for it. Hence the circular restriction would still leave us with the problem that Kaplan's common currency conception of words does not license us to apply our own disquotational truth predicates to other speakers' sentences.

To avoid the problem yet still preserve Kaplan's insight that our criteria for sameness and difference of words are at root public and practical, we need to elucidate practical criteria for sameness of word types that keep track of the word types relevant to generalizing on other speakers' sentences, and hence relevant to our pragmatic explication of truth and satisfaction. We *actually* keep track of the relevant word types by relying on our PJSSs. When we make such practical judgements, we take ourselves to be using, hence in some sense repeating, words that we read or hear, and so we are relying on our ordinary criteria for word repetition. But we are doing so in a context that disciplines our understanding of the word types that we repeat. To conceive of word types in a way that is relevant to satisfaction and truth, we need to pay careful attention to such contexts. I therefore propose that we conceive of words in a way that obeys what I call

> *The context principle (first version): never ask for the word type of a word token in isolation, but only in the context of one's PIWs and PJSSs for that word token.*

This principle is meant to refine Kaplan's insight that we have no grip on sameness and difference of words apart from our practical criteria for identifying and distinguishing between words. The idea behind the refinement is that my PJSS for Alice's word 'robin', for instance, is simultaneously (i) *licensed by* my PIW that Alice's word token 'robin' is of the same type as my word token 'robin' and (ii) *a constraint on* my understanding of the word type of which I take Alice's word token 'robin' and my word token 'robin' to be tokens. Hence to obey the context principle is to conceive of words in such a way that we accept a sentence that expresses a PIW, such as

(1′) Alice's word 'robin' is the same as my word 'robin',

if and only if we take it to license a corresponding PJSS.

Against this, one might be inclined to reason as follows: "If I have no understanding of PIWs expressed by sentences like (1′) independent of the PJSSs that I take them to license, then if I want to know whether to accept ($1'$), I am caught in a vicious circle: to obey the context principle, I need to know whether to make a PJSS for Alice's word 'robin', but I will make a PJSS for it only if I *already* accept ($1'$)." This reasoning overlooks the fact that both PIWs and PJSSs are *non-deliberative*—we make them independent of any conscious decisions about whether to make them. We can subsequently revise them, should we see reason to do so. But to get started, one should ask not *whether to* make a PIW and corresponding PJSS for Alice's word 'robin', but *whether one actually does* make them. Given an *actual record* of PIWs and PJSSs, the context principle constrains our understanding of word types. To obey the context principle is to seek a reflective equilibrium between our understanding of word types and our PIWs and PJSSs—an account of word types that fits with all and only the PIWs and PJSSs we see no reason to reject.[28]

To keep track of the word types relevant to truth and satisfaction, however, it is not enough to obey the first version of the context principle. For our practical criteria for sameness and difference of word type may also include other speakers' PIWs and PJSSs. Suppose, for instance, that Alice *mumbles* as she utters the sentence 'There is a goldfish in the bird bath' and, as a result, her utterance sounds to me like an utterance of 'There is a goldfinch in the bird bath.' Then I will I take her to have said that there is a goldfinch in the bird bath. I will take the fourth word of the sentence she mumbled to be of the same type as my word 'goldfinch', and thereby conclude that like my word 'goldfinch', the fourth word of the sentence she mumbled satisfies x if and only if x is a goldfinch. Now suppose that after looking for a goldfinch in the bird bath, I say to Alice "Where is the goldfinch? I don't see it," and she replies, with clearer diction, "I said there is a gold*fish* in the bird bath!" I will then take Alice to have corrected my PIW and PJSS for the mumbled word by *repeating* what she said more clearly. In this case I rely not only on my own PIW and PJSS for the word 'gold*fish*' that Alice uses to correct me, but also, and crucially, on *Alice's* PIWs (and corresponding PJSSs, if she makes any) for the word I use in my reply to her, and for the words in the sentence she mumbled.

---

[28] The reflective equilibrium I have in mind is modelled on Nelson Goodman's classic account of the justification of deductive inferences: "How do we justify a *deduction*? . . . *A rule is amended if it yields an inference we are unwilling to accept; an inference is rejected if it violates a rule we are unwilling to amend.* The process of justification is the delicate one of making mutual adjustments between rules and accepted inferences; and in the agreement achieved lies the only justification needed for either" (Goodman 1983: 63–4).

In some contexts we make a PIW *solely* because we accept that there is a chain of PIWs made by other speakers that implies it. Recall, for instance, that if I learn that, in 1820, John Audubon pointed to a bird and said, "That is a robin," I will take for granted that there is a chain of PIWs that can be traced from my word 'robin' all the way back to Audubon's unregimented word 'robin'. In these circumstances, I will make a PIW for his word 'robin'. I cannot ask Audubon whether I've understood him correctly. But I assume that English-speakers who interacted with Audubon in 1820 and made PIWs for his word 'robin' were in a position to correct those PIWs if they had any reason to doubt them, and that *their* tokens of that word are related to mine by a chain of PIWs across time. Similarly, when we take ourselves to have made a discovery about gold, for instance, we assume there are chains of PIWs that links our current uses of 'gold' to uses of 'gold' long ago. In such cases, our non-deliberative (yet revisable) assumption that such chains exist commits *us* to making PIWs (and corresponding PJSSs) for words used by speakers long ago.

These cases illustrate that in practice we typically keep track of words in part by relying on *other* speakers' PIWs and PJSSs. And when we rely on other speakers' PIWs and PJSSs, we commit ourselves to making PJSS-based judgements of sameness of truth value for other speakers' *sentences*. To explicate truth in a way that captures this aspect of our inquiries, we need to replace the first version of the context principle with

> *The context principle (second version): never ask for the word type of a word token in isolation, but only in the context of one's own PIWs and PJSSs for that word token and other speakers' PIWs and PJSSs for that word token, if such judgements exist.*

I shall henceforth take this to be the context principle. Since there are other English-speakers, and we rely on their PIWs (and corresponding PJSSs, if they exist) for all of the word types we use, the context principle implies that we have no conception of the word types we use apart from our reliance on other English-speakers' PIWs (and corresponding PJSSs, if they exist) for those word types. The context principle does not by itself imply that I do not use any word that no one else uses, but only that if I do use such a word, then my own PIWs and PJSSs for it exhaust my criteria for keeping track of it.

As before, I propose that we regard word tokens as marks (word replicas) and word types as equivalence classes of marks (word replicas). The *context principle* then becomes: *never ask for the equivalence-class of a mark (word replica) in isolation, but only in the context of one's own PIWs and PJSSs for that mark (word replica) and other speakers' PIWs and PJSSs for that mark (word replica), if such judgements exist.* When it is restated in this way, the context principle amounts to a constraint on one's explication of what I call *PJSS-based* word types, which license our intersubjective applications of truth and logic. To explicate Kaplan's common currency word types, we used the phrase 'is a repetition replica of'. To explicate PJSS-based word types, I propose that we use the phrase 'is a PJSS-based replica of'.

From the pragmatic perspective that I have stressed, the question of how to explicate our PJSS-based word types arises only after we have each regimented our own words, so that we can distinguish between the word replicas we ourselves utter or write by their spelling alone. After regimentation, for instance, I can use the string of letters r-o-b-i-n to produce and identify my own current replicas of my word 'robin'. To explicate PJSS-based word types as equivalence classes of replicas, however, I must respect the context principle. I must therefore identify my PJSS-based word type 'robin' with $\{x: x$ is a PJSS-based replica of **robin**$\}$, where I identify the word replica in boldface by its spelling alone and I understand the phrase 'is a PJSS-based replica of' in accordance with the second context principle.

But how does the context principle constrain my understanding of the phrase 'is a PJSS-based replica of'? To address this question, let us first stipulate that a statement of the form 'x satisfies my PJSS-based word type _____' is an abbreviation of 'x satisfies every word replica in the set $\{x: x$ is a PJSS-based replica of_____ $\}$'. For instance, 'x satisfies my PJSS-based word type **robin**' is an abbreviation for 'x satisfies every word replica in the set $\{x: x$ is a PJSS-based-replica of **robin**$\}$'. Now if I make a PJSS of the form 'x satisfies my PJSS-based word type **robin** if and only if x is a robin and x satisfies A's word type **r** if and only if x is a robin', and I accept the context principle, I thereby take my word type **robin** to be identical to A's word type **r**, and conclude that **r** is a PJSS-based replica of **robin**. I might later revise the PJSS and regard it as false, but if I accept the context principle I have no grip on whether or not a given mark is a PJSS-based replica of another given mark apart from my PIWs and PJSSs for those marks.

The central virtue of the context principle is that it respects the PIWs and PJSSs on which we rely when we identify our agreements and disagreements with others, take ourselves to learn from others, or make discoveries—PIWs and PJSSs of the sort that I highlighted above (§§3.2–3.6) in support of the second formulation of the intersubjectivity constraint. Consider again, for instance, the first situation I described in Chapter 3: I am on a walk with Alice, a bird lands on a branch in front of us, and Alice says, "That is a robin," pointing to the bird on the branch. Without hesitation or reflection, I take her to have said that the bird is a robin, and, in so doing, I take her word 'robin' to be the same as my word 'robin'—the word that I use to express what I take her to have said. In this sense of "same word"—the sense the I propose to explicate as an equivalence class of word tokens—I accept

(1′) Alice's word 'robin' is the same as my word 'robin'

Now suppose, again, that I also (already) accept

(4) x satisfies my word 'robin' if and only if x is a robin.

Then my unreflective acceptance of (1′) will lead me to accept

(5) x satisfies Alice's word 'robin' if and only if x is a robin.

I thereby commit myself to accepting the conjunction of (4) and (5), namely,

(6) (x satisfies my word 'robin' if and only if x is a robin) and (x satisfies Alice's word 'robin' if and only if x is a robin).

In this way, my unreflective commitment to (1′) and my explicit commitment to (4), together with the inference from (1′) and (4) to (5), commit me to (6), a PJSS. Let 'r' name the word token that Alice uttered and that I take to be a token of my PJSS-based word type **robin**. I propose that we explicate (6) as

(6′) x satisfies my PJSS-based word type **robin** if and only if x is a robin and x satisfies Alice's PJSS-based word type **r** if and only if x is a robin.

and (1′) as

(1″) Alice's PJSS-based word type **r** is the same as my PJSS-based word type **robin**.

But (1″) abbreviates

(1‴) {x: x is a PJSS-based-replica of Alice's mark **r**} = {x: x is a PJSS-based replica of my mark **robin**},

and (6′) abbreviates

(6″) For every word replica w in the set {x: x is a PJSS-based replica of my mark **robin**}, x satisfies w if and only if x is a robin, and for every word replica w in the set {x: x is a PJSS-based replica of Alice's mark **r**}, x satisfies w if and only if x is a robin.

If I accept the context principle, then when I accept (6″) for the reasons given above, I will regard Alice's mark **r** to be a PJSS-based replica of my mark **robin**. I will therefore accept (1‴). At the same time, I will take my unreflective acceptance of (1‴) to license my acceptance of (6″). To accept the context principle is to have no understanding of sentences like (1‴) independent of the sentences like (6″) that one takes them to license. In general, to obey the context principle is to eschew any criteria for sameness and difference of words that can be specified without using any sentences that express our PJSSs, and hence to view one's understanding of sameness and difference of words as inextricably linked to one's PJSS-based use of words. It is to adopt what I call the *PJSS-based conception of words*.

4.9. How to Satisfy the Intersubjectivity Constraint without Rejecting the Tarski–Quine Thesis

Let us now consider whether the Tarski–Quine thesis and intersubjectivity constraint are compatible if we adopt the PJSS-based conception of words. There are three crucial considerations. First, if we adopt the PJSS-based conception, we will regard any criterion for sameness of word types that violates the context principle as irrelevant to truth and satisfaction. Any criterion for sameness of word types that implies

(P) Sentences that express our PJSSs are factual only if they have truth values that are determined by facts about the ex-uses of the word tokens they contain violates the context principle, because it presupposes that there are criteria for sameness and difference of word type that do not presuppose the truth of any sentences that express our PJSSs. Hence if we adopt the PJSS-based conception of words, we will regard any criterion for sameness of word types that implies (P) as irrelevant to truth and satisfaction. But, as we saw in §4.5, all token-and-explanatory-use conceptions of words imply (P). Hence if we adopt the PJSS-based conception of words, we will regard all token-and-explanatory-use conceptions of words as irrelevant to truth and satisfaction, and thereby discredit the reasoning (explained in §4.5) that initially led us to think the Tarski–Quine thesis and intersubjectivity constraint are incompatible.

Second, if we adopt the PJSS-based conception, then we can explain why it is epistemically reasonable for us to regard our PJSSs as factual and trustworthy. For this purpose, I propose that we place three constraints on our understanding of 'epistemically reasonable' and related epistemic terms. The first two of these constraints are

(T1) A person has a *reason* for believing that S only if she can say *why* she believes that S *without presupposing that S*.[29]

(T2) A person has an *entitlement* (or is *entitled*) to believe that S if and only if she has no reason (in the sense of 'reason' constrained by (T1)) for believing that S—she cannot say *why* she believes that S without presupposing S—but it is *epistemically reasonable* for her to believe that S.

One might think that

(*) For every statement S, it is epistemically reasonable for a person to accept S only if she has a *reason* for believing that S,

which, together with (T1) and (T2), implies that there is no statement S that anyone has an *entitlement* (or is *entitled*) to believe. But there are some statements, such as the statement that *not every statement is both true and false*, that no one has any (independent) reason to accept, yet no one can make sense of doubting, either. I assume it is epistemically reasonable to accept such statements. But we have no reason (in the sense of 'reason' constrained

---

[29] Although we sometimes say that a person has a reason for believing that S even if all her best attempts to explain why she believes S presuppose that S, I will not use 'reason' in this way.

by (T1)) for believing them—we cannot say *why* we believe them without presupposing them. By (T2), then, we are epistemically *entitled* to accept these statements, including the statement that not every statement is both true and false.

This argument for the existence of epistemic entitlements depends heavily on the assumption that there are some statements we cannot make sense of doubting. Let us try to make this assumption more precise. To make sense of doubting a statement S, one must be able to specify a way in which S may be false. For this it is not enough just to say 'it is not the case that' before an uttered token of S, or to prefix a negation sign to a written token of S. We are unable to specify how 'Not every statement is both true and false' could be false, even though we are able to write and utter the sentence 'It is not the case that not every statement is both true and false'. In short, to specify how a statement may actually be false, one must do more than just negate it.[30]

One might be tempted to conclude that for every statement S, if a person cannot specify a way in which S may be false, then she is epistemically entitled to accept S. But this goes too far. For if a person has no understanding of a statement, then it trivially follows that she cannot specify a way in which it may be false. And of course it is *not* epistemically reasonable for a person to believe any statement of which she has no understanding just on the grounds she is unable to specify a way in which it may be false. The saving consideration is that we do not take ourselves or others to *believe* or *disbelieve* a statement if we or they have no understanding of it. (How much understanding is required for belief/disbelief depends on the statement and the circumstances. I shall discuss these nuances in Chapter 9.) If we have no understanding of a statement S, then the question of whether our supposed belief in S is epistemically reasonable does not arise, since we do not satisfy minimum conditions for *believing* or *disbelieving* a statement if we have no understanding of it.

To accommodate these observations I propose the following additional constraint:

(T3) If a person understands a statement S well enough to raise the question of whether or not she believes S and she cannot specify

---

[30] If it is unclear whether a given speaker is able to specify a way in which her statement that S may be false, then it will also be unclear whether (T3) applies to her statement that S.

a way in which a statement *S* may actually be false, then it is epistemically reasonable for her to accept *S*.[31]

If we adopt (T1)–(T3), we may conclude that we are each epistemically entitled (in a sense constrained by (T2)) to accept that not every statement is both true and false, since we cannot provide a reason (in the sense of 'reason' constrained by (T1)) for accepting that not every statement is both true and false, but by (T3) it is nevertheless epistemically reasonable for us to accept that not every statement is both true and false, because we cannot specify a way in which *the statement that not every statement is both true and false* may actually be false.

One might worry that there will be circumstances in which (a) a person *P* satisfies minimal conditions for believing or disbelieving a statement *S*, (b) *P* has so little understanding of *S* that *P* cannot specify a way in which *S* may be false, but (c) it is *not* epistemically reasonable for *P* to accept *S*. For instance, one might be inclined to reason as follows: "Suppose that without any proof, or other grounds, you simply claim (not having heard of Goldbach's conjecture) that *every even number greater than 2 is the sum of two primes.* You know that a prime number is a whole number larger than 1 that is divisible only by itself and 1. But you know too little to be very specific about how it may actually be false. By (T3), apparently, it is epistemically reasonable for you to accept the claim. But it is obviously *not* epistemically reasonable for you to accept the claim, which was for you no better than a guess. Hence (T3) is false."

This reasoning involves a misapplication of (T3). For even if you don't know much mathematics, if you understand what a prime number is, you can specify a way in which that statement may be false. You understand the statement well enough to see that it may be false if there is a number *k* greater than 2 such that *k* is not the sum of two prime numbers. This is not just a matter of negating the statement. For you can be more specific. A quick Google search can lead you to a list of the known prime numbers less than 10,000. You can then specify that the statement is false if 6,121, for instance, is not the sum of two prime numbers. In this case, then, you *can* specify a way in which the statement may actually be false. You might

---

[31] This constraint is inspired by (but is not meant as an interpretation of) Ludwig Wittgenstein's remark that "From its *seeming* to me—or to everyone—to be so, it doesn't follow that it *is* so. What we can ask is whether it can make sense to doubt it" (Wittgenstein 1969: §2).

later discover that 6,121 is the sum of two primes. But unless you have a proof of Goldbach's conjecture, at any given time you will be able to specify some prime number (or other) that at that time you don't know to be the sum of two primes. The moral is that in applying (T3), we must pay careful attention to whether we can specify a way in which the statement in question may be false. Although I do not have the space to list and reply to them here, all the alleged counter-examples to (T3) that I have encountered overlook some of the ways in which the subject may specify how the claim in question may actually be false.

Even if (T3) is not undermined by alleged counter-examples like the one just described, however, many will be inclined to reject it, reasoning as follows. "It is epistemically reasonable for a person to accept a particular statement only if she has epistemic grounds for accepting it. But a person's inability to specify a way in which a statement may actually be false gives her no reason to think it is likely to be true, hence no epistemic grounds for accepting it. Therefore, if the epistemic role of the statement for her is exhausted by her inability to specify a way in which the statement may actually be false, it is not epistemically reasonable for her to accept it." Those who find this reasoning compelling typically assume that if we want to show that it is epistemically reasonable to accept some statement *S* without evidence, we must try to explain how it is possible for a person to have *grounds* for thinking *S* is likely to be true that are not based on any evidence she could offer in support of *S*. Motivated by this conclusion, some philosophers would argue that we can have such grounds for accepting a given statement if the psychological processes that led us to accept it reliably yield true beliefs (Rey 1998). Others hypothesize that we have a capacity for "rational insight" that enables us to know directly, without reasons, that a given statement is likely to be true (Bonjour 1998, Katz 1998). Yet others argue that we are entitled to accept some statements without providing any reasons for accepting them, because our acceptance of them is constitutive of the meanings of the words we use to express them (Boghossian 2000 and 2001, Peacocke 2000).

These positions are all problematic in well-known ways that we need not rehearse here. For present purposes the crucial point is that these problematic positions are motivated by the orthodox assumption that if we want to show that it is epistemically reasonable to accept some statement *S* without evidence, we must to try to explain how it is possible for a person to have *grounds* for thinking S is likely to be true that are not based on any evidence she could offer in support of S. But I see no good reason to accept this assumption. In my view, if one cannot specify a way in which a statement S may be false, it is epistemically reasonable to accept S, even if the fact that one cannot specify a way in which S may be false does not imply that S is likely to be true. Hence, contrary to the orthodox positions just sketched, I propose that we accept (T3) as a further constraint on our understanding of 'epistemically reasonable'.

These reflections bear directly on the question whether it is epistemically reasonable for us to regard our PJSSs as both factual and trustworthy. For if we adopt the PJSS-based conception of words, we will take ourselves to have no grip on sameness of satisfaction apart from our PJSSs, and hence we will be epistemically entitled to regard them as both factual and trustworthy. To see why, let us first consider the question whether we are epistemically entitled to regard our PJSSs as *factual*. If we adopt the PJSS-based conception of words, we will have no conception of how sentences that express our PJSSs could fail to be declarative sentences of a regimented language for which we can define a Tarski-style disquotational truth predicate. Hence we will be unable to specify a way in which the statement

(f) Sentences that express our PJSSs are declarative sentences of a regimented language for which we can define a Tarski-style disquotational truth predicate

could be false. By (T3), then, it is epistemically reasonable for us to accept (f). But to accept (f) is to accept that sentences that express our practical judgements of sameness of satisfaction are factual, in the sense of 'factual' defined by (H) above (§3.9). Hence it is epistemically reasonable for us to regard sentences that express our PJSSs as factual. Since the sentences that express our practical judgements of sameness of satisfaction are factual if and only if our PJSSs are factual, it is epistemically reasonable for us to regard our PJSSs as factual. Nevertheless, we have no *reason* to regard our PJSSs as factual, in the sense of 'reason' constrained by (T1). Hence, by (T2), we are epistemically *entitled* to regard our PJSSs as factual.

Let us now consider the question whether we are epistemically entitled to regard our PJSSs as *trustworthy*. I assume that (def) Our PJSSs are trustworthy if and only if it is epistemically reasonable for us to trust sentences that express our PJSSs unless we have particular, local reasons in a given context for not doing so.

Now we may reason as follows. If we adopt the PJSS-based conception of words, we will take ourselves to have no grip on sameness of satisfaction apart from our PJSSs. More specifically, we will take ourselves to be unable to raise a doubt about any particular PJSS unless we simultaneously trust a number of other PJSSs. We will suppose that in principle we may come to doubt any given PJSSs, but we will not be able to make sense of simultaneously doubting all of them. We will regard our trust in the PJSSs that we presuppose when we raise doubts about other PJSSs as epistemically reasonable, since we cannot see how to assess particular PJSSs without it. In short, we will be unable to specify a way in which the statement

(t) It is epistemically reasonable for us to trust sentences that express our PJSSs unless we have particular, local reasons in a given context for not doing so

could be false. By (T3), then, it is epistemically reasonable for us to accept (t).[32] By (def), it is epistemically reasonable for us to accept (t) if and only if it is epistemically reasonable for us to accept that our PJSSs as trustworthy. Hence, we may conclude that it is epistemically reasonable for us to accept that our PJSSs are trustworthy. Nevertheless, we have no *reason* to accept that our PJSSs are trustworthy, in the sense of 'reason' constrained by (T1). Hence, by (T2), we are epistemically *entitled* to regard our PJSSs as trustworthy.

Third, if we adopt the PJSS-based conception, we will regard our PJSS-based use of words, including our PJSSs, as integral to our grasp of the word types to which our own Tarski-style disquotational definitions of satisfaction and truth apply. Recall that if I make a PJSS of the form "x satisfies my word type **robin** if and only if x is a robin and x satisfies A's word type **r** if and only if x is a robin," I will thereby take my word type **robin** to be identical to A's word type **r**, and conclude that A's mark **r** is a PJSS-based

[32] This reasoning may seem circular, because (t) itself contains an occurrence of the phrase 'epistemically reasonable'. But I do not aim to *define* this phrase; (T1)–(T3) are *constraints* on our use of it, not definitions. Hence they leave open the possibility that other considerations, such as whether we can make sense of doubting (t), can help us to discover what it is or is not epistemically reasonable for us to believe.

replica of **robin**. In general, if we adopt the PJSS-based conception we will identify the word types to which our own Tarski-style disquotational definitions of satisfaction apply with the word types that we take others to be using when we make PJSSs for their words.[33] We will therefore distinguish between the orthographic criteria that we each set up when we regiment our words, and that we use to keep track of our own regimented word types *intra*subjectively when we construct disquotational definitions of satisfaction for them, on the one hand, and the PJSS-based word types to which our disquotational definitions of satisfaction apply, on the other. Finally, if we adopt the PJSS-based conception and we explicate our regimented sentence types as finite *sequences* of our regimented word types, as I proposed above (§4.3), then we will identify the sentence types to which our own Tarski-style disquotational definitions of true-in-L apply with the sentence types that we take others to be using when we make PJSSs for their words.

I propose that we adopt the PJSS-based conception of words. By doing so, we transform our understanding of the word types to which our own Tarski-style disquotational definitions of satisfaction and truth apply: we come to see our PJSSs as factual and trustworthy, yet also integral to our grasp of our Tarski-style disquotational truth predicates. Viewed in this way, the Tarski–Quine thesis does not leave open the possibility that our PJSSs are not both factual and trustworthy. By adopting the PJSS-based conception of words, therefore, we discredit (C) (of §4.1): we supplement our understanding of our own Tarski-style disquotational truth predicates with an account of why we are entitled to regard our PJSSs as both factual and trustworthy *without* undermining the Tarski–Quine thesis that there is no more to truth than what is captured by a Tarski-style disquotational truth predicate defined for one's own sentences.

4.10. Preliminary Objections and Replies

One might doubt that the PJSS-based conception of words, which is at root practical, is clear enough to be considered integral to our understanding of

---

[33] How then should we think of quotation, as it is used in our definitions of satisfaction and truth? I favour a modified Davidsonian account of quotation, according to which a quotation in which a given mark, such as **robin**, is displayed refers to the corresponding PJSS letter or word type, such as {x: x is a PJSS-based replica of my mark **robin**}. (See Davidson 1984: 79–92 and Bennett 1988 for considerations that favour a "display" conception of quotation.)

truth. I will address this concern indirectly in later chapters by elucidating in more detail the central idea behind the PJSS-based conception of words—the idea that we have no understanding of the word types relevant to satisfaction and truth independent of the PJSSs on which we rely when we apply our disquotational definitions of satisfaction and truth to other speakers' sentences and to our own sentences as we use them in the past. Given my proposed explication of the word types relevant to satisfaction and truth, the task is to elucidate what it is for a given mark to be a PJSS-based replica of another mark by looking at how we actually keep track of word types in the midst of our inquiries. This task can seem worth pursuing only if one already has a preliminary understanding of how the PJSS-based conception of words differs from token-and-explanatory-use conceptions of words, and that is what I have tried to convey in this chapter.

I will end this chapter by considering four objections that are easier to address. First, one might object that if we take the PJSS-based conception of words to be integral to our understanding of truth, as I propose, then we cannot make sense of generalizing over sentences of foreign languages, such as French or German. This objection overlooks the fact that we can learn how to use words of other languages, and thereby come to make PJSSs for those words.[34] An English-speaker may also be a French speaker, so an English-speaker may be in a position to construct Tarski-style disquotational definitions of satisfaction for words of French and to apply the definitions unreflectively to other French speakers' words. The same reasoning applies to any language that we can learn.[35]

Second, one might object that my proposal conflicts with our intuition that even *before* we learn a given foreign language, we can make sense of applying a truth predicate to its sentences. I concede that my proposal does not respect this intuition. But I don't see this as a problem for the proposal, since we do not need to respect the intuition in order to use logic to clarify our agreements and disagreements with other inquirers. For this purpose, it is sufficient that we be able to learn the language of our fellow inquirers, if we do not already know it.

---

[34] Quine proposed this way of applying Tarski-style definitions of satisfaction and truth to expressions of a foreign language in Quine 1961a: 130–8. Hartry Field endorses Quine's proposal in Field 1994: 273–4.

[35] Michael Resnik suggests that "we think of our truth-predicate as applying immanently to the human polyglot" (Resnik 1997: 38). I have argued, in effect, that to make sense of this suggestion without giving up the Tarski–Quine thesis, we need to embrace the PJSS-based conception of words.

Third, one might think we need a general explanation of how we make the transition from not knowing anything about a language to being able to make PJSSs for its words, and that any such explanation will presuppose or support the token-and-explanatory-use conception of words. I grant that for every word of every language we learn, there is some (and usually more than one) way in which we learn to use that word. But this truism does not imply or even suggest that there is a general explanation of how we learn to use words, or that to describe how we learn to use a given word we must presuppose the token-and-explanatory-use conception of words.

Finally, if our understanding of truth is inextricable from our PJSS-based conception of words, as I believe, then every sentence to which we can apply a truth predicate contains word types for which we can make PJSSs. This will seem counter-intuitive to philosophers who think there may be true sentences (used by a super-intelligent alien species, perhaps) that contain word types for which we could never make PJSSs.[36] As I argued in §2.5, however, given my purposes in this book I do not find it fruitful to evaluate theses about truth by asking whether they successfully capture a concept that our ordinary uses of 'true' express. I recommend that we ask, instead, "Do we need a truth predicate?" and "If so, what sort of truth predicate do we need?" My answer to the first of these questions is that we need a truth predicate to formulate logical laws that we can use to clarify our agreements and disagreements with other inquirers. For this purpose, we do not need a truth predicate that applies to sentences that contain word types for which we could never make PJSSs. Instead, we need to be entitled to affirm every given sentence of the form 'X is true-in-L if and only if S', where 'X' is replaced by a name of a declarative sentence of our regimented language L, 'S' is replaced by the sentence that 'X' names, or a paraphrase of it that we explicitly adopt when we decide to use sentences of L in place of sentences of ordinary English, and *the sentence types and word types of L are conceived of as PJSS based, in accordance with the context principle.* We can satisfy this need by merging our

---

[36] To make this intuition vivid, Wolfgang Künne imagines that "there could be intelligent beings, Alpha-Centaurians, say, endowed with modes of sensory awareness and conceptual abilities that we and our descendants constitutionally lack.... Why should the fact that some of their utterances are forever incomprehensible to members of our species prevent them from being true?" (Künne 2003: 246)

own Tarski-style disquotational definitions of satisfaction and truth with our PJSS-based conception of words. If we understand truth and words in this way, we cannot help but regard our PJSSs as factual and trustworthy. We thereby come to see that the Tarski–Quine thesis and intersubjectivity constraint are compatible.

5

Learning from Others, Interpretation, and Charity

5.1. Is the Intersubjectivity Constraint Compatible with the Negation of the Tarski–Quine Thesis?

As I stressed in Chapter 2, our desire to clarify and facilitate our rational inquiries motivates us to regiment our sentences so that we can formulate logical generalizations, such as "Every regimented sentence of the form '$S \vee \sim S$' is true." A Tarski-style truth predicate defined disquotationally for our own regimented sentences enables us to formulate such generalizations for the regimented sentences we can directly use. One might therefore be inclined to embrace the Tarski–Quine thesis that there is no more to truth than what is captured by a Tarski-style truth predicate defined disquotationally for our own regimented sentences. But to clarify and facilitate our rational inquiries we also need to generalize on the other speakers' sentences, so that we can apply logical generalizations to their utterances. As I emphasized in Chapter 3, however, when we generalize on other speakers' sentences, we regard our practical judgements of sameness of satisfaction (PJSSs) for their words as both factual and trustworthy. This may lead us to adopt the *intersubjectivity constraint: a Tarski-style disquotational definition of truth for one's own sentences is satisfactory only if it is supplemented by an account of why it is epistemically reasonable for us to regard our PJSSs as both factual and trustworthy.* But a Tarski-style disquotational definition of truth for one's own sentences tells us nothing about our PJSSs. Hence the intersubjectivity constraint appears incompatible with the Tarski–Quine thesis.

I argued in Chapter 4 that this appearance is illusory. If one adopts the PJSS-based conception of words, one can endorse the Tarski–Quine thesis yet still explain why it is epistemically reasonable to regard one's PJSSs as both factual and trustworthy. In short, the intersubjectivity constraint is compatible with the Tarski–Quine thesis. But my arguments for the compatibility of the Tarski–Quine thesis and intersubjectivity constraint apparently leave it open that one can explain why it is epistemically reasonable to regard one's PJSSs as both factual and trustworthy if one endorses a token-and-ex-use conception of words, and one thereby rejects both the Tarski–Quine thesis and the PJSS-based conception of words. In short, my arguments so far apparently leave it open that the intersubjectivity constraint is compatible with the negation of the Tarski–Quine thesis.

It appears that we now face a choice: either (i) we adopt the PJSS-based conception of words and embrace *both* the Tarski–Quine thesis and intersubjectivity constraint, as I recommend, or (ii) we embrace a token-and-ex-use conception of words, reject both the Tarski–Quine thesis and the PJSS-based conception of words, and try to explain why it is epistemically reasonable to regard one's PJSSs as both factual and trustworthy by hypothesizing that facts about language ex-use somehow constrain or determine the truth values of sentences that express our PJSSs. For all I have argued so far, many (perhaps even most) philosophers will still be inclined to choose option (ii) over option (i).

My goals in Chapters 5–8 are (first) to present examples and thought experiments that discredit option (ii), and (second) to elucidate the PJSS-based conception of words by showing how it makes sense of examples and thought experiments that seem puzzling or paradoxical if we assume a token-and-ex-use conception of words. By the end of Chapter 8, I hope to have convinced you that contrary to what you might have thought at first, option (ii) is unacceptable—the intersubjectivity constraint is not compatible with the negation of the Tarski–Quine thesis—and (i) is the only genuine option we have if we seek to fit our disquotational truth predicates with our PJSSs. I begin in this chapter by examining the relationship between our PJSSs and Donald Davidson's influential principle of charity.

5.2. Language Ex-Use and Interpretation

If we adopt the PJSS-based conception of words, as I propose, we will regard all token-and-ex-use conceptions of words as irrelevant to truth and satisfaction. It would be absurd to claim that language ex-use is irrelevant to our practical judgements of sameness of satisfaction, however. These judgements reflect our robust but subtle ability to distinguish between situations in which we would take a word uttered by another English speaker to be of the same type as one of our own words, and similar situations in which we would not do so. From these truisms it is tempting to infer both that there is a systematic relationship between language ex-use and our PJSSs and that we need a philosophical theory of that relationship.

A number of such theories have been proposed, but I shall focus in this chapter on what is perhaps the most influential of all of these theories—the theory of interpretation developed by Donald Davidson. Davidson assumes that an interpreter who does not already know a given language L can nevertheless describe circumstances under which a given speaker of L holds her sentences true. In effect, Davidson presupposes a token-and-ex-use conception of words according to which an interpreter's specifications of satisfaction for another speaker's words are constrained by facts about the circumstances under which the speaker of L holds her sentences true. The main goal of Davidson's theory of interpretation is to explain how an interpreter can construct a satisfactory interpretation of a language based only on his knowledge of facts about when its speakers hold its sentences true. For this purpose, Davidson posits a principle of charity that takes up the slack between the evidence about language ex-use available to an interpreter and interpretations of sentences of L. In its simplest form, the principle of charity requires that we interpret a speaker's words in such a way that if the speaker holds a sentence true, then that sentence is true under the assigned interpretation. A crucial consequence of the principle of charity is that error only makes sense against a background of massive agreement, understood as an optimal fit between sentences held true and truth (Davidson 1984: Essays 2, 9, 10).

To evaluate Davidson's theory of interpretation, I shall ask whether it is compatible with our PJSSs. It is clearly incompatible with many of our PJSSs *across time*. Suppose we learn, for instance, that in 1750 David Hume uttered the sentence "This is gold" while pointing at a bit of platinum. Relying on our PIWs and PJSSs across time for our word 'gold', we unreflectively judge that Hume's tokens of g-o-l-d are of the same word type as our tokens of g-o-l-d, and hence that x satisfies both his and our tokens of g-o-l-d if and only if x is a bit of gold. We know that no bit of platinum is a bit of gold. Hence we judge that Hume's utterance was false. Since by hypothesis, Hume held his utterance of "This is gold" true while pointing at a bit of platinum, our PJSS for his word 'gold' will lead us to judge that his utterance was false, and hence (for reasons I shall clarify below) to violate Davidson's principle of charity. In a similar way, many of our PIWs and PJSSs across time violate Davidson's principle of charity.

Such conflicts between our PIWs and PJSSs across time and Davidson's principle of charity are unlikely to persuade anyone who accepts Davidson's principle of charity to abandon it, however, since the most compelling applications of Davidson's theory of interpretation do not involve cases in which we try to interpret speakers who lived long ago, but cases in which we try to interpret our contemporaries. Hence, to discredit Davidson's principle of charity, one must show that it prevents us from accommodating the PIWs and PJSSs on which we rely in our linguistic interactions with our contemporaries. I shall focus on cases in which we learn from our contemporaries by relying on our PIWs and PJSSs for their words and trusting what they write or say.

Many philosophers assume that Donald Davidson's principle of charity is at least *compatible* with trusting what others write or say.[1] Against this, I will argue that if Davidson's principle of charity is a constraint on correctly interpreting what others write or say, then our ordinary impression that we can learn from others by relying on our PIWs and PJSSs for their words and trusting what they write or say is an illusion created by habitual but unjustified misinterpretations of their utterances.[2] The reason is that in a large number of cases in which we take ourselves to be learning from others

[1] And some philosophers are committed to the stronger claim that we can *justify* our trust in what others write or say by appealing to Davidson's principle of charity. See, for instance, Coady 1992: chapter 9. For a similar argument, see Burge 1993. Burge argues that our trust in testimony is justified by an a priori principle that is "clearly similar to what is widely called a 'Principle of Charity' for translating or interpreting others" (Burge 1993: 487). Burge rejects Davidson's assumption that speakers of the same natural language should use the methods of radical interpretation to interpret each other. But Burge suggests that something like a Principle of Charity provides an a priori entitlement to accept what others say as true.

[2] In Fricker 1995, Elizabeth Fricker also raises doubts about Coady's attempt to use Davidson's principle of charity to justify our reliance on testimony, but not by raising doubts about Coady's assumption that Davidson's principle of charity is a constraint on correctly interpreting what others write or say. Fricker's point is that testimony may be unreliable even if many of our beliefs are true (Fricker 1995: 409–10).

by accepting what they write or say, what we *take* them to write or say, given (what Davidson sees as) our tacit interpretations of what we read or hear, is *not* true by our own lights. In such cases, when we take ourselves to be learning from others, we violate Donald Davidson's principle of charity.

We must therefore either reject Davidson's principle of charity, or conclude that what others write or say cannot conflict with what we believe. I propose that we reject Davidson's principle of charity. For reasons I'll explain, this requires that we also reject the token-and-ex-use conception of words that underlies his conception of the problem of interpretation. I propose that we adopt the PJSS-based conception of words and trust our PIWs and PJSSs, both at a given time and across time, as in the Hume case described above, unless we have good reason in a given context not to do so. Unlike Davidson's principle of charity, my proposal that we combine the PJSS-based conception of words with our own Tarski-style disquotational of truth and satisfaction both allows for and illuminates the familiar phenomenon of learning from others.

5.3. A Case in which One Person Learns from Another

My discussion of learning from others will focus on the following case.[3] A competent English speaker named Al accepts a number of English sentences that contain the word 'arthritis', including such sentences as 'Arthritis can cause pain in one's joints', 'Several members of my family have arthritis', and 'I have arthritis in my left knee.' Al does in fact have arthritis in his left knee. He also has a pain in his thigh that resembles the arthritic pain in his left knee. He tells his friend Joe, "I have arthritis in my thigh." Joe replies, "You don't have arthritis in your thigh—arthritis afflicts the joints only." "I bet you're wrong, Joe," Al says, "but I'll ask my

---

[3] This is an elaboration on the arthritis case that Tyler Burge first presented in Burge 1979. I chose to elaborate on Burge's arthritis case, and not to construct a completely new case of my own, because many philosophers now accept our initial, commonsense description of Burge's case, even though this description conflicts with some theories of meaning that were once widely accepted. This consensus about how to describe Burge's case aids my argument.

doctor—I have an appointment with her tomorrow." The next day, Al asks his doctor, "Do I have arthritis in my thigh?" She replies "You don't have arthritis in your thigh—arthritis afflicts the joints only." Later that day, Al tells Joe, "I was wrong—the pain in my thigh is not arthritis."

To begin with, let me draw your attention to several obvious but important aspects of this case. First, since Al accepts the sentences "Arthritis can cause pain in one's joints," "Several members of my family have arthritis," and "I have arthritis in my left knee," it is natural to say that Al *believes* that arthritis can cause pain in one's joints, that several members of his family have arthritis, and that he has arthritis in his left knee. Second, it is natural to suppose that since Al, Joe, and the doctor are all at least minimally competent English-speakers, they are at least minimally competent in the use of the English words 'thigh' and 'joint', so that if they were asked, "Is a thigh a joint?" they would each say, "No, a thigh is not a joint," thereby expressing their belief that a thigh is not a joint.

Third, Al makes *practical identifications of words* (PIWs) for Joe's and the doctor's words 'arthritis', 'in', 'thigh', 'only', and 'joint'. In Chapter 3 I emphasized that speakers of the same language typically take one another to utter words tokens of which they can each use to express one another's assertions, thereby making PIWs for one another's words. In doing so, they attribute beliefs to each other and identify points on which they agree and disagree. In this case, Al takes Joe and the doctor to disagree with his belief that he has arthritis in his thigh.

Against this background, two aspects of the case stand out. First, Al does not think he can learn anything from Joe about arthritis, and so when Joe says, "You don't have arthritis in your thigh—arthritis afflicts the joints only," Al continues to believe that he has arthritis in his thigh. In contrast, Al assumes that his doctor knows more than he does about arthritis, and so when the doctor says, "You don't have arthritis in your thigh—arthritis afflicts the joints only," Al takes himself to have *learned* from her that arthritis afflicts the joints only. The key observation is that

(1) Al makes PIWs for his doctor's words and accepts what she says.

Al thereby takes himself to have learned from her that arthritis afflicts the joints only. Since Al believes that a thigh is not a joint, he takes himself to have learned from his doctor that he does not have arthritis in his thigh.

Second, after his conversation with the doctor, Al tells Joe, "I was wrong—the pain in my thigh is not arthritis." Al and Joe remember that the previous day, Al said to Joe, "I have arthritis in my thigh." When we hear this story, we naturally assume that after Al takes himself to have learned from his doctor that arthritis afflicts the joints only, he *also* makes PIWs for words that occur in his previous utterance of 'I have arthritis in my thigh', but rejects the belief that he thereby takes himself to have expressed. Hence Al takes for granted that for several days, up until he spoke with his doctor, he believed that the pain in his thigh was arthritis, and that he learned from his doctor that that belief was false. The key observation here is that

   (2) After Al talks with his doctor, he makes PIWs for words that occur in his previous utterance of 'I have arthritis in my thigh', thereby taking himself to have expressed the belief that he had arthritis in his thigh, but he rejects that belief.

Al thereby takes himself to have learned from his doctor that his belief that he had arthritis in his thigh was false.

It seems a small step from these observations to the conclusion that by making PIWs for his doctor's words and accepting what she says, Al learns from her. But there is more to learning from another than making PIWs for her words and accepting what she says. What she says must also be true. From $\ulcorner A$ learns that $p\urcorner$, one may infer $\ulcorner p\urcorner$.[4] I shall largely ignore this further condition and focus on cases in which we take for granted that what a given subject is told is true. I shall highlight and explore the consequences of aspects (1) and (2) of Al's situation, which is typical of situations in which we take ourselves to have learned from others that some of our previous beliefs were false. In such cases we make PIWs for others' words and accept what we thereby take them to have said, while at the same time relying on PIWs for words in our previous utterances,

---

   [4] There is also an ordinary sense in which one can be said to "learn" that p, even if p is false. This sense of "learn" goes with the ordinary sense in which a person may be said to "teach" another that p, even if p is false. For example, a person who accepts Darwin's theory of evolution may say "Zack is teaching Mary (and Mary is learning) that Darwin's theory of evolution is false." I will not be concerned with this sense of "learn" in this chapter.

thereby taking ourselves to have expressed beliefs that we now reject because they conflict with what we take ourselves to have learned.

These aspects of ordinary cases in which we take ourselves to be learning from others, encapsulated for Al's case by (1) and (2), seem almost too obvious to state. We ordinarily take such observations for granted without any sense that they are in tension with each other, or that they violate any commonsense constraints on understanding others. It is therefore natural to assume that the conjunction of (1) and (2) is compatible with Davidson's principle of charity.

In fact, however, the conjunction of (1) and (2) *violates* Davidson's principle of charity. To see why, one must focus on the intimate relationship between (1) and (2), on the one hand, and Al's PJSSs for his doctor's words, as well as his PJSSs for his own words as he used them in the past, on the other. I shall describe this relationship in the next section, and then sketch a strategy for showing that the conjunction of (1) and (2) violates Davidson's principle of charity.

5.4. Two Conditionals

Recall the following pattern for defining satisfaction for one's own words disquotationally:

(Sats) x satisfies my word '___' if and only if x is ___.[5]

Anyone who understands (Sats) can apply it to his own regimented words. For instance, I accept the results of writing my word 'arthritis' in the blanks of (Sats), so I accept that x satisfies my word 'arthritis' if and only if x is (an instance of) arthritis. If, in addition, I apply (Sats) to another speaker's word 'arthritis', I make a practical judgement of sameness of satisfaction (PJSS). More generally, any speaker who accepts applications of (Sats) to his own words, and who makes a PIW for a speaker A's word w while he is talking with A, thereby makes a PJSS for A's word w. And any speaker who accepts applications of (Sats) to his own words, and who

---

[5] Applications of (Sats) are short for corresponding disquotational definitions of satisfaction of sentences by sequences of objects. See §3.3.

makes a PIW for a given word w that he used at some previous time t, thereby makes a PJSS across time for the word w that he used at t.

Let's assume that Al accepts applications of (Sats) to his own words, so that, in particular, Al accepts the following sentence:

(a) x satisfies my word 'arthritis' if and only if x is (an instance of) arthritis.

Then we can establish two conditionals, the first with (1) as antecedent, and the second with (2) as antecedent.

To establish the first conditional, suppose that

(1) Al makes PIWs for his doctor's words and accepts what she says.

This trivially implies that Al makes PIWs for his doctor's words. Given that Al accepts (a), when he makes PIWs for his doctor's words he accepts the following sentence

(b) x satisfies the doctor's word 'arthritis' if and only if x is (an instance of) arthritis

and thereby commits himself to the conjunction of (a) and (b), which is a PJSS *at a given time* for the doctor's word 'arthritis'. Now, given that Al accepts (a) and (b), we can infer that

(3) Al accepts that x satisfies his word 'arthritis' if and only if x satisfies the doctor's word 'arthritis'.

These reflections show that whether or not we accept (1), if Al accepts applications of (Sats) to his own words, then

(C1) If (1) then (3).

This is the first conditional.

To establish the second conditional, suppose that

(2) After Al talks with his doctor, he makes PIWs for words that occur in his previous utterance of 'I have arthritis in my thigh,' thereby taking himself to have expressed the belief that he had arthritis in his thigh, but he rejects that belief.

This implies, in particular, that Al makes a PIW for the word 'arthritis' that occurred in his previous utterance of 'I have arthritis in my thigh.' Given that Al accepts (a), when he makes a PIW for his past use of the word 'arthritis', he accepts the following sentence

(c) x satisfies the word 'arthritis' that I used before talking to the doctor if and only if x is (an instance of) arthritis.

and thereby commits himself to the conjunction of (a) and (c), which is a PJSS *across time* for the word 'arthritis' that he used before talking to the doctor. Now, given that Al accepts (a) and (c), we can infer that

(4) Al accepts that an object x satisfies the word 'arthritis' that he used before talking to the doctor if and only if x satisfies the word 'arthritis' that he uses after talking with her.

These reflections show that whether or not we accept (2), if Al accepts applications of (Sats) to his own words, then

(C2) If (2) then (4).

This is the second conditional.

5.5. Strategy

The conjunction of (1) and (2), together with (C1) and (C2), truth functionally implies the conjunction of (3) and (4). I will use this implication to argue that if we accept Davidson's principle of charity, then we must reject the conjunction of (1) and (2). The heart of my argument, which I will present in the next several sections, is that if we accept Davidson's principle of charity, then we must reject the conjunction of (3) and (4). Since the conjunction of (1) and (2), together with (C1) and (C2), truth functionally implies the conjunction of (3) and (4), we may infer that if we accept Davidson's principle of charity, then we must reject the conjunction of (1), (2), (C1), and (C2). That is, we must reject either (1) or (2) or (C1) or (C2). But, as we shall see, (C1) and (C2) are unproblematic consequences of Davidson's methodology of interpretation. Hence if we accept Davidson's principle of charity, we must reject the conjunction of (1) and (2).

5.6. What is Davidson's Principle of Charity?

To understand Davidson's principle of charity, one must see how it fits with his project of constructing empirically testable theories of interpretation for natural languages. Davidson's project is to try to bridge an assumed gap between data about linguistic behaviour, on the one hand, and semantic interpretations of that data, on the other. In practice speakers of the same natural language typically ignore this gap—they typically make PIWs for one another's words without reflecting about whether they are justified in doing so. But Davidson thinks that if we want to interpret another speaker's words fairly and accurately, it is almost always wrong to rely on our PIWs for her words. Instead, he thinks, we should suspend our unreflective trust in our PIWs, acknowledge the epistemological gap between data about linguistic behaviour, on the one hand, and semantic interpretations of that data, on the other, and interpret speakers in accordance with a principle of charity.[6]

To explain how Davidson arrives at this conclusion, I will answer three questions about his approach: (i) What are the philosophical roots of Davidson's project of constructing a theory of interpretation? (ii) What is Davidson's conception of the task and test of a theory of interpretation? (iii) How is Davidson's conception of the task and test of a theory of interpretation related to his principle of charity? The answer to question (i) puts constraints on the answer to question (ii), which in turn puts constraints on the answer to question (iii). I'll address them in order, starting with question (i).

Like many others, Davidson is convinced by W. V. Quine that traditional philosophical attempts to make sense of the idea of meaning are hopelessly obscure. Quine argues that all such attempts make use of notions such as *synonymy* (sameness of meaning), analyticity (truth "in virtue of" meaning), and *semantical rule* that are themselves no clearer than the idea of meaning. This would not be a problem if the idea of meaning were clear. But Quine argues that unlike the sentences used in the mature sciences, including logic, psychology, and physics, sentences that contain the term 'meaning'

---

[6] In this respect Davidson's theory of interpretation differs from Quine's account of translation, which implies that our PIWs and PJSSs are trustworthy, for reasons I explained in §3.9. The difference is due to Davidson's principle of charity, which is related to, but, much stronger than Quine's.

have no explanatory import. For Quine, explanatory import is the criterion of clarity, and so he concludes that the terms 'meaning', 'synonymy', 'analyticity', and 'semantical rule' are hopelessly obscure.

Quine recommends that we replace the obscure idea of meaning with the more tractable idea of translation, understood as a mapping from sentences of one language to sentences of another. To explicate the translation relation, Quine constructs an empirical theory of translation that makes no essential appeal to the notion of meaning. In Quine's view, as I explained in §3.6, a translation of one language into another is acceptable if it preserves the relevant speakers' dispositions to assent to and dissent from sentences under various stimulus conditions.[7]

Like Quine, Davidson proposes that we replace the obscure idea of meaning with an idea that has clearer empirical consequences.[8] But Davidson seeks a theory of interpretation that states the meanings of expressions of a natural language. A translation of one language A into another B comprises a syntactical correlation of the expressions of A with the expressions of B, and so it does not actually state the meanings of the expressions of A (Davidson 1984: 129). Davidson agrees with Quine that the notions of truth and satisfaction are clearer than the traditional idea of meaning,[9] he thinks that "to give truth conditions is a way of giving the meaning of a sentence" (Davidson 1984: 24), and he endorses Quine's suggestion that "in point of *meaning* . . . a word may be said to be determined to whatever extent

[7] For a more thorough and accurate account of Quine's views on meaning and translation, see chapter 2 of Ebbs 1997.

[8] For a different interpretation of Davidson, see Lepore and Ludwig 2005, especially chapters 3–6. Lepore and Ludwig claim that Davidson seeks not an explication that replaces the ordinary notions of translation and meaning, but an account of truth for natural languages that is faithful to our prior and independent intuitions about translation and meaning. Their interpretation implies that Davidson's account of how to test theories of meaning is *wrong by his own standards*. In my view, however, Davidson's account of how to test theories of truth for natural languages is part of an explication that is meant to *replace* the ordinary notion of meaning. On the pragmatic view of explication that I endorse, this distinction is itself blurred, since there is no more to meaning than what can be salvaged by an explication we find useful for a particular purpose, such as clarifying and facilitating rational inquiry. Whether or not the distinction is blurred, however, Davidson presents his account of how to test theories of truth for natural languages as a new standard for judging all questions in the theory of meaning, and embraces its counter-intuitive consequences, including the one I shall soon highlight in this chapter. I think this shows that Davidson's goal is not to construct an account of truth for natural languages that is faithful to our prior and independent intuitions about translation and meaning, but to explicate what he finds useful and clear in the ordinary notion of meaning and translation.

[9] But note that unlike Davidson, Quine thinks it makes no sense to apply a truth predicate to sentences that we have not translated and do not understand.

the truth or falsehood of its contexts is determined" (Quine 1976b: 82). Combining these considerations, Davidson claims that the "meaning" of a sentence *S* of language *L* may be specified by an empirically tested theory of truth for *L*.

This brings us to question (ii)—"What is Davidson's conception of the task and test of a theory of interpretation?" Davidson is impressed by Noam Chomsky's approach to constructing an empirically testable theory of the *syntax* of a speaker's language:

> While there is agreement that it is the central task of semantics to give the semantic interpretation (the meaning) of every sentence in the language, nowhere in the linguistic literature will one find, so far as I know, a straightforward account of how a theory performs this task, or how to tell when it has been accomplished. *The contrast with syntax is striking.* The main job of a modest syntax is to characterize meaningfulness (or sentencehood). We may have as much confidence in the correctness of such a characterization as we have in the representativeness of our sample and our ability to say when particular expressions are meaningful (sentences). *What clear and analogous task and test exist for semantics?*   (Davidson 1984: 21–2)

Davidson's answer is that the *task* of a theory of meaning for an infinitary natural language *L* is to specify the meanings of all the sentences of *L* on the basis of the meanings of a finite number of simple expressions of *L* without using the obscure notion of meaning. His conception of the *test* of such a theory is modelled on Chomsky's approach to testing theories of syntax. Chomsky's approach is to test a proposed theory of the syntax of a given speaker's language by checking evidence about whether or not the speaker himself regards particular sentences that the theory entails as grammatical. We can clarify the obscure notion of meaning, Davidson argues, if we can propose a conception of meaning and evidence that is structurally similar to the linguists' conception of theories of syntax and the evidence to which such theories must be faithful.

Davidson begins with the idea that "to give truth conditions is a way of giving the meaning of a sentence". He proposes that the task of a theory of meaning for a natural language *L* is to construct a Tarski-style truth theory for *L* that has a finite number of clauses which together specify the denotations of all the simple expressions of *L*. He stipulates that "a theory of meaning for a language *L* shows 'how the meanings of sentences depend on

the meanings of words' if it contains a (recursive) definition of truth-in-*L*"
(Davidson 1984: 23).

This proposed clarification of the task of a theory of meaning suggests
a simple test of such a theory. According to Davidson, a Tarski-style
truth theory for a natural language *L*, relativized to persons, times, and
circumstances, entails biconditionals of the following general form:

> (T) Sentence *s* is true-in-*L* (speaker *p*'s language) at *t* if and only if
> conditions *c* obtain at *t*.

In order to test a Tarski-style truth theory for a natural language, "all that
is needed is the ability to recognize when the required biconditionals are
true". This conception of the test for empirical theories of meaning puts
them "on as firm a footing empirically as syntax" (Davidson 1984: 62).[10]

To answer question (iii) — "How is Davidson's conception of the task and
test of a theory of interpretation related to his principle of charity?" — we
must look more closely at Davidson's account of how an empirical theory
of truth is tested. A theory of truth for a German speaker, stated in English,
might entail the following biconditional:

> (t) 'Es schneit' is true-in-*L* (speaker *p*'s language) at *t* if and only if it is
> snowing in the vicinity of *p* at *t*.

But how can we test (t) if we do not (yet) know what the sentence 'Es
schneit' means? According to Davidson,

> A good place to begin is with the attitude of holding a sentence true, of accepting
> it as true. This is, of course, a belief, but it is a single attitude applicable to
> all sentences, and so does not ask us to be able to make finely discriminated
> distinctions among beliefs. It is an attitude an interpreter may plausibly be taken
> to be able to identify before he can interpret, since he may know that a person
> intends to express a truth in uttering a sentence without having any idea *what*
> truth.   (Davidson 1984: 135)

Suppose that statements of our evidence about which sentences a given
speaker holds true have the following general form:

> (E) Sentence *s* is held-true-in-*L* by speaker *p* at *t* if and only if conditions
> *c* obtain at *t*.

[10] For a later affirmation of the same basic view of the task and test of a theory of interpretation, see
Davidson 1994b: 126–7.

Then one bit of evidence might be:

> (e) 'Es schneit' is held-true-in-L by speaker p at t if and only if it is snowing in the vicinity of p at t.

To test a proposed theory of truth for a language L, we must determine whether the biconditionals it entails are true. This is where Davidson's principle of charity comes in: *to determine whether* (t) *is true, we must in effect treat the phrase 'true-in-L' as roughly equivalent to 'held-true-in-L'*. As Davidson puts it, "I propose that we take the fact that speakers of a language hold a sentence to be true (under observed circumstances) as prima facie evidence that the sentence is true under those circumstances" (Davidson 1984: 152). According to this proposal, for instance, (e) is evidence for (t).

The key point is that to test a theory of truth for a natural language, we must link our understanding of when the phrase 'true-in-L' applies to a given sentence to our understanding of when the phrase 'held-true-in-L' applies to that sentence. The link we need is the principle of charity. In Davidson's view, this principle is not optional: the gap that Davidson describes between data about linguistic behaviour, on the one hand, and semantic interpretations of that data, on the other, can only be bridged "by assigning truth conditions to alien sentences that make native speakers right when plausibly possible, according, of course, to our own view of what is right" (Davidson 1984: 137). Davidson sometimes recommends that we "maximize" the number of alien sentences that come out true by our own lights, and sometimes that we "optimize" that number. No matter how the principle of charity is formulated, however, its role is to give content to Davidson's leading idea that the consequences of a particular theory of truth for a natural language L can be *tested* against evidence available to an interpreter who does not already know what the sentences of L mean.

5.7. Davidson's Framework for Evaluating (3) and (4)

If we view Al as a Davidsonian interpreter of the doctor's language (idiolect) and of the language (idiolect) he used on the previous day, then (3) and (4) (introduced in §5.4) imply that Al accepts particular interpretations of the doctor's words at the time he is learning from her, and of his own words on the previous day, respectively, so those interpretations are acceptable or not according as they are permitted by Davidson's principle of charity. This can be seen in three steps.

First, suppose that Al has the resources to construct a Davidsonian theory for another speaker's language. Then he has the resources to define satisfaction for his own words disquotationally. Hence we may assume (as before) that Al accepts applications of (Sats) to his own words, and, in particular, that Al accepts the sentence

(a) x satisfies my word 'arthritis' if and only if x is (an instance of) arthritis.

We would ordinarily make a PIW for Al's word 'arthritis' and assume that Al's assertion of (a) expresses Al's belief that x satisfies his word 'arthritis' if and only if x is (an instance of) arthritis. But Davidson thinks that if we are trying to understand Al, we should at first *suspend* our inclination to make a PIW for Al's word 'arthritis', and interpret Al in that way only if it is justified by the principle of charity.[11] Even if we suspend our inclination to make a PIW for Al's word 'arthritis', however, we know that when Al makes a PIW for his doctor's word 'arthritis', he accepts

(b) x satisfies the doctor's word 'arthritis' if and only if x is (an instance of) arthritis

and thereby makes a PJSS at a given time for the doctor's word 'arthritis'. Similarly, we know that when Al makes PIWs for the word 'arthritis' that he used before talking to the doctor, he accepts

(c) x satisfies the word 'arthritis' that I used before talking to the doctor if and only if x is (an instance of) arthritis

and thereby makes a PJSS across time for the word 'arthritis' that he used before talking to the doctor. From here the reasoning presented earlier (§5.4) will take us the rest of the way to (C1) and (C2). In this sense, (C1) and (C2) are unproblematic consequences of Davidson's approach to interpretation.

---

[11] This is the main reason that I have emphasized (3) and (4), which we (theorists describing Al's situation) can state without making a PIW for Al's word 'arthritis', not the practical judgements that Al would express by affirming sentences (a), (b), and (c), the meanings of which, according to Davidson, we cannot take ourselves to know in advance of interpretation.

Second, suppose Al is constructing a Davidsonian theory of truth for the doctor's language (idiolect) at the time he is learning from her, or for his own language (idiolect) at some previous time. Then his PJSSs for the doctor's word 'arthritis' at the time he is learning from her, and for his own word 'arthritis' at some previous time, imply what Davidson calls "base clauses" that define satisfaction for, and thereby *interpret*, the doctor's word 'arthritis' at the time Al is learning from her, and Al's own word 'arthritis' at that previous time. These are the same PJSSs that imply the conditionals (C1) and (C2), which, together with (1) and (2), imply (3) and (4).

Finally, Davidson thinks his principle of charity governs all interpretation. From Davidson's perspective, then, (3) and (4) are acceptable or not according as the PJSSs that they presuppose are permitted by his principle of charity.

5.8. Why the Conjunction of (3) and (4) Violates Davidson's Principle of Charity

We are now in a position to see that the conjunction of (3) and (4) is not permitted by Davidson's principle of charity. I'll show (first) that if (4) is permitted, then (3) is not, and (second) that if (3) is permitted, then (4) is not. These two conditionals are truth-functionally equivalent, but it is nevertheless instructive to see the symmetrical arguments that support them.

Suppose that Al is trying to construct a Davidsonian theory of truth for his doctor's language at the time when she says, "You don't have arthritis in your thigh—arthritis afflicts the joints only," and that Davidson's principle of charity does not rule out (4), according to which Al accepts that *x* satisfies the word 'arthritis' that he used before talking to the doctor if and only if *x* satisfies the word 'arthritis' that he uses after talking with her. It's part of the story that before Al talks with his doctor, Al takes the ailment in his thigh to satisfy his word 'arthritis'. And, as I stressed above, Davidson thinks we can solve the problem of interpretation only "by assigning truth conditions to alien sentences that make native speakers right when plausibly possible, according, of course, to our own view of what is right" (Davidson 1984: 137). Hence, since Davidson thinks that radical interpretation begins at home, his principle of charity implies that Al must judge satisfaction and truth by his own lights. Given (4), then, according to Davidson's principle of charity, Al must take the ailment in his thigh to satisfy his own word 'arthritis' even after he talks with his doctor.

Now suppose in addition that

(3) Al accepts that x satisfies his word 'arthritis' if and only if x satisfies the doctor's word 'arthritis'.

Then Al accepts that the ailment in his thigh satisfies the doctor's word 'arthritis'. Hence, in effect, Al interprets the doctor's word 'arthritis' in such a way that the ailment in Al's thigh satisfies it. But Al can see from the doctor's linguistic behaviour that she believes that the ailment in Al's thigh does not satisfy her word 'arthritis'. Thus Al interprets the doctor's words in such a way that under the interpretation, the doctor's utterance expresses the belief that Al doesn't have (what Al calls) arthritis in his thigh. This interpretation of the doctor's utterance is unacceptable, according to Davidson, because it attributes what Al takes to be a false belief to the doctor, and thereby violates the principle of charity.

Davidson sometimes says that the principle of charity permits us to attribute false beliefs to other speakers, as long as the error is, by Davidson's standards, explicable. (Davidson 1984: 136, 153, 168–9). In this case, however, the error that Al would be attributing to the doctor if he were to trust his PIWs for the doctor's words is not, by Davidson's standards, explicable. To see why, consider the following passage, in which Davidson describes a problem of interpretation that is similar to Al's:

If you see a ketch sailing by and your companion says, 'Look at that handsome yawl', you may be faced with a problem of interpretation. One natural possibility is that your friend has mistaken a ketch for a yawl, and has formed a false belief. But *if his vision is good and his line of sight favorable it is even more plausible that he does not use the word 'yawl' quite as you do, and has made no mistake at all about the position of the jigger on the passing yacht.* (Davidson 1984: 196, my emphasis)

In other words, Davidson thinks that under the circumstances described, if your friend's vision is good and his line of sight is favourable, you should not take his word 'yawl' to be satisfied by an object x if and only if x is a yawl, since that would be to attribute an inexplicable error to him—the error of believing that the ketch sailing by is a yawl.

You might object to Davidson's treatment of this example on the grounds that it is natural to assume that your friend intends to speak "correctly"—to apply the word 'yawl' in the same way that other competent English-speakers apply it. In Davidson's view, however, your friend's intention to speak "correctly" in this sense does not settle how his word 'yawl' should be interpreted. Davidson would agree that we should interpret speakers in the way that they intend to be interpreted.[12] But according to Davidson, our grasp on how the speaker intends to be interpreted is ultimately rooted in our evidence of which sentences he holds true. By this criterion, together with the principle of charity, we must conclude that your friend intends to be interpreted in such a way that the ketch sailing by is what he calls a 'yawl'. Your friend may also intend to apply the word 'yawl' in the same way that other competent English-speakers apply it, but according to Davidson this metalinguistic intention is less fundamental to our understanding of what he means. As Davidson puts it, "A failed intention to speak 'correctly', unless it foils the intention to be interpreted in a certain way, does not matter to what the speaker means."[13]

Davidson's treatment of his ketch–yawl example reflects his methodological assumption that we can't explain a speaker's error simply by attributing other false beliefs to her, since our attribution of *any* false beliefs to the speaker is precisely what needs explaining. Instead we must appeal to factors that can be checked independently of the interpretation, such as whether or not a speaker's vision is good and his line of sight is favourable. In the ketch–yawl case, by hypothesis, the speaker's vision is good and his line of sight is favourable, so, Davidson suggests, if you were to attribute to your friend the mistaken belief that the passing yacht is a yawl, you would be attributing an inexplicable error to him. The clear implication

---

[12] Davidson writes that "if the speaker is understood he has been interpreted as he intended to be interpreted" (Davidson 1986: 436). In Davidson 1986, he endorses some of H. P. Grice's views about the relationship between a speaker's intentions and the literal meanings of her words. But Davidson thinks that a speaker's intentions to be interpreted in a certain way cannot have the status that Grice attributes to them, since "making detailed sense of a person's intentions and beliefs cannot be independent of making sense of his utterances. . . . an inventory of a speaker's sophisticated beliefs and intentions cannot be the evidence for the truth of a theory for interpreting his speech behaviour" (Davidson 1984: 144).

[13] Davidson 1992: 261. Davidson elaborates on this attitude towards "incorrect" usage in "A Nice Derangement of Epitaphs", where he writes that "error or mistake of this kind, with its associated notion of correct usage, is not philosophically interesting. We want a deeper notion of what words, when spoken in context, mean . . ." (Davidson 1986: 434).

of the passage is that you should interpret your friend's word 'yawl' in such a way that, unlike your word 'yawl', it is satisfied by the ketch sailing by.

By hypothesis, both Al's and the doctor's vision is good and their lines of sight are favourable—they can both see Al's thigh clearly. Hence, by Davidson's standards, Al could not cite these facts to explain what (according to Davidson) Al *should* regard as the doctor's error, *if* he accepts that x satisfies his word 'arthritis' if and only if x satisfies the doctor's word 'arthritis'. Moreover, I don't see how there could be *any* facts about Al's and the doctor's situation that by Davidson's standards Al could cite to explain this. I conclude that just as according to Davidson you should interpret your friend's word 'yawl' in such a way that, unlike your word 'yawl', it is satisfied by the ketch sailing by, so according to Davidson Al should interpret the doctor's word 'arthritis' in such a way that, unlike Al's word 'arthritis', it is *not* satisfied by the ailment in Al's thigh.[14]

These considerations show that if (4) is permitted by Davidson's principle of charity, then (3) is not. One might think, however, that *before* Al speaks with his doctor, Al's word 'arthritis' is satisfied by the ailment in his thigh, but *after* he speaks with her and accepts the sentence 'One can't have arthritis in one's thigh', Al's word 'arthritis' is no longer satisfied by the ailment in his thigh. For instance, one might think that when

---

[14] One might think that Davidson can avoid this conclusion by claiming that 'arthritis' is a theoretical term. Davidson himself has claimed that "Disagreement about theoretical matters may (in some cases) be more tolerable than disagreement about what is more evident . . ." (Davidson 1984: 169). One might try to use this commonsense observation to argue that Davidson could allow both Al's word 'arthritis' does not denote the ailment in Al's thigh, and that Al believes that he has arthritis in his thigh. There are two main problems with this objection. First, given Davidson's conception of the task and test of a theory of interpretation, he has no grounds for thinking that Al's word 'arthritis' is a theoretical term. Second, even if we did have some reason to regard Al's word 'arthritis' as theoretical, that would not show that the error that we would be attributing to him if we were to take his word 'arthritis' to be satisfied by an object x if and only if x is arthritis is, by Davidson's standards, explicable. Recall that to explain a given false belief of a speaker, according to Davidson, it is not enough simply to attribute other false beliefs to the speaker in light of which her mistake makes sense. Despite Davidson's occasional suggestions to the contrary, his principle of charity implies that it is no easier to accept error among theoretical beliefs than among observational ones.

Simon Evnine thinks that distinction between theoretical beliefs and observational beliefs can be invoked to defend Davidson against the charge that on his view error is impossible. See Evnine 1991: chapter 6, especially section 6.5. At the crucial point, however, Evnine simply quotes Davidson's commonsense remark about the likelihood of error among our theoretical beliefs, and concludes that Davidson can accommodate error. For the reasons I just sketched, I don't see how Davidson's remark can help him to avoid the consequence that according to his theory of interpretation, Al can't be mistaken about whether he has arthritis in his thigh.

Al accepts the doctor's assertion, he unwittingly exchanges his old word 'arthritis' for a new word that is spelled the same way but is satisfied by a different range of objects. If we accept this description of what happens when Al accepts the doctor's sentence 'One can't have arthritis in one's thigh', then (3) may be permitted by Davidson's principle of charity.

Let's turn now to the second way of formulating the conflict between the conjunction of (3) and (4) and Davidson's principle of charity: if (3) is permitted by Davidson's principle of charity, then (4) is not.

Suppose that Al is trying to construct a Davidsonian theory of truth for the language he used just a few minutes before he spoke with his doctor, and that Davidson's principle of charity does not rule out (3), according to which Al accepts that x satisfies his word 'arthritis' if and only if x satisfies the doctor's word 'arthritis'. Al can see from the doctor's linguistic behaviour that she believes that her word 'arthritis' is *not* satisfied by the ailment in Al's thigh. Hence Al believes that his own word 'arthritis' is not satisfied by the ailment in his thigh.

Now suppose, in addition, that

(4) Al accepts that an object x satisfies the word 'arthritis' that he used before talking to the doctor if and only if x satisfies the word 'arthritis' that he uses after talking with her.

Then Al accepts that before he talked to his doctor, his word 'arthritis' was not satisfied by the ailment in his thigh. But Al remembers that he accepted the sentence 'I have arthritis in my thigh', so he can see that he believed that his word 'arthritis' *was* satisfied by the ailment in his thigh. Thus Al interprets his own words in such a way that under the interpretation, his previous utterance of 'I have arthritis in my thigh' expressed the belief that he has (what Al now calls) arthritis in his thigh. But when Al said, "I have arthritis in my thigh," he did not make any mistakes that we could discern simply by observing the pattern of sentences he held true and using this data to construct a Davidsonian truth theory for his language (idiolect) at that time. By Davidson's standards, then, the mistake that Al attributes to himself—the mistake of believing that he had arthritis in his thigh—is inexplicable. In short, Al's interpretation of his own previous utterance violates the principle of charity. Hence if (3) is permitted by Davidson's principle of charity, then (4) is not.

I conclude that if (4) is permitted by Davidson's principle of charity, then (3) is not, and if (3) is permitted by Davidson's principle of charity, then (4) is not. In other words, the conjunction of (3) and (4) violates Davidson's principle of charity.[15]

5.9. My Conclusion Drawn, Generalized, and Explained

We can now see that if we accept Davidson's principle of charity, then we must reject the conjunction of (1) and (2). Recall that the conjunction of (1) and (2), together with (C1) and (C2), truth functionally implies the conjunction of (3) and (4). We have now seen that the conjunction of (3) and (4) violates Davidson's principle of charity. We may infer that the conjunction of (1), (2), (C1), and (C2) violates Davidson's principle of charity. But, as we saw earlier (§5.7), (C1) and (C2) are unproblematic consequences of Davidson's methodology of interpretation. Hence we must conclude that the conjunction of (1) and (2) violates Davidson's principle of charity.

There is no way of avoiding this conclusion while still embracing Davidson's conception of the task and test of a theory of interpretation. Recall that according to that conception, the *task* of such a theory is to interpret another speaker's words by constructing a truth theory for her language without relying on any evidence about what her words mean, and the *test* is to determine whether the consequences of the theory—the biconditionals it entails—are true. The very idea of such a test builds in Davidson's principle of charity, which links evidence plausibly available to an interpreter—evidence about when speakers hold their sentences true—with particular biconditionals entailed by the theory. When we

---

[15] One anonymous reader for OUP suggested to me that since Davidson's principle of charity must be understood as a global constraint on the interpretation of the speaker's utterances, it does not have the consequences I describe in this section. As I observe in the text, however, given Davidson's conception of the task and test of a theory of interpretation, Davidson does not have the resources to explain away the error that Al must attribute either to himself or the doctor if he accepts both (3) and (4). This observation about Davidson's approach to interpretation does not imply that the principle of charity has only local application, since what Davidson call's "formal" constraints, especially the compositionality of a Davidsonian truth theory, remain in place, and require that the application of charity be systematic and global.

apply this principle we cannot take for granted that we understand what others are telling us. If we are to obey the principle, we must suppose that at any given time, our entire grip on truth is exhausted by what we currently believe at that time. This does not imply we cannot acquire new beliefs by using words in the way that others do. As I noted above, Davidson allows for the possibility that when Al accepts the doctor's assertion, he unwittingly exchanges his old word 'arthritis' for a new word that is spelled the same way but is satisfied by a different range of objects. But, as I also noted above, Davidson's principle of charity does imply that if Al accepts the doctor's assertion, he should not also take himself to *correct* the belief that he expressed yesterday by saying, "I have arthritis in my thigh." Instead, he should conclude that his word 'arthritis', as he used it yesterday, is satisfied by a range of objects that is different from the range of objects that satisfy his word 'arthritis', as he uses it now, after talking with the doctor. Hence Davidson's principle of charity implies that we cannot learn from others by trusting our PIWs for their words and accepting what we thereby take them to say, where this is understood to involve *correcting* one's previous beliefs.

Why have so many philosophers missed or ignored this consequence of Davidson's approach to interpretation? The main reason, I think, is that our practice of trusting our PIWs for one another's words is so deeply entrenched that it is largely unresponsive to Davidson's a priori criticisms. Even those who have studied and absorbed Davidson's approach to interpretation apparently overlook the extent to which their PIWs for other speakers' words shape their "interpretations" of other speakers' utterances. Most interpreters who think they are following Davidson's recommendations in fact unwittingly rely on their PIWs for other speakers' words even when those PIWs commit them to PJSSs that conflict with Davidson's principle of charity. They take comfort in Davidson's claim that his principle of charity makes room for error, but they do not realize that the errors that they are inclined to attribute to themselves or to others are not in fact compatible with his principle of charity.

There is also a tendency to conflate *charity* with *trust*—to assume that it is *charitable* to rely on one's PIWs for another speaker's words and accept what one thereby takes her to have said solely because we *trust* her. Unlike trust, however, charity is something we think of ourselves as exercising only if we take ourselves to be in a position *superior* in some respects to the position of the person to whom we aim to be charitable. Hence Davidson's principle of charity is well named: if we obey it, *we will have no choice but to regard ourselves as ultimate authorities on truth*, so we will always interpret others in such a way that what they say or write is compatible with what we already believe.[16] As we have seen, however, when I make PIWs for another speaker's words and accept what I thereby take her to have said solely because I *trust* her, I do not always interpret her words in accordance with Davidson's principle of charity. When I trust another speaker in such contexts, I take her position to be *superior* to mine for judging truth about the salient topic of discussion, and in that respect, do not treat her with charity.

Many philosophers of language nevertheless take for granted that to understand or make sense of other speakers *just is* to interpret them with charity. For Davidson, these come to the same thing, because in his view we should *explicate* (and, in effect, replace) the vague words 'meaning', 'synonymy', and 'belief' by describing how to construct an empirically testable theory of interpretation governed by his principle of charity. One who dislikes the consequences of Davidson's explication described above could still suppose that to understand or make sense of other speakers just is to interpret them with ''charity''. To suppose this in a way that challenges my conclusions, however, one would need to articulate a principle of charity that is different from Davidson's, yet can nevertheless be used at least to *clarify* the vague words 'meaning', 'synonymy', and 'belief' that Davidson sought to clarify. I know of only three main types of alternatives to Davidson's principle of charity, however, and none of them satisfies the condition just stated. The first main alternative is to explicate the

---

[16] This consequence of Davidson's view—that we have no choice but to regard ourselves as ultimate authorities on truth—does not imply that for Davidson our confident applications of our words *make true* the assertions that we express by using them. My point here is epistemological, not metaphysical: it follows from Davidson's theory of interpretation that we are never justified in interpreting another's assertions in such a way that those assertions conflict with our own beliefs. It may be tempting to try to explain this by saying that our confident applications of our words *make true* the assertions that we express by using them. But even if Davidson's principle of charity implies that I must take myself to be an *authority* on whether or not my word 'arthritis' is satisfied by a given object x, it does not follow that Davidson is committed to the metaphysical claim that my *confidence* that a given object x is an instance of arthritis *makes true* my judgement that x is an instance of arthritis. At most the point about authority raises the question of whether Davidson is entitled to the distinction between belief and truth. This is an important and interesting question, but I need not settle it to show that Davidson's principle of charity precludes learning from others. I grant for the sake of argument that Davidson is entitled to the logical distinction between belief and truth.

phrase 'principle of charity' in terms of our ordinary intuitions about what expressions mean, when two expressions are synonymous, and related intuitions about what speakers believe. (See Lewis 1974 for what is, in effect, if not in rhetoric, one version of this alternative. Grandy 1973 offers another version, but uses a different phrase—'the principle of humanity'.) If we accept this alternative, then the phrase 'principle of charity' cannot be explained and applied independently of our ordinary intuitions about meaning, synonymy, and belief.

A second alternative is to suppose that the expressions 'principle of charity', 'meaning', 'synonymy', and 'belief' can somehow be used to clarify each other, even if our pre-theoretical uses of any one of them are not completely independent of our pre-theoretical uses of the others. According to a version of this alternative proposed by Gareth Evans and John McDowell, for instance,

the idea would be that a detailed account of the complex network of beliefs and intentions involved in conversation, in the characteristic Gricean style (but purged of the reductionist refusal even to entertain the possibility that semantic matter might figure in the specification of the content of the beliefs and intentions), might yield a richer set of simultaneous equations for us to consider ourselves as solving when we construct a theory of meaning: and hence a richer set of constraints, imposed, not necessarily in a reductive spirit, by bringing general psychological principles to bear upon determinations of meaning in order to make the constructed theory fit the data on the basis of which is constructed. Apart from this greater richness, the constraints would operate in much the same way as that already considered in connection with the Davidsonian picture.   (Evans and McDowell 1976: xix.)

In this passage, Evans and McDowell reject Davidson's conception of the task and test of a theory of interpretation, calling it "reductive". While they do not explicitly mention a principle of charity, they claim to model their account of constructing an interpretation on "the Davidsonian procedure", and may thereby be taken to be proposing that we understand (some revised version of) Davidson's principle of charity as among "the constraints that would operate" when we construct a "non-reductive" theory of interpretation for a given speaker. The problem with this sort of proposal is that there is no established pre-theoretical practice of applying "charity" in interpretation, and hence no such use to appeal to when trying to clarify the phrases 'meaning', 'synonymy', and 'belief'.

A third alternative is to take the fact that a speaker holds-true sentences that express her PIWs and PJSSs as a prima-facie reason for an interpreter to suppose that such sentences are true.[17] If we adopt this alternative, we will take the fact that Al holds-true sentences (3) and (4), for instance, as a prima-facie reason to suppose that (3) and (4), as Al uses them, are true. The main problem with this alternative to Davidson's principle of charity is that to accept it is to reject the assumption that semantic claims such as the ones expressed by (3) and (4) need empirical support by evidence that is available independent of them, and thereby leave no substantive role for charity to play in semantic interpretation. (I examine and criticize a version of this alternative in more detail in Chapter 8.)

In short, I see no way to articulate a plausible substantive principle of charity that does not have the consequences of Davidson's principle of charity that I described above. I conclude that the shortcomings with Davidson's principle of charity illustrate shortcomings with *any* plausible substantive principle of charity. Davidson points out that in his view "The methodology of interpretation is...nothing but epistemology seen in the mirror of meaning" (Davidson 1984: 169). We can now see that his methodology of interpretation, and, more generally, *any* methodology of interpretation that relies on a substantive principle of charity to clarify the ordinary vague phrases 'meaning', 'synonymy', and 'belief', is individualistic: it precludes learning from others by making PIWs for another speaker's words and accepting what we thereby take her to say solely because we trust them.[18]

5.10. Is the Principle of Charity Optional?

Is this a *criticism* of the idea that interpretation is governed by a principle of charity? The answer to this question depends on whether or not interpreting in light of a principle of charity is optional. Davidson insists that we have no choice but to accept a principle of charity in interpretation, since otherwise

---

[17] Bill Brewer, Henry Jackman, and an anonymous reader for OUP each independently urged me to consider this objection.

[18] This shows what is wrong with C. A. J. Coady's attempt (in Coady 1992: chapter 9) to use Davidson's principle of charity to *justify* our practice of taking ourselves to learn from others. Coady does not realize that Davidson's principle of charity presupposes a radical epistemological individualism.

we would not be able to solve the problem of interpretation. He would insist that even though we are inclined to trust our PIWs and PJSSs, careful reflection about linguistic interpretation shows we should not trust them. If that undermines our assumption that we learn from others by making PIWs for other speakers' words and accepting what we thereby take them to say solely because we trust them, he reasons, then so much the worse for this assumption, which must be rejected along with other tempting but unfounded assumptions, such as the assumption that synonymy (sameness of meaning) is an objective relation, or that some sentences are analytic (true "in virtue of" their meaning).

I agree that we cannot accept Davidson's conception of the task and the test of a theory of interpretation without also accepting his principle of charity. If Davidson's token-and-ex-use conception of words, and the conception of the task and the test of a theory of interpretation that goes with it, were not optional, then his principle of charity would not be optional either.[19] The question, therefore, is whether Davidson's token-and-ex-use conception of words and the conception of the task and his proposed test of a theory of interpretation are optional.

Like most philosophers, Davidson simply presupposes a token-and-ex-use conception of words. Given this presupposition, he was driven to his conception of the task and the test of a theory of interpretation by his disenchantment with traditional approaches to meaning, which rely on such obscure notions as meaning, synonymy, and analyticity. I agree with Davidson that an adequate philosophical description of our practice of interpreting each other should not make use of such notions. The question, therefore, is whether we can find a way of understanding linguistic interpretation that accommodates our PIWs and PJSSs, and thereby makes sense of the familiar phenomenon of learning from others, without relying

[19] Thus I disagree with some critics of Davidson's principle of charity, such as Richard Grandy (in Grandy 1973) and David Lewis (in Lewis 1974), who think they can avoid counter-intuitive consequences of that principle by reformulating it slightly, without questioning Davidson's conception of the problem of interpretation. In fact, both Grandy and Lewis reject Davidson's conception of the problem of interpretation. Grandy takes many of our PJSSs for granted in his characterizations of our evidence for interpretations, and Lewis posits the existence of whatever constraints on interpretation are needed in order to rule out interpretations he doesn't find intuitive, or to break a tie between two that he does find intuitive. These alternative "principles of charity" simply *presuppose* ordinary notions of sameness of meaning and reference—the very notions that Davidson's principle of charity is supposed to help us to clarify in other, independent terms—and are therefore not my target in this chapter.

on such obscure notions as meaning, synonymy, and analyticity. The answer to this question, I believe, is "yes".

5.11. An Alternative to Davidson's Principle of Charity

I proposed in Chapter 4 that we combine the PJSS-based conception of words with our own Tarski-style disquotational definitions of satisfaction and truth. To adopt this proposal is in effect to regard our PIWs and PJSSs as part of the data that our account of interpretation must accommodate. As I explained in Chapter 4, if we adopt the PJSS-based conception of words it is epistemically reasonable for us to trust our PJSSs unless we have some reason in a given context for not doing so. Hence if we adopt the PJSS-based conception of words, we will conclude that neither our PIWs nor the PJSSs they commit us to need special independent justification. Instead, we will conclude that it is local *divergences* from our PIWs and PJSSs that need justification. But the sort of justification that such divergences need cannot be derived from an abstract principle of interpretation; it must be based in a description of how we actually proceed when we are trying to understand utterances that puzzle us.

The first thing we typically do is *ask our interlocutor what he or she is saying*. This is only possible if we take for granted some shared vocabulary with which we may discuss the question. Davidson describes the problem of interpretation in such a way that no common vocabulary can be assumed, and so every identification of one person's word with another's must be justified by some abstract principle that links linguistic behaviour to theory. The key to my alternative is to build some of what Davidson regards as "interpretations" into the data with which we begin when we try to understand others.[20]

To see in more detail how my approach differs from Davidson's, recall first that if we combine applications of (Sats) to our own regimented words

[20] My approach to interpretation is in some ways similar to Rudolf Carnap's approach to it in his paper "Meaning and Synonymy and Natural Languages", reprinted in Carnap 1956: 233–47. Carnap assumes that to determine what a speaker's words mean, we must ask him whether he would apply it in various different possible circumstances—circumstances that we describe by using words of his whose translations we take as settled. At the same time, however, Carnap also assumes (wrongly, in my view) that the extensions and intensions of a speaker's words are fixed by her linguistic dispositions.

with our PIWs for a speaker's words, we thereby make corresponding PJSSs for the speaker's words. This simple observation can help us to describe the arthritis case. If Al accepts the results of writing his word 'arthritis' in the blanks of (Sats), he can see that when he takes his word 'arthritis' to be the same as the doctor's word 'arthritis', he in effect takes for granted that an object x satisfies the doctor's word 'arthritis' if and only if x is arthritis, and thereby makes a PJSS for the doctor's word 'arthritis'. Similarly, if the doctor accepts the results of writing her word 'arthritis' in the blanks of (Sats), she can see that when she takes her word 'arthritis' to be the same as Al's word 'arthritis', she in effect takes for granted that an object x satisfies Al's word 'arthritis' if and only if x is arthritis, and thereby makes a PJSS for Al's word 'arthritis'.

If we adopt the PJSS-based conception of words, as I recommend, then we will accept such PJSSs unless we have some concrete reason in a given context for not doing so. We do not and should not begin with the assumption that we cannot trust our PIWs for another speaker's words unless we can provide some independent justification for doing so. Since we need not begin with this assumption, our practice of interpreting each other does not commit us to Davidson's principle of charity. If there are reasons in a given context for suspending or rejecting a PIW or PJSS, they are not abstract reasons derived from a principle of charity, but concrete reasons rooted in our ordinary practice of interpreting each other.

But what counts as a "concrete reason" for suspending or rejecting a PJSS? The context principle implies that there can be no correct, informative, and general account of the reasons that should lead us to suspend or reject our PJSSs, so I can only offer examples. I have given some examples already (see §3.2), but here is another. Suppose John invites his friend Sally over for dinner, and asks her if she has any dietary restrictions. Sally says, "I don't eat meat; anything else would be fine." John serves chicken. Sally, who is fastidious about her diet, objects, saying, "John, I thought I told you that I don't eat meat." John replies, "Chicken is not meat, Sally—it's poultry." Assume that both are sincere and at first make PIWs for one another's words. They consult the *Shorter Oxford English Dictionary* (*SOED*), and discover that according to one of the *SOED* entries for 'meat'—'The flesh of animals used as food, now esp. excluding fish and poultry . . .'—John is right. Sally regards this dictionary entry for 'meat' as the definition of a word that is different from, even if related to, her word 'meat'. Both Sally's and John's uses of the word 'meat' are established among competent English users; there is good reason to think that the word is ambiguous between a looser use that encompasses chicken, and a more restricted use that does not. In this case, when Sally says, "John, I thought I told you that I don't eat meat," and regards the dictionary definition of 'meat' as the definition of a word that is different from her word 'meat', it becomes clear to John that he was wrong to identify his word 'meat' with Sally's word 'meat'.[21]

In this and other cases in which we suspend or revise a previous PJSS, we presuppose other PIWs and PJSSs. For instance, Sally and John rely on their PIWs for one another's words 'chicken' and 'poultry' in their discussion of whether or not poultry is meat. But we typically rely on our PIWs and PJSSs, doubting or revising them only if there are good reasons for doing so. We trust our PIWs and PJSSs unless we have some concrete reason in a given context for not doing so.[22]

If we adopt the PJSS-based conception of words, as I recommend, then we can make sense of our trust in our PIWs and PJSSs, including Al and his doctor's PIWs and PJSSs. And if we also think Al is entitled to *accept* what his doctor tells him, we can describe Al as having learned that arthritis applies to the joints only, and as being relieved that what he previously believed about his thigh is false. We can also describe the doctor as having corrected Al's false belief about arthritis. We therefore can describe this as a clear case of what I call *learning from others*.

Davidson's argument against describing the case in this way presupposes his conception of the problem of interpretation, as we have seen. We can resist Davidson's argument by adopting a different description of our practice of interpreting each other. As I see it, our understanding of satisfaction and truth is inextricable from our practice of making PIWs and PJSSs. Divergences from this practice are local, as are the reasons for those divergences. No single abstract principle of interpretation is needed,

---

[21] Sometimes two speakers will disagree about the proper definition of the word without concluding that they are actually using different words with different satisfaction conditions. This possibility is crucial to the attempt to provide good definitions of words already in use. See Burge 1986a, and Ebbs 1997: chapter 8.

[22] Although I think it is typical that speakers make PIWs for each other's words, under certain unusual circumstances we may come to the conclusion that we should *not* make PIWs for most of a given English speaker's words. Still, if we arrive at this conclusion, we will have worked our way towards it by relying on PIWs for the words we use to pose *questions* to the speaker about what she means by certain *other* words.

since particular interpretations always presuppose some background of momentarily unquestioned assumptions, and are therefore never generated completely from scratch.[23]

5.12. Frontiers of Translation

Davidson's conception of the problem of interpretation goes hand in hand with his assumption that we need a fully general philosophical theory of how we interpret others. Such a theory must cover all cases, including cases in which we know nothing about the language we are attempting to interpret. These are cases in which we must engage in what Davidson calls radical interpretation. Since he assumes that all interpretation must proceed by the same principles that we use in radical interpretation, he thinks that all interpretations are ultimately based on evidence that is available to an interpreter who knows nothing about the language he is interpreting. Even when we interpret our fellow English-speakers, Davidson believes, we employ the same abstract principles of interpretation that govern radical interpretation.[24]

I propose that we turn this reasoning on its head—assume not that radical interpretation is the model for all interpretation, but that ordinary interpretation, in which we take for granted a shared vocabulary for

---

[23] My approach also allows us to describe Al as having the sort of self-knowledge (or first-person authority) that goes with minimal competence in the use of language, even though he does not know that arthritis afflicts the joints only. Davidson's conception of the problem of interpretation and principle of charity prevents him from accepting this description of Al. As Davidson points out, his principle of charity implies that "A belief is identified by its location in a pattern of beliefs; it is this pattern that determines the subject matter of the belief, what the belief is about. . . . false beliefs tend to undermine the identification of the subject matter; to undermine, therefore, the validity of the description of the beliefs as being about that subject" (Davidson 1984: 168). To take Al to believe that one can't have arthritis in one's thigh would "tend to undermine the validity of the description of the belief as being about that subject," arthritis. In short, as I stressed earlier, the principle of charity implies that each individual is the ultimate authority on whether or not one of his words denotes a contextually salient object, such as a boat sailing by, or a painful condition in one's thigh. According to Davidson, to accept the commonsense view that Al's belief that he has arthritis in his thigh is false is in effect to deny that Al is an authority on whether or not his word 'arthritis' denotes the painful condition in his thigh, and thereby to deny that Al has first-person authority about what thoughts he expresses when he uses the word 'arthritis'. Once again, however, if we reject Davidson's conception of the task and test of a theory of interpretation, we are not committed to his principle of charity, so we are not committed to his assumption that each individual is the ultimate authority on whether or not one of his words denotes a contextually salient object. We are free to accept that Al has self-knowledge or first-person authority, even if he believes falsely that he has arthritis in his thigh. I develop this consequence of my view below, in Chapter 9.

[24] Davidson stresses that "All understanding of the speech of another involves radical interpretation" (Davidson 1984: 125).

raising questions about what other speakers mean, is the model for all interpretation. My proposal is best understood in stages, beginning with the familiar cases in which questions arise about how to interpret other speakers' words.

For instance, in the case involving John and Sally that I described above, John's question about Sally's word 'meat' arises against the background of PIWs for Sally's words. John's and Sally's discussion of the *SOED* entry for the word 'meat' was prompted by Sally's protest that John ignored her request that he not serve 'meat'. This discussion led John and Sally to conclude that an object x satisfies Sally's word 'meat' if and only if x satisfies John's expression 'meat or poultry'. Once they come to this agreement, however, they could just as well begin to use each other's words directly, each now treating the word form m-e-a-t as ambiguous. But suppose they keep track of the ambiguity by using subscripts. Then they will agree that an object x satisfies 'meat$_J$' if and only if x is meat$_J$, and that an object x satisfies 'meat$_S$' if and only if x is either meat$_J$ or poultry. (They will also both accept the disquotational statement that an object x satisfies 'meat$_S$' denotes x if and only if x is meat$_S$, but this would not help them to keep track of the difference between 'meat$_J$' and 'meat$_S$'.)

If John and Sally begin to assimilate these regimented words into their respective regimented languages and make PIWs for these words in appropriate circumstances when they discuss food together, then their explicit interpretations of the word 'meat' will fade into the background. If and when this occurs, they will no longer question their PIWs for these words. They will therefore no longer be involved in what I call *interpreting* each other's uses of these words. In this way it can happen that an interpretation agreed on at one time may later become unproblematic, and hence no longer be an interpretation, but simply part of the background against which new questions about how to interpret other words can be formulated and addressed.[25]

This approach to interpretation says nothing about what Davidson calls radical interpretation, which is supposed to be necessary when we seek to

---

[25] There is a parallel here with what Quine calls legislative postulation (Quine 1963: 394–5). But Quine would regard our trust in our PIWs as a tacit endorsement of a homophonic translation manual, and hence as just one of many acceptable "translations" of our fellow English-speakers' words. Moreover, his notion of legislative postulation is individualistic, having nothing in principle to do with linguistic collaboration, understanding, or translation.

understand the utterances of a language that we have never encountered before, and for which there are no manuals of translation. If there were a case of what Davidson calls radical interpretation, it would lie at the frontier of entrenched translation practice, where hitherto unknown languages are encountered. In my view, all interpretation proceeds against a background of PIWs and PJSSs, and so interpretation cannot begin until some basic ways of taking other speakers' words are adopted and relied on. In short, what Davidson calls radical interpretation is not what I call interpretation.

One might be willing to accept this terminological point, yet still insist that we need a general *method* for pushing back the frontiers of entrenched translation practice, so that we can get into the position in which we make PIWs and PJSSs, and can therefore interpret puzzling utterances in the way I described above. If we accept the demand for such a method, then Davidson's attempt to provide one will look attractive. Recall that according to his method, a radical interpreter can identify the attitude of holding a sentence true without knowing anything about how to translate the sentence. Davidson's method describes how we can use evidence of when the native speakers "hold true" sentences of their language to test particular proposed "interpretations" of this evidence. Since this evidence must be available independent of any prior translation of the language, our understanding of what it is to "hold true" a given sentence cannot be explained disquotationally. Davidson's method therefore commits him to accepting a non-disquotational notion of truth. (Davidson himself stresses this in Davidson 1990.) In contrast, I have been urging that we adopt a disquotational Tarski-style method of defining truth for the pragmatic reasons sketched above, we have no need for a non-disquotational notion of truth. In particular, we have no need for a notion of "holding true" that we can grasp independent of our practice of making PIWs and PJSSs for each others' words.

This conception of translation practice may seem to imply that we cannot criticize particular translations. For it is tempting to think that we can criticize a particular translation only if there are valid principles for translation that are independent of our actual PIWs and PJSSs. That there are such principles seems to be supported, for instance, by Quine's influential criticism of Levy-Bruhl's doctrine that there are pre-logical peoples who accept certain contradictions as true. To illustrate Levy-Bruhl's doctrine, Quine imagined that a group of speakers of a newly encountered language accept as true a certain sentence of the form 'q ka bu q', which is translated into an English sentence of the form 'p and not p'. Quine remarked that "If any evidence can count against a lexicographer's adoption of 'and' and 'not' as translations of 'ka' and 'bu', certainly the natives' acceptance of 'q ka bu q' counts overwhelmingly" (Quine 1963: 387). Quine's criticism rests on the obviousness of elementary logic. One might think that it depends on the more general assumption that all translation is governed by a principle of obviousness, according to which speakers of a language should not be translated in such a way that some of the sentences they accept are translated by English sentences that we regard as a obviously false. In a similar way, one might think that any criticism of actual translation practice presupposes that there are valid principles of translation that are independent of our PIWs and PJSSs. This would be an objection to my proposal, since I accept that we can criticize particular translations, yet I deny that there are valid principles for translation that are independent of our PIWs and PJSSs.

The trouble with this objection is that for any general principle of translation, there are bound to be cases in which our PIWs and PJSSs conflict with the requirements of the principle. For instance, both Quine's principle of obviousness and Davidson's principle of charity apparently imply that we cannot learn from others that something we took to be obviously true is in fact false. The principles are therefore vulnerable to the criticism I made in this chapter of Davidson's principle of charity. Echoing Quine, we might say that if any evidence can count against these principles, certainly their conflict with the phenomenon of learning from others counts overwhelmingly.

5.13. The Method behind these Conclusions

I started this chapter by describing a typical case in which one speaker learns from another by trusting his PIWs for her words and accepting what he thereby takes her to say. I then explained why Davidson's principle of charity is incompatible with our ordinary observations about this typical case. If Davidson is right, then we can't learn from another by making PIWs for her words and accepting what we thereby take her to say. The problem is that according to Davidson's understanding of interpretation, each individual is the ultimate authority on whether or not one of his words is satisfied by a contextually salient object, such as a boat sailing by, or a painful condition in one's thigh.[26] But if we learn from others, then we are not the ultimate authorities on whether or not one of our words is satisfied by a contextually salient object. There is no way to avoid this consequence without rejecting Davidson's conception of the problem of interpretation.

I argued that this conception is not mandatory—there is an alternative. In particular, I proposed that we accept our PIWs and PJSSs as part of the data that any account of interpretation must accommodate. I proposed that we adopt the PJSS-based conception of words and trust our PIWs and PJSSs unless we find concrete reasons in a particular context for revising them. I then briefly sketched the consequences of this approach for our understanding of learning from others. I argued that if we take this alternative approach to describing our linguistic practices, we can accept our ordinary observations about typical cases, such as Al's, in which we take ourselves to have learned from others. We have seen that Davidson's understanding of the word 'word' leads him to embrace his principle of charity, which conflicts with the PIWs and PJSSs on which we rely when we take ourselves to learn from others by accepting what they say. My proposal that we adopt the PJSS-based conception of words is expressly designed to explicate the word 'word' in a way that fits with our PIWs, and thereby to clarify and preserve the phenomenon of learning from others. I conclude that if we wish to make sense of those aspects of learning from others that matter to us when we see ourselves as engaged in rational inquiry, then we should reject Davidson's conception of the problem of interpretation, as well as the token-and-ex-use conception of words that it presupposes, and combine the PJSS-based conception of words with a Tarski-style disquotational account of satisfaction and truth.

---

[26] Recall that this does not imply that for Davidson our confident applications of our words *make true* the assertions that we express by using them. See note 16 of this chapter.

6

A Puzzle about Sameness
of Satisfaction across Time

6.1. An Intuition about Sameness of Satisfaction across Time

I argued in the previous chapter that we should reject Davidson's principle of charity because it conflicts with the practical judgements of sameness of satisfaction (PJSSs) on which we rely when we take ourselves to have learned from others by accepting what they write or say. I also argued that we can accommodate these PJSSs if we reject all token-and-ex-use conceptions of words and adopt the PJSS-based conception of words instead. I want now to examine the objection that it would be wrong to adopt the PJSS-based conception of words because it conflicts with a deeply entrenched intuition about sameness of satisfaction across time that can only be accommodated by an account of sameness of satisfaction across time that presupposes a token-and-ex-use conception of words.

The intuition is best introduced with an example. Suppose that in 1650 John Locke bought a ring from a jeweller who said, "This ring is gold," and today, three and a half centuries later, a chemist performs various tests on the ring, and says, "This ring is not gold." When told this story, we make a complex PIW (practical identification of a word) for the jeweller's word 'gold', trusting that there is a chain of simple PIWs that link our present use of 'gold' back through time to the jeweller's word 'gold', thereby taking for granted that the jeweller's word 'gold' and the chemist's word 'gold' are the same as our word 'gold', in the sense of 'same word' that licenses us to make corresponding PJSSs for the jeweller's word 'gold' and the chemist's word 'gold'. These PJSSs together imply that

(1) An object x satisfies the jeweller's word 'gold' if and only if x satisfies the chemist's word 'gold'.

The PJSS-based conception of words licenses us to accept the PJSSs that imply (1) *whether or not* the facts about the ex-use of the jeweller's word 'gold' in 1650 determined that x satisfies the jeweller's word 'gold' if and only if x is gold. This consequence of the PJSS-based conception of words conflicts with the intuition I want to highlight. The intuition implies that

(2) If (1) then the ex-use of the jeweller's 'gold' in 1650 determined that x satisfies the jeweller's word 'gold' if and only if x is gold.

From (1) and (2), it follows that

(3) The ex-use of the jeweller's 'gold' in 1650 determined that x satisfies the jeweller's word 'gold' if and only if x is gold.

In short, if one accepts (2), one cannot accept (1) without also committing oneself to (3). Those who feel they cannot give up (2) will therefore feel compelled to reject the PJSS-based conception of words, which licenses us to accept (1) even if we reject (3).

To state the intuition in a more general form, it helps first to recast the gold example in terms not of one's PJSSs across time, but of one's corresponding practical judgements of sameness of *extension* across time (PJSEs). One's PJSSs across time commit one to corresponding PJSEs across time by a series of simple steps. First, one can use

(Sats) x satisfies my word '___' if and only if x is ___.[1]

to specify the extension of one's word 'gold'—the set of objects that satisfy one's word 'gold'—as follows:

x is a member of the extension of 'gold'
        iff $x \in \{x\colon x$ satisfies my word 'gold'$\}$ [by definition]
        iff $x \in \{x\colon x$ is gold$\}$ [by (Sats)]
        iff x is gold.[2]   [by concretion][3]

---

[1] Recall that applications of (Sats) are short for corresponding disquotational definitions of satisfaction of sentences by sequences of objects. See §3.3.

[2] 'Gold' is a mass term, true of each gold thing, and also of each aggregate of gold things. In contrast, 'elm', for example, is what I call a count term (also known as a count noun), true of each elm, but not of aggregates of elms. Putting 'elm' in the blanks of (E) yields: 'elm' is true of x if and only if x is (an) elm. From "'elm' is true of x if and only if x is (an) elm', for example, I can infer '$\{x\colon$ 'elm' is true of $x\} = \{x\colon x$ is (an) elm$\}$'.

[3] The terminology is from Quine 1982: 134.

Once one makes this simple derivation, one can see that when one makes a PJSS across time for another speaker's word 'gold', or for one's own word 'gold' as one used it in the past, one thereby also commits oneself to a corresponding PJSE across time for the same word. Hence a person who accepts (1) commits himself to accepting

(1′) The extension of the jeweller's word 'gold' in 1650 is the same as the extension of the chemist's word 'gold' today.

The PJSS-based conception of words licenses us to accept (1′) *whether or not* the facts about the ex-use of the jeweller's word 'gold' in 1650 and the chemist's word 'gold' today determine that (1′) is true. In contrast, the intuition I am trying to articulate implies that

(2′) If (1′) then facts about the ex-use of the jeweller's 'gold' in 1650 determined that the extension of the jeweller's word 'gold' was the set of all and only gold things.

From (2′) and (3′), it follows that

(3′) The ex-use use of the jeweller's 'gold' in 1650 determined that the jeweller's 'gold' was the set of all and only gold things.

Again, if one accepts (2′), one cannot accept (1′) without also committing oneself to (3′). Those who feel they cannot give up (2′) will therefore feel compelled to reject the PJSS-based conception of words, which licenses us to accept (1′) even if we reject (3′).

Behind (2′) lies the intuition that

(M) For any two word tokens w and w' such that the utterance or inscription of w occurs at some time t before the utterance or inscription of w', a PJSE *across time* for w and w' is true only if for some set E,

(a) E is the extension of both w and w', and

(b) the totality of facts about the ex-use of w at times prior to or identical with t (hence prior to the utterance or inscription of w') determines that E is the extension of w.[4]

---

[4] By assigning a set as the extension of a predicate, (M) presupposes that the predicate is determinately true or false of any given object. Hartry Field, among others, rejects this presupposition. I consider Field's views in Chapter 7, where I present a revised formulation of (M) that allows for an assignment of what I call a core extension to a predicate.

Recall that the only restriction on what counts as a fact about the ex-use of a word token w is that the fact can in principle be described without using any sentence that expresses a PJSS or PJSE for w. The facts about the ex-use of a word token w may include, for instance, facts about the dispositions and functional states, if any, that are causally responsible for a speaker's application of w, facts about causal relations that exist between w, other speakers, objects, and events in the social and physical environment in which w is uttered, as well as irreducible facts about the intentions of the speaker who uttered w or about what w means, and even the sorts of facts posited by a theory that asserts that the ex-use of w determines that w has a Fregean sense, and thereby determines w's extension. In short, (M) encompasses all *substantive* theories of, or conjectures about, what determines the extension of a word token w at the time of its utterance or inscription.

The intuition captured by (M) challenges my proposal that we adopt the PJSS-based conception of words. For the PJSS-based conception commits us to clause (a) of (M), but not to clause (b) of (M). The PJSS-based conception implies that a PJSE may be true *whether or not* the relevant instantiation of clause (b) is true. We must therefore either reject (M) or the PJSS-based conception of words.

Faced with this choice, one might be inclined to reject the PJSS-based conception of words. Against this, in this chapter I shall present a thought experiment that discredits (M). In this and the next two chapters, I shall try to show that we are attracted to (M) only because we mistake certain logical consequences of our PJSSs and PJSEs for commitments to (M). I conclude in Chapter 8 that we have no grounds for accepting (M). Any residual temptation we may feel to accept (M) should therefore not prevent us from adopting the PJSS-based conception of words.

6.2. Methodological Analyticity

To appreciate the problems with (M) that I will raise below, it helps to see first that most contemporary philosophers of language who are committed to (M) nevertheless regard their PJSSs and PJSEs as more trustworthy than particular versions of (M) that conflict with them. Consider, for instance, the relationship between our PJSEs and the tempting thesis that some of our sentences are "analytic", in the sense that we cannot abandon them

without changing the subject. Standard versions of this thesis, including
the psychologistic versions of it held by such figures as John Locke and
David Hume, are versions of (M). The most radical version of the thesis is
that we *make* some of our sentences true by instituting a convention about
how they are to be evaluated.[5] The main problem with this version of the
thesis is that it conflates truth and belief. As Frege observed in a different
connection, "Being true is different from being taken to be true, whether
by one or many or everybody, and in no case is to be reduced to it. There
is no contradiction in something's being true which everybody takes to be
false" (Frege 1964: 13).

One way to support the thesis that some of our sentences are analytic
without conflating truth and belief is to derive the thesis from a description
of how we evaluate sentences. To see how this might be done, consider
W. V. Quine's account of the deviant logician's predicament. Against the
idea that deviant logicians may "reject the law of non-contradiction and
accept an occasional sentence and its negation both as true", Quine argues
as follows:

[They] think they're talking about negation, '∼', 'not'; but surely the notation
ceased to be recognizable as negation when they took to regarding some conjunctions of the form 'p. ∼ p' as true, and stopped regarding such sentences as implying
all others. Here, evidently, is the deviant logician's predicament: when he tries to
deny the doctrine he only changes the subject.   (Quine 1986: 81)

The moral is that even though truth is not up to us, for some words,
including '∼', 'not', we can agree on criteria that settle whether or not a
speaker is using them to talk about the same subjects that we talk about
when we use them.

This is the truism behind what I call methodological analyticity—the
idea that even though truth is not up to us, there are sentences we

<hr>

[5] This version of the thesis goes hand in hand with what Paul Horwich calls "the strategy of implicit
definition", according to which "terms may be provided with their meanings by the assertion of
statements containing them" in such a way that some of the asserted statements could not be abandoned
without changing the extensions of the terms they contain. Horwich rejects this position, for reasons
he explains in chapter 6 of Horwich 1998b. I am sympathetic with Horwich's objections, but I think
he does not expose the deepest problem with the strategy of implicit definition—that it ignores the
diachronic dimension of our pursuit of truth. My arguments in this section, as well as in §§6.7–6.11,
highlight the diachronic dimension of our pursuit of truth, and indicate how I would argue against the
stronger and even less plausible thesis that we *make* some of our sentences true by agreeing on how
they are to be evaluated.

cannot reject without changing the subject. The least problematic version of the idea, due to Rudolf Carnap, makes sense only for sentences of an artificial language system (Carnap 1990). If we accept Quine's textbook explanations of negation and conjunction (symbolized here by '$\sim$' and '$\wedge$', respectively), sentences of the form '$\sim(S \wedge \sim S)$' come close to being 'analytic' in Carnap's strict sense of that troublesome word.

The sort of methodological analyticity I want to discuss is also supposed to be a feature of natural language sentences, such as 'Bachelors are unmarried adult males', and 'Gold is a yellow metal'. The idea is that we *tacitly* agree on criteria that settle whether or not a speaker is using 'bachelor' to talk about bachelors, 'adult' to talk about adults, 'gold' to talk about gold, and so on. We tacitly agree that no one can reject 'Bachelors are unmarried adult males' or 'Gold is a yellow metal', for instance, without changing the subject. Moreover, the criteria on which we tacitly agree are in principle obvious to us without any special empirical investigations and without awaiting the development of as yet unimagined scientific theories—we can tell by reflecting on our own present usage of the terms whether or not an explicit statement of the criteria is correct. If there are any natural language sentences that are analytic in this sense, then they can play a methodological role in our inquiries that is analogous to the more strictly defined methodological role of analytic sentences in Carnap's artificially constructed language systems. That is why I call this sort of analyticity *methodological*.

One might be inclined to dismiss methodological analyticity (even the pure form of it that is restricted to artificial languages) with the claim that for any sentence we accept, we can imagine that it's false. This claim may seem to follow immediately from Frege's distinction between truth and belief. But that distinction has no direct bearing on whether we can imagine that a sentence we now accept is false. What would it be, for instance, to imagine that a sentence of the form '$\sim(S \wedge \sim S)$' is false?

One might reply that even if we cannot imagine that a sentence of the form '$\sim(S \wedge \sim S)$' is false, we can still employ the strategy just described to undermine the claim that, for instance, 'Gold is a yellow metal' is analytic. Thus consider the following objection by Saul Kripke:

Could we have discovered that gold was not in fact yellow? . . . Suppose there were an optical illusion which made the substance appear to be yellow; but, in fact, once the peculiar properties of the atmosphere were removed, we would see that it is actually blue. . . . Would there on this basis be an announcement in the newspapers: 'It has turned out that there is no gold. Gold does not exist. What we took to be gold is not in fact gold?' . . . It seems to me that there would be no such announcement. On the contrary, what would be announced would be that although it appeared that gold was yellow, in fact gold has turned out not to be yellow, but blue.   (Kripke 1980: 118)

This objection relies on the supposition that we *could have* discovered that gold is not in fact yellow, but blue. A person who thinks that 'Gold is a yellow metal' is analytic might not find that supposition intelligible. How then might we try to persuade such a person that 'Gold is a yellow metal' is not analytic?

One way would be to remind him that we may at one time feel confident that one could not reject a given statement without changing the subject, but later realize that we were wrong. He might still insist that he is not wrong about the analyticity of 'Gold is a yellow metal', even if he has proved wrong about other cases of analyticity. Ultimately, the best way to undermine his confidence is simply to point out that gold in its pure form is not yellow, but white. He could dig in his heels and insist that 'Gold is a yellow metal' is true. But to do so would be to reject the PJSSs and PJSEs on which members of our own community relied when they took themselves to have discovered that pure (unalloyed) gold is white.

To accept that we discovered that gold is white, we must trust our PJSSs for the term 'gold' more than we trust our previous speculation that one cannot reject the statement that gold is a yellow metal without changing the subject. Trusting these judgements, we realize that we might be wrong about gold—perhaps it's yellow after all. But we take ourselves to have *discovered* that gold is white, and we realize that to do so is to accept our PJSSs and PJSEs across time for 'gold'. Our present uses of 'gold' link it to earlier uses of 'gold', and those earlier uses of 'gold' are linked to even earlier uses of it. Taken together, these uses of 'gold' constitute a trans-temporal chain of PIWs for 'gold' that licenses corresponding PJSSs and PJSEs across time for 'gold'. In a similar way, every inquiry brings with it some chain or other of PJSSs and PJSEs across time.

One might think that this reasoning only shows that we can be radically wrong about our own tacit criteria for applying our terms, not that methodological analyticity is incorrect. As I defined it four paragraphs above, however, methodological analyticity implies that whether or not a given statement is analytic is in principle obvious to us without any special empirical investigations or the development of as yet unimagined scientific theories—we can tell just by reflecting on our own current usage of a term whether or not a given explicit statement of how it should be applied is correct. Our discovery that gold is white shows that we can't tell just by reflecting on our own current usage of a term whether not a given explicit statement about how it should be applied will survive a conflict with our PJSSs. This discovery, and the ever-present possibility of others like it, undermines methodological analyticity.

6.3. Causal–Historical Theories

The failure of methodological analyticity, combined with an unreflective trust in our PJSSs and PJSEs and a tacit commitment to (M), led Saul Kripke and Hilary Putnam to adopt a radically different picture of how facts about ex-use determine the truth or falsity of our PJSSs and PJSEs. In *Naming and Necessity*, Saul Kripke sketched a causal-historical account of reference for proper names and the extensions of natural kind terms, including 'gold'. Hilary Putnam further developed the idea. Both Kripke's and Putnam's causal-historical accounts of what determines the extensions of proper names and natural kind terms can be seen as a response to the failure of methodological analyticity—a response to the fact that beliefs that we take at one time to be definitive of a given topic may later be revised without changing the topic. In this section I will briefly explain how Kripke's and Putnam's causal-historical accounts of what determines the extensions of proper names and natural kind terms can be seen as attempts to make sense of our PJSSs and PJSEs in light of their commitment to (M).

Kripke's version of the causal-historical theory of extension should be distinguished from his thesis that names are rigid designators. Rigidity is a modal notion defined as sameness of reference in all possible worlds, whereas the causal-historical theory of extension is intended to explain sameness of extension across time in the actual world. The motivating intuition behind the causal-historical theory is the one I emphasized above—the intuition that there must be something about the use of a term prior to a discovery that settles its extension. Kripke highlights features of our practice that suggest that the extension of a natural kind term used by a given speaker is not settled by the speaker's beliefs about how to apply it. His account of how the extension of a kind term is settled has the same structure as his account of how the reference of a proper name is settled. The following passage contains his most explicit statement of how the extension of a kind term is settled:

> In the case of proper names, the reference can be fixed in various ways. In an initial baptism it is typically fixed by an ostension or a description. Otherwise, the reference is usually determined by a chain, passing the name from link to link. The same observations hold for such a general term as 'gold'. If we imagine a hypothetical (admittedly somewhat artificial) baptism of the substance, we must imagine it picked out by some such 'definition' as, 'Gold is the substance instantiated by the items over there, or at any rate, by almost all of them'.   (Kripke 1980: 135)

Thus Kripke suggests that the extension of 'gold' is fixed by a "baptism" that combines a "definition"—"Gold is the substance instantiated by the items over there, or at any rate, by almost all of them"—with pointing gestures that identify items that exemplify the kind of things that we intend our kind term 'gold' to denote. A speaker who was not present at this "baptism" may nevertheless be able to use 'gold' to denote gold things, if she picked up her use of that term from other speakers who have links with speakers who have links with speakers . . . who were present at the "baptism". The "links" between speakers that Kripke posits must track what I call practical judgements of sameness of extension for 'gold', which constitute the data Kripke is attempting to explain.

Kripke's account of how the extension of a kind term is determined is ambiguous between two different readings. On one reading, Kripke is saying that a kind term such as 'gold' refers to a kind (of stuff), and treats *kinds* as items in the world that we can name. But it is clearer and less problematic to recast Kripke's account so that the extension of a kind term is simply the set of objects of which the kind term is true—bits of gold, for instance, in the case of 'gold'.[6] If we accept this modification, then we

---

[6] I propose that we treat natural kind terms as predicates, not as names for kinds. I do not claim that this way of thinking of natural kind terms captures the way Kripke himself thought about kind terms when he wrote *Naming and Necessity*. The crucial consideration is that, as Scott Soames has recently

can recast Kripke's account as follows: the extension of the term 'gold' is fixed by the following "ostensive definition":

(K) x is gold if and only if for most things y that I and other speakers in my linguistic community have on other occasions called 'gold', x is (a bit of) the same substance as y.

The key point is that the question whether a given object x is (a bit of) the same substance as y is not settled by our current beliefs about x or y. Yet if we adopt the ostensive definition (K), we can then inquire into what makes an object x (a bit of) the same substance as some sample object y. We may then come to accept that x is (a bit of) the same substance as some sample object y if and only if x and y both have the atomic number 79. Looking back at our previous uses of the word 'gold', we can say that all along it was true of all and only the objects with atomic number 79, even if we did not know this when we first accepted (K).

Inspired by Kripke's causal-historical theory of extension, Hilary Putnam devised a thought experiment that highlights (among other things) the relationship between our natural kind terms and our external environment.[7] The details of Putnam's Twin Earth thought experiment are now very well known, but I will briefly review them here in preparation for further applications below.

Suppose there is a planet called Twin Earth which is just like Earth except that wherever there is water on Earth, there is another substance, twin water, on Twin Earth. Twin water is indistinguishable from water in ordinary circumstances, but the molecular structure of twin water is different from the molecular structure of water. Putnam supposes that just as we have discovered the molecular structure of water, our contemporaries on Twin Earth have discovered the molecular structure of twin water. If earthlings were able to visit Twin Earth, they might at first mistake twin water for water. But after talking with the chemists on Twin Earth, they will learn that twin water is not water, even though in ordinary circumstances

---

explained, "the natural kind terms with which Kripke is concerned include many expressions that function primarily as predicates" (Soames 2002: 248). This fits with W. V. Quine's observation that for predicative uses of mass terms, among them natural kind terms such as 'water' and 'gold'—predicative uses such as "That puddle is water"—"we can view the mass terms ... as general terms, reading 'is water' ... in effect as 'is a bit of water'" (Quine 1960: 97–8).

[7] In 1973, Putnam wrote, "Kripke's work has come to me second hand; even so, I owe him a large debt for suggesting the idea of causal chains as the mechanism of reference" (Putnam 1973: 198).

it is indistinguishable from water. Twin Earthlings use a language called Twin English that is almost indistinguishable from English. Just as we apply the English word 'water' to water, they apply their Twin English word 'water' to twin water. Putnam observes that in these circumstances, we would say that an object x satisfies the English word 'water' if and only if x is (a bit of) water, not twin water, and an object x satisfies the Twin English word 'water' if and only if x is (a bit of) twin water, not water. The extension of the English word 'water' is the set of things (puddles, pools, raindrops, ice cubes, etc.) that are (portions of) water, and the extension of the Twin English word 'water' is the set of things (twin puddles, twin pools, twin raindrops, twin ice cubes, etc.) that are (portions of) twin water.

Putnam then asks us to "roll the time back" to an earlier time, say 1650, when chemistry was not developed on either Earth or Twin Earth. Even though the chemical structure of water and twin water was not yet known, the Twin English word 'water' was applied to twin water, and the English word 'water' was applied to water. We take for granted in the English-speaking community that the extension of our (English) word 'water' has not changed since 1650, and members of the Twin English-speaking community take for granted that the extension of their (Twin English) word 'water' has not changed since 1650. We (members of the English-speaking community) take ourselves to have discovered the molecular structure of water, so we naturally conclude that in 1650 the extension of the English word 'water' was the set of things (puddles, pools, raindrops, ice cubes, etc.) that are (portions of) water, even though no member of our community had enough chemical knowledge in 1650 to distinguish water from qualitatively similar liquids, such as twin water. Members of the Twin English-speaking community take themselves to have discovered the molecular structure of twin water, so they naturally conclude that in 1650 the extension of the Twin English word 'water' was the set of things (puddles, pools, raindrops, ice cubes, etc.) that are (portions of) twin water, even though no member of their community had enough chemical knowledge in 1650 to distinguish twin water from qualitatively similar liquids, such as water. In short, members of both communities take for granted that the extension of their term 'water' did not change since 1650. They trust their PJSEs across time, from 1650 to today, for their word 'water'.

Putnam's version of Kripke's causal theory of the reference of natural kind terms is meant to explain and justify these PJSEs across time. Putnam presents his theory in the following passage:

Suppose I point to a glass of water and say 'this liquid is called water'...My "ostensive definition" of water has the following empirical presupposition: that the body of liquid I am pointing to bears a certain sameness relation (say, x *is the same liquid as* y, or x *is the same$_L$ as* y) to most of the stuff I and other speakers in my linguistic community have on other occasions called 'water'. If this presupposition is false because, say, I am without knowing it pointing to a glass of gin and not a glass of water, then I do not intend my ostensive definition to be accepted. Thus the ostensive definition conveys what might be called a defeasible necessary and sufficient condition: the necessary and sufficient condition for being water is bearing the relation same$_L$ to the stuff in the glass; but this is the necessary and sufficient condition only if the empirical presupposition is satisfied.   (Putnam 1975: 225)

Putnam's idea is that in 1650, English-speakers ostensively defined the denotation of the English word 'water' as follows: 'x is (a bit of) water if and only if for most things y that I and other speakers in my linguistic community have on other occasions called 'water', x is the same liquid as y'. This ostensive definition is designed to explain and justify the practical judgements of sameness of denotation across time, from 1650 to today, of the English word 'water'. The key point is that whether or not x is the same liquid as y "may take an indeterminate amount of scientific investigation to determine" (Putnam 1975: 225). If members of the English-speaking community had somehow been transported to Twin Earth in 1650, they would have believed that bodies of twin water bear the same liquid relation to bodies of water. This would have been a mistake even though they did not at the time know enough chemistry to avoid or correct it.

Putnam thinks that a parallel definition explains and justifies the practical judgements of sameness of extension across time—from 1650 to today—of the Twin English word 'water'. In 1650, Twin English-speakers ostensively defined the extension of the Twin English word 'water' as follows: 'x is (a bit of) water if and only if for most things y that I and other speakers in my linguistic community have on other occasions called 'water', x is the same liquid as y'. Since their linguistic community is different from ours, and the bodies of liquid to which they apply the word 'water' are bodies of twin water, not water, Putnam thinks that this "definition" determines in 1650 that their word water denotes (as we would say it) twin water. Exactly parallel reasoning applies: if members of the Twin English-speaking community had somehow been transported to Earth in 1650, they would have believed that bodies of water bear the same liquid relation to bodies of twin water. This would have been a mistake even though they did not at the time know enough chemistry to avoid or correct it.

According to Putnam's version of the causal-historical theory, for instance, the extension of 'gold' in 1650 was fixed by an "ostensive definition" such as the following:

(P) x is gold if and only if for most things y that I and other speakers in my linguistic community have on other occasions called 'gold', x is (a bit of) the same metal as y.

This is slightly more explicit than (K), because the 'same metal' relation is not as vague as the 'same substance' relation that (K) relies on. Nevertheless, whether or not x is (a bit of) the *same metal* as some sample y takes an indeterminate amount of scientific investigation to discover. Putnam thinks this partly explains how we can now say that the extension of 'gold' in 1650 was the set of things with atomic number 79, even though no one in 1650 had the theoretical knowledge even to state or understand this claim.

6.4. A Thought Experiment

I shall now argue that despite its appeal, the causal-historical theory of reference fares no better than methodological analyticity as an explanation or justification for our PJSSs and PJSEs across time. Moreover, the problem I shall raise for the causal-historical theory cannot be solved by *any* version of (M). I shall present a thought experiment that shows that even our most deeply trusted PJSSs and PJSEs across time are incompatible with (M).

The historical background for the thought experiment is that platinum was not discovered until the mid-eighteenth century, when chemists called it 'white gold' because of its striking similarities to what they previously called gold. Platinum has a higher melting point than gold. But platinum and gold have a similar resistance to attack by acids.[8] In 1650, a chemist

---

[8] See Crosland 1962: 97. Crosland writes that platinum was compared with gold "because of several similarities including its resistance to attack by acids", especially *aqua regia*.

applying the best current acid tests to a sample of platinum might have concluded that it should be called 'gold'.[9] We now know that platinum and gold are different elements: platinum is the element with atomic number 78, and gold is the element with atomic number 79.

Against this background, my thought experiment proceeds as follows. Suppose that there is a Twin Earth that is indistinguishable from Earth up until 1650, when large deposits of platinum are uncovered in Twin South Africa, and that once it is established by Twin Earth chemists that the newly uncovered metal passes the best current acid tests for gold, members of the Twin English-speaking community call it 'gold', treating it in the same way we treat gold: the platinum is mined as gold, hammered (and later melted) together with gold to produce coins and bars that are valued by Twin Earthlings just as we value gold. Everyone on Twin Earth trusts the Twin Earth chemists' judgement that the newly uncovered metal is properly called 'gold'.

Suppose also that on Twin Earth chemistry develops in almost exactly the same way in which it develops in our community, except that when chemists in the Twin Earth community investigate what they call 'gold', they conclude that there are two kinds of 'gold': one of these kinds of 'gold' is gold, which they know only as the element with atomic number 79, and the other is platinum, which they know only as the element with atomic number 78. Long after their discovery, we visit their planet, and learn their language. We conclude that their word 'gold' is true of an object x just in case x is gold, the element with atomic number 79, or platinum, the element with atomic number 78, or a mixture of the two.

Note that until 1650, the linguistic dispositions and mental states of members of the two communities, as well as the relations the members bear to their respective environments, are virtually the same.[10] Moreover, until 1650, the physical constitution of the things to which members of the

---

[9] Crosland reports that in 1752, a Swedish chemist named Scheffer concluded that the close similarity of (what we now call) platinum to gold justifies the claim that (what we now call) platinum is white gold (Crosland 1962: 97). Crosland also points out that "the distinct nature of new substances was not always easy to demonstrate by elementary analytical methods and the skeptics could always maintain that any apparent discovery was really a substance previously known..." (Crosland 1962: 97–8), and that among alchemists in the mid-eighteenth century, platinum "was considered to be a kind of gold" (ibid. 235, n. 33).

[10] This judgement presupposes, as demanded by (M), that we describe these dispositions, states, and relations independently of future developments in either linguistic community. In Chapter 8 I will consider and reject a modified version of (M) according to which we must describe the community

two communities are causally related is also the same. For we supposed that Twin Earth is just like Earth with a slightly different future after platinum is first uncovered in Twin South Africa in 1650. To see the possibility of this Twin Earth scenario, it is enough to imagine a few accidental differences between the two communities—such as a chance decision in the Twin Earth community of a few individuals to dig for gold in the hills where platinum lies hidden—that allow for the accidental uncovering of large amounts of platinum in the Twin Earth community.[11]

The crucial point is that just as members of our English-speaking community take for granted that the extension of the English word 'gold' did not change as a result of the discovery that it is true of x if and only if x is (a bit of) the element with atomic number 79, so members of the Twin English-speaking linguistic community take for granted that the extension of their Twin English word 'gold' did not change as a result of their discovery that it is true of x if and only if x is (a bit of) the element with atomic number 78 or x is (a bit of) the element with atomic number 79 (or a mixture of the two). Members of the two communities assign different extensions to their respective tokens of g-o-l-d, even when they are evaluating utterances made in 1650—before the uncovering of platinum in the Twin Earth community—by speakers using sentences that contain tokens of g-o-l-d.

To highlight this strange consequence of the thought experiment, let us suppose that in 1650 John Locke and his twin on Twin Earth both

members' dispositions, states, and relations in a way that *includes* future developments in their respective linguistic communities.

[11] This thought experiment is similar to Mark Wilson's Druid thought experiment: "A B-52 full of regular American types landed on their uncharted Island and the Druids exclaimed, 'Lo, a great silver bird falleth from the sky.'... [After this event]...the extension of the predicate 'is a bird' for the cosmopolitan Druidese is something like the set of flying devices (including animal varieties). ... [But]...If the hapless aviators had crashed in the jungle unseen and were discovered by the Druids six months later as they camped discontentedly around the bomber's hulk, their Druid rescuers would have proclaimed, 'Lo, a great silver house lieth in the jungle.'... [In this alternative linguistic community] airplanes are no longer [read: are not] held to be 'birds'. ... Which extension should be assigned to 'bird' in cosmopolitan Druidese thus depends upon the *history* of the introduction of B-52's to the island..." (Wilson 1982: 549–50). See also Dennett 1987: 312. Despite the similarities of Wilson's and Dennett's (much briefer) thought experiments, however, neither Wilson nor Dennett emphasize what I regard as crucial to my thought experiment: there may be two *isolated* communities whose ex-uses of a term are the same up until a given time, and then diverge later, while members of both communities continue to make and to trust their PJSSs and PJSEs for previous uses of those terms in their respective linguistic communities. I shall highlight this feature of my thought experiment in this and the next two chapters.

uttered the sentence 'There are huge deposits of gold in those hills', with Locke indicating South African hills, and Twin Locke indicating the corresponding Twin South African hills, both of which contain platinum but no gold. We take Locke's word 'gold' to be true of an object x just in case x is gold, whereas members of the Twin Earth community take Locke's word 'gold' to be true of an object x just in case (as we would say it) x is either gold or platinum (or a mixture of the two). We conclude that Locke's utterance is false, and our contemporaries in the Twin Earth linguistic community conclude that Twin Locke's utterance is true. And yet by supposition, in 1650, before the uncovering of large deposits of platinum on Twin Earth, Locke's and Twin Locke's linguistic dispositions and mental states, as well as the non-semantic relations that Locke and Twin Locke bear to their respective external environments and the physical constitutions of the things to which Locke and Twin Locke are causally related, are the same.[12]

6.5. The Standard Conception of the Options for the Thought Experiment

The following diagram displays the standard conception of the options for characterizing the extensions of tokens of g-o-l-d as used by members

---

[12] This way of illustrating the odd consequences of the first thought experiment is adapted from Donnellan 1983: 103. Lance and O'Leary-Hawthorne 1997: 44–54 also present a thought experiment in which a single sentence—'There are witches'—is evaluated as true by one group of speakers and false by another. But I find their witch thought experiment much less plausible than my gold–platinum thought experiment, for two related reasons. First, it concerns hypothetical, deliberate *translations* of the term 'witch', as tokens of that term were ex-used in Salem, Massachusetts, in the 1600s, into two *different* languages used at some *later* time by linguistic communities that are unconnected by chains of PJSSs or PJSEs across time to tokens of the Salemites' term 'witch'. (In my gold–platinum thought experiment, in contrast, there are no deliberate translations of previous uses of 'gold' in either community; members of each community simply trust their own chains of PJSSs and PJSEs across time for their respective words.) Second, Lance and O'Leary-Hawthorne regard it as "clear" that a linguist from either of the later communities they describe would translate the Salemites' term 'witch' into her own language "homophonically" (Lance and O'Leary-Hawthorne 1997: 47). I don't find this plausible, given the supposition that the linguists' uses of their term 'witch' are not connected to the Salemites' tokens of 'witch' by chains of PJSSs or PJSEs across time. Finally, Lance and O'Leary-Hawthorne suggest that "either translation would be correct from the perspective in which they would be given" (Lance and O'Leary-Hawthorne 1997: 51), thereby endorsing the idea that translation, hence also truth value and extension, are in some way perspective relative. I investigate and reject a sophisticated version of this kind of view in §8.8.

of the two linguistic communities described in the first thought experiment:[13]

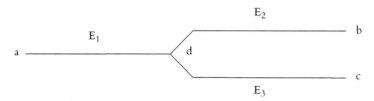

Line ab represents the ex-use of tokens of g-o-l-d in our English-speaking community, line ac represents the ex-use of tokens of g-o-l-d in the Twin English-speaking community, and line ad, where lines ab and ac overlap, represents the supposition that before the accidental uncovering of large amounts of platinum on Twin Earth in 1650—an event represented by point d—members of the two communities have virtually the same dispositions to ex-use of tokens of g-o-l-d, associate the same mental states with their tokens of g-o-l-d, and bear the same relations to the things and substances in their environment, provided that these dispositions, states, and relations are described independently of future developments in either linguistic community. 'E_1', 'E_2', and 'E_3' represent the extension of tokens of g-o-l-d at various points in the histories of the two communities.

Note that 'E_1' is the only symbol that represents the extension of tokens of g-o-l-d during the period *before* the accidental uncovering of large amounts of platinum on Twin Earth—the period when by supposition the ex-use of tokens of g-o-l-d is the same in both communities. In this way the standard commitment to (M) is built into the diagram.[14] The rest of the diagram is straightforward: the extension of tokens of g-o-l-d in the actual English-speaking community after the branching is represented by 'E_2', and the extension of tokens of g-o-l-d in the counterfactual English-speaking community after the branching is represented by 'E_3'.

Given this diagram and the natural assumption that $E_2 \neq E_3$—the extension of tokens of g-o-l-d is different in the two linguistic communities

[13] This diagram (but not my thought experiment or my interpretation of the diagram) is adapted from Larson and Segal 1995: 534.

[14] Recall that I understand the ex-use of 'gold' in 1650 to encompass all non-semantic relations that speakers in 1650 bore to speakers who used 'gold' before 1650, and the physical constitution of the things to which these earlier speakers were causally related.

after the branching—it appears that there are only three options for characterizing the extension of tokens of g-o-l-d before the branching: either (1) $E_1 = E_2$ and $E_1 \neq E_3$, or (2) $E_1 = E_3$ and $E_1 \neq E_2$, or (3) $E_1 \neq E_2$ and $E_1 \neq E_3$.[15]

6.6. A Preview of why Options (1) and (2) are Unacceptable

Options (1) and (2) are both unacceptable for symmetrical reasons. To see why, suppose first that $E_1 = E_2$—the extension of the word type 'gold' in English before the branching is the same as the extension of word type 'gold' in English today. This accords with our practical judgement that the extension of our word type 'gold' has remained the same despite our discovery that gold is the element with atomic number 79. Since sameness of extension is an equivalence relation, and by supposition $E_2 \neq E_3$, we must conclude that $E_1 \neq E_3$, and hence we must accept option (1).

The trouble is that members of the Twin English-speaking community take for granted that the extension of *their* word type 'gold' has not changed either. If we accept option (1), we are committed to saying they are wrong. But by supposition, before the branching, there is no difference in external environment or in linguistic dispositions or mental states, described independently of the branching futures. It seems that *nothing about the ex-use of tokens of g-o-l-d before the branching determines that we are right and they are wrong.*

It is difficult to accept this conclusion. We are strongly inclined to think that there is some independent explanation or justification for our conviction that our PJSEs across time for our tokens of g-o-l-d are correct and their PJSEs across time for their tokens of g-o-l-d are incorrect. Should we trust this inclination? To find out, we must look carefully at the most promising strategies for explaining or justifying our PJSEs across time for our tokens of g-o-l-d, beginning with the causal-historical theory that I sketched above.

---

[15] This abstract characterization of the options (but not my thought experiment or my interpretation of the options) is also adapted from Larson and Segal 1995: 534.

6.7. A Dilemma for the Causal-Historical Theory

One might think that one could appeal to the causal-historical theory to explain or justify our PJSEs across time for our tokens of g-o-l-d, and thereby to defend option (1). To explore this idea, suppose that in 1650 members of both linguistic communities affirmed the Kripke-style "ostensive definition" (K):

> (K) x is gold if and only if for most things y that I and other speakers in my linguistic community have on other occasions called 'gold', x is (a bit of) the same substance as y.

Does it follow that on both Earth and Twin Earth, it was already determined in 1650 that the extension of tokens of g-o-l-d is the set of all and only (bits of) gold—i.e. (bits of) the element with atomic number 79? The answer, as I shall now try to show, is "No."

To see why, note first that to explain our practical judgement that the extension of the English word 'gold' did not change since 1650 by appealing to (K), we must assume that

> (A) for all x and y, if x and y are gold, then x is (a bit of) the same substance as y

is true in English and Twin English. But even if (A) is true in Twin English, and members of the Twin English-speaking community accept (A), it may be that for some x and y, 'x is (a bit of) the same substance as y' is true in Twin English of the ordered pair (x, y), but x does *not* have the same atomic number as y. One might try to rule this out by stipulating that

> (B) for all x and y, if x is (a bit of) the same substance as y, then x has the same atomic number as y

is true in both in English and Twin English. One problem with this strategy is that in 1650 no one was in a position to formulate (B), since analytical chemistry had not yet been developed. A deeper problem is that even if we suppose that (B) is true in English and Twin English, and that members of both communities accept (B), we have no guarantee that (A) is true in Twin English. One may "ostensively define" 'gold' by affirming (K) without thereby guaranteeing that (A) is true. Members of the Twin English-speaking community described in the thought experiment may conclude that despite their previous affirmation of (K), gold is not a substance, and so (A) is false.

Alternatively, they may reject (B), and conclude that the "substance" that was picked out by their affirmation of (K) in 1650 was *platigold*, not the element with atomic number 79 (which we call gold). They may take for granted that tokens of their word 'gold' are satisfied by all and only bits of some particular kind of 'substance', and conclude that since x satisfies their word 'gold' x if and only if x is (a bit of) the element with atomic number 79 or x is (a bit of) the element with atomic number 78 (or a mixture of the two), not all 'substances' map neatly onto the periodic table.

It is natural to suppose that just as members of both linguistic communities take for granted that the extension of their term 'gold' has not changed since some time before 1650, so members of both linguistic communities take for granted that the extension of their expression 'x is (a bit of) the same substance as y'—the set of ordered pairs of which 'x is (a bit of) the same substance as y' is true in their language—has not changed since some time before 1650. Under the circumstances described in the previous paragraph, the extensions of 'x is (a bit of) the same substance as y' in English and Twin English are *different* yet *equally compatible* with the affirmation of (K) prior to the branching in 1650.[16]

One might think it strange to suppose that the Twin English word 'gold' was true of samples of gold and platinum even *before* the accidental uncovering of large amounts of platinum, when tokens of g-o-l-d were actually applied only to samples of gold, and not to samples of platinum. But this possibility does not seem so strange when one focuses on the practical and social aspects of the use of a term. The sense of strangeness all but disappears when we see that there are terms whose *actual* use resembles the use of tokens of g-o-l-d in the Twin Earth community described above. To take one famous (but superficially understood) example, our word 'jade' is true of both jadeite and nephrite. The Chinese character *yu*

---

[16] Under the circumstances described in the first thought experiment, the mental states, including the recognitional capacities and linguistic dispositions, of the speakers in 1650, do not determine the extension of 'x is (a bit of) the same metal as y'. For examples of theories that are undermined by this observation, see Berger 2002, Brown 1998, Devitt and Sterelny 1987: 72–5, Horwich 1998b, Kitcher 1982: 341–2, and Kitcher 1993: 79–89.

that we translate as 'jade' was actually applied only to nephrite until the eighteenth century, when the Chinese first encountered jadeite and started carving it. The mineralogical differences between nephrite and jadeite were discovered in 1863, a century after the Chinese practice of applying *yu* to both nephrite and jadeite became entrenched (Hansford 1968: 26–9). They (and we) take for granted that the extension of the term *yu* did not change when it was applied to jadeite. Similarly, Twin English-speakers take for granted that the extension of their term 'gold' did not change when it was applied to the element with atomic number 78.[17]

These considerations show that affirmations of (K) can settle the extension of tokens of g-o-l-d only if we know that (K) *could not turn out to be false*. As I emphasized earlier, however, we trust our PJSEs across time, so we have no guarantee that any given sentence, including (K), is analytic, in the methodological sense that we cannot revise it without changing the subject.[18] I conclude that affirmations of (K) in 1650 do not rule out either the Earthlings' or Twin Earthlings' discoveries about the nature of the objects that satisfy their tokens of g-o-l-d, and therefore do not justify the PJSEs for tokens of g-o-l-d in either linguistic community.

[17] My argument in this and the previous four paragraphs challenges the thesis that the extension of a natural kind term such as 'gold' is *determined* by indexical applications of such descriptions as 'gold is whatever bears the same metal relation to the stuff which I and other speakers in my linguistic community typically call "gold".' Hilary Putnam apparently endorses this thesis in, for instance, Putnam 1975: 225, and Putnam 1988: chapter 2. But Putnam simply takes for granted that the extension of 'gold' in previous centuries was the same as the extension of our word 'gold'. In describing individuals who at some previous time "mistakenly" apply the word 'gold' to an alloy, Putnam asserts that "what they meant by 'gold' was what we mean by 'gold'" (Putnam 1988: 37), but he offers no account, independent of our actual judgements of sameness of extension across time, of when the extension of a term used at one time is the same as the extension of a term used at some other time. If, as I'll argue later, our best grip on sameness of extension across time is given by our practical judgements of sameness and difference of extension across time, then my first thought experiment shows that the extension of 'gold' was not determined by the way it was ex-used in 1650.

[18] Similarly, we have no guarantee that a "recognitional capacity" that we associate with a given term determines the extension of the term, in this sense proposed by Jessica Brown in Brown 1998. On any non-semantic account of a "recognitional capacity", the members of the Earth and Twin Earth linguistic communities in my thought experiment associate the same "recognitional capacity" with their tokens of g-o-l-d in 1650. Yet they later characterize the extension of their tokens of g-o-l-d differently, and revise the "recognitional capacities" they respectively associate with their tokens of g-o-l-d, without taking themselves to be changing the subject. If we take our practical judgements of sameness of denotation across time as our best guide to when we have changed the subject and when we haven't, then my thought experiment undermines Brown's theory of what determines the extension of natural kind terms. For similar reasons, it also undermines Alan Berger's theory that the extension of certain terms, such as 'gold', is determined in part by what a baptizer of the term "focuses" on. For Berger's theory of the reference-determining role of what he calls "focusing", see Berger 2002.

One natural response to this argument is that (K) is too *vague* to settle the extension of 'gold'. This might lead one to replace the vague word 'substance' with the more precise word 'metal', for example, and to affirm (P).

> (P) x is gold if and only if for most things y that I and other speakers in my linguistic community have on other occasions called 'gold', x is (a bit of) the same metal as y.

Suppose that in 1650 members of both linguistic communities affirmed (P). Does it follow that on both Earth and Twin Earth, it was already determined in 1650 that the extension of 'gold' is the set of all and only (bits of) gold—i.e. (bits of) the element with atomic number 79? The answer, once again, is "No."

To explain our practical judgement that the extension of the English word 'gold' did not change since 1650 by appealing to (P), we must assume that

> (C) for all x and y, if x and y are gold, then x is (a bit of) the same metal as y

is true in English and Twin English. But even if (C) is true in Twin English, it may be that for some x and y, 'x is (a bit of) the same metal as y' is true in Twin English of the ordered pair (x, y), but x does *not* have the same atomic number as y. One might try to rule this out by stipulating that

> (D) for all x and y, if x is (a bit of) the same metal as y, then x has the same atomic number as y

is true in both English and Twin English. But if members of both linguistic communities accept (D) they may reject (C). If for some reason they stick with (C), then they may reject (D). Their trust in their PJSEs across time for 'gold' may lead them to re-evaluate a number of beliefs they formerly expressed by using their term 'gold'. In such cases, none of their antecedent commitments—even their supposed commitment to (P)—shows that these re-evaluations are incorrect. This is just another application of the lesson learned from the counter-examples to methodological analyticity.

One could try to state an "ostensive definition" of 'gold' that is more precise than (P). The trouble is that the more precise one's "definition" of 'gold' is, the more likely it is that it will later be rejected without changing the extension of 'gold'. The causal-historical theory of extension therefore faces a dilemma: the more informative the supposed ostensive definitions are, the more likely it is that they will later be revised without changing the subject; but the less informative they are, the less likely it is that there is only one way of correctly applying them. I conclude that even if, contrary to what most philosophers believe, sentences such as (K) or (P) of §6.3 were actually affirmed in 1650, these supposed "ostensive definitions" could not rule out either the Earthlings' or Twin Earthlings' discoveries about what their word form 'gold' denotes, and therefore could not explain or justify our PJSEs for 'gold'. Despite appearances, causal-historical theories do not support option (1).

6.8. Dispositions

Perhaps we can support option (1) by supplementing the assumption that members of both communities affirmed (K) or (P) before 1650 with facts about their linguistic dispositions. Putnam uses this strategy when he tries to defend his claim that our discovery that gold is the element with atomic number 79 implies that some of Archimedes' assertions about gold—assertions made by using a Greek word that we now translate as 'gold'—might have been false. Putnam explains his claim as follows:

[suppose] there were or are pieces of metal...which we can distinguish from gold quite easily with modern techniques. Let X be such a piece of metal. Clearly X does not lie in the extension of gold in standard English; my view is that it did not lie in the extension of [the Attic Greek word we translate as 'gold'] either, although an ancient Greek would have *mistaken* X for gold...When Archimedes asserted that something was gold...he was not just saying that it had the superficial characteristics of gold...; he was saying that it had the same general hidden structure (the same 'essence', so to speak) as any normal piece of local gold. Archimedes would have said that our hypothetical piece of metal X was gold, but he would have been *wrong*. (Putnam 1975: 235–6)

Putnam is aware that it may seem as though we are *imposing* our current standards onto our description of Archimedes' hypothetical claim that X was gold. To try to dispel this impression, Putnam relies on a *counterfactual* claim about how Archimedes *would have* reacted to our experiments and theories if he *had been* exposed to them:

> ...there are a host of situations that *we* can describe (using the very theory that tells us that X isn't gold) in which X would have behaved quite unlike the rest of the stuff Archimedes classified as gold. Perhaps X would have separated into two different metals when melted or would have had different conductivity properties, or would have vaporized at a different temperature, or whatever. If we had performed the experiments with Archimedes watching...he would have been able to check the empirical regularity that 'X behaves differently from the rest of the stuff I'd classify as [gold] in several respects'. Eventually he would have concluded that 'X may not be gold'. ...If, now, we had gone on to inform Archimedes that gold had such and such a molecular structure (except for X), and that X behaved differently because it had a different molecular structure, is there any doubt that he would have agreed with us that X isn't gold?   (Putnam 1975: 237–8)

This thought experiment is designed to convince us that an individual's "ostensive definitions" of the denotations of his natural kind terms implicitly express theoretical commitments that he would *explicitly* endorse if he were presented with the relevant evidence and theories. Thus Putnam suggests that "ostensive definitions" of the denotations of natural kind terms, together with facts about what speakers *would* say if they *were* presented with new theories or evidence, explain and justify many of our practical judgements of sameness of denotation across time for natural kind terms.

Applying this reasoning to the thought experiment above, one might think that we can support option (1) by citing Locke's and Twin Locke's affirmation of (P), together with facts about what they are *disposed* to say if they are presented with the evidence we now have for the claim that x is gold if and only if x is (a bit of) the element with atomic number 79. There are two serious problems with this strategy. The first problem is that whether or not an individual would accept or reject certain sentences may depend on the *order* in which he is presented with evidence that supports those sentences.[19] It is plausible to suppose that Locke and Twin Locke would have affirmed the sentence 'x is gold if and only if x is (a bit of)

---

[19] This formulation of the challenge my thought experiment poses for dispositional theories is due to Bill Robinson. The point was already implicit in Mark Wilson's Druid thought experiment (see n. 11).

the element with atomic number 79' if they had been presented with the same evidence that later English-speakers encountered, *in the same order* in which they actually encountered it. But by hypothesis members of the Twin English-speaking community described in the gold–platinum thought experiment came to affirm the sentence '*x* is gold if and only if either *x* is the element with atomic number 79 or *x* is the element with atomic number 78 (or a mixture of the two)' without thinking at any point that they had changed the extension of their term 'gold'. It is therefore plausible to suppose that Locke and Twin Locke would have affirmed the sentence '*x* is gold if and only if either *x* is the element with atomic number 79 or *x* is the element with atomic number 78 (or a mixture of the two)' if they had been presented with the same evidence that later Twin English-speakers encountered, *in the same order* in which they actually encountered it. We have no independent grounds for saying that one of these presentations of the evidence is correct and the other is incorrect, and so an appeal to dispositions cannot show that our community's PJSSs and PJSEs for 'gold' are correct and theirs are incorrect.[20]

The second and deeper problem with this strategy is that it is unclear *how* a speaker's dispositions could settle sameness of extension across time. Our understanding of whether or not Locke and Twin Locke had dispositions to *agree* or *disagree* with later investigators in the two communities depends on our *prior* judgement of whether their terms have the same extension as the similarly spelled terms used by later investigators in the two communities. There is no obvious criterion in terms of dispositions *alone*, apart from our PJSEs, for settling when two individuals are using a term with the same extension. One difficulty for any proposed criteria is that

[20] The observations in this section suggest an argument against Paul Horwich's use theory of meaning. According to that theory, the meaning of a term is constituted by its possession of a certain "acceptance property" that can be specified independently of its meaning or denotation. Candidates for such properties are facts about a speaker's linguistic behaviour, in particular, facts about which sentences the speaker is disposed to accept under various circumstances. For instance, according to Horwich, "the acceptance property that governs a speaker's overall use of 'and' is (roughly) his tendency to accept '*p* and *q*' if and only if he accepts both '*p*' and '*q*'" (Horwich 1998b: 45). Moreover, according to Horwich, two words express the same concept if they have the same basic acceptance property (Horwich 1998b: 46), and any two words that express the same concept must have the same denotation (Horwich 1998b: 69). Since Horwich can only appeal to linguistic dispositions, described in non-semantic terms, he is apparently committed to saying that the term 'gold' expresses the same concept, and therefore has the same denotation, in 1650 in both of the linguistic communities of my thought experiment. This aspect of his use theory clearly conflicts with our confidence that the extension of our term 'gold' today is the same as the extension of 'gold' in 1650.

204 A PUZZLE ABOUT SAMENESS OF SATISFACTION

individuals sometimes stubbornly *disagree* with each other about issues that
are important to both of them. This suggests that Locke's and Twin
Locke's dispositions to accept or reject certain *sentences*, even if they were
well defined and perfectly objective, do not by themselves determine how
we should evaluate our PJSEs in the two linguistic communities.

Suppose we could somehow objectively determine that Locke and Twin
Locke are disposed to *accept* the sentence 'x is gold if and only if x is (a
bit of) the element with atomic number 79' and disposed to *reject* the
sentence 'x is gold if and only if either x is the element with atomic
number 79 or x is the element with atomic number 78 (or a mixture
of the two)', even after they are presented with the evidence on which
members of the Twin English-speaking community after 1850 based their
conclusion that 'gold' is true of (bits of) the elements with atomic number
79 or (bits of) the elements with atomic number 78. If we accept the
PJSEs across time in both communities, we should conclude that Locke
is right, but Twin Locke is wrong. Hence the supposed dispositions
cannot by themselves show that we should not accept the PJSEs in both
communities.

6.9. Epistemic Possibilities and Primary Intensions

Frank Jackson and David Chalmers have recently developed a framework
for relating ostensive definitions of the sort exemplified by (K) and (P) to
individual speakers' judgements about how they would apply kind terms
under various possible circumstances. They both present their view as a
justification of what I call our practical judgements of sameness of extension
(PJSEs) across time for natural kind terms, such as 'water' and 'gold'. Their
view is more complicated than the two I have examined so far, but it fails
for similar reasons. Because of its greater complexity, it is more difficult to
see exactly where it goes wrong. In this section I will briefly sketch their
view, beginning with an account of the underlying motivation for it. In
the next section I will argue that their view cannot support option (1), and
is actually in direct conflict with it.

Jackson and Chalmers are not always explicit about the underlying
motivation for their view. I assume, however, that Jackson speaks for both
of them when he writes that

Language...is a convention generated set of physical structures that has as a principle function making it easy to articulate, and in consequence easy to record, transmit in communication, debate the consequences of, and so on, how someone...takes things to be.   (Jackson 1998b: 201–2)

This conception of language implies that when we rely on our PJSSs and PJSEs, we take for granted that they enable us to report accurately how our fellow English-speakers take things to be. In addition, on this view, how our fellow English-speakers take things to be is *independent* of our PJSSs and PJSEs. According to Jackson and Chalmers, a speaker's *beliefs* about how to apply the term settle how she takes things to be when she applies it. As Jackson explains it, "... a name [or kind term] *T* used by *S* refers to whatever has the properties that *S* associates with *T*" (Jackson 1998b: 203). This is not just one plausible account among others, according to Jackson; any alternative theory according to which the reference of a name [or kind term] *T* used by *S* is *not* determined by the properties that *S* associates with *T* leaves reference unexplained and mysterious:

... the crucial point here, and generally, it is that our classifications of things into categories—grooming behavior, belief, pain, and so on and so forth—is not done at random and is not a miracle. There are patterns underlying our conceptual competence. They are often hard to find—we still do not know in full detail the rules that capture the patterns underlying our classification of sentences into the grammatical and the ungrammatical, or of inferential behavior into the rational and the irrational—but *they must be there to be found. We do not classify sentences as grammatical, or inferential behavior as rational, by magic or at random!*   (Jackson 1998b: 64, my emphasis)

In this passage Jackson emphasizes that our linguistic behaviour is guided by our beliefs about how to apply our terms. In his view, language itself is merely a conventional device for conveying beliefs, and hence any adequate account of a speaker's linguistic competence must explain it without presupposing a public language, solely in terms of beliefs that speakers associate with their words.

Jackson and Chalmers are aware that this conception of language seems at first to be refuted by Putnam's and Kripke's arguments against the description theory of reference. In response, Jackson and Chalmers offer a new interpretation of what Kripke's and Putnam's arguments show. Jackson and Chalmers first introduce a criterion for determining what properties a speaker S associates with a given term T. The key assumption behind this criterion is that *before one can even begin to make empirical inquiries about a particular kind T, one must first be able to identify a particular item as a sample of T, without presupposing any empirical beliefs.* To discover how we identify items to which a given term applies, they believe, we must ask ourselves *what we would say* in various different epistemically possible circumstances.

When they characterize this epistemological task, Jackson and Chalmers presuppose what has now become a widely accepted account of epistemic possibility. Putnam's method of describing Twin Earth scenarios (as described, for instance, in §6.3 above) suggests that for each person we can specify countless *subjectively equivalent* circumstances in which everything seems the same, but the external environments are different from what they are on Earth. Putnam assumed that Twin Earth actually exists. Nevertheless, if I try to imagine that I am my twin on Twin Earth, I am in effect imagining that I am in a different (but subjectively equivalent) possible world. The difference between the actual world and this other possible world in this case is simply the difference between occupying my current perspective, and occupying the perspective of my twin on Twin Earth. More generally, to specify an epistemic possibility we must specify a subjectively equivalent world centred on a particular agent. I will call these *agent-centred* subjectively equivalent possible worlds. On one standard view, epistemic possibilities are explained in terms of agent-centred possible worlds.

This way of thinking about epistemic possibility yields a corresponding understanding of *a priority*: a speaker's belief is a priori if it is true in all subjectively equivalent agent-centred worlds. According to this way of thinking about epistemic possibility, a speaker's belief is empirical if it is not a priori.

David Chalmers (Chalmers 1996) defines the *primary intension* of a word as a special sort of function from (agent-centred) worlds to extensions: in a given (agent-centred) world w, the primary intension of a word picks out what the extension of the word would be if w turned out to be actual (Chalmers 1996: 57). To grasp the primary intension of 'water', for instance, we must grasp a function that yields the set of all and only portions of *water* as value if the actual (agent-centred) world has water in its rivers, lakes, and oceans, but yields the set of all and only portions of *twin water* as value if the actual (agent-centred) world has twin water in its rivers, lakes, and oceans.

What is distinctive of a primary intension, according to Chalmers, is that our grasp of it is independent of any assumptions we make about which of our agent-centred subjectively equivalent worlds we are actually in. He argues that there *must be* a primary intension for any word that we can use to express a discovery. If we are to express a discovery about water that is based on our examination of a given sample of what we take to be water, he reasons, we must be able to say *why* it counts as a sample of *water* by appealing to rules that we can grasp without going through any empirical investigation or presupposing any empirical beliefs (Chalmers 1996: 62).

This reasoning moves from a truism to a substantive epistemological claim. The truism is that we take ourselves to express a discovery about water by using the term 'water' only if we make a PJSE for 'water', and thereby suppose that the extension of 'water' does not change as a result of our supposed discovery. The substantive epistemological claim is that we are entitled to take ourselves to express a discovery about water by using the term 'water' only if we can *justify* our PJSEs for 'water' by appealing to rules that we can grasp without going through any empirical investigation or presupposing any empirical beliefs. This substantive epistemological claim is a natural consequence of the conception of language that motivates the Jackson–Chalmers account of primary intensions. The fundamental point is that all linguistic relationships between speakers, both at a given time and across time, must ultimately be grounded in the speakers' *beliefs* about how their terms are correctly applied.

A primary intension is well suited to this justificatory role, according to Chalmers. "The intension specifies how reference depends on the way the external world turns out, so does not itself depend on the way the external world turns out" (Chalmers 1996: 57). By reasoning about "what our words *would* refer to if the actual world turned out in various ways", Chalmers thinks, we can simultaneously *see* that our words have primary intensions and *discover* what they are.

According to Jackson and Chalmers, the existence of primary intensions for our words makes it possible for us to identify items to which our words apply, and to begin empirical inquiries into the nature of those items. They grant that Kripke and Putnam describe one way in which these inquiries can result in discoveries about the nature of those items. For instance, they grant that once we can identify samples of water by means of our primary intension for the word 'water' we can go on to discover that in fact in the actual world water is H_2O. Moreover, once one has made such a discovery, Jackson and Chalmers agree, it is natural to say that if there is no H_2O in a given world, then there is no *water* in that world. They explain this by introducing the idea of *secondary intensions* for our terms. According to Chalmers, for instance, "The *secondary intension* of 'water' picks out the water in every counterfactual world; so if Kripke and Putnam are correct, the secondary intension picks out H_2O in all worlds" (Chalmers 1996: 57). More generally, the secondary intension of a term is a function that settles the extension of that term in counterfactual worlds, given its extension in the actual world. It is called *secondary* because it is defined in terms of the primary intension of the term, which, according to Jackson and Chalmers, must be fixed before an empirical inquiry into the extension of the term in the actual world can even begin.

Jackson and Chalmers present this theory as an interpretation and clarification of the epistemological status of "ostensive definitions" of the sort exemplified by (K) and (P), and the relationship of these definitions to individual speakers' judgements about how they would apply kind terms under various possible circumstances. For any given speaker S and natural kind word T, an "ostensive definition" of the *secondary intension* expressed by T is defined as whatever explains the underlying unity of all the objects or items to which T *actually* applies, given its *primary intension*. S knows the primary intension of T without any empirical inquiry—without presupposing anything about which subjectively equivalent world S is actually in. According to this view, a speaker may revise her understanding of the *primary intension* of T, but only if she believes she has made a mistake about the circumstances under which she would correctly apply T, independent of any assumptions about which world is actual. Nevertheless, according to Jackson and Chalmers, the primary intension and the secondary intension of a given term T by definition yield exactly the same extension for T in the actual world.

6.10. Problems with Primary Intensions

Can we appeal to Jackson's and Chalmers's theory of primary intensions to defend option (1)? They claim that their view is consistent with Kripke's and Putnam's causal-historical theory of extension, and that it yields the conclusion, for instance, that the actual extension of 'water', and hence also (by definition) its secondary intension, is H_2O. But Kripke and Putnam claim that the extension of the word type 'gold' in English is the set of objects that are (bits of) the element with atomic number 79, and that this is an empirical discovery that did not change the extension of the word type 'gold' in English since at least as far back as 1650. To justify these claims, hence to justify option (1), a person who accepts Jackson and Chalmers's theory of primary intensions would have to show that in 1650, the primary intension of the English word 'gold', together with facts about the world in 1650, determined that the extension of the English word 'gold' was the set of objects that are (bits of) the element with atomic number 79, and not the set of objects that are (bits of) the element with either atomic number 78 or atomic number 79 (or mixtures of the two).

The first main problem with this strategy is that primary intensions are apparently too *vague* to support (1). Since Locke and Twin Locke are by hypothesis physical and behavioural twins, and future developments in either linguistic community are not relevant to the primary intensions they associate with the respective word types that they spell g-o-l-d, those primary intensions must be identical. As I explained above, neither Locke's nor Twin Locke's linguistic dispositions entail that platinum is not in the extension of both of their respective tokens of g-o-l-d. If primary intensions are settled by what a speaker would say under various circumstances, then, the primary intension that Locke and Twin Locke associated with their respective tokens of g-o-l-d does not support option (1).

Chalmers and Jackson might be willing to agree that the primary intension that Locke and Twin Locke associated with their respective tokens of g-o-l-d was too vague to support option (1). In a footnote, Jackson asserts that "In the mouths and from the pens of the folk it is indeterminate whether [water] is H_2O or the watery stuff on Twin Earth that counts as water on Twin Earth" (Jackson 1998a: 38 n. 12). If he accepts this, it seems he would be more inclined to accept that the primary intension that Locke and Twin Locke associated with their respective tokens of g-o-l-d was too vague to support option (1). If Jackson makes this move, and (1)–(3) exhaust the options for describing the thought experiment, then Jackson must embrace option (3). I will examine this kind of reaction to the gold–platinum thought experiment in the next chapter.

Another possible reply is that the primary intensions that Locke and Twin Locke associated with their tokens of g-o-l-d in 1650 did *in fact* determine that the extension of their tokens of g-o-l-d is the set of objects that are bits of the element with atomic number 79, but that Locke and Twin Locke may have been confused or unclear about this. According to this reply, they could *in principle* have discovered the precise primary intension of their tokens of g-o-l-d without going through any empirical investigation, if they had attended carefully enough to what they would say in various different epistemically possible circumstances.

One main problem with this reply, and with Jackson's and Chalmers's account of primary intensions more generally, is that what we *actually* say when we find ourselves in a previously imagined situation almost always trumps our earlier speculations about what we *would* say if we *were to* find ourselves in that situation. What we actually say when we find ourselves in a previously imagined situation reflects our best current judgement of what is true in that situation. When we are actually in the previously imagined situation, our best judgement of what is true in that situation brings with it PJSSs and PJSEs. If those PJSSs and PJSEs conflict with earlier speculations, then so much the worse for those speculations. Recall, for instance, in the seventeenth century scientists took for granted that gold is a yellow metal. A person living at the time might well have believed that one cannot reject the statement that gold is a yellow metal without changing the subject. But we now know that in its pure form gold is white, not yellow. Later scientists took themselves not to have *changed the topic*, but to have *discovered* that gold is white. To accept this description of the case, we must trust the later scientists' complex PJSSs and PJSEs for the word 'gold' more than we trust any previous judgement that one could not reject the statement that gold is a yellow metal without changing the subject.

This example shows that statements we can't imagine giving up without changing the subject are not thereby *guaranteed* to be true. But one might think that to accept Chalmers's claim that some of our words have primary intensions that we can know a priori, we need only suppose that some of the statements that we can't imagine giving up without changing the subject actually *are* true. The trouble with this thought, however, is that Chalmers's primary intensions are supposed to "back *a priori* truths"—statements that are "true no matter how the actual world turns out" (Chalmers 1996: 59). Hence to accept Chalmers's claim that some of our words have primary intensions that we can know a priori, it is not enough to suppose that some of the statements that we can't imagine giving up without changing the subject are true.[21]

Like Chalmers, Jackson tries to defend the inference from 'we don't understand how we could give up statement S without changing the subject' to 'we could not give up statement S without changing the subject'. "[S]urely it *is* possible to change the subject," Jackson reasons, "and how else could one do it other than by abandoning what is most central to defining one's subject? Would a better way of changing the subject be to abandon what is less central?" (Jackson 1998a: 38). The mistake here is to suppose that our best *current* judgement about what counts as changing the subject is immune to future revisions. It is a truism that if we want to change the subject, we must rely on our understanding of what is most central to defining it. But this truism does not establish that our current understanding of what is most central to defining our subject cannot be revised without changing the subject. This claim is discredited by many actual cases in which we were once confident that we could not revise a given statement without changing the subject, but discovered later that we were wrong. For reasons I noted earlier, provided we regiment our words and define truth for them disquotationally, each of our discoveries brings with it some chain or other of PJSEs across time. In this sense, our PJSEs are of a piece with our pursuit of truth.[22]

One might agree that our PJSEs across time can in practice lead us to revise our beliefs about the extension of a given term, but insist that in such cases our PJSEs partly constitute our coming to see the a priori conditions for applying our terms more clearly than we saw them before. Both Chalmers and Jackson insist that we can be mistaken about a priori

---

[21] One can define a function F from words and (agent-centred) worlds to extensions so that for any ordered pair of words and agent-centred worlds, the value of F for that ordered pair is the extension of the word as used by the agent in that agent-centred world. Suppose we know a priori that for each pair of words and agents, there exists such a function. It does not follow, as Chalmers seems to assume, that we can know a priori what the value of the function is for the world we are actually in. For a similar criticism of a related position, see Stalnaker 1990: 131–45.

[22] The link between our pursuit of truth and our PJSEs does not imply that the underlying traits of the universe are somehow ultimately syntactical. My argument against Chalmers and Jackson suggests, on the contrary, that "the syntactic construction of a quantity name may not reveal its actual ties to other quantities adequately", as Mark Wilson has stressed. See Wilson 1993: 82. I agree with Wilson that we may *discover* that many of our terms have what he calls honourable intensions. Unlike Chalmers's hypothetical primary intensions, *honourable* intensions are not known a priori.

claims, so the fact that in practice we have revised many of our beliefs about how to apply our terms does not show that those beliefs are not a priori.

The main problem with this reply is that it implies that in practice we may be no more confident of a so-called a priori claim about how to apply our terms than we are of many of our empirical beliefs. From an epistemological perspective, then, on this view, a priori beliefs have no distinctive role, no special methodological significance. The category of a priori beliefs about extension has metaphysical significance, perhaps, but no practical epistemological significance. Moreover, the emptiness of this metaphysical–epistemological distinction becomes clear when one reflects about particular examples of revisions in our beliefs about how to apply our terms. It is plausible to suppose, for instance, that for centuries before the discovery of the chemical composition of water, it was widely assumed that the term 'water' applied only to liquids. But now that we have discovered that the extension of 'water' is H_2O, we believe that ice is in the extension of 'water', too. Trusting our PJSEs across time, we are prompted, according to the present theory, to revise our prior, incorrect beliefs about the preconditions for applying the term 'water'. Here it seems obvious that we revise those prior beliefs because of an empirical discovery. The claim that the revision is nevertheless purely "a priori", because it follows from one's theory that it *must* be a priori if it concerns our "primary" understanding of how to apply the term, is strained and ultimately empty.[23]

Someone might insist that the primary intension that Locke and Twin Locke associated with their respective tokens of g-o-l-d in 1650 actually determined that our PJSEs across time for tokens of g-o-l-d in our linguistic community are correct, and the PJSEs across time for tokens of g-o-l-d in the Twin Earth community are incorrect. But this claim ultimately rests on the mysterious and empty assumption that even though the Locke and Twin Locke were confused about the primary intension that they actually associated with their own tokens of g-o-l-d, and even though as far as they are understood, it might be applied either to gold or platinum, nevertheless

[23] In Russell 2008, Gillian Russell presents an account of 'truth in virtue of reference determiner' that is structurally similar to Chalmer's and Jackson's account of truth in virtue of primary intensions. Unlike Chalmers and Jackson, however, Russell sees clearly that her account "has no hope of meeting any kind of special epistemic condition" (Russell 2008: 67) and hence that we cannot in general know a priori that a sentence is 'true in virtue of reference determiner'.

there was something about how they used tokens of g-o-l-d in 1650 that determined that the extension of those tokens of g-o-l-d was the set of objects that are bits of the element with atomic number 79. This is not so much a theory in support of option (1), as a stubborn insistence that option (1) is correct, combined with an uninformative account of why this is so. In fact, as I noted earlier, Jackson himself would not attempt to defend option (1) in this way. This is not surprising, given that the theory of primary intensions stems from an account of language that strongly suggests that most of our PJSEs are incorrect, whether or not we focus on long spans of time across which we have certainly lost track of past English-speakers' beliefs about how to apply their terms. I conclude that the theory of primary intensions proposed by Jackson and Chalmers does not support option (1).

6.11. Implicit Conceptions

One might be convinced by these objections to Jackson's and Chalmers's theory of primary intensions, yet still feel there is something right about the idea that prior states of understanding determine the extensions of our terms. Perhaps the main source of the problems with Jackson's and Chalmers's theory is that they define a speaker S's state of understanding a term T at time t in terms of how S would apply tokens of T under various different circumstances she can entertain hypothetically at t. Let's agree that this equation is incorrect for the reasons presented above, the most important of which is that what a speaker accepts in a particular, actual situation almost always trumps her prior speculations about what we she *would* say in that such a situation if it *were* actual. Still, one might think, this does not show that when a speaker does encounter a new situation, her application of tokens of T is not determined in some way by her prior understanding of how to apply tokens of T. To maintain this position despite the objections to Jackson's and Chalmers's theory of primary intensions, we need only reject the theoretical claim that such prior states of understanding can always in principle be fully and accurately articulated by the speakers who have them. In other words, to maintain this position it may be enough to say that the mental states that determine correct application are implicit.

Christopher Peacocke has recently argued that in order to explain the fact that speakers can arrive at new understandings of their own claims by reasoning, we must posit implicit conceptions that *guide* a speaker's reasoning. Peacock focuses on cases in logic and mathematics, but his reasoning, if it were correct, would also apply to the clarification of natural kind terms. He seems to be guided by the thought that the only way to explain how it is possible for a given speaker S to use tokens of a term T to inquire into the truth of sentences in which such tokens occur is to theorize that S associates with the tokens of T an implicit conception that determines S's evaluation of the truth of sentences in which such tokens occur.

Peacocke claims, for instance, that Newton and Leibniz had an implicit conception of the limit of a series that guided their discovery of the calculus, even though they could not provide an explicit account of the limit of a series, and, in fact, no one at that time had the mathematical resources to provide an explicit account of the limit of a series. Peacocke claims we can explain Newton's and Leibniz's deep understanding of calculus only if we attribute to them an implicit conception of the notion of the limit of a series that predetermined a single, correct, and *explicit* account of that notion.

Peacocke wants to accommodate what he calls the Phenomenon of New Principles—"the rational, justified acceptance of new principles involving a given concept, new in the sense that these principles do not follow from those principles (if any) immediate acceptance of which is required for possession of the concept" (Peacocke 1998: 65). This requires, he argues, that implicit conceptions not be understood as "personal-level conceptual-roles" (Peacocke 1998: 64).

Can an appeal to something like implicit conceptions help us to justify or explain option (1)? The proposal would be that in 1650, prior to the branching of the two linguistic communities described above, Locke associated with his tokens of g-o-l-d an implicit conception that guided him in his applications of the term, and determined that the extension of the tokens is the set of objects that are bits of the element with atomic number 79, not the set of objects that are either bits of the element with atomic number 78 or bits of the element with atomic number 79 (or mixtures of the two).

One problem with this suggestion is that if Locke associated a given conception with his tokens of g-o-l-d in 1650, by hypothesis, Twin Locke simultaneously associated a conception with *his* tokens of g-o-l-d in 1650.

Since Peacocke wants his implicit conceptions to guide and predetermine correct linguistic usage, he cannot appeal to *later* developments in the two communities to distinguish between the conceptions that Locke and Twin Locke associate with their respective tokens of g-o-l-d. By hypothesis, however, if we disregard later developments in either community, we must conclude that the implicit conception that Locke associated with his tokens of g-o-l-d in 1650 is the same as the implicit conception that Twin Locke associated with his tokens of g-o-l-d in 1650.

As I stressed above, however, it seems that nothing in the linguistic behaviour or mental states of Locke and Twin Locke supports option (1) or option (2). The bald assertion that in this case the implicit conception associated by Locke and Twin Locke with their respective tokens of g-o-l-d in 1650 supports option (1) leaves it mysterious how we can ever know what the implicit conceptions associated by a speaker with his terms actually are. To see the problem, note that when Peacocke claims that the implicit conception that Locke associated with his tokens of g-o-l-d in 1650 determined that option (1) is correct, Twin Peacocke on Twin Earth simultaneously claims (when translated into English) that the implicit conception that Twin Locke associated with his tokens of g-o-l-d in 1650 determined that option (2) is correct. Suppose Peacocke and Twin Peacocke were to try to decide which of these two claims is correct. What could possibly settle this? The thought experiment implies there is nothing independent of their contested, hypothetical implicit conceptions to ground (or undermine) either of their incompatible assertions.

Peacocke is sensitive to the possible charge that implicit conceptions are mysterious and unknowable. He rejects this charge in the following passage:

> nothing in what I have said should encourage the view that implicit conceptions . . . somehow transcend the knowable. There would be a commitment to such transcendence if it were allowed as the possibility that there could be two speakers whose rational judgements about particular applications of an expression, and about principles involving it, are in actual and counterfactual circumstances identical, and yet have differing implicit conceptions. Nothing I have said entails that that is a possibility.   (Peacocke 1998: 57)

It seems, however, as I have argued, that if Peacocke attempts to justify option (1) by appeal to implicit conceptions, he will commit himself to the existence of mysterious, unknowable implicit conceptions. For his twin on Twin Earth will presumably attempt to justify the PJSEs on Twin Earth in the same way, thus generating the fruitless "dispute" that I just described. Although Peacocke and his twin disagree, and are therefore not asserting that Locke and Twin Locke had different implicit conceptions, they are nevertheless unable to appeal to anything except their confidence in the PJSEs across time in their respective communities to support their claims about the implicit conceptions that Locke and Twin Locke associate with their respective tokens of g-o-l-d.

If Peacocke retains his commitment to (M) yet does not insist on making mysterious ungrounded claims of the sort just described, he must reject both options (1) and (2), and thereby reject the PJSEs in both linguistic communities. We thereby arrive, once again, at the conclusion that if we accept (M) we must reject options (1) and (2). If we hang on to (M), the only remaining option is (3), according to which $E_1 \neq E_2$ and $E_1 \neq E_3$. We must now consider whether it is more attractive to endorse option (3) than to abandon (M) and the intuitions that support it.

7

Sense and Partial Extension

7.1. Option (3)

We have now seen that if we accept

(M) For any two word tokens w and w' such that the utterance or inscription of w occurs at some time t before the utterance or inscription of w', a practical judgement of sameness of extension (PJSE) *across time* for w and w' is true only if for some set E,

    (a) E is the extension of both w and w', and

    (b) the totality of facts about the ex-use of w at times prior to or identical with t (hence prior to the utterance or inscription of w') determines that E is the extension of w

then we cannot accept *either* option (1), according to which $E_1 = E_2$ and $E_1 \neq E_3$, or option (2), according to which $E_1 \neq E_2$ and $E_1 = E_3$, in the gold–platinum thought experiment. We naturally find option (1) more attractive than option (2), because it accords with *our* PJSEs across time for 'gold'. But we have no basis independent of these judgements for claiming that the extension of the English word 'gold' in 1650 was the same as the extension of the English word 'gold' in our linguistic community today. To insist on option (1) is to beg the question against option (2), which members of the Twin English-speaking community today will no doubt prefer, because it accords with *their* PJSEs across time for the Twin English word 'gold'.

Given (M), the only remaining option is (3), according to which $E_1 \neq E_2$ and $E_1 \neq E_3$. To embrace the option (3) is to abandon our PJSEs across time for 'gold'. Moreover, it is not difficult to construct thought experiments that challenge our PJSEs across time for other natural kind terms. To reject the corresponding options (1) and (2) for all of these terms is to reject a vast number of our PJSEs across time, and thereby to undermine our confidence in the way we actually conduct ordinary and scientific inquiries.

Those who accept (M) only because they think it might enable them to explain and justify their PJSEs across time, including their PJSEs across time for tokens of g-o-l-d, should therefore now be inclined to reject (M) because it implies option (3). For all I have argued so far, however, it may still seem reasonable to embrace option (3).[1] In this chapter I'll examine two different strategies for making sense of option (3), and explain why one might be tempted to endorse these different strategies for making sense of option (3), even though they commit us to rejecting many of our PJSSs and PJSEs across time. I shall argue that although both strategies are initially appealing, closer examinations reveal that neither one provides a plausible alternative to trusting our PJSEs across time.

7.2. Dummett on Sameness of Satisfaction across Time

Suppose you are studying a proof written in English that a plane intersects a cylinder in an ellipse.[2] When you read the sentence 'A plane intersects a cylinder in an ellipse', you take the author to be asserting that a plane intersects a cylinder in an ellipse, and you take the word 'ellipse' that occurs in the author's sentence to be the same word 'ellipse' that occurs in your present affirmations of

(e) x satisfies my word 'ellipse' if and only if x is an ellipse.

---

[1] Many philosophers who wish to explain and ground our PJSEs whenever possible would endorse option (3). Mark Wilson, for example, writes that "in some common situations the proper ground for determining whether a predicate is true of a particular individual becomes uncertain or ambiguous. One kind of situation in which this can happen ... is one in which the linguistic community is unaware of the existence of kinds of objects to which a predicate might be thought to apply. It is frequently indeterminate whether such unexpected objects should be assigned to the extension or to the counter-extension of the predicate" (Wilson 1982: 549). Wilson's intuition that "it is frequently indeterminate whether such unexpected objects should be assigned to the extension or to the counter-extension of the predicate" suggests that he is committed to (M). Moreover, a commitment to (M) would explain Wilson's proposed "adequacy condition" on assignments of extensions: "The evidence for assignment of an extension to a predicate should be limited to such linguistic behavior as can be reasonably extrapolated from the community's contemporaneous practice and should not reflect accidental features of the society's later history" (Wilson 1982: 553).

[2] I get this example from Dummett 1978a: 300. See also Hacking 1985; Hilbert and Cohn-Vossen 1956: 7–8; and Spivak 1994: chapter 4, Appendix 2, Problem 2.

You thereby also accept that x satisfies the word 'ellipse' that occurs in the author's sentence if and only if x is an ellipse. Conjoining these two acceptances, you make a PJSS for the author's word 'ellipse'.

As you work through the proof, you occasionally glance back at earlier parts of the proof that contain tokens of e-l-l-i-p-s-e, and you continue to take those tokens of e-l-l-i-p-s-e to be tokens of the same word 'ellipse' that occurs in your own affirmations of (e). Given your acceptance of (e), you accept that x satisfies the word 'ellipse', as it occurs earlier in the proof, if and only if x is an ellipse, and thereby make a PJSS across time for the author's word 'ellipse'.

Now suppose you are convinced by the proof. You take yourself to have learned something new about ellipses. When you accept the proof, you continue to trust your PJSSs across time for tokens of e-l-l-i-p-s-e. Some of these practical judgements reach back to your own tokens of e-l-l-i-p-s-e that existed before you worked through the proof. It is tempting to assume that these practical judgements are correct or incorrect according as your criteria for applying 'ellipse' *before* you worked through the proof determined an extension for 'ellipse' that is identical to the extension determined by the new criterion for applying 'ellipse' that you accept *after*, and *as a result of*, working through the proof. According to Michael Dummett, from whom I borrow this example,

> The standard view of the effect of the proof [that a plane intersects a cylinder in an ellipse] is that the new criterion which it provides enables us to recognize as ellipses only figures which could already have been so recognized by the criteria we already had: what the proof establishes is precisely that the new criterion, where applicable, must always agree extensionally with that given by the original definition of 'ellipse'; that is why the proof persuades us to adopt the new test as a criterion.   (Dummett 1978a: 301)

This way of thinking about sameness of satisfaction across time is especially gripping when we are trying to understand reasoning about abstract objects, such as ellipses, that we feel we can only identify by means of definitions.[3] But it is also natural to think that a new *empirical* claim made by using a term T counts as a discovery only if the new criterion for applying T that it introduces agrees extensionally with the relevant previous criteria for

---

[3] Recall Meno's paradox: we cannot inquire into the definition of virtue unless we can *already* define it, for otherwise we cannot even identify the topic whose definition we seek.

applying T. Consider, for instance, the original announcement (in English) that gold is the element with atomic number 79. The English-speaking chemists who made this announcement continued to take their previous uses of tokens of g-o-l-d to be occurrences of the word type 'gold' that they take themselves to be using to make their announcement. Now suppose some of them affirmed

(g) x satisfies 'gold' if and only if x is (a bit of) gold.

Then when they took their previous tokens of g-o-l-d to be tokens of their word 'gold', they made a PJSS across time for their previous tokens of g-o-l-d—they accepted both that x satisfies 'gold' if and only if x is (a bit of) gold and that x satisfies their previous tokens of g-o-l-d if and only if x is (a bit of) gold. But, just as in the ellipse case, the standard view is that their trust in this judgement would be misplaced unless the criteria for applying 'gold' to which they were committed *before* they made their supposed discovery agree extensionally with the new criterion, according to which x satisfies the word 'gold' if and only if x is (a bit of) the element with atomic number 79.[4]

The standard view amounts to a version of (M). Taking this version of (M) for granted, Dummett argues, in effect, that the ex-use of tokens of g-o-l-d in 1650 on Earth and Twin Earth in the gold–platinum thought experiment did not settle that x satisfies those tokens if and only if x is (a bit of) the element with atomic number 79, or that x satisfies those tokens if and only if x is either (a bit of) the element with atomic number 78 or a bit of the element with atomic number 79, and hence that the PJSSs and PJSEs across time for tokens of g-o-l-d made by members of the English-speaking community on Earth and the Twin English-speaking community on Twin Earth are false. To see why, one must examine Dummett's accounts of sense and implicit knowledge.

7.3. Dummett on Sense and Implicit Knowledge[5]

Dummett argues that a speaker's uses of her words are guided by her knowledge of her language, and that at the core of a speaker's knowledge

---

[4] This implies not that all their previous applications of 'gold' are correct according to the new criterion, but that if one or more of their previous applications of 'gold' is incorrect according to the new criterion, it is also incorrect according to their previous criteria for applying 'gold'.

[5] I am indebted to Imogen Dickie for very helpful criticisms of two earlier drafts of §§7.3–7.6

of her language is her knowledge of the *senses* of the logically significant expressions of her language, where "the sense of an expression—which is part, and often the whole, of its meaning—is given to us as a means of determining its reference (or its semantic value)" (Dummett 1991: 148). In particular, the sense of a *sentence* is given to us as the grasp of the condition that must be satisfied for the sentence to be true. The sense of a *predicate* is given to us as the grasp of the contribution of the predicate to our grasp of the senses of *sentences* in which it occurs. Dummett reasons as follows: "If to grasp the sense of the predicate is to grasp something that determines its reference, and if it is to lead us to apprehend the condition for a sentence formed by means of the predicate to be true, then it must be given to us as the grasp of the condition that must be satisfied, by any object, for it to be mapped onto the value *true* or for it to be mapped onto the value *false*."[6] The idea can be expressed without treating truth values as objects. For instance, we can say that the sense of our word 'gold' is given to us as the grasp of the conditions under which an object x satisfies our word 'gold'.

If the *sense* of (tokens of) a given predicate P at a given time t settles, for every object x, the conditions under which a given object x satisfies (tokens of) P at t, then the sense determines the *extension* of (tokens of) P at t—the set of all and only the objects that satisfy (tokens of) P at t. For instance, if the *sense* of tokens of g-o-l-d used by English-speakers in 1650 settles, for every object x, the conditions under which a given object x satisfies those tokens of g-o-l-d, then it settles the *extension* of those tokens of g-o-l-d—the set of objects of which those tokens of g-o-l-d are true.

On Dummett's interpretation of sense, (i) the sense of (tokens of) a predicate P at t is given to speakers at t as a grasp of the conditions under which a given object x satisfies (their tokens of) P, and (ii) the speakers' grasp at t of these conditions must be among (or, at least, settled by) the speakers' mental states at t, hence part of the *ex-use* of (their tokens of) P at t.[7] In short, the ex-use of (tokens of) a predicate P at time t determines

---

[6] Dummett 1991: 143. This interpretation of the sense of a predicate contrasts with P. T. Geach's view that the sense of a predicate is a function from the senses of names to the senses of sentences. See Dummett 1991: 141–5.

[7] Dummett emphasizes that "the function [of a theory of sense] is solely to present an analysis of the complex skill which constitutes mastery of a language, to display, in terms of what he may be said to know, just what it is that someone who possesses that mastery is able to do ... [and] not ... to describe any inner psychological mechanisms which may account for his having those abilities" (Dummett 1993b: 37). In this passage Dumment may *seem* at first look to be rejecting the claim that facts about

the *sense* of (tokens of) P at t. As we saw in the previous paragraph, if the *sense* of (tokens of) P at t settles, for every object x, the conditions under which a given object x satisfies (tokens of) P, it determines the *extension* of (tokens of) P at t. We can conclude that if the sense of (tokens of) P at t settles, for every object x, the conditions under which a given object x satisfies (tokens of) P, then its *ex-use* at t determines the *extension* of (tokens of) P at t.

A speaker's knowledge of the sense of a word is *explicit* only if she states and deliberately consults criteria for applying it. But no speaker is ever in a position to state non-circularly, for *every* word in her language, the criteria for correctly applying it. At any given time, a speaker's knowledge of the criteria for correctly applying some of her words must be *implicit*.

One might object that if a speaker does not state and deliberately consult criteria for applying her words, then it makes no sense to say, as Dummett does, that her application of her own words is *guided by* criteria. Dummett tries to answer this objection by tying implicit knowledge closely to linguistic behaviour: a speaker's implicit knowledge of how to ex-use her words, he writes, "shows itself partly by . . . a readiness to acknowledge as correct a formulation of that which is [implicitly] known when it is a presented" (Dummett 1993b: 96). According to Dummett, we can convince ourselves that a speaker's implicit knowledge shows itself in this way by reflecting on ordinary cases in which we come to accept explicit formulations of rules as formulations of rules we have been following. He reasons, for instance, as follows:

> If a speaker always uses the pairs 'I'/'me', 'he'/'him', 'she'/'her' and 'who'/'whom' correctly, but, never having been taught the rudiments of formal grammar, has never heard the words 'nominative' and 'accusative', can he be said to have an implicit grasp of the concepts they express? A statement of the rule he tacitly follows will involve an explicit formulation of those concepts and will necessarily be somewhat lengthy. Still, *we may credit the speaker with an implicit knowledge of that rule, provided that, when he understands the statement of it, he acknowledges it as accurately describing his existing practice.*   (Dummett 1991: 96, my emphasis)

the ex-uses of word tokens settle what senses those word tokens express, especially when such facts are assumed to be specifiable in purely physical or psychological terms. What he is rejecting, however, is that it is the function of a theory of sense to describe the particular physical and psychological facts about ex-uses of word tokens that actually settle the senses that those word tokens express, or to hypothesize more generally about how facts about ex-use settle the senses of word tokens.

In this passage Dummett suggests the *form* of a sufficient condition for a speaker to be credited with an implicit knowledge of a *grammatical* rule—roughly, the speaker's willingness to accept an explicit formulation of it. But if a speaker's implicit knowledge of a grammatical rule can be manifested by the speaker's willingness to accept an explicit formulation of it, it should also be possible for a speaker's knowledge of a *semantical* rule to be manifested by the speaker's willingness to accept an explicit formulation of it. For instance, consider the following observation, which parallels Dummett's observation about the grammatical rule:

If a speaker always uses 'gold' in such a way that it is satisfied by x if and only if x is (a bit of) the element with atomic number 79, but, never having been explicitly taught the rudiments of chemistry, has never heard the words 'atomic number', we may still credit the speaker with an implicit knowledge of that rule, provided that, when he understands the statement of it, he acknowledges it as accurately describing his existing practice.

More generally, if we accept Dummett's recipe for tying implicit knowledge to an explicit formulation of it, we should also accept the following weak constraint on our understanding of implicit knowledge of a semantical rule of the form "an object x satisfies A's (unambiguous) word w if and only if x is F".

> *Acceptance constraint*: Speaker A has implicit knowledge that an object x satisfies A's (unambiguous) word w if and only if x is F
> IF
> if A were presented in appropriate circumstances with an explicit statement that x satisfies w if and only if x is F, A understood that statement, and A carefully considered whether to accept it, then A would explicitly accept that x satisfies w if and only if x is F.

To apply this constraint, one would need to have some idea of when circumstances are *appropriate*, what it is for a person to *understand* a statement of the form "x satisfies w if and only if x is F", and how long and in what way she must *consider* such a statement for her acceptance of it to show that she has implicit knowledge of the conditions under which an object x satisfies her tokens of a given word. I shall not try to explicate these crucial terms of the acceptance constraint. To understand the acceptance constraint, however, it helps to see that it as a partial interpretation of Dummett's more fundamental *manifestability constraint* on a theory of implicit knowledge:

> *Manifestability constraint*: If a speaker's use of a given word is guided by her implicit knowledge of criteria for correctly applying it then there is some practical ability by means of which her implicit knowledge of those criteria for correctly applying it may be manifested.[8]

To apply this crucial constraint, we must have some idea of what it would take for a speaker's implicit knowledge of criteria for applying her terms to be manifested. The acceptance constraint presents the schematic form of one type of sufficient condition for a speaker's implicit knowledge of criteria for applying her terms to be manifested. More generally, Dummett argues that a speaker's implicit knowledge of criteria for applying a given word is manifested by her practical ability to use whole sentences in which that word occurs (Dummett 1993a: 38). It is a further question what sense of "practical ability" Dummett has in mind. I shall not try to explicate Dummett's use of this term, or to formulate, on his behalf, necessary and sufficient conditions for a speaker's use of a given word to be guided by her implicit knowledge of criteria for applying it in terms of her practical ability to use whole sentences in which that word occurs. I shall assume for now that we have some idea of how to apply the acceptance constraint, seen as a partial interpretation of the manifestability constraint, and raise difficulties for that assumption in §7.6.

In addition to the acceptance and manifestability constraints, there is a constraint that implicit knowledge must satisfy if it is to be compatible with (M). The roots of this third constraint are evident in Dummett's commentary on the proof that a plane intersects a cylinder in an ellipse. Dummett's commentary on that proof is designed in part to persuade us of his view that an individual's new applications of her words are *guided* by her implicit knowledge, which must therefore exist *prior to and independently of* those new applications. The criteria that she adopts as a result of accepting a proof or discovery should determine satisfaction conditions for her words that are extensionally equivalent to the satisfaction conditions determined for those words by the implicit knowledge of how to apply them that she

---

[8] Dummett's commitment to the manifestability constraint is evident in most of his writings, but see, in particular, Dummett 1993a: 37–8, 46, and 92.

had *prior to* her acquaintance with the proof or discovery. But any two criteria for applying a given word that agree extensionally with the criteria for applying it that are determined by the implicit knowledge of how to apply it that she had prior to her acquaintance with the proof or discovery will agree extensionally with each other. In short, according to Dummett, attributions of implicit knowledge to a speaker A must satisfy the

> *Extensional equivalence constraint*: If w is not ambiguous for A, A has implicit knowledge that x satisfies w if and only if x is F, and A has implicit knowledge that x satisfies w if and only if x is G, then x is F if and only if x is G.

7.4. Why Dummett's Constraints Rule out Options (1) and (2)

Dummett rejects Putnam's claim that the extension of English-speakers' tokens of g-o-l-d has not changed since the development of chemistry and the discovery that gold is the element with atomic number 79. To discredit Putnam's claim, Dummett constructs the following thought experiment:

Suppose that, when chemical analysis became possible, it had been discovered that there were two chemically distinct substances, one an element and the other a compound, both satisfying both the ordinary criteria for being gold and indistinguishable save by the most refined tests. Of those things ordinarily said to be made of gold, some were composed of one substance, some of the other, and a few of a mixture of the two. It is clear that the term 'gold' would then have become useless for theoretical chemistry, so long as it continued to be applied as before, e.g. in such a way that people now said that there were two kinds of gold. Of course, an alternative would have been to reserve the term 'gold', in its everyday application, for one or other of these two types of substance: since that would entail considerable upheaval in social practice, in view of the symbolic and economic significance of gold, it would be the more unlikely outcome of the discovery. *What is clear, at any rate, is that the word 'gold' did not, in advance of the introduction of a theory and technique of chemical analysis, have a meaning which determined the course to be followed.*   (Dummett 1978b: 428–9, my emphasis)

In this passage Dummett equates 'meaning' with 'sense'; the italicized conclusion of his thought experiment is that the word 'gold' did not, in advance of the introduction of a theory and technique of chemical analysis, have a *sense* that determined the course to be followed. Dummett makes this explicit as follows:

The thesis that the adoption of technical means for distinguishing gold from other substances involves some alteration in the sense of 'gold' ought not to be resisted. To resist it would be to hold it was determined in advance what we ought to have done if what were ordinarily classified as gold had proved to comprise two chemically distinct substances; and this is not the case.   (Dummett 1978b: 429)

Dummett concludes that the *sense* of 'gold' did not "determine in advance" the course to be followed after the development of chemical analysis. By this he means that in 1650, for instance, prior to the development of chemical analysis, the practical ability to apply tokens of g-o-l-d was not *guided by* implicit knowledge of *either* of the two rules for applying 'gold' that might be adopted after the development of chemical analysis. His thought experiment is intended to show that these two criteria for applying tokens of g-o-l-d determine extensions that are different from the extension determined by the criteria for applying tokens of g-o-l-d that English-speakers relied on in 1650. So the differences in criteria that guide speakers' use of tokens of g-o-l-d determine corresponding differences in the *extensions* of tokens of g-o-l-d. By the extensional equivalence constraint, then, we must conclude that in 1650, the sense of tokens of g-o-l-d did not determine that tokens of g-o-l-d in 1650 had either of the extensions that tokens of g-o-l-d come to have after the development of chemistry in the two alternative futures that Dummett describes.

The same goes for the gold–platinum thought experiment. Recall that members of both communities in the gold–platinum thought experiment take themselves to be *guided* by their understanding of how to apply their tokens of g-o-l-d—they each find their own applications of their tokens of g-o-l-d natural and inevitable. After about 1850, when their chemical discoveries become entrenched, they would not be persuaded by members of the other community that they have made any mistakes about the conditions under which an object x satisfies their tokens of g-o-l-d. Moreover, by hypothesis in 1650 the samples to which they actually applied their tokens of g-o-l-d, and their dispositions to apply such tokens in various different situations, were in all relevant respects the same. Hence, if the ex-use of tokens of g-o-l-d settles the senses of those tokens in 1650, as Dummett's theory assumes, there are no grounds for distinguishing between the senses that members of the two communities associated with their tokens of g-o-l-d in 1650. Nevertheless, members of the two linguistic communities reach different verdicts about the extensions of their respective tokens of g-o-l-d.

One might wonder *how* they could reach these different verdicts, if their ex-use of tokens of g-o-l-d in 1650 are by hypothesis the same. A key consideration, emphasized above in §6.8, is that whether or not an individual would accept or reject certain sentences may depend on the *order* in which he is presented with evidence and theories that are relevant to his evaluation of those sentences. It is plausible to suppose that Locke and Twin Locke (and other members of their respective linguistic communities, including jewellers and chemists) would have affirmed the sentence '*x* is gold if and only if *x* is (a bit of) the element with atomic number 79' if they had been presented with the same evidence and theories that English-speakers have encountered since 1650, *in the same order* in which they actually encountered them. But it is equally plausible to suppose that Locke and Twin Locke (and others in their respective linguistic communities) would have affirmed the sentence '*x* is gold if and only if *x* is either (a bit of) the element with atomic number 79 or (a bit of) the element with atomic number 78' if they had been presented with the same evidence and theories that Twin English-speakers have encountered since 1650, *in the same order* in which they actually encountered them. We have no independent grounds for saying that one of these presentations of evidence and theories is correct and the other is incorrect.[9]

---

[9] One might reply that even if Locke would accept the sentence '*x* is gold if and only if *x* is either (a bit of) the element with atomic number 79 or (a bit of) the element with atomic number 78' under certain conditions, he could nevertheless appeal to his *archetypical* applications of g-o-l-d, which would lead him to say, of a particular piece of platinum, "That is not gold." If so, then this recognitional capacity should lead him to *reject* the above sentence. The problem with this suggestion is that the order in which Locke and Twin Locke are presented with evidence and theories also affects their archetypical applications of g-o-l-d and the recognitional capacities they associate with g-o-l-d. It is plausible to suppose that if they had been presented with the same evidence and theories that English-speakers have encountered since 1650, *in the same order*, both Locke and Twin Locke would have *denied* that 'gold' is true of what they recognize to be a piece of platinum. But it is equally plausible to suppose that if they had been presented with the same evidence and theories that Twin English-speakers have encountered since 1650, *in the same order*, they would have *affirmed* that 'gold' is true of that same piece of platinum, which they would recognize to be a piece of what they call 'gold'. Again, we have no independent grounds for saying that one of these presentations of evidence and theory is correct and the other is incorrect.

If we focus just on the acceptance constraint, it may seem permissible to attribute to Locke and Twin Locke *both* (i) the implicit knowledge that x satisfies their tokens of g-o-l-d if and only if x is the element with atomic number 79, *and* (ii) the implicit knowledge that x satisfies their tokens of g-o-l-d if and only if x is the element with atomic number 78 or x is the element with atomic number 79. But these accounts of the conditions under which an object x satisfies their tokens of g-o-l-d are not coextensive. Hence the attributions of implicit knowledge just described do not satisfy the extensional equivalence constraint. Dummett's acceptance of (M), his account of sense, and the constraints he lays down on attributions of implicit knowledge together commit him to the conclusion that the sense that Locke and Twin Locke associated with tokens of g-o-l-d in 1650 rules out options (1) and (2). If we accept Dummett's premises, the only remaining option is (3).

7.5. Dummett's Version of Option (3)

But how shall we make sense of option (3) if we accept Dummett's premises? To answer this question, we must first look more closely at Dummett's understanding of the sense of the English word 'gold'. Dummett observes that

The criteria for the application of 'gold' used by ordinary speakers are sufficient for ordinary purposes, but . . . such speakers are willing to yield to the criteria employed by the experts, and unknown to themselves, in extraordinary cases. (Dummett 1978b: 427)

But Dummett argues that the sense of 'gold' for ordinary speakers is not different from the sense of 'gold' for the experts. How could this be? Dummett's answer is that

The meaning of the word 'gold', as a word of the English language, is fully conveyed neither by a description of the criteria employed by the experts nor by a description of those used by ordinary speakers; it involves both, and the grasp of the relationship between them.   (Dummett 1978b: 427)

If one accepts this view of the sense of 'gold', then to understand option (3) one must characterize the sense that Locke and Twin Locke associated with their tokens of g-o-l-d in 1650 partly in terms of a criterion (a rule, requirement, or test) that was actually *taken* by experts at that time to settle whether or not an object x falls in the extension of tokens of g-o-l-d at that time. It is not enough, however, to note that experts in 1650 take some criterion to settle whether or not an object x falls in the extension of tokens of g-o-l-d. If the criterion is to be part of the *sense* of that Locke and Twin Locke associated with their tokens of g-o-l-d in 1650, it must settle whether or not an object x falls in the extension of those tokens of g-o-l-d in a way that cannot be extensionally incorrect.

Dummett typically uses the word 'criterion' to mean a rule, requirement, or test that settles whether or not an object x falls in the extension of particular tokens of w in a way that cannot be extensionally incorrect. In contrast, I use the word 'criterion' to mean a rule, requirement, or test that speakers *take* to settle, for their purposes at a given time, whether or not an object x falls in the extension of tokens of w at that time, but that *may* be extensionally incorrect. To keep track of the distinction introduced in the previous paragraph, I shall say that a criterion for using tokens of w is *weak* if it may be extensionally incorrect, and *strong* if it cannot be extensionally incorrect. Hence what Dummett calls a criterion is what I shall call a *strong* criterion.

Suppose, provisionally, that there was a strong criterion for using tokens of g-o-l-d in 1650, that it was explicitly endorsed by those who counted in 1650 as experts in the proper use of tokens of g-o-l-d—jewellers and chemists, for instance—and that it is part of the characterization of the *sense* for tokens of g-o-l-d in 1650, a sense that settles, for every object x, whether or not x is in the extension of tokens of g-o-l-d, as used by English-speakers in 1650.[10] Suppose, also, that the ex-use of English-speakers' tokens of g-o-l-d in 1650 settled that those tokens expressed the sense just

---

[10] Let us not worry about what makes it the case that Locke's and Twin Locke's tokens of g-o-l-d in 1650 have the same sense as the experts' tokens of g-o-l-d in 1650. Dummett writes that "I shall not be deterred, by the thought that he may not know what a gasket is, from telling someone that the gasket in my car is leaking, any more than I am deterred by the fact that I myself do not know. The reason is that I know that he will know how to find out what a gasket is if he needs to. The occurrence of this word in our dialogue cannot be explained in terms of his idiolect or mine; it can only be explained by reference to the English language, ... A language is not to be characterized as a set of overlapping idiolects. Rather, an idiolect is constituted by the partial and imperfect grasp that a speaker has of a language." (Dummett 1991: 87) I shall not try to explain how this observation fits with Dummett's account of sense and implicit knowledge. The problem I raise below for Dummett-style versions of

hypothesized, and that the corresponding extension of tokens of g-o-l-d in 1650 is not identical with the extension of tokens of g-o-l-d today in either the English-speaking community or the Twin English-speaking community. Then it seems we can endorse what I'll call *Dummett's version of option (3)*, according to which

> (i) there is a sense S_1 of tokens of g-o-l-d in 1650 that is settled by the ex-uses of tokens of g-o-l-d in 1650,
>
> (ii) there is a sense S_2 of tokens of g-o-l-d on Earth today that is settled by the ex-uses of tokens of g-o-l-d on Earth today,
>
> (iii) there is a sense S_3 of tokens of g-o-l-d on Twin Earth today that is settled by the ex-uses of tokens of g-o-l-d on Twin Earth today, and
>
> (iv) each of S_1, S_2, and S_3 is different from the others, and determines an extension that is different from the extensions determined by the others.

If we accept (i)–(iv), we will conclude that the ex-uses of tokens of g-o-l-d in 1650 settle that those tokens have a determinate extension that is different from the extensions that tokens of g-o-l-d later come to have in the two linguistic communities of the gold–platinum thought experiment.[11]

7.6. Two Problems for Dummett's Version of Option (3)

As I see it, there are two main problems with Dummett's version of option (3). The first is that it conflicts with PJSSs and PJSEs on which we confidently rely. The second is that it leaves us without any clear practical criterion for sorting "good" PJSSs and PJSEs from "bad" ones, and hence

option (3) suggests a related problem for Dummett's view that a natural language is conceptually prior to particular idiolects, but I shall not take the time to investigate that problem in this book.

[11] A minor variant of this interpretation is that according to Dummett the sense of tokens of g-o-l-d was *indeterminate* in 1650 and therefore did not determine a classical extension for tokens of g-o-l-d in 1650. An apparent advantage of viewing the sense of tokens of g-o-l-d as indeterminate in 1650 is that by doing so we would be able to regard later uses of tokens of g-o-l-d in both linguistic communities of my gold–platinum thought experiment as *rationally permitted* by that indeterminate sense, and hence as (in a way) rationally *guided* by speakers' grasp of it. I shall not explore this interpretation of Dummett's account of the sense of 'gold' in 1650, however, because I think it faces essentially the same problems as what I call *Dummett's version of option (3)* and adds mostly unilluminating complications that make those problems more difficult to discern.

leaves us with no clear grasp of the distinction between strong and weak criteria for using our words. I'll discuss these problems in order, devoting a subsection to each.

The first problem

Recall that according to Dummett's acceptance constraint,

> Speaker A has implicit knowledge that an object x satisfies A's (unambiguous) word w if and only if x is F
>
> IF
>
> if A were presented in appropriate circumstances with an explicit statement that x satisfies w if and only if x is F, A understood that statement, and A carefully considered whether to accept it, then A would explicitly accept that x satisfies w if and only if x is F.

As I noted above, this acceptance constraint presents the schematic form of one type of sufficient condition for a speaker's implicit knowledge of criteria for applying her terms to be manifested. As I also noted above, the key terms in the acceptability constraint are unclear, so it is unclear exactly how we are to apply it. Even so, we know from the *extensional equivalence* constraint that neither 'x satisfies tokens of g-o-l-d in 1650 if and only if x is (a bit of) the element with atomic number 79' nor 'x satisfies tokens of gold in 1650 if and only if x is either (a bit of) the element with atomic number 78 or (a bit of) the element with atomic number 79' characterize the sense of tokens of g-o-l-d in 1650.

The extensional equivalence constraint therefore implies that while speakers of both linguistic communities *take* themselves to be using their respective tokens of g-o-l-d correctly as they develop their different accounts of the extension of their tokens of g-o-l-d and rely on their PJSSs and PJSEs across time for their own previous tokens of g-o-l-d and for tokens of g-o-l-d previously produced by other speakers in their respective linguistic communities, they gradually and unwittingly *change* the senses of their tokens of g-o-l-d. Without noticing, they gradually cease to be guided by the sense that guided speakers' uses of tokens of g-o-l-d in 1650. It is easy to see how *ordinary* users of tokens of g-o-l-d, who by assumption don't know the experts' criteria for applying those tokens, might make such a mistake. But in the circumstances described in the gold–platinum thought experiment, the extensional equivalence constraint implies that even the *experts* gradually and unwittingly change the senses of their tokens of g-o-l-d.

The first problem for Dummett is that the experts' PJSSs and PJSEs across time for tokens of g-o-l-d are among the PJSSs and PJSEs on which we confidently rely in our inquiries. We take these PJSSs and PJSEs to be *guided* by our *understanding* of the topics they concern. Dummett's theory of sense does not explain what this "guidance" or "understanding" consists in, but instead presents a theory of sense that is designed to explain a *different* sort of "guidance" and "understanding", one that *conflicts* with many of the PJSSs and PJSEs across time on which we confidently rely. If we were convinced that Dummett's theory of sense explains a sort of "guidance" and "understanding" that matters to our inquiries, we would have to reject a vast number of the PJSSs and PJSEs across time on which we confidently rely.

The second problem

As we saw in §7.3, according to Dummett's theory the sense of an expression at a given time is settled by the ex-uses of its tokens at that time. One might therefore suggest that even if members of the two linguistic communities gradually and unwittingly change the senses of their tokens of g-o-l-d, members of the two linguistic communities today could in principle *discover* and *correct* their alleged mistakes by reflecting more carefully on the differences between their ex-uses of tokens of g-o-l-d today and the ex-uses of tokens of g-o-l-d in 1650. Let us now try to evaluate this suggestion.

Note first that we can take the suggestion seriously only to the extent that we understand the assumption that (i)–(iv) of the previous section are true. But do we understand *how it could be* that the ex-uses of tokens of g-o-l-d at various times in the histories of the two linguistic communities in the gold–platinum thought experiment *settle* the senses of tokens of g-o-l-d at various times in such a way that (i)–(iv) are true? To address this question, we must face a very difficult and obscure question that lies behind it: What, if anything, settles whether or not a given criterion for using tokens of a word *w* is a *strong* criterion for using those tokens, not a *weak* one?[12] This

---

[12] This is one version of the question of what it is to follow a rule. I discuss this question at length in Ebbs 1997. For a sampling of other interpretations of the question and attempts to answer it, see Miller and Wright 2002 and Wilson 2006.

question is especially difficult for any theory which, like Dummett's, implies that a vast number of our PJSSs and PJSEs across time are mistaken. We can begin to see why the question is difficult for such theories if we focus not on deductions or discoveries, as Dummett usually does, but on *mistakes*. In many cases, the best indication of whether or not a speaker has made a mistake is his own linguistic behaviour—in particular, his willingness to acknowledge that he made a mistake, in part by accepting an explicit formulation of a criterion that he takes himself to have misapplied. For instance, a speaker who at time *t* writes the phrase 'for who the bell tolls' may later come to acknowledge that relative to the grammatical rule that he was implicitly committed to following at *t*, he *should* have written 'for whom the bell tolls'. As we saw above, Dummett himself emphasizes that "we may credit the speaker with an implicit knowledge of [such a] rule, provided that, when he understands the statement of it, he acknowledges it as accurately describing his existing practice" (Dummett 1991: 96). In such a case we take the speaker's acceptance of an explicit formulation of the grammatical rule to express his commitment to it when he wrote 'for who the bell tolls', hence to imply that he made a *mistake* when he wrote 'for who the bell tolls'.

The same kind of reasoning shows that in some cases a speaker's explicit formulation of a semantical rule licenses us to conclude that one of his previous utterances was false. Suppose (first) that a speaker utters "That's gold," while he was pointing at a piece of platinum, and (second) that a few moments later, after some prompting, he says, "My word 'gold' is satisfied by x if and only if x is (a bit of) the element with atomic number 79," thereby expressing a rule to which he takes himself to have been implicitly committed when he said, "That's gold," while pointing at that piece of platinum. Then he will rely on his PJSSs and PJSEs across time for the token of g-o-l-d that occurs in his earlier utterance of 'That's gold': if he learns that the piece of platinum is not (a bit of) the element with atomic number 79, he will conclude that his utterance of 'That's gold' was false.

This example shows that to take a speaker's acceptance of an explicit formulation of a semantical rule to express his own *prior* implicit commitment to that rule, we must accept at least some of the speaker's PJSSs and PJSEs across time for word tokens he used in the past. And it seems that even Dummett must concede that in some cases, at least, a speaker's acceptance of an explicit formulation of a semantical rule is indispensable to us, in the sense that without it we would lose our grip on which rules the speaker was implicitly committed to at some earlier time. In such cases we would lose our grip on which rules the speaker was implicitly committed to at some earlier time if we did not rely in part on the speaker's PJSSs and PJSEs across time for some of his previous word tokens.

Against this, one might think that a speaker's actual applications of his sentences and words at a given time *t* always settle what criteria we should use to evaluate those applications at *t* completely *independently* of his own later acceptance of an explicit formulation of a semantical rule to which he takes to have been implicitly committed at *t*. But this does not fit well with the fact (stressed in Chapter 6) that in the midst of our inquiries we trust our PJSSs and PJSEs across time more than we trust any prior judgements that a particular criterion for applying our words cannot be extensionally incorrect. If we are to base our understanding of how a speaker's commitment to a rule is manifested partly on our own commonsense judgements about when a speaker is committed to a given rule, then we must at least sometimes rely on a speaker's PJSSs and PJSEs across time.

This poses a second problem for the Dummettian claim that the experts' PJSSs and PJSEs across time for tokens of g-o-l-d are mistaken. The problem is that Dummett's constraints on implicit knowledge and sense don't provide us with any criteria for judging in particular cases whether or not our *new* applications of a word are properly guided by the (Dummettian) sense of our own previous tokens of the word. The constraints therefore leave us with no practical grip on when we can and when we cannot rely on a speaker's PJSSs and PJSEs across time. Dummett's constraints on implicit knowledge sense are supposed to motivate our acceptance of (i)–(iv). On closer scrutiny, however, it is unclear how they *could* do so, because they do not tell us exactly when we can and we cannot rely on our PJSSs and PJSEs across time.

One might think it is *easy* to identify the Dummettian strong criterion that guided English and Twin English-speakers' applications of their tokens of g-o-l-d in 1650—the criterion is '*x* satisfies a token of g-o-l-d in 1650 if and only if *x* dissolves in aqua regia'. But this thought overlooks the crucial distinction between taking a criterion such as 'dissolves in aqua regia' to be *strong*—to settle the extension of tokens of g-o-l-d in 1650 in a way that cannot be extensionally incorrect—and taking the criterion to be *weak*—to settle at best how such sentence tokens were *actually* evaluated in 1650, without thereby guaranteeing that the criterion is extensionally correct. As we saw in detail in Chapter 6, most chemists in 1650 were inclined to take 'dissolves in aqua regia' as a criterion for applying their tokens of g-o-l-d. But this observation does not by itself settle whether the criterion was weak or strong. And further details about their attitude to the criterion make it difficult, at best, to defend the view that the criterion was strong. When they confronted platinum for the first time, some were inclined to call it 'gold', but others hesitated, because they noticed, for instance, that samples of platinum have a different melting point than paradigm samples of what they called 'gold'. The gold–platinum thought experiment is plausible because there are different reasonable ways of weighing the various factors that implicitly or explicitly inclined a person to apply tokens of g-o-l-d to samples of platinum in 1650. The chemists and other speakers in the two different linguistic communities in the gold–platinum thought experiment apply their tokens of g-o-l-d differently, because, deliberately or not, they weigh those factors differently. And so far we have found no good reason to think that one way of weighing the factors is correct and the other incorrect. Again, as I emphasized in Chapter 6, we trust our PJSSs and PJSEs across time more than we trust any prior judgements that a particular criterion for applying our words cannot be extensionally incorrect. The chemists and other speakers in the two linguistic communities in my gold–platinum thought experiment illustrate this general point. Trusting their own PJSSs and PJSEs across time for their prior tokens of g-o-l-d, they take speakers on Earth and on Twin Earth to have been committed to different criteria for applying tokens of g-o-l-d in 1650. In short, we cannot discredit the PJSSs and PJSEs across time for tokens of g-o-l-d that are accepted on Earth or Twin Earth simply by noting that chemists in 1650 applied their tokens of g-o-l-d to an object x if and only if x dissolves in aqua regia, since we have good grounds for concluding that 'dissolves in aqua regia' was only a weak, defeasible criterion for applying tokens of g-o-l-d in 1650.

To satisfy Dummett's constraints on implicit knowledge and sense in a way that addresses this problem, we would need to find compelling *practical* grounds for concluding that a given speaker's application of our word tokens is guided by strong criteria and for distinguishing in practice between a speaker's strong and weak criteria for applying her word tokens. As the gold–platinum thought experiment shows, however, speakers *themselves* are unable to distinguish between strong and weak criteria for applying their word tokens in a way that meets the extensional equivalence requirement. One might hope to save the extensional equivalence requirement by second-guessing PJSSs and PJSEs that span very long periods of time. But that would not be enough. For PJSSs and PJSEs that span very long periods of time are sustained by chains of PJSSs and PJSEs that span very short periods of time. Hence one would have to second-guess PJSSs and PJSEs that span very short periods of time, including those we rely on in proofs, such as the proof that a plane intersects a cylinder in an ellipse. As we have seen, however, Dummett's constraints leave us without any concrete practical grounds for saying which, if any, of these PJSSs and PJSEs across time are doubtful. His constraints therefore leave us in the dark about when we should and when we should not trust our PJSSs and PJSEs—the very judgements that his theory of sense is supposed to explain and justify.

7.7. Field on Partial Extension

Let us now examine a very different version of option (3), according to which we should assign what Hartry Field (in Field 1973) calls *partial extensions* to tokens of g-o-l-d in 1650. To see how, let's suppose (first) that the ex-use of 'gold' in 1650 did not *rule out* either of the extensions that the members of the English-speaking community on Earth and the Twin English-speaking community on Twin Earth would later assign to it, (second) that *both* of these extension assignments are *acceptable*, and *equally* so. These suppositions look attractive after our discussion of the difficulties with Dummett's version of (3). Assuming that both extension assignments are acceptable, one might treat the set of gold things and the set of things that are either gold or platinum as *partial extensions* of 'gold' in 1650. To show how Field's idea of a partial extension can be used to clarify option (3), I shall also suppose that no *other* partial extension assignment is acceptable. Nothing we have said so far supports this supposition. For now I accept it without argument. I'll evaluate it in §7.10 below.

Field's idea of partial extension can be used to clarify the intuition that in 1650 some sentences containing occurrences of g-o-l-d are determinately true, others are determinately false, and the rest are neither determinately true nor determinately false. Field proposes that we explain what it is for a sentence to be determinately true or determinately false in terms of structures that correspond to a sentence:

a *structure* for a sentence is a function that . . . maps each predicate [in the sentence] into some set. The structure *m corresponds* to the sentence if . . . each predicate [in the sentence] partially signifies the set that *m* assigns to it. Now, for each structure *m*, we can apply the standard referential (Tarski-type) semantics to determine whether the sentence is *m-true* or *m-false*, i.e., true or false *relative to m*. (To say that the sentence is *m*-true is to say that it *would* be true if the . . . extensions of its terms were as specified by *m*.) We can then say that a sentence is [determinately] true (false) if it is *m*-true (*m*-false) for every structure *m* that corresponds to it. Putting all these definitions together, we get definitions of [determinate] truth and [determinate] falsity in terms of . . . partial signification.   (Field 1973: 477)

We can apply this strategy to describe the indeterminacy in the extension of tokens of g-o-l-d in 1650 as follows. What Field calls a *structure* for an English or Twin English sentence used in 1650 is fixed by a *translation* of that sentence into contemporary English. To simplify matters, let's suppose that the *only* English or Twin English predicate that is indeterminate in 1650 is 'gold'. If we translate this predicate as 'gold' in contemporary English, then we in effect assign the set of gold things as the partial extension of 'gold' in 1650. But if we translate 'gold' as 'either gold or platinum', we in effect assign the set of gold or platinum things to the partial extension of 'gold' in 1650. Assume that all *other* English and Twin English predicates that are ex-used in 1650 are translated into contemporary English homophonically, thereby in effect assigning to those predicates, as ex-used in 1650, the same extensions that the corresponding contemporary English words have. Holding these homophonic translations fixed, one structure for an English sentence used in 1650, structure m_1, is determined by adding the homophonic translation of 'gold' into contemporary English, and another structure for the sentence, structure m_2, is determined by adding the translation of 'gold' as 'either gold or platinum'. Finally, let's suppose that both m_1 and m_2 *correspond* to any English or Twin English sentence containing tokens of g-o-l-d ex-used in 1650, in the sense that they are each equally acceptable assignments of partial extensions to the respective tokens of g-o-l-d in the sentences, and (again, without argument) that no *other* partial extension assignments, and hence no other structures, are acceptable.

Now suppose that in 1650 Locke said, "This is gold," pointing at his gold ring. Since a gold ring is also either gold or platinum, the sentence 'This is gold', as used in 1650 by Locke as he pointed at his gold ring, is both m_1-true and m_2-true, and hence by Field's criterion *determinately true*. Suppose that in 1650 Locke said, "This is gold," pointing at a bar of iron pyrites. Since a bar of iron pyrites is neither gold nor platinum, the sentence 'This is gold', as used in 1650 by Locke as he pointed at the bar of iron pyrites, is both m_1-false and m_2-false, hence by Field's criterion *determinately false*. Finally, consider again the case described above: in 1650, Locke says, "There's gold in those hills," while pointing at hills in South Africa that contain platinum but no gold. Under these circumstances, the sentence 'There's gold in those hills' is m_1-false and m_2-true, and hence by Field's criterion, neither determinately true nor determinately false. The same points hold for Twin Locke's utterances of these sentences. The only difference is that the ring and the hills to which Twin Locke refers while uttering those sentences are twins of the ring and the hills to which Locke refers on Earth.

7.8. A Field-Style Argument against Options (1) and (2)

Field's strategy for assigning partial extensions to indeterminate predicates does not tell us how to interpret the symbol E_1 if we adopt option (3). I propose that we use Field's concepts of *partial extension, structure, determinate truth*, and *determinate falsity* to define two different sets—T_1, the set of objects of which tokens of g-o-l-d are determinately true in 1650, and F_1, the set of objects of which tokens of g-o-l-d are determinately false in 1650. T_1 and F_1 are well defined only if it is determinate which partial extension assignments for 'gold' are acceptable. We supposed that the set of *gold* things and the set of *either gold or platinum* things are the *only* acceptable partial extension assignments for the English and Twin English word 'gold' as it was used in 1650. I'll question this assumption below, after I explain how one might combine it with Field's methods to reject options (1) and (2) for the gold–platinum thought experiment.

Let $E_1 = <T_1, F_1>$. Under this interpretation, E_1 is not an extension, but it is like an extension in one crucial respect: it settles which objects tokens of g-o-l-d are determinately true of in 1650, and which objects tokens of g-o-l-d are determinately false of in 1650. We can call E_1 *the determinate core of an extension*, or an *extension core*, for short. Similarly, let $E_2 = <T_2, F_2>$, where T_2 is the set of objects of which tokens of g-o-l-d are determinately true in English today, and F_2 is the set of objects of which tokens of g-o-l-d are determinately false in English today. Finally, let $E_3 = <T_3, F_3>$, where T_3 is the set of objects of which tokens of g-o-l-d are determinately true in Twin English today, and F_3 is the set of objects of which tokens of g-o-l-d are determinately false in Twin English today. (Note that if tokens of g-o-l-d have an extension in English today, the extension is T_2, and if tokens of g-o-l-d have an extension in Twin English today, it is T_3.)

Under this interpretation of the diagram, $E_2 \neq E_3$, which is to say that $<T_2, F_2> \neq <T_3, F_3>$. Ordered pairs are identical just in case their first members are identical and their second members are identical. In this case, $T_2 \neq T_3$, since 'gold' is determinately true of platinum things in Twin English today, but 'gold' is not determinately true of platinum things in English today; moreover, $F_2 \neq F_3$, since 'gold' is determinately false of platinum things in English today, but 'gold' is not determinately false of platinum things in Twin English today.

From this interpretation of 'E_1', 'E_2', and 'E_3', it follows that we must reject both option (1), according to which $E_1 = E_2$ and $E_1 \neq E_3$, and option (2), according to which $E_1 \neq E_2$ and $E_1 = E_3$. Here's why. $E_1 = E_2$ amounts to $<T_1, F_1> = <T_2, F_2>$. But $F_1 \neq F_2$. In particular, tokens of g-o-l-d are determinately false of platinum things in English today, but tokens of g-o-l-d are not determinately false of platinum things in English in 1650. Hence $<T_1, F_1> \neq <T_2, F_2>$, so (by definition) $E_1 \neq E_2$. Similarly, $E_1 = E_3$ amounts to $<T_1, F_1> = <T_3, F_3>$. But $T_1 \neq T_2$. In particular, in English in 1650 tokens of g-o-l-d are *not* determinately true of platinum things, but in Twin English today, tokens of g-o-l-d are determinately true of platinum things. Hence $<T_1, F_1> \neq <T_3, F_3>$, so (by definition) $E_1 \neq E_3$.

By conjoining these results we arrive at a version of option (3), according to which $E_1 \neq E_2$ and $E_1 \neq E_3$. Hence it seems we can use Field's concepts of *partial extension, structure, determinate truth*, and *determinate falsity* to define extension cores $<T_1, F_1>$, $<T_2, F_2>$, $<T_3, F_3>$, whose assignment to E_1, E_2, and E_3, respectively, yields a version of option (3).

7.9. A Field-Style Defence of Option (3)

Let us now see if we can defend option (3), interpreted in the way just described. We were driven to reject options (1) and (2) in part by (M), the entrenched metaphysical assumption that the ex-use of word tokens determines their extension. Recall that in the diagram of §6.5, 'E_1' is the only symbol assigned to tokens of g-o-l-d during the period *before* the accidental uncovering of large amounts of platinum in the Twin Earth community—the period when by supposition the ex-use of tokens of g-o-l-d is the same in English and Twin English. If 'E_1' represents an *extension* assignment, the standard presupposition that *the ex-use of tokens of g-o-l-d determines their extensions* is built into the diagram. But in the previous section we saw that we can interpret 'E_1' as the *extension core* $<T_1, F_1>$, where T_1 is the set of objects of which tokens of g-o-l-d were determinately true in 1650, and F_1 is the set of objects of which tokens of g-o-l-d were determinately false in 1650. If 'E_1' is interpreted in this way, then instead of the presupposition that *the ex-use of tokens of g-o-l-d in 1650 determines their extensions*, a slightly weaker metaphysical presupposition is built into the diagram—the presupposition that *the ex-use of tokens of g-o-l-d in 1650 determines their extension cores—the (identical) sets of objects which tokens of g-o-l-d, as ex-used in 1650, are determinately true of and the (identical) sets of objects which tokens of g-o-l-d, as ex-used in 1650, are determinately false of.*

More generally, if we adopt my proposed Field-style interpretation of the standard diagram of options for the gold–platinum thought experiment, we should replace (M) with the following metaphysical principle for predicates

(M′) For any two word-tokens w and w' such that the utterance or inscription of w occurs at some time t before the utterance or inscription of w', a PJSE *across time* for w and w' is true only if for some set E,

(a) E is the extension core of both w and of w', and

(b) the totality of facts about the ex-use of w at times prior to or identical with t (hence prior to the utterance or inscription of w') determines that E is the extension core of w.

This seems to be the strongest metaphysical principle that we can endorse if we accept the standard diagram of options for the gold–platinum thought experiment.[13] If we adopt (M′), then we must reject options (1) and (2) of the gold–platinum thought experiment for the reasons sketched in the previous section. In particular, if w is a token of g-o-l-d that Locke uttered, and $w′$ is a token of g-o-l-d that I utter today when I make a PJSE for w, then clause (a) fails, since there is no E that is the extension core of w and the extension of $w′$. Similarly, if w is a token of g-o-l-d that Twin Locke uttered and $w′$ is a token of g-o-l-d that my twin on Twin Earth utters today, then clause (a) fails, since there is no E that is the extension core of w and the extension of $w′$.

One might try to defend option (3), under the proposed Field-style interpretation, by appeal to (M′). The gold–platinum thought experiment might be taken to show that m_1 and m_2 (as defined in §7.7) are equally acceptable structures for sentences used in 1650 that contain tokens of g-o-l-d. It would then be tempting to conclude that any acceptable interpretation of tokens of g-o-l-d in 1650, whether on Earth or Twin Earth, must identify their core extensions—the sets of objects of which those tokens were then determinately true and the sets of objects of which they were then determinately false.

7.10. A Problem for the Field-Style Defence of Option (3)

Although this Field-style defence of option (3) may seem more plausible than a Dummett-style defence of option (3), it faces similar problems. To see why, recall that T_1 and F_1 are well defined only if it is determinate which structures correspond with sentence tokens that contained tokens of g-o-l-d

---

[13] My goal in proposing (M′) is not to provide an accurate interpretation of Field's position in Field 1973, but to use his methods to articulate the metaphysical intuition behind option (3). It is not clear that Field himself accepts (M′). He writes, for instance, that "[Newton's term] 'mass' would have undergone a simple refinement rather than a double refinement if everyone had followed Einstein's example in adhering to (4R) [which interprets 'mass' as 'relativistic mass']" (Field 1973: 479). This suggests that, according to Field, what counts as an acceptable partial extension assignment for a term T as used at some time t, and hence which objects are elements of what I call the core-extension of T at t, depends *not only* on the ex-use of T up to and including t, but *also* on how members of the relevant linguistic community *later* interpret T. If this is indeed what Field believes, then he is committed to rejecting (M′). And if he rejects (M′), then the account of option (3) that I offer in this section applies Field's technical apparatus in ways that he himself would not apply it—namely, to try to articulate the metaphysical intuition behind option (3).

in 1650. To illustrate my proposed Field-style interpretation of option (3), in the previous section I supposed that it is somehow settled which partial extension assignments to tokens of g-o-l-d in 1650 are acceptable. I gave no argument for this supposition, and noted that it does not follow from my thought experiment. In the context of the proposed Field-style defence of option (3), this supposition becomes especially important. The crucial point is that the proposed Field-style defence of option (3) assumes that the totality of facts about the ex-use of tokens of g-o-l-d at times prior to and included in the year 1650 uniquely determines the *core extension* of tokens of g-o-l-d in 1650—the set of objects of which those tokens were determinately true and the set of objects of which they were determinately false in 1650. Since core extension is defined in terms of acceptable *partial extensions*, this assumption implies that the totality of facts about the ex-use of tokens of g-o-l-d at times prior to and included in the year 1650 uniquely determines which partial extensions for tokens of g-o-l-d in 1650 are acceptable and which ones are not. If the totality of facts about the ex-use of tokens of g-o-l-d at times prior to and included in the year 1650 leaves it *indeterminate* which partial extension assignments to those tokens are acceptable, then, given (M'), the *core extension* of tokens of g-o-l-d in 1650 is undefined. Hence the proposed Field-style interpretation of option (3) stands or falls with the assumption that the totality of facts about the ex-use of tokens of g-o-l-d at times prior to and included in the year 1650 uniquely determines which partial extensions for tokens g-o-l-d in 1650 are acceptable and which ones are not.

The problem is that this assumption is no more plausible than the assumption that the totality of facts about the ex-use of tokens of g-o-l-d at times prior to and included in the year 1650 uniquely determines a *classical* extension for tokens of g-o-l-d in 1650. If the gold–platinum thought experiment discredits the latter assumption, similar thought experiments will discredit the former assumption. To see why, it is enough to focus on how the proposed Field-style defence of option (3) would define the first component of the core extension of tokens of g-o-l-d in 1650, namely, T_1, the set of objects of which tokens of g-o-l-d are determinately true in 1650. Suppose we initially conclude that according to Field's theory of partial extensions, the gold–platinum thought experiment implies that T_1 is the set of all and only gold things—all and only bits of the element with atomic number 79. To discredit this specification of T_1, it is enough to describe two linguistic communities whose ex-uses of tokens of g-o-l-d are identical to the ex-uses of tokens of g-o-l-d on Earth until sometime in the nineteenth century, when scientists in the two communities examine paradigm instances to which they apply their tokens of g-o-l-d, but the samples that are central and salient for the scientists are different in the two communities, and so scientists in one of the communities conclude that their tokens of g-o-l-d apply to *any* bit of the element with atomic number 79, whereas scientists in the other community conclude that their tokens of g-o-l-d apply not to any bit of the element with atomic number 79, but *only* to any bit of the naturally occurring *isotope* of the element with atomic number 79.[14] As before, we can stipulate that members of the two communities encounter each other *after* scientists in the two communities arrive at their respective analyses of the stuff to which they apply tokens of g-o-l-d, and they see no conflict between their scientists' conclusions. Moreover, members of both communities trust their PJSEs across time for tokens of g-o-l-d, and therefore assign different extensions to tokens of g-o-l-d used in 1650. Faced with this scenario, it seems we must conclude that both of these partial extension assignments are acceptable, and hence that contrary to our initial supposition, T_1 is *not* the set of all and only gold things—all and only bits of the element with atomic number 79—but the set of all and only bits of the naturally occurring *isotope* of the element with atomic number 79.

But now we can easily describe a scenario that discredits this new speculation about T_1. For instance, we can describe two communities whose ex-uses of tokens of g-o-l-d are the same at least up to the end of 1650, but whose scientists later come to different conclusions about how *much* of the naturally occurring isotope of the element with atomic number 79 counts as an object of which tokens of g-o-l-d are true. The scientists in one of the two communities conclude that some clusters of atoms of the naturally occurring isotope of the element with atomic number 79 are too *small* to be in the extension of their tokens of g-o-l-d, whereas the scientists in the other community conclude that *no* portion of such atoms is too small to be in the extension of that community's tokens of g-o-l-d—even a single such atom is in the extension of that community's tokens of g-o-l-d.

[14] This is a variation on a thought experiment in Donnellan 1983. Donnellan describes a possible future in which scientists take themselves to have discovered that their tokens of g-o-l-d are true of x if and only if x is a bit of a particular isotope of the element with atomic number 79.

Again, we may suppose that members of both communities trust their PJSEs across time for tokens of g-o-l-d, and accordingly assign different extensions to tokens of g-o-l-d used in 1650. Field's theory then apparently implies that T_1 is not the set of all and only bits of the naturally occurring isotope of the element with atomic number 79, but the set of all and only large enough *portions* of the naturally occurring isotope of the element with atomic number 79.

And now we can easily exploit the vagueness of 'large enough' to construct a thought experiment that discredits this new speculation about T_1. More generally, it is plausible to suppose that for *any* claim that the totality of facts about the ex-use of tokens of a given orthographic word type w at times prior to or identical with some given time t uniquely determines that the core extension of tokens of w at t is identical with some *specified* set S, we can construct a thought experiment that discredits the claim. The problem is that given (M'), the core extension of tokens of w at t is fixed only if the range of acceptable partial extension assignments for tokens of w at t is fixed by the totality of facts about the ex-use of w at times prior to or identical with t. But the range of acceptable partial extension assignments for tokens of w at t is *not* fixed by the totality of facts about the ex-use of w at times prior to or identical with t. To suppose that the totality of facts about the ex-use of w at times prior to or identical with t fixes a *core* extension for tokens of w at t one must suppose that this totality of facts uniquely determines the boundary between acceptable and unacceptable partial extension assignments, even if we cannot always tell where that boundary lies. But the thought experiments show that this supposition is no more plausible than the assumption that the totality of facts about the ex-use of w at times prior to or identical with t uniquely determines w's (classical) extension. Hence the Field-style version of option (3), whose main principle, (M'), rests on this assumption, is not a stable and satisfying response to the thought experiments.

Some philosophers assume that languages have built-in *rules* that set constraints on acceptable partial extension assignments. For instance, the super-valuation approach to vague predicates, such as 'heap', 'bald', and 'thin', uses *meaning postulates* to settle the boundary between accept- able and unacceptable partial extension assignments. To rule out what is called "higher order" vagueness—vagueness in the boundary between

acceptable and unacceptable partial extension assignments to vague predicates—proponents of the super-valuation approach simply *adopt* meaning
postulates that settle whether or not a partial extension assignment is
acceptable. According to the Field-style version of option (3) that we
are considering here, however, meaning postulates are irrelevant: the
ex-use of a predicate must *by itself* settle the boundary between acceptable and unacceptable partial extension assignments.[15] But we have now
seen that if the ex-use of a predicate does not uniquely determine its
classical extension, the ex-use of the predicate does not uniquely determine the boundary between acceptable and unacceptable partial extension
assignments, either.

Option (3) has content only if we suppose that totality of facts about
the ex-use of tokens of g-o-l-d at times prior to and included in the year
1650 settles something that we could plausibly regard as an interpretation
of E_1 on the standard diagram for the gold–platinum thought experiment.
As we have seen, however, if we adopt Dummett's approach, we are
left with no principled way to specify the implicit rules that guide a
speaker's use of an expression, and thereby settle its supposed sense and
extension at a given time. Similarly, if we adopt the Field-style approach,
we are left with no principled way to settle which objects a particular
expression is determinately true of or determinately false of at a given
time. Like any version of option (3), Dummett's version of option (3) and
the Field-style version of option (3) both imply that we must suspend
or reject our PJSEs across time for tokens of g-o-l-d. We could perhaps

---

[15] One might be inclined to agree with Field that

the vagueness of our semantic terms serves no useful purposes, and as semantic theory develops we can
expect these terms to become more precise. On some ways of making them precise, [a claim near the
perceived borderline] will be absolutely true, on other ways of making them precise, it will not be
absolutely true but will have an extremely high degree of truth … The fact that there is no fact of the
matter as to whether [such a claim] is absolutely true, as we currently use 'absolutely true', is simply
due to the fact that our current use of 'absolutely true' is imprecise.   (Field 1974: 227)

This kind of response does not address the problem raised in the text. According to the particular
application of Field's approach that I am challenging, what a word token w ex-used at t is determinedly
true of is well defined only if

(*) the set of acceptable partial extensions for w at t is uniquely determined by the totality of facts
about the ex-use of w at times prior to or identical with t.

But the thought experiments I sketched show that the truth value of (*) cannot plausibly be settled
just by stipulating new, more precise meanings for 'acceptable', 'partial extension', and 'uniquely
determined'.

accept this extreme consequence if principles such as (M) or (M′) provided us with plausible alternative criteria for sameness of extension or partial extension across time. As we have seen, however, they do not. To adopt option (3) is to lose one's grip on the very idea of sameness of extension across time.

8

The Puzzle Diagnosed and Dissolved

8.1. The Puzzle Reviewed

We saw in Chapter 6 that the token-and-ex-use model of words underlies the apparently unobjectionable intuition that

(M) For any two word tokens w and w' such that the utterance or inscription of w occurs at some time t before the utterance or inscription of w', a PJSE *across time* for w and w' is true only if for some set E,

    (a) E is the extension of both w and w', and

    (b) the totality of facts about the ex-use of w at times prior to or identical with t (hence prior to the utterance or inscription of w') determines that E is the extension of w

where the only restriction on what counts as a fact about the ex-use of a word token w is that the fact can in principle be described without using any sentence that expresses a PIW, PJSS, or PJSE for w. Guided by the token-and-ex-use the conception of words, we feel sure that (M) provides the only possible framework for legitimating our PJSSs and PJSEs. But if we accept (M) we are committed to the following diagram of options for the gold–platinum thought experiment:

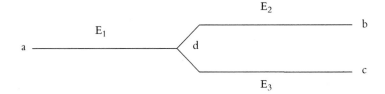

Line ab represents the ex-use of tokens of g-o-l-d in our English-speaking community, line ac represents the ex-use of tokens of g-o-l-d in the Twin English-speaking community, and line ad, where lines ab and ac overlap, represents the supposition that before the accidental uncovering of large amounts of platinum on Twin Earth in 1650—an event represented by point d—members of the two communities have virtually the same dispositions to ex-use tokens of g-o-l-d, associate the same mental states with their tokens of g-o-l-d, and bear the same relations to the things and substances in their environment, provided that these dispositions, states, and relations are described independently of future developments in either linguistic community. 'E_1', 'E_2', and 'E_3' represent the extension of tokens of g-o-l-d at various points in the histories of the two communities.

Recall that by hypothesis the two communities are isolated from each other until after the development of analytical chemistry in the two communities. Nevertheless, the standard diagram of options provides only one symbol, 'E_1', that represents the extension of tokens of g-o-l-d during the period *before* the accidental uncovering of large amounts of platinum on Twin Earth—the period when by supposition the ex-use of tokens of g-o-l-d is the same in both communities. In this way the standard commitment to (M), and hence to a token-and-ex-use conception of words, is built into the diagram.[1] The rest of the diagram is straightforward: the extension of tokens of g-o-l-d in the actual English-speaking community after the branching is represented by 'E_2', and the extension of tokens of g-o-l-d in the counterfactual English-speaking community after the branching is represented by 'E_3'.

Given this diagram and the natural assumption that $E_2 \neq E_3$—the extension of tokens of g-o-l-d is different in the two linguistic communities after the branching—it appears that there are only three options for characterizing the extension of tokens of g-o-l-d before the branching: either (1) $E_1 = E_2$ and $E_1 \neq E_3$, or (2) $E_1 = E_3$ and $E_1 \neq E_2$, or (3) $E_1 \neq E_2$ and $E_1 \neq E_3$.[2] In Chapter 6 we saw that options (1) and (2) are arbitrary

---

[1] Recall that I understand the ex-use of tokens of g-o-l-d in 1650 to encompass all facts about tokens of g-o-l-d in 1650 that can in principle be stated without using any sentence that expresses a PIW, PJSS, or PJSE.

[2] As I noted in Chapter 6, this abstract characterization of the options (but not my thought experiment or my interpretation of the options) is also adapted from Larson and Segal 1995: 534.

and unacceptable for symmetrical reasons. And in Chapter 7 we saw that to adopt any version of option (3) is to suspend or reject one's PJSEs and thereby to lose one's grip on the very idea of sameness of extension across time.

The problems with the options (1)–(3) stem from our commitment to (M), and to token-and-ex-use conceptions of words more generally, which sets the standard framework for our attempts to explain or justify our PJSSs and PJSEs. Hence we face a puzzle: it seems that none of our options—none of (1)–(3)—is acceptable. I see the puzzle as a *reductio ad absurdum* of the token-and-ex-use model of words, which leads us to accept (M) and the standard diagram of options.

In this chapter I shall elucidate the PJSS-based conception of words by showing how it dissolves the apparent puzzle raised by the gold–platinum thought experiment. I shall also investigate and reject the superficially similar idea that the extension of tokens of a PJSS-based word type *w* at time *t* can be settled by facts about how other tokens of *w* are ex-used at some time after *t*.

8.2. The First Gold–Platinum Thought Experiment and the Context Principle

Recall that at the heart of the PJSS-based conception of words lies the *context principle: never ask for the word type of a word token in isolation, but only in the context of one's own PIWs and PJSSs for that word token and other speakers' PIWs and PJSSs for that word token, if such judgements exist.* To accept the context principle is to think of word types in such a way that one has no conception of the word type of a given word token apart from one's own PIWs and PJSSs for that word token and other speakers' PIWs and PJSSs for that word token, if such judgements exist. I explained in §4.5 how we can explicate words in accordance with the context principle by defining equivalence classes of word tokens, or marks. For present purposes, however, we need not be explicit about what words are on the PJSS-based conception; it is enough to note that the proper explication of words is constrained by the context principle.

How will we identify and individuate the word types used by the two linguistic communities of the first gold–platinum thought experiment if we adopt the context principle? To address this question we must first highlight the relevant suppositions of the thought experiment:

(i) Members of both linguistic communities trust their PIWs, PJSSs, and PJSEs across time for their respective tokens of g-o-l-d, and continue to do so even after they learn of each other's diverging ex-uses of their tokens of those words.

(ii) The two linguistic communities are isolated from each other until after the development of chemistry in each community.

(iii) Sometime after their contemporaneous development of chemistry, members of the two communities encounter each other and come to make PIWs, PJSSs, or PJSEs for some of each others' word tokens.

(iv) After members of the two communities encounter each other and come to make PIWs, PJSSs, or PJSEs for some of each other's word tokens, they distinguish between the English word 'gold' and the Twin English word 'gold', and take the two words to have different extensions.

If we adopt the PJSS-based conception of words, then supposition (iii) is crucial to the intelligibility of the gold–platinum thought experiment.[3] The crucial consideration is that if we (English-speakers) supposed, contrary to supposition (iii), that the Twin Earth community were forever isolated from us, then our understanding of the Twin English would be exhausted by our stipulations about how members of the Twin English-speaking community ex-use their word tokens. But the context principle implies that we have no PJSS-based conception of word types used by members of the Twin English-speaking community apart from the PIWs, PJSSs, and PJSEs we come to make once we encounter them for the first time. In particular, our grasp on the word types they used in 1650 is dependent on PIWs, PJSSs, and PJSEs that link tokens of our word types to tokens of their word types, both at a given time and across time. In short, the context principle implies that our grasp on the word types used by members of the Twin English-speaking linguistic community in 1650 is dependent on their PIWs, PJSSs, and PJSEs across time.

[3] I am indebted to Robert Gooding-Williams for helping me to see the importance of adding supposition (iii) to my gold–platinum thought experiment.

The principle also implies that our grasp on word types used by members of our English-speaking linguistic community in 1650 is dependent on our PJSSs and PJSEs across time, and those of other members of the English-speaking community, through chains of such judgements that in some cases extend from the present to at least as far back as 1650. Given the context principle, supposition (i) licenses us to trust the PJSSs and PJSEs of members of both linguistic communities for their respective tokens of g-o-l-d, provided there are no special reasons for revising or rejecting those PJSSs and PJSEs. Suppositions (ii)–(iv) together suggest (and I shall hereafter assume) that there are no such reasons in the story for revising or rejecting either of the two community's PJSSs and PJSEs across time. Hence given the context principle and suppositions (i)–(iv), we may trust the PJSSs and PJSEs across time in the two linguistic communities.

For instance, in our English-speaking community today, speakers make PJSSs and PJSEs across time for Locke's tokens of g-o-l-d, and in the Twin English-speaking community today, speakers make PJSSs and PJSEs across time for Twin Locke's tokens of g-o-l-d. We group these tokens into different PJSS-based word types. Hence we (English-speakers) take for granted that the extension of *our* PJSS-based word type 'gold' is the same as the extension of Locke's PJSS-based word type 'gold', and they (Twin English-speakers) take for granted that the extension of *their* PJSS-based word type 'gold' is the same as the extension of Twin Locke's PJSS-based word type 'gold'. By the context principle and suppositions (i)–(iv) of the thought experiment, we may simultaneously accept our PIWs, PJSSs, and PJSEs for Locke's PJSS-based word type 'gold' and the Twin-English speakers' PIWs, PJSSs, and PJSEs for Twin Locke's PJSS-based word type 'gold'.

This will seem impossible to us if we accept the token-and-ex-use model of word types, and principles such as (M) that follow from it. Since by hypothesis Locke's tokens of g-o-l-d and Twin Locke's tokens of g-o-l-d have exactly the same ex-use, the token-and-ex-use model of word types implies that Locke's tokens of g-o-l-d and Twin Locke's tokens of g-o-l-d are tokens of the same token-and-ex-use word type. As we have seen, this consequence of the token-and-ex-use model of word types is built into the standard diagram of options for describing the gold–platinum thought experiment. If we adopt the context principle, however, we will not take the facts about ex-use of tokens of g-o-l-d to settle questions about whether two word tokens of the same PJSS-based word type. We will instead base our identifications of and distinctions between word types on our PIWs, PJSSs, and PJSEs. And, as we have seen, our PIWs, PJSSs, and PJSEs in the thought experiment lead to the conclusion that Locke's tokens of g-o-l-d and Twin Locke's tokens of g-o-l-d are tokens of different *PJSS-based* word types.

Hence if we adopt the PJSS-based conception of words, we can accept a new diagram of options for the thought experiment:

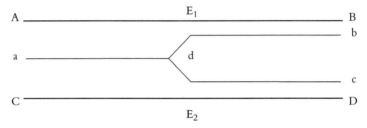

where line AB represents the PJSS-based word type 'gold' in the English-speaking community, line CD represents the PJSS-based word type 'gold' in the Twin English-speaking community, E_1 represents the extension of the PJSS-based word type 'gold' in the English-speaking community, E_2 represents the extension of the PJSS-based word type 'gold' in the Twin English-speaking community, and, as before, line ab represents the ex-use of tokens of g-o-l-d in our English-speaking community, line ac represents the ex-use of tokens of g-o-l-d in the Twin English-speaking community. This diagram of the options for the gold–platinum thought experiment leaves open the possibility that we will accept the PIWs, PJSSs, and PJSEs made by members of the English-speaking community *and* the PIWs, PJSSs, and PJSEs made by members of the Twin English-speaking community. In short, if we reject the token-and-ex-use model of word types and adopt the PJSS-based conception of words, we will come to see that there is no conflict between the two communities' PIWs, PJSSs, and PJSEs.

8.3. The Second Gold–Platinum Thought Experiment

To understand the new diagram of options for the gold–platinum thought experiment, it helps to consider a superficially similar thought experiment in which tokens of g-o-l-d that come to have different ex-uses in two isolated communities are all nevertheless tokens of the same PJSS-based word type.[4] Suppose that on Earth in 1651 the population of English-speakers divides into two large groups that are from then on for many years completely isolated from each other. In one of the groups the ex-use of tokens of g-o-l-d is virtually the same as the ex-use of tokens of g-o-l-d in the actual English-speaking community, and in the other the ex-use of tokens of g-o-l-d is like the ex-use of tokens of g-o-l-d in the Twin English-speaking community on the Twin Earth described in the first gold–platinum thought experiment (described in §6.4). Suppose also that just as on Earth and Twin Earth in the first thought experiment, members of the two communities rely on their PIWs, PJSSs, and PJSEs across time for their respective tokens of g-o-l-d. Finally, suppose that the isolation between the two groups ends, and they learn that their PIWs, PJSSs, and PJSEs across time for tokens of g-o-l-d extend back to tokens of g-o-l-d used by members of the English-speaking community on Earth before the split.

In this case members of the two groups are not likely to relinquish their PIWs, PJSSs, or PJSEs across time for their respective tokens of g-o-l-d. They will take themselves to *disagree* about the extension of a single PJSS-based word type 'gold', and try to persuade each other of their views. Even if they fail to come to an agreement about the extension of their PJSS-based word type 'gold', they will not necessarily reject their PIWs, PJSSs, or PJSEs across time for its tokens: members of each group may stand by their judgements about the extension of their PJSS-based word type 'gold' and reject those of the other group.

This thought experiment therefore contrasts with the first gold–platinum thought experiment, in which by hypothesis the two linguistic communities are isolated until after their contemporaneous discovery of chemistry and their subsequent accounts of the extensions of their respective tokens of g-o-l-d. The context principle implies that in the first thought experiment the tokens of g-o-l-d used by members of the two communities are tokens of different PJSS-based word types. But in the second thought experiment by hypothesis the divergent ex-uses of tokens of g-o-l-d are linked by chains of PIWs, PJSSs, and PJSEs to tokens of a single unambiguous PJSS-based

[4] This thought experiment is a development of one sketched in Ebbs 2000: n. 27.

word type that was used prior to 1651, when the English-speaking community split into two isolated ones. Let's suppose, in addition, that there are no contextually salient reasons for revising those PIWs, PJSSs, or PJSEs. Then in the second thought experiment, unlike in the first, the context principle implies that tokens of g-o-l-d that are ex-used in the two isolated communities are tokens of a single unambiguous PJSS-based word type.

One might object that if we can make sense of the new diagram of options for the first gold–platinum thought experiment, then we should also be able to make sense of the possibility that in the second gold–platinum thought experiment, in 1650, hence *prior* to the formation of the two isolated communities, tokens of g-o-l-d had *both* of the two extensions that English-speakers later come to attribute to it after the original English-speaking community splits into two isolated ones. But this objection overlooks the fact that the new diagram of options applies to the first gold–platinum thought experiment only if we adopt the context principle, which implies that the tokens of g-o-l-d on Earth in 1650 are tokens of a PJSS-based word type that is different from the PJSS-based word type of which the tokens of g-o-l-d on Twin Earth in 1650 are tokens. But, for reasons I explained above, if we adopt the context principle, we have no grounds for doubting that in the second thought experiment, the tokens of g-o-l-d on Earth in 1650 are tokens of a single PJSS-based word type. To suppose that in 1650, prior to the split, tokens of g-o-l-d had both of the two extensions that English-speakers later come to attribute to it would be to suppose, contrary to the context principle, that the English-speakers' PIWs, PJSSs, and PJSEs do not keep track of the word types they use. Against this, I have urged that we adopt the context principle, which implies that if members of both linguistic communities are apprised of all of the relevant facts about their PIWs, PJSSs, and PJSEs, both at a given time and across time, at least as far back as 1650, and they continue to regard tokens of g-o-l-d as unambiguous in 1650, there are no good grounds for questioning that tokens of g-o-l-d as unambiguous in 1650.[5]

---

[5] This leaves open the possibility that the speakers themselves conclude that their tokens of g-o-l-d have different extensions, despite their initial confidence in their PJSSs and PJSEs, and hence that the entrenched beliefs in the two communities are compatible. I take for granted that the members of the two communities will resist this conclusion not because they presuppose a general metaphysical

If we adopt the context principle, we will diagram the options for the second gold–platinum thought experiment as follows:

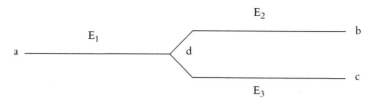

where, just as in the diagram of the options for the first gold–platinum, line ab represents the ex-use of tokens of g-o-l-d in one of the two branches of the English-speaking community, line ac represents the ex-use of tokens of g-o-l-d in the other branch of the English-speaking community, and line ad, where lines ab and ac overlap, represents the ex-uses of tokens of g-o-l-d before the original English-speaking community splits into two isolated ones—an event represent by point d—and 'E_1', 'E_2', and 'E_3' represent the extension of tokens of g-o-l-d at various points in the histories of the two communities. In this diagram, unlike in the diagram of the options for the first gold–platinum, however, *both* lines ab *and* ac represent continuity of a *single* PJSS-based word type 'gold'.

The lines and letters of the diagram of the options for the second gold–platinum thought experiment and the standard diagram of options are identical to the lines and letters of the diagram of the first gold–platinum thought experiment. In both diagrams, there is only one symbol, 'E_1', that represents the extension of tokens of g-o-l-d during the period before the events represented by the forking lines at their respective points d. There is a fundamental difference between what the two diagrams convey, however. The diagram of options for the first thought experiment reflects the standard commitment to (M), and hence to a token-and-ex-use conception of words, whereas the diagram of options for the second thought experiment is a reflection of our adoption of the context principle, which, as we have seen, is incompatible with (M).

In the second gold–platinum thought experiment, unlike in the first, the context principle commits us to denying that $E_2 \neq E_3$ unless the speakers themselves come to relinquish some of their PIWs, PJSSs, or PJSEs, a

principle such as (M), but because they trust their PJSSs and PJSEs unless they see some special reason in a given context for not doing so.

possibility we have hypothetically ruled out. As I have emphasized, in the circumstances described in the second gold–platinum thought experiment the context principle implies that there is a single unambiguous PJSS-based word type 'gold' that members of both communities use. A single PJSS-based word type has only one extension. Hence the context principle implies that $E_1 = E_2$ and $E_1 = E_3$. By the transitivity of identity, $E_1 = E_2$ and $E_1 = E_3$ together imply $E_2 = E_3$. Hence the context principle implies that in the second gold–platinum thought experiment, unlike in the first, members of the two linguistic communities *disagree* with each other about the extension of a single, unambiguous, PJSS-based word type 'gold'. In practice, however, they are likely to focus not on this metalinguistic disagreement, but on the disagreement about whether gold is the element with atomic number 79 that it mirrors.

We are now in a position to see that if we accept the token-and-ex-use model of words, we are likely to mistake some of the commitments that result from our PIWs, PJSSs, and PJSEs with commitments to (M). From our perspective as participants in inquiries about gold, we cannot help but find our PJSSs, and PJSEs for 'gold' factual and trustworthy. As we have seen, these judgements themselves naturally incline us to diagram the options for the second thought experiment in a way that looks superficially like the standard diagram of options of the first thought experiment. The token-and-ex-use conception of words implies that in both the first *and* second gold–platinum thought experiments, all the tokens of g-o-l-d used in 1650 have the same extension. Therefore, if we tacitly accept the token-and-ex-use model of words, we will naturally but unwittingly conflate the conclusion we draw from our PIWs, PJSSs, and PJSEs in the second gold–platinum thought experiment—the conclusion that all the tokens of g-o-l-d used in 1650 have the same extension—for a *metaphysical* intuition that in the first gold–platinum thought experiment all the tokens of g-o-l-d used in 1650 have the same extension. Once we adopt the context principle, however, we become aware of the conflation, and can therefore distinguish between the conclusion that in the second gold–platinum thought experiment all the tokens of g-o-l-d used in 1650 have the same extension, on the one hand, and the dubious metaphysical intuition that in the first gold–platinum thought experiment all the tokens of g-o-l-d used in 1650 have the same extension, on the other.

8.4. The Thesis that the Extension of a PJSS-Based Word Type is Determined by Facts about the Ex-Uses of Some of its Tokens

You might now be persuaded that we should reject the token-and-ex-use model of words, and embrace instead the PJSS-based conception of words, according to which the question whether or not two word tokens are tokens of the same word type cannot be raised or settled independent of our PIWs, PJSSs, and PJSEs for the tokens. You might still be tempted to suppose, however, that the extension of a PJSS-based word type is determined by facts about the ex-uses of *some* of its tokens. You might suppose, in particular, that

(a) In the first gold—platinum thought experiment, the extension of the English PJSS-based word type 'gold' is determined by the ex-use of 'gold' on Earth in 1750, after speakers on Earth doubted that they should apply their word 'gold' to samples of (what we now call) platinum, but before scientists on Earth agree on a chemical analysis of the stuff they call 'gold'.

and

(b) In the first gold—platinum thought experiment, the extension of the Twin-English PJSS-based word type 'gold' is determined by the ex-use of 'gold' on Twin Earth in 1750, after speakers on Twin Earth began confidently applying their word 'gold' to samples of (what we now call) platinum, but before scientists on Twin Earth agree on a chemical analysis of the stuff they call 'gold'.

You might have been inclined to accept that the extension of the English PJSS-based word type 'gold' is different from the extension of the Twin English PJSS-based word type 'gold' *because* they presuppose (a) and (b). If so, it may seem to you that my argument against the token-and-ex-use model of words presupposes that *the extension of a PJSS-based word type is settled by facts about the ex-uses of some of its tokens.*

It is important to see, however, that the first gold—platinum thought experiment does not commit us to (a) or (b). The thought experiment assumes that members of the English-speaking community find it natural to conclude that

(*) The extension of the English PJSS-based word type 'gold' is different from the extension of the Twin English PJSS-based word type 'gold'.

One might suppose that if (*) is true, its truth must somehow be settled by the ex-uses of tokens of the respective words in the two communities. But this supposition is as dubious as the thesis that the ex-uses of word tokens in 1650 determined the extension of those tokens. To see why, it is enough to construct a thought experiment in which two linguistic communities whose ex-uses of tokens of their respective PJSS-based word types are identical to the ex-uses of tokens of the PJSS-based word type 'gold' on Earth until sometime in the nineteenth century, when they examine paradigm instances to which they apply their word types, and reach different conclusions partly because the samples that are central and salient for the scientists are different in the two communities.[6] As before, we can stipulate that after they arrived at their respective analyses of the stuff to which they apply tokens of their respective PJSS-based word types, the members of the two communities encounter each other, and conclude that there is no conflict between their conclusions. We may suppose, finally, that members of both linguistic communities are right about the extensions of their words.

A thought experiment of this sort could be used to show that if we adopt the context principle and endorse the PJSS-based conception of words, we should give up (a). A similar thought experiment could be used to discredit (b). More generally, for any claim that some specified set of ex-uses of tokens of a PJSS-based word type w determines that w's extension is some specified set we can construct a thought experiment that undermines the claim. To resist the conclusions of the thought experiments simply because they conflict with the metaphysical idea that some facts about ex-uses of tokens of a PJSS-based word type w determine w's extension, one would have to question our PIWs and PJSSs for word tokens used by members of the two communities, either before or after they encounter each other, simply because these PIWs and PJSSs conflict with the metaphysical idea. And this would be to reject the context principle.

---

[6] I presented one such thought experiment in Ebbs 2000: §11.

This reasoning does not establish that the context principle is incompatible with the idea that some facts about ex-uses of tokens of a PJSS-based word type *w* determine *w*'s extension, but it does suggest a weaker, methodological conclusion that is directly relevant to the pragmatic approach to truth and words that I favour: even if it is possible that some facts about ex-uses of tokens of a PJSS-based word type *w* determine *w*'s extension, this possibility makes no difference to our actual assessments of our PIWs, PJSSs, and PJSEs, since by the context principle, we have no better grounds for evaluating sameness and difference of extension than by relying on our PIWs, PJSSs, and PJSEs, together with our investigations into the truth or falsity of particular statements we express by using our words. I conclude that we can adopt the context principle without committing ourselves to the thesis that the extension of a PJSS-based word type is determined by facts about the ex-uses of some of its tokens.

We may nevertheless still wonder whether the thesis that extension of a PJSS-based word type is determined by facts about the ex-uses of some of its tokens is compatible with the version of the Tarski–Quine thesis that I have sketched. Either the thesis that the extension of a PJSS-based word type is determined by facts about the ex-uses of some of its tokens is compatible with the PJSS-based conception of words or it isn't. If it is compatible with the PJSS-based conception of words, then for reasons I have explained, the context principle implies that it is irrelevant to truth and satisfaction. If the thesis is incompatible with the PJSS-based conception of words, then, since it presupposes the PJSS-based conception of words, it is self-undermining. Either way, the thesis is not a threat to my version of the Tarski–Quine thesis.

Still, the thesis is intriguing. If it is coherent, it may be true. And if it is both coherent and true, then the extension of tokens of the PJSS-based word type 'gold' uttered in 1650 may be determined by facts about how other tokens of the PJSS-based word type 'gold' are ex-used at some time after 1650. More generally, if the extension of a PJSS-based word type is determined by facts about the ex-uses of some of its tokens, then

(TE) *For some PJSS-based word types w, the extension of tokens of w at a given time t is or will be determined by facts about how other tokens of w are ex-used after t.*

(Here 'TE' is short for 'temporal externalism', a phrase coined by Henry Jackman, whose views I shall discuss below.) In the next three sections I shall investigate two recent discussions of sameness of extension across time that apparently support (TE). I shall try to show that these attempts fail because (TE) both presupposes and is incompatible with the PJSS-based conception of words.

8.5. George Wilson's Riverdale Olympics Case

George Wilson describes a case in which a committee of high-school coaches settles standards for qualifying to participate in a local athletic contest, the Riverdale Olympics. Athletes who want to qualify must perform in April, but the precise standards for qualification are not decided by the committee until May. Wilson stipulates that everyone who participates in the try-outs agrees to this arrangement. In these circumstances, he points out, it would be misleading to say that the standards for qualifying *changed* from April to May, since all along it was understood that they would be decided by the committee in May. Wilson thinks this is a case in which what happens later *fixes* standards for an earlier time, yet does not *change* those standards. Analogously, he reasons, it may be that our discoveries about the extension of 'gold' *fix* the extension of 'gold' in 1650 without *changing* its extension. Wilson expresses his conclusion as follows: "uses of 'gold' before *t* may be answerable to truth standards that came to be fixed only after *t*" (Wilson 2000: 95).

This way of phrasing the thesis is ambiguous between a weaker, epistemological version, and a stronger, metaphysical one. The ambiguity is due to ambiguities in the words 'use' and 'fixed'. To say that uses of 'gold' before *t* may be answerable to truth standards that came to be fixed only after *t* may be just to say that beliefs we express by (transparently) using a PJSS-based word type *w* at some time after *t* *settle how we should (at that later time) evaluate* beliefs that we or others expressed by using *w* before *t*. I am committed to this epistemological thesis by my adoption of the context principle. However, to say that uses of 'gold' before *t* may be answerable to truth standards that came to be fixed only after *t* may be to say something stronger: that certain *ex-uses* of tokens of a PJSS-based word type *w* that come to exist after *t* *metaphysically determine w*'s extension before *t*. Wilson apparently endorses this stronger thesis as well.

Wilson endorses my recommendation that we accept the PIWs, PJSSs, and PJSEs in both linguistic communities of the first gold–platinum thought experiment.[7] I argued above that we cannot accept these PIWs, PJSSs, and PJSEs unless we adopt the PJSS-based conception of words. If this argument is correct, then Wilson's metaphysical thesis amounts to a version of (TE). Let us now examine this thesis.

To begin with, we should acknowledge that Wilson's Riverdale Olympics case is similar in *some* respects to the first gold–platinum thought experiment. For instance, we find it natural to say that in 1650 John Locke did not know whether there was gold in the hills of South Africa, in part because those hills had not yet been mined. Similarly, in April of the year of the Riverdale Olympics, athletes who performed in the try-outs do not know whether they qualify for the Riverdale Olympics.

But the similarity is superficial: the reasons why Locke did not know in 1650 whether there was gold in the hills of South Africa are fundamentally different from the reasons why athletes who performed in the try-outs do not know in April whether they qualify for the Riverdale Olympics high jump contest. To see why, it helps to look more closely at the details of Wilson's story. According to Wilson, prior to the meeting of the committee of coaches in May, it is already settled that to qualify to participate in the high jump contest, one must jump at least as high as 6 feet in the try-outs in April. Moreover, it's already settled that any jump in the try-outs of over 6 ft 3 in qualifies. What the coaches must decide in May is where within the range from 6 ft to 6 ft 3 in to set the standard for qualifying for the high jump contest. In Wilson's story, they finally settle on 6 ft 2 in. Now suppose one of the athletes, Fred, jumped 6 ft 1 in during the try-outs in April. Suppose that right after he jumps, he sees that he jumped 6 ft 1 in; we then ask him, "Did you qualify?" and he replies, "That's not yet decided—the coaches will decide in May whether 6 ft 1 in is enough

---

[7] More precisely, Wilson grants that my gold–platinum thought experiment shows that the use of the term 'gold' up to 1650 does not determine that 'gold' was true of *x* iff *x* was (as we say) gold. He does not challenge the PJSSs and PJSEs in either linguistic community, and takes them for granted in his account of how later usage can settle the extensions of the two terms spelled g-o-l-d that are used on Earth and Twin Earth, respectively, in 1650. See Wilson 2000: 90–1.

to qualify for the high jump contest." This remark is true, according to Wilson's story.[8]

In contrast, however, whether in 1650 there was gold in the hills of South Africa is not settled by anyone's *decision* about the standards for applying the word 'gold'. If we trust our PIWs, PJSSs, and PJSEs, we will not regard Locke's utterance of 'There is gold in those hills' as a *prediction* about future language ex-use or about the beliefs of chemists—we will not regard Locke's predicate 'is gold' as equivalent to 'will be called 'gold' in the future by some experts in my linguistic community', for example.[9] We will take for granted that Locke's utterance of 'There is gold in those hills' was true or false in 1650, before later developments in either of the two future groups of speakers that can trace their word 'gold' back to his in a chain of PIWs, PJSSs, and PJSEs. By trusting our PIWs, PJSSs, and PJSEs across time for 'gold', we commit ourselves to rejecting the idea that the truth values of claims we make by using our PJSS-based word type 'gold' at a given time *t* are settled by facts about how tokens of that PJSS-based word type are ex-used *after t*.

Note also that someone may coherently challenge the current view that in 1650 there was no gold in the hills of South Africa. It makes sense, even if it is false, to say, "Gold is not in fact the element with atomic number 79, despite what the experts say now or will say in the future." The currently entrenched belief that gold is the element with atomic number 79 is not an analytic claim made true by stipulation; it is deeply held, but possibly false. By contrast, in Wilson's story the coaches could not be wrong about the standards for qualifying for the high jump contest: Fred's jump of 6 ft 1 in could not qualify him for the high jump contest if the coaches decide otherwise in May. Fred may feel that the coaches' decision is unfair, or that it should have been different. But the coaches cannot be *wrong* about whether he qualifies: their decision *settles* whether Fred qualifies.

The contrast disappears on the weaker, epistemological, reading of Wilson's claim that "uses of 'gold' before *t* may be answerable to truth

---

[8] Wilson asserts that "It is not the case that facts about the coaches' guidelines and about regular season high jumps determined that a tryout jump qualifies the jumper for the Riverdale Olympics iff that jump is 6'2" or higher" (Wilson 2000: 93).

[9] Here I agree with Jessica Brown, who objects to Jackman's view on the grounds that evidence about the usage of a word *w* at time *t* would not generally be regarded as relevant to the truth of an utterance made by using *w* at some time before *t*. See Brown 2000: 178–88.

standards that came to be fixed only after *t*" (Wilson 2000: 95). For on this weaker reading, we need not suppose that the analogue of the coaches' decision for the case of 'gold' is a *metaphysical* determination of the extension of 'gold' by its use after 1650. One need only maintain that sometime after 1650, speakers come to agree on a characterization of the extension of 'gold'. Their agreement need not be thought to settle the extension of 'gold' in a metaphysical way, and therefore need not be vulnerable to the criticism of the previous two paragraphs.

Nevertheless, Wilson takes the high jump case to establish (TE), according to which *for some PJSS-based word types w, the extension of tokens of w at a given time t is or will be determined by facts about how other tokens of w are ex-used after t.* Wilson's description of the role of the coaches in settling the standards for qualifying for the high jump contest implies that if the coaches had never met to settle the standards, it would have been *indeterminate* whether or not a high jump of 6 ft 1 in meets the standards for qualifying for the contest. At the same time, Wilson maintains that in the actual world the coaches' decision did not actually *change* standards for qualifying in April. Hence he seems committed to the curious claim that given how things actually developed, it was always the case in April that the qualifying standards for the high jump were 6 ft 2 in, even though in the world in which the coaches never decide the standard, it is indeterminate in April what the qualifying standards for the high jump are.

Similarly, on the metaphysical reading, Wilson's thesis that "uses of 'gold' before *t* may be answerable to truth standards that came to be fixed only after *t*" (Wilson 2000: 95) implies that if the English-speaking community had ceased to exist in 1650 (perhaps because a large asteroid destroyed life on Earth in 1650), then the extension of the tokens of g-o-l-d would have been indeterminate between (at least) the two extensions described in the first thought experiment. At the same time, according to Wilson, developments in the ex-use of tokens of g-o-l-d in the actual world did not *change* the extensions of tokens of g-o-l-d in 1650. Hence he is committed to saying *both* that in the actual world it was always the case that the extension of the English word 'gold' in 1650 was the set of all and only bits of the element with atomic number 79, just as it is now, *and* that later uses of the word 'gold' fixed, or made it the case that, the extension of the English word 'gold' in 1650 was the set of all and only bits of the element with atomic number 79. But how could one determine (in the sense of "make it the case") that p is true if it is *already* determined that p is true?

8.6. Henry Jackman's Temporal Externalism

This puzzle is only apparent, according to Henry Jackman, whose view of sameness of extension across time is similar to Wilson's. Jackman distinguishes between the question whether in 1650 the extension of 'gold' was the set of all and only bits of the element with atomic number 79, on the one hand, and the question whether it was *settled* in 1650 that the word 'gold' was the set of all and only bits of the element with atomic number 79, on the other. According to Jackman, the ex-uses of the English word 'gold' *after* 1650 settled that the extension of 'gold' in 1650 was the set of all and only bits of the element with atomic number 79. In the actual world in 1650 the extension of the English word 'gold' was *unsettled*, but nevertheless the same as, the extension of the English word 'gold' today.

This distinction does not entirely remove the puzzle, however. For Jackman's theory implies that in the counterfactual world in which the English-speaking community ceases to exist in July of 1650, the extension of the English word 'gold' was both *unsettled* in July of 1650 and *different from* its extension in the actual world in July of 1650—namely, the set of all and only bits of the element with atomic number 79.[10] To recover the puzzle, we need only ask *why* the extension of the English word 'gold' in July of 1650 in this counterfactual world is *different from* its extension in July of 1650 in the actual world. The answer implied by Jackman's theory is it is never *settled* in that counterfactual world that the extension the English word 'gold' is the set of all and only bits of the element with atomic number 79. It follows that if one settles, at some time t_2, what the extension of a word w is at some previous time t_1 one thereby *makes it the case that* the extension of w at t_1 is different from what it would have been at t_1 if it had not been settled at some time after t_1.

---

[10] As Jackman himself notes, it follows from his theory that in Mark Wilson's Druid thought experiment, "If the Druids' use of 'ave' died out before they encountered planes, the meaning of 'ave' would have been indeterminate between flying thing and bird" (Jackman 1999: 168). He embraces the consequence.

Jackman explicitly compares this consequence of his theory with the observation that the truth values of statements that contain what he calls "temporally loaded expressions" depend on what happens in the future (Jackman 1999: 162). Suppose, for example, that Cheney shoots Whittington at time *t*, and Whittington dies later from the gunshot wounds. If Whittington had not died of the gunshot wounds that Cheney caused by shooting him at *t*, then Cheney would not have killed Whittington by shooting him at *t*. Looking back, we might loosely say that since Cheney caused Whittington's later death by shooting him at *t*, Cheney killed Whittington at *t*. This apparently implies, paradoxically, that *Cheney killed Whittington before he died*. Analogously, on Jackman's view, in the actual world the extension of the English word 'gold' was the set of all and only bits of the element with atomic number 79 in 1650, before the extension of the English word 'gold' in 1650 was *settled*, hence, paradoxically, before it *became true* that the extension of the English word 'gold' in 1650 was the set of all and only bits of the element with atomic number 79.

Jackman thinks that this paradox is no more problematic than the misleading statement that *Cheney killed Whittington before he died*. In both cases, he thinks, we can avoid genuine paradox by noting that some words, such as 'killed', are "temporally loaded". The sentence 'Cheney killed Whittington' is not true *until* Whittington dies. Strictly speaking the sentence 'Cheney killed Whittington' was *not* true at *t*; the sentence became true after *t*, when Whittington died from his wounds. Looking back, we can see that at *t*, Cheney initiated the events that would eventuate in Whittington's death, hence that the sentence 'Cheney killed Whittington' was true at *t*. Similarly, Jackman supposes, the token of the sentence 'There's gold in those hills' that Locke uttered while pointing at hills in South Africa is not true (or false) until after some members of his community settled the meaning of Locke's word 'gold' in such a way that the word is true (or false) of some of the metal in those hills. In this case, according to Jackman, time affects not just the truth value of the claim, but the meanings of the words used to express it: Locke said something that was determinedly true or false in 1650, even though *what* Locke said was not settled until some time *after* 1650.

The superficial similarity between these two cases does not dispel the air of paradox surrounding Jackman's account of what Locke said in 1650. The problem is that our understanding of what Locke said in 1650 is not like our understanding of what Cheney did at time *t*. We take for granted that future events may change our *understanding* of what Locke said in 1650, not its truth value. Yet Jackman claims that future events change the *truth value* of what Locke said in 1650, in the modal sense that if we had settled the meaning of his tokens of g-o-l-d differently at some time after 1650, what Locke said in 1650, hence also the truth value of his utterance, would have been different. Thus it seems we must conclude that what Locke said in 1650 is not settled until the meaning of his tokens of g-o-l-d is settled some time after 1650, and therefore that in 1650 it was not (yet) true that Locke's utterance was true or false.

This puzzling description of Locke's utterance is an inevitable consequence of Jackman's assumption that if members of a linguistic community arrive at an entrenched and stable set of beliefs that they express by using a given term, say 'gold', then the combined ex-uses of that term in the community constitute an 'equilibrium' for the term that settles (a) the term's meaning, and hence also (b) the contents of the entrenched beliefs that members of the community express by using the term, in such a way that (c) most of the entrenched beliefs that members of the community express by using the term are true. For many of our terms, according to Jackman, there is more than one accessible equilibrium—more than one way in which the ex-use of the term could be extended and developed into a coherent practice of ex-uses of the term that settle its meaning (Jackman 1999: 160–1). In the first gold–platinum thought experiment (described in §6.4), for instance, the ex-use of tokens of g-o-l-d in the two communities in 1650 is identical, yet, after gradual and plausible extensions of that ex-use, each community arrives at different entrenched beliefs expressed by using tokens of g-o-l-d. In this and many other similar cases, Jackman supposes, the two communities arrive at different but equally valid equilibria for their respective tokens of g-o-l-d. Their different ex-uses thereby settle different meanings for their respective tokens of g-o-l-d, and those meanings settle that the entrenched beliefs they express by using their respective tokens of g-o-l-d, though different, are mostly true.[11]

Jackman combines this theory of meaning-settling equilibria with our PIWs, PJSSs, and PJSEs, and infers that "the future behavior of an

---

[11] This description presupposes that members of each community sort its respective word tokens into PJSS-based word types.

individual or his society can affect the content of his [previous] thoughts and utterances" (Jackman 1999: 160). In 1650 on Earth, for instance, when Locke said, "There is gold in those hills," it was not yet *settled* that an object *x* satisfies Locke's word 'gold' if and only if *x* is a bit of the element with atomic number 79. Jackman supposes that on Earth today there is an equilibrium for the English word 'gold' that settles that an object *x* satisfies 'gold' if and only if *x* is a bit of the element with atomic number 79. We *also* trust our PIWs, PJSSs, and PJSEs for Locke's term 'gold'. Looking back, we say that even in 1650, before the meaning of Locke's term 'gold' was settled, an object *x* satisfied Locke's word 'gold' if and only if *x* was a bit of the element with atomic number 79. Members of the Twin English-speaking community today will reach an analogous conclusion for Twin Locke's term 'gold'. If we accept the PIWs, PJSSs, and PJSEs in both communities, then if the equilibria reached in the two communities *settle* the meanings of the respective terms used in those communities, as Jackman assumes, the equilibria somehow also retroactively settle the meanings of Locke's and Twin Locke's terms.[12]

Suppose provisionally that we can make sense of the idea that the ex-uses of 'gold' today retroactively settle the meaning of Locke's word 'gold' in 1650. Does this fit with our PIWs, PJSSs, and PJSEs for Locke's word 'gold'? I have stressed that to accept these PIWs, PJSSs, and PJSEs is to suppose that in 1650 the beliefs that Locke expressed by using 'gold' were not indeterminate, but true or false. Jackman tries to accommodate this consequence of our PIWs, PJSSs, and PJSEs by distinguishing between the question whether in 1650 an object *x* satisfies Locke's word 'gold' if and only if *x* is a bit of the element with atomic number 79, on the one hand, and the question whether it was *settled* in 1650 that an object *x* satisfies Locke's word 'gold' if and only if *x* is a bit of the element with atomic number 79, on the other. He wants to say "Yes" to the first question and "No" to the second question. This way of answering the two questions does not directly conflict with our PIWs, PJSSs, or PJSEs in

---

[12] Jackman's theory of meaning equilibria is not unlike Tim McCarthy's neo-Davidsonian theory of reference, which yields "a policy favoring the stability of the reference of natural kind terms over time" (McCarthy 2002: 152), where the facts that are relevant to determining the reference of a term at a given time *t* may include facts about how tokens of the same syntactic type are used in that linguistic community at some *after t*. Although I shall focus just on Jackman's theory, I think similar criticisms would also discredit McCarthy's.

the first gold–platinum thought experiment, because we supposed in that experiment that each community arrives at a *single* equilibrium for 'gold'. But Jackman concedes that a single linguistic community could split into two communities, "with each sub-community developing accessible but incompatible equilibria from the original community's usage" (Jackman 1999: 167–8). Let us now consider what his theory commits us to saying about such a case.

Recall that in the second gold–platinum thought experiment (§8.3), a single linguistic community splits into two isolated linguistic communities, members of which arrive at different but equally entrenched beliefs about the extension of their PJSS-based word type 'gold', while continuing to take for granted their PIWs, PJSSs, and PJSEs for the PJSS-based word type 'gold' used in the original community before the split. Jackman is inclined to suppose that members of the two isolated communities in this second gold–platinum thought experiment have developed "accessible but incompatible equilibria from the original community's usage" (Jackman 1999: 167–8). Since the supposed equilibria in the two communities are both valid, Jackman's theory implies that in *both* linguistic communities after the split the entrenched beliefs that members of the two communities express by using sentences that contain the PJSS-based word type 'gold' are mostly true. As we saw above, however, we cannot say that prior to the split, the word 'gold' had *both* the extensions that members of the two later communities believe it to have. In such cases, I argued, we should accept the PIWs, PJSSs, and PJSEs in both communities, and conclude that members of the two communities *disagree* about the extension of a single PJSS-based word type 'gold'. But this description of the thought experiment is not open to Jackman, given his supposition that each community has reached a valid equilibrium for its tokens of g-o-l-d. His theory of meaning-determining equilibria leads him to conclude that in the second gold–platinum thought experiment and other similar cases, "the existence of a rival community undermines each community's entitlement to say what their predecessors meant" (Jackman 1999: 168). In particular, if the two later communities in the second gold–platinum thought experiment reach different but equally valid equilibria for their respective tokens of g-o-l-d, as Jackman is inclined to suppose, then Jackman's theory implies that neither of the two communities is entitled to say what their predecessors meant. Members of the two communities are therefore not entitled to suppose that they *disagree* about the extension of the PJSS-based word type 'gold' that was in use before the split.

In the second gold–platinum thought experiment there is a conflict between our PIWs, PJSSs, and PJSEs, on the one hand, and Jackman's theory of how meaning is determined, on the other. Forced to choose between our PIWs, PJSSs, and PJSEs and his theory of meaning, Jackman chooses his theory of meaning.[13] This shows that his theory of meaning is incompatible with the context principle and the PJSS-based conception of words. Yet Jackman rejects the token-and-ex-use conception of words when he supposes that ex-uses at a given time can settle the extensions of terms at an earlier time. The only way to justify such a retrospective extension assignment, I submit, is to accept the context principle and PJSS-based conception of words. Any other way of individuating words would conflict with our own practical way of keeping track of words across time. Hence Jackman's position appears to be self-undermining. It both tacitly presupposes the context principle and explicitly presupposes a theory of meaning that violates the context principle by sometimes conflicting with, and supposedly trumping, our PIWs, PJSSs, and PJSEs.

8.7. Counterfactuals about the Past and the Third Gold–Platinum Thought Experiment

I argued above (§8.3) that if we adopt the context principle we will suppose that in the second gold–platinum thought experiment, Locke's utterance of 'There's gold in those hills' was already true or false in 1650. As we've seen, this description of the second thought experiment conflicts with Jackman's theory of equilibria, according to which some ex-uses of terms *settle* their meanings, in the metaphysical sense explained above. If we adopt

---

[13] Henry Jackman suggested to me in a personal communication that he finds my second thought experiment implausible, since it builds in the stipulation that members of the two later linguistic communities will take themselves to disagree about gold when they discover that their PJSSs and PJSEs across time for their tokens of g-o-l-d link both communities to the same tokens of g-o-l-d used in 1650, prior to their isolation from each other. He believes that even after a short discussion about their differences, both sides would conclude that they mean something different by 'gold', and if they disagree at all, it would be over which of the two means by 'gold' what was originally meant in 1650. To me, however, this looks like a disguised expression of Jackman's commitment to his theory of how meaning is determined.

the context principle, we must therefore resist the claim that the two later communities in the second gold–platinum thought experiment each reach a different meaning-settling equilibrium in the ex-use of their respective terms. We must therefore distinguish between (1) the supposition that members of the two communities described in the second gold–platinum thought experiment express different entrenched beliefs by using their respective tokens of g-o-l-d, on the one hand, and (2) the supposition that these entrenched beliefs constitute two different meaning-settling equilibria for those respective tokens of g-o-l-d, on the other. Jackman is tempted to move from (1) to (2). But if we adopt the context principle, we commit ourselves to resisting this temptation.

By adopting a theory of meaning that tempts us to move from (1) to (2), we run the risk of conflating belief with truth. This is not to say that Jackman's theory implies there is no difference between belief and truth, however. His theory leaves open the possibility that in any given circumstance, a group of speakers can be wrong about whether they have arrived at a meaning-settling equilibrium for their words. This leaves open the possibility that members of at least one of the two linguistic communities in the second gold–platinum thought experiment have *not* arrived at a meaning-settling equilibrium for their term 'gold', even if they think they have. In this way, one might think one can reconcile Jackman's theory of meaning-settling equilibria with the supposition that there is a disagreement between the two linguistic communities that they express by using a single unambiguous PJSS-based word type that they trace back to the linguistic community from which they both evolved.

There are two related problems with this attempted reconciliation. First, to claim that only one of the two linguistic communities in the second gold–platinum thought experiment has arrived at a meaning-settling equilibrium for their PJSS-based word type 'gold' would be ad hoc. For Jackman's theory of meaning-settling equilibria is supposed to explain why we think that in the *first* gold–platinum thought experiment, *both* linguistic communities are right about what they respectively call 'gold': the explanation is supposed to be that both linguistic communities have arrived at a meaning-settling equilibrium for the PJSS-based word types that they typically spell g-o-l-d. What difference is there between the meaning-settling facts about ex-use in the first and second gold–platinum thought experiments? It seems that Jackman's theory of meaning-settling equilibria is unable to offer a principled answer to this question, and it cannot be invoked in support of a claim that only one of the two linguistic communities in the second gold–platinum thought experiment has arrived at a meaning-settling equilibrium for their PJSS-based word type 'gold'.

A related problem is that to accept such a claim is in effect to concede that our beliefs about whether a given pattern of ex-uses constitute a meaning-settling equilibrium for one of our words will be no more secure than our beliefs about the extensions of our terms. But, as we saw in §8.4, our speculations about what determines extensions of our words are no more secure than beliefs we express by using those words. Hence if we adopt this suggestion, the claim that a range of ex-uses of tokens of a given PJSS-based word type w is meaning-settling will be methodologically on a par with the claim that the entrenched beliefs we express by using tokens of w are true, hence equally open to revision. Why not then reject all speculations about which ex-uses of a given term are meaning-settling, and obey the context principle, as I recommend?

One tempting answer is that we cannot abandon such speculations, because we need a theory of how ex-uses settle meanings and extensions in order to describe certain counterfactual circumstances. Consider again the counterfactual world in which the English-speaking community ceases to exist in July 1650. One might suppose that we settle the facts about the extensions of tokens of g-o-l-d in this world just by stipulating that the ex-uses of tokens of g-o-l-d in that counterfactual world are the same as the ex-uses of tokens of g-o-l-d in the actual English-speaking community until July 1650, when the counterfactual community ceases to exist. But if the extensions of those tokens are settled by their ex-use, we reason, their extensions must be different from the extensions of tokens of g-o-l-d in the actual English-speaking community.

If we adopt the PJSS-based conception of words, however, we will conclude that we cannot stipulate counterfactuals about extensions of words by stipulating facts about the ex-uses of their tokens and asking what extensions are determined by those facts. Instead, to make sense of a counterfactual situation in which a group of speakers uses word tokens of some PJSS-based word type, we must directly stipulate that the speakers use tokens of that PJSS-based word type in that counterfactual situation.[14] To make sense of the counterfactual described in the previous paragraph, for instance, we must stipulate that members of the counterfactual English-speaking community in June 1650 use the same PJSS-based word type 'gold' that members of the actual English-speaking community use in June 1650. We can then specify the extension of their word 'gold' simply by using it, hence without speculating about the relationship between ex-use and extension.

This way of specifying of a counterfactual situation in which a group of speakers uses word tokens of some PJSS-based word type is an application of Kripke's point that to make sense of trans-world identity, we need (first) to identify what we wish to talk about, and (second) to say how things might have been for that thing (Kripke 1980: 15–20). Starting with this conception of trans-world identity, Kripke argues for a necessity of origins thesis, according to which each thing has the properties of its origin essentially. To find these properties, we must trace the thing back to the earliest *actual* moment at which we could have identified it and said how things might have been for it. PJSS-based word types don't have origins in the same sense in which physical objects do, but we obey something like Kripke's necessity of origins constraint when we stipulate how things might have been for a particular PJSS-based word type if it is part of our stipulation that the counterfactual world's history overlaps with our world's history at all points prior to some given time. When we describe the world in which our English-speaking community ceased to exist in July 1650, for instance, we identify a PJSS-based word type 'gold' and say of it that it might have been used by a community that was just like ours *until* July 1650.[15]

If the necessity of origins constraint applies to PJSS-based word types in the way just described, however, and there are no further constraints on how things might have been for particular PJSS word types, then we can

[14] To allow for the possibility of such stipulations, some modification would be needed in my Goodman-style explication of PJSS-based word types. We can perhaps still think of such word types as sets of their tokens if we allow such sets to include possible as well as actual word tokens. An adequate specification of such sets would require an extension of the context principle to encompass possible PIWs and PJSSs, so long as these can be seen to bear the relation 'is a PJSS-based replica of' to some of our own actual PIWs and PJSSs.

[15] John MacFarlane helped me to see that I need to be explicit about what kinds of constraints there are on our descriptions of worlds in which speakers use some of our PJSS-based word types.

stipulate that there is a counterfactual world w in which Locke exists, and hence uses our PJSS-based word type 'gold', but future members of his temporally extended linguistic community use tokens of g-o-l-d in just the way that members of the linguistic community on Twin Earth in the first gold–platinum thought experiment use their tokens of g-o-l-d.[16] I shall call this the third gold–platinum thought experiment.

One might be inclined to doubt that the world w just described is a possible word. The trouble is that, by hypothesis, there is no *non-semantic* difference between the ex-uses of tokens of g-o-l-d in world w and the ex-uses of tokens of g-o-l-d on Twin Earth in the first gold–platinum thought experiment. And we concluded that in the circumstances described in the first gold–platinum thought experiment we have no grounds to criticize or disagree with the verdict of scientists on Twin Earth that x satisfies their PJSS-based word type 'gold' if and only if either x is a bit of the element with atomic number 78 or x is a bit of the element with atomic number 79. But in the previous paragraph we stipulated that in world w members of the English-speaking community use *our* PJSS-based word type 'gold'. Hence, if, as we suppose, it is not the case that x is gold if and only if either x is a bit of the element with atomic number 78 or x is a bit of the element with atomic number 79, then it follows from our description of world w that members of the linguistic community on Earth in w are wrong about gold. But how could our stipulation that in world w members of the English-speaking community use our PJSS-based word type 'gold' make it the case that we are right and they are wrong about gold? Would it perhaps be better to say that there is no possible world like w, hence that our stipulations about how our PJSS-based word types might have been used must satisfy further constraints, beyond the constraint suggested by Kripke's thesis of the necessity of origins?

These doubts about w rest on a mistake. It cannot be part of our description of a counterfactual world such as w that *we* are *actually* right about gold. Hence it does not follow from our description of w that members of the linguistic community on Earth in w are wrong about gold. In this respect, the relationship between the actual English-speaking community today and the counterfactual English-speaking community today in the third

---

[16] Henry Jackman pointed out to me that my view of PJSS-based word types apparently allows us to describe this possible world, and raised the challenge I present in the next paragraph. It is my addition to highlight the relationship of Jackman's challenge to Kripke's necessity of origins thesis.

gold–platinum thought experiment is similar to the relationship between the two later branches of our English-speaking community in the second gold–platinum thought experiment, prior to their discovery that they both use the same PJSS-based word type 'gold'. Just as members of the two later branches of our English-speaking community in the second gold–platinum thought experiment use the same PJSS-based word type 'gold' to express their respective judgements about the make-up of gold, so members of the actual English-speaking community today and members of the counterfactual English-speaking community today in the third gold–platinum thought experiment use the same PJSS-based word type 'gold' to express *their* respective judgements about the make-up of gold. Naturally, we assume we are right about gold, but this does not follow from our descriptions of either of these two possible worlds. What follows, it seems, is just that the respective judgements made by using our PJSS-based word type 'gold'—namely, the judgement (made by members of our actual English-speaking community today in the third gold–platinum thought experiment, and by members of one of the two branches of our English-speaking community in the second gold–platinum thought experiment) that x is gold if and only if x is a bit of the element with atomic number 79, and the judgement (made by members of the counterfactual English-speaking community today in the third gold–platinum thought experiment, and by members of the *other* branch of our English-speaking community in the second gold–platinum thought experiment) that x is gold if and only if x is either a bit of the element with atomic number 78 or a bit of the element with atomic number 79—cannot both be true.

But even this last statement of what follows is too strong. For just as we left it open in the second gold–platinum thought experiment that members of either of the two branches might later come to think some of their PJSSs and PJSEs for their tokens of g-o-l-d were false, so we should leave it open in the third gold–platinum thought experiment that members of either the actual English-speaking community or the counterfactual English-speaking community might come to think that some of their PJSSs and PJSEs for their tokens of g-o-l-d were false. It is easy to allow for this possibility in the counterfactual circumstances after 1650 in the third gold–platinum thought experiment. All we need to do is to stipulate that members of that counterfactual linguistic community make PIWs, PJSSs, and PJSEs that together link their current utterances of sentences containing tokens of g-o-l-d back to their ancestors' utterances of sentences containing tokens of g-o-l-d in 1650, without also stipulating that those practical judgements are true. It is less obvious how to accommodate the qualification in the actual English-speaking community of the third gold–platinum thought experiment. For if we come to think that some of our past PIWs, PJSSs, and PJSEs for our tokens of g-o-l-d are false, we might conclude that Locke did not actually use our current PJSS-based word type 'gold', despite our initial assumption that he did. But if we were to come to this conclusion, then due to the necessity of origins constraint discussed above, we could no longer describe the counterfactual world as one in which Locke uses our PJSS-based word type 'gold'. Hence my original presentation of the third gold–platinum thought experiment, in particular, the claim that we can simply stipulate that w is a world in which Locke uses our PJSS-based word type 'gold', needs to be qualified. We must now say that if Locke uses our PJSS-based word type 'gold', as we actually suppose, then he might have used that PJSS-based word type even in a world in which Earth ceased to exist in 1650, or in a world in which the English-speaking community develops after 1650 in exactly the same way that the linguistic community on Twin Earth develops in my first gold–platinum thought experiment. Let us understand the third gold–platinum thought experiment from now on in this way.

Jackman's theory of meaning-determining equilibria apparently commits him to the conclusion that the tokens of g-o-l-d used by members of the Twin English-speaking linguistic community on Twin Earth in the first gold–platinum thought experiment and the tokens of g-o-l-d used by members of the counterfactual English-speaking linguistic community in the third gold–platinum thought experiment must be satisfied by all and only the same objects, because the ex-uses of those tokens are by hypothesis exactly the same. Hence his theory of meaning-determining equilibria apparently commits him to rejecting the possibility that members of the counterfactual English-speaking linguistic community in the third gold–platinum thought experiment today use our PJSS-based word type 'gold', and that their judgements about gold disagree with ours. His theory definitely commits him to rejecting the possibility that members of the English-speaking community that ceases to exist in July 1650 use our PJSS-based word type 'gold'. By committing us to doubting and or rejecting these possibilities on fully general theoretical grounds, Jackman's theory of meaning-determining equilibria conflicts with the context principle and PJSS-based conception of words.

As I emphasized above, however, Jackman rejects the token-and-ex-use conception of words when he supposes that ex-uses at a given time can settle the extensions of terms at earlier times. I've argued that the only way to justify such a retrospective extension assignment is to accept the context principle and PJSS-based conception of words. Any other way of individuating words would conflict with our own practical way of keeping track of words across time and with our strong sense that statements expressed by using natural kind terms are true or false at the time of utterance, even if it may take a great deal of further investigation to discover their truth value. Hence we now have additional reasons to conclude that Jackman's position both tacitly presupposes the context principle and explicitly presupposes a theory of meaning that violates the context principle by sometimes conflicting with, and supposedly trumping, our PIWs, PJSSs, and PJSEs.

8.8. Temporal Externalism and Relative Truth[17]

Let us now see if we can reconcile Jackman's metaphysical speculations about what determines the extensions of one's terms with the context principle and PJSS-based conception of words by *relativizing* our evaluations of our utterances and beliefs about the extensions of our PJSS-based word types to different *contexts of assessment*. To see how this might be motivated, recall the problematic suggestion that only one of the two linguistic communities in the second gold–platinum thought experiment has arrived at a meaning-settling equilibrium for its PJSS-based word type 'gold'. As I noted above, by accepting this suggestion one might think one can reconcile Jackman's theory of meaning-settling equilibria with the supposition that the two linguistic communities use a single unambiguous PJSS-based word type 'gold' that they trace back to the linguistic community from which they both evolved. But we noted that the suggestion faces two serious problems. The first is that Jackman's theory of meaning-settling equilibria

---

[17] I am indebted to John MacFarlane for his advice about how to approach the main issues of this section.

is unable to offer a principled, independent reason for thinking that one of the two linguistic communities in the second gold–platinum thought experiment has arrived at a meaning-settling equilibrium for its PJSS-based word type 'gold' and the other has not. The second is that the claim that a range of ex-uses of tokens of a given PJSS-based word type is meaning-settling will be methodologically on a par with the claim that the entrenched beliefs we express by our corresponding transparent uses of those tokens are true; both claims stand or fall together and are equally open to revision. For this reason I suggested that we give up the metaphysical speculations about what determines the extensions of our terms.

One might nevertheless find it repugnant to give up such metaphysical speculations, and therefore seek some relief from the worry that they are ad hoc. Let us focus first on the third gold–platinum thought experiment. It would be odd just to put one's foot down, and claim without independent justification that the ex-uses of tokens of the PJSS-based word type 'gold' determine that x satisfies the PJSS-based word type 'gold' if and only if x is a bit of the element with atomic number 79, and hence that, contrary to what members of the counterfactual English-speaking community in the third gold–platinum thought experiment believe, it is not the case that x satisfies the PJSS-based word type 'gold' if and only if either x is a bit of the element with atomic number 78 or x is a bit of the element with atomic number 79. For members of the counterfactual English-speaking community in the third gold–platinum thought experiment are in an equally strong epistemic position to claim that x satisfies the PJSS-based word type 'gold' if and only if either x is a bit of the element with atomic number 78 or x is a bit of the element with atomic number 79, and hence that, contrary to what we (members of the English-speaking community) believe, it is not the case that x satisfies the PJSS-based word type 'gold' if and only if x is a bit of the element with atomic number 79.

Instead of claiming without independent justification that only one of the two linguistic communities in the third gold–platinum thought experiment is right and the other wrong, one might be tempted to think that *each of the two communities is right in its own way*.[18] John MacFarlane has

---

[18] Mark Lance and John O'Leary-Hawthorne suggest that in their witch thought experiment, "either translation would be correct from the perspective in which they would be given" (Lance and O'Leary-Hawthorne 1997: 51), thereby endorsing the idea that translation, hence also truth value and extension, are in some way perspective relative. They are apparently committed to claiming that in all my

recently developed a semantics according to which the truth values of some utterances are defined only *relative* to contexts of assessment. Let us now see if we can use MacFarlane's semantics to make sense of the idea that in the third gold–platinum thought experiment the two linguistic communities' conflicting claims about the extension of their shared PJSS-based word type 'gold' are true relative to different contexts of assessment. We can then ask if the same kind of approach can help us to make sense of the second gold–platinum thought experiment.

To begin with, consider MacFarlane's treatment of sentences about future contingencies, such as 'Whittington will die tomorrow from the gunshot wounds that Cheney caused by shooting him today.' Let us avoid the temporal complications introduced by verbs such as 'kill'—complications that are important to Jackman's defence of his view that on Earth in 1650 the extension of 'gold' was the set of all and only bits of the element with atomic number 79, even though the extension of 'gold' was not yet *settled* in 1650, but play no role in MacFarlane's account of relative truth—and focus instead on pure predictions. Consider, for instance, the sentence 'It will be sunny here tomorrow', which I will write as

(1) Sunny (here, tomorrow)[19]

Suppose I now utter (1). Call this utterance of (1) u_1. How should I evaluate u_1? Let us assume that it is objectively indeterminate whether it will be sunny here tomorrow. MacFarlane argues that to make sense of this assumption, I must suppose that I am now actually in at least two overlapping worlds that diverge tomorrow, and perhaps also diverge sometime between now and tomorrow. To simplify, suppose I am now actually in exactly two worlds that contain u_1—world, w_1, in which it is sunny here tomorrow, and world w_2, in which it is not sunny here tomorrow. If we evaluate u_1 now, before w_1 and w_2 diverge, it seems natural to conclude that u_1 is neither true nor false, hence *indeterminate*. But if we evaluate u_1 tomorrow in w_1, we will conclude that u_1 is true,

gold–platinum thought experiments, including the third one, members of each of the later communities is right in its own perspective-relative way. As I shall explain in the text below, this vague idea can be made precise by using MacFarlane's semantics for relative truth. (For a brief description of the main differences between my gold–platinum thought experiments and the Lance–O'Leary-Hawthorne witch thought experiment, see Chapter 6, n. 12.)

[19] This is (23) from MacFarlane 2008: 91, with the addition of the indexical 'here', which MacFarlane leaves implicit.

and if we evaluate u_1 tomorrow in w_2, we will conclude that u_1 is false. More generally, as MacFarlane puts it, if we suppose there are branching worlds in the sense just explained, it is natural to say both that "present claims concerning the future can be shown to be untrue by a proof of present unsettleness", and that "past claims concerning the present cannot be shown to have been untrue by a proof of past unsettleness" (MacFarlane 2008: 90).

To highlight these observations about how we evaluate utterances of (1), MacFarlane contrasts (1) with

(2) Settled$_{now}$: Sunny (here, tomorrow).[20]

where $\ulcorner$Settled$_t$: $s\urcorner$ means that the truth value of $\ulcorner s\urcorner$ is settled by how things are at t. Suppose I now utter (2). Call this utterance of (2) u_2. How should I evaluate u_2? Since by assumption I am now actually in w_1 and w_2, it is not now settled that it will be sunny here tomorrow. Hence unlike u_1, which is now *indeterminate* in truth value, u_2 is now *false*. And, since u_2 makes a claim about what is *now* settled, unlike u_1, u_2 is false when evaluated at all future times and contexts in either in w_1 or w_2, the two worlds that by hypothesis contain it.

MacFarlane explicates these intuitive evaluations by modifying and extending a semantics in the style of Lewis 1980 and Kaplan 1989a that relativizes truth to a *point of evaluation*—an ordered triple $<C, w, a>$, where C is a *context*, understood as "a possible occasion on which a sentence might be used", w is an *index*, which for now we can take to be a possible world, and a is an *assignment function* from variables to objects in the domain (MacFarlane 2008: 83). For instance, a semantic theory that relativizes truth to points of evaluation might include the following two clauses:

(Q) $\ulcorner\forall x\Phi\urcorner$ is true at $<C, w, a>$ if and only if Φ is true at every point $<C, w, a'>$ such that a' differs from a at most in the value it assigns to x.

(N) $\ulcorner\Box\Phi\urcorner$ is true at $<C, w, a>$ if and only if Φ is true at every point $<C, w', a>$ such that w' is accessible from w.

One way to relate the concept of the truth of a formula at a point of evaluation to the concept of the truth of a closed sentence s (i.e.

---

[20] This is (24) from MacFarlane 2008: 91, with the addition of 'here'.

one that contains no free variables) as used in a particular context is as follows:

(A) An occurrence of s in a context C is true if and only if s is true at $<C, w_C, a>$, where w_C is the world of C and a is an arbitrary assignment.[21]

In contrast, MacFarlane develops a framework for characterizing truth relative to *two* contexts—a context of utterance and a context of assessment. To capture our intuition that statements about future contingencies are objectively indeterminate, he assumes a metaphysics of branching worlds, as described above. This by itself requires some departure from (A), since the definite description 'the world of C' in (A) fails to pick out any world if there is more than one world that contains C, as in the example above, in which a single occurrence (utterance) u_1 of 'Sunny (here, tomorrow)' is in *both* worlds w_1 and w_2 (where $w_1 \neq w_2$). In addition, as we have seen, we find it natural to say that u_1 is indeterminate as assessed now, before w_1 and w_2 diverge, that u_1 is true as assessed tomorrow in w_1, and that u_1 is false as assessed tomorrow in w_2. MacFarlane explicates these and other similar assessments of utterances by constructing a semantics that clarifies what it means to say that an utterance is true-at-a-context-of assessment.

Suppose that C, C_1, and C_2 are contexts. Let $W(C)$ be the set of worlds that overlap at C, and let $W(C_1/C_2)$ be $W(C_1)$, if $W(C_1) \cap W(C_2) = \emptyset$, and $W(C_1) \cap W(C_2)$, otherwise (MacFarlane 2008: 91). We can then explain when an occurrence of a sentence at a context—the context of utterance, here represented as C_U—is true *as assessed in a context of assessment*—here represented as C_A—as follows (I shall call this 'Assessment Relative Truth', hence the acronym 'ART'):

(ART) An occurrence of a sentence s at C_U is true as assessed at C_A if and only if for every $w \in W(C_U/C_A)$, s is true at $<C_U, w, a>$.[22]

To see how (ART) works, let us first apply it to utterance u_1 discussed above. Let C_1 be the context in which I uttered u_1, let C_2 be the context in which I assess u_1 tomorrow in w_1, and let C_3 be the context in which I assess u_1 tomorrow in w_2. To simplify, as before, assume that

[21] Clauses (Q), (N), and (A) are, with minor notational changes, essentially the same as clauses (1), (2), and (3), respectively, from MacFarlane 2008: 83.
[22] This is clause (22) from MacFarlane 2008: 91.

$W(C_1) = \{w_1, w_2\}$. Then $W(C_1/C_1) = W(C_1) = \{w_1, w_2\}, W(C_1/C_2) = W(C_2) = \{w_1\}$, and $W(C_1/C_3) = W(C_3) = \{w_2\}$. Applying (ART), we find that

> u_1 is indeterminate as assessed at C_1
> u_1 is true as assessed at C_2
> u_1 is false as assessed at C_3.

Now let us apply (ART) to utterance u_2 discussed above. To do this we need an account of truth at a point of evaluation for sentences of the form ⌜Settled$_t$: s⌝. McFarlane proposes the following:

> (B) ⌜Settled$_t$: s⌝ is true at $<C, w, a>$ if and only if s is true at all points $<C, w', a>$ such that w' overlaps with w at t.[23]

To apply (B) to the above-described utterance u_2 of (2), namely, 'Settled$_{now}$: Sunny(here, tomorrow)', we suppose that C is the context of utterance for u_2. Hence, if w_1 and w_2 overlap at $t =$ now, the occurrence of 'Sunny(here, tomorrow)' that u_2 contains is true at $<C, w_1, a>$ and the occurrence of 'Sunny(here, tomorrow)' that u_2 contains is not true at $<C, w_1, a>$, then by (B) we may conclude that u_2 is not true, i.e. false, at $<C, w, a>$ for every w. Applying (ART), then, we find that

> u_2 is false as assessed at C_1, C_2, and C_3.

These results accord with our intuition that if we presuppose a metaphysics of branching possible worlds, the truth value for u_1 is *not* the same for all contexts in which it is assessed, whereas the truth value of u_2 *is* the same for all contexts in which it is assessed. MacFarlane summarizes this observation by saying that (1) is *assessment-sensitive*, whereas (2) is not (MacFarlane 2008: 92).

MacFarlane's account of assessment-sensitivity can be seen as an explication of the idea that truth is relative, not absolute. Previous attempts to explain relative truth can at best muster only very weak replies to the objection that they conflate belief with truth. For instance, Jack Meiland recommends that a relativist about truth reply to this objection by insisting that, for instance, Jones's belief that p is just a *criterion* for p's being *true-for-Jones*, not what p's being true-for-Jones *consists in* (Meiland 1977: 580).

---

[23] This is clause (8) from McFarlane 2008: 84. As McFarlane notes, this clause yields a supervaluational semantics of the sort presented in Thomason 1970.

But the distinction between being a *criterion* for truth-for-Jones and being what truth-for-Jones *consists in* is strained and legalistic; it is not much of a defence against the charge that relativists about truth conflate truth with belief. MacFarlane's semantics promises to do better. And it clearly *does* do better if we assume a metaphysics of branching worlds. As we saw when we applied (ART) to an utterance of (1), if a single context of utterance is contained within many worlds, MacFarlane's notion of assessment-sensitivity can be explicated without remainder in terms of contexts of utterance, contexts of assessment, and truth at a point of evaluation, which is not itself relativistic.

Let us now try to use MacFarlane's method to make sense of the idea that in the third gold–platinum thought experiment, the two linguistic communities' conflicting claims about the extension of their shared PJSS-based word type 'gold' are *true relative to different contexts of assessment*. To apply the method, let us add some detail to the third gold–platinum thought experiment. Suppose, as we did in the first gold–platinum thought experiment, that while pointing at some South African hills represented on a map, Locke utters the sentence

(3) There is gold in those hills.

Call his utterance of (3) u_3. How should we evaluate u_3? Let w_3 be a world we are now actually in, in which we judge that u_3 is false, based on our present account of the extension of our PJSS-based word type 'gold', and let w_4 be the counterfactual world of the third gold–platinum thought experiment—the world in which we now judge that u_3 is false, based on our present account in that world of the extension of our PJSS-based word type 'gold'. Suppose that w_3 and w_4 overlap at 1650, hence both contain u_3. Let C_4 be the context in which Locke uttered u_3, let C_5 be the context in which I evaluate u_3 today in w_3, and let C_6 be the context in which I evaluate u_3 today in w_4. To simplify again, assume that $W(C_4) = \{w_3, w_4\}$. Then $W(C_4/C_4) = W(C_4) = \{w_3, w_4\}$, $W(C_4/C_5) = W(C_5) = \{w_3\}$, and $W(C_4/C_6) = W(C_6) = \{w_4\}$. Applying (ART), we find that

   u_3 is indeterminate as assessed at C_4
   u_3 is true as assessed at C_5
   u_3 is false as assessed at C_6.

A temporal externalist who is willing to apply (ART) can therefore make sense of the idea that u_3 is true as assessed by one of the linguistic communities at C_5, and false as assessed by the other linguistic community at C_6.

The resulting assessment-sensitivity of our evaluations of u_3 contrasts with our evaluations of utterances of sentences prefixed by 'Settled$_{now}$:' Thus suppose that while pointing at some South African hills represented on a map, Locke utters the sentence

(4) Settled$_{now}$: there is gold in those hills.

Call this utterance of (4) u_4. By clause (B), u_4 is false. Hence by (ART) it is false for every context of utterance/context of evaluation pair. In short, (3) is *assessment-sensitive*, whereas (4) is not.

Is a temporal externalist treatment of the third gold–platinum thought experiment more plausible if it is combined with (ART) in the way just sketched? We are still left with a hard question of why we should think that if a community has entrenched, stable beliefs about the extension of a PJSS-based word 'gold', then the community has reached a meaning-determining equilibrium for that word. With (ART), however, one can make the mystery symmetrical. If we apply (ART), we are not showing bias or favouritism towards one of the two linguistic communities of the third gold–platinum thought experiment over the other, since we get different truth values—indeterminate, true, false, respectively—when we assess the two communities' evaluations of u_3 from C_4, C_5, and C_6.

I think this is the best that can be said for combining temporal externalism with (ART). And it comes at a cost—several new problems for temporal externalism arise as a direct result of combining it with (ART). First, when temporal externalism is combined with (ART), we lose our grip on our initial intuition that members of the two linguistic communities of the third gold–platinum thought experiment *disagree* about *gold*. The problem is that by hypothesis each side to the dispute ascribes different meanings and extensions to occurrences of the PJSS-based word type 'gold', including the occurrences of that word in u_3. Each side takes the other to mean what it means by 'gold', but the two sides do not agree about the meaning or extension of 'gold', and that is what explains their different assessments of u_3. They disagree about the *extension* of their common PJSS-based word type 'gold', but their disagreement about its *meaning* prevents them from concluding that they disagree about gold itself. In contrast, the different evaluations of u_1 discussed above do not depend on different assessments of the *meanings* of the words ('Sunny', 'Here', 'Tomorrow') that occur in (1); and to the extent that the different evaluations of u_1 reflect different assignments of *extension* to one of those words ('Sunny'), the differences in the assignments are due to differences in the *worlds* that contain the different contexts from which u_1 is assessed, not to differences in the *meaning-determining ex-uses* of words, as in the temporal externalist's evaluations of u_3. In the application of (ART) to the temporal externalist's evaluations of u_3, if we have any grip at all on there being a common subject matter about which both linguistic communities disagree, that grip is secured by the existence of a single PJSS-based word type 'gold' that members of both communities both take themselves to use, despite the different meanings and extensions that they assign to it. (For this reason, I shall not consider how one might apply (ART) to PJSSs themselves.) But if we apply (ART) in the way just sketched, the existence of that shared PJSS-based word type 'gold' does not bring with it either a shared meaning or a shared extension for the word, and so there's no longer any clear basis for taking the two communities to disagree about gold.

We face a second problem if we try to use (ART) to explicate the *second* thought experiment sketched above, in which two parts of a given linguistic community become isolated from each other and develop different entrenched beliefs about the extension of a single PJSS-based word type 'gold'. To explicate the different evaluations of u_3 made by members of the two linguistic communities in the second gold–platinum thought experiment, one cannot appeal to branching possible worlds, since, by hypothesis, both communities are in the *same* possible world. To apply (ART) to the second gold–platinum thought experiment, then, we need to find an appropriate interpretation of the variable in (ART) that ranges over *indices*—the variable 'w'. But I suspect that there is no way to do this without conflating *truth-at-a-context-of-assessment* with *belief*. To back up my suspicion, I would need to present and evaluate several interpretations of 'w' in (ART). I don't have the space here for such an investigation. The basic reason for my suspicion, however, is easy to state: I don't see how the different *assessments* of u_3 by members of the two linguistic communities in the second gold–platinum thought experiment can be explained by anything other than the different *beliefs* that members of those communities have about how to evaluate sentences that contain their PJSS word type 'gold'. I therefore find it difficult to see how a relativist about truth who wishes to apply (ART) to u_3 under the circumstances described in the second gold–platinum thought experiment can avoid conflating truth-at-a-context-of-assessment with belief.[24]

If there's no good answer to this second problem, as I suspect, then to apply MacFarlane's (ART) without conflating truth-at-a-context-of-assessment with belief, we must presuppose a metaphysics of branching worlds. If, in addition, we accept temporal externalism, according to which the meaning and extension of a word depends on future ex-uses of that word, we thereby commit ourselves to the conclusion that *most of our utterances are assessment-sensitive*. There will be some exceptions, including utterances of sentences prefixed by 'Settled$_{now}$'. But in general we will not be able to avoid assessment-sensitivity even in sentences such as (3) whose truth values we normally regard as determinate at the time of utterance. In my view, this consequence is unacceptable, since we easily avoid it by rejecting both absolute and relative forms of temporal externalism and embracing the PJSS-based conception of words.[25]

I conclude that we cannot make temporal externalism more appealing by combining it with a MacFarlane-style assessment-sensitive semantics. I recommend that we eschew both absolute and relative forms of temporal externalism and solve the puzzles raised by the gold–platinum thought experiments by combining the Tarski–Quine thesis with the PJSS-based conception of words.

---

[24] In Lasersohn 2005, Peter Lasersohn argues on *empirical linguistic* grounds that the truth value of sentences containing what he calls predicates of personal taste, such as 'fun' or 'tasty', must be relativized to individuals, whose judgements about what is fun or tasty differ. Lasersohn's account of such relativity is structurally parallel to MacFarlane's (ART). I am not fully persuaded by Lasersohn's arguments, but if they were successful, they would provide an interesting defence against the objection that Lasersohn's account conflates relativity of truth value with belief—the defence that English-speakers actually *do* conflate relativity of truth value with belief, and hence any adequate theory of meaning must attribute that conflation to them. Richard 2004 can be read in a similar way. My goal in this book is not to provide a theory of meaning for English, however, but to find a truth predicate that enables us to clarify and facilitate our inquiries. Given this goal, I see no advantage to combining temporal externalism with (ART) in a way that conflates truth-at-a-context-of-assessment with belief.

[25] In addition, as John MacFarlane pointed out to me, if most of our sentences are assessment-sensitive for the reasons just sketched, then we cannot take for granted, as MacFarlane does in MacFarlane 2005: 338 n. 19, that the meta-language in which we *state* (ART) is "devoid of assessment-sensitivity," and so cannot easily rule out the possibility that our attempts to state (ART) are self-refuting.

8.9. Immanent Realism

In the midst of our collaborative inquiries, we do not speculate about what, if anything, determines the extensions of our words; instead, we take for granted that our PIWs, PJSSs, and PJSEs are both factual and trustworthy, and inquire directly into the questions that interest us. If we wish to try to clarify and resolve a disagreement about whether there is gold in certain specified hills in South Africa, for instance, we do not speculate about what if anything determines the extensions of our term 'gold', but trust our PIWs, PJSSs, and PJSEs for 'gold', and try to find out whether there is gold in those hills in South Africa. We may come to agree on an answer, and may even take it to be beyond doubt. But we do not and we need not suppose that our answer metaphysically determines the extensions of our terms. We treat any claim about what actually determines the extensions of our terms as just another belief, more or less firmly accepted, and hence in principle open to review and revision. After reviewing a given belief we may conclude that it was false, taking for granted that our PIWs, PJSSs, and PJSEs for the words we used to express the belief are trustworthy and factual. As Quine emphasizes,

> We should and do currently accept the firmest scientific conclusions as true, but when one of these is dislodged by further research we do not say that it had been true but became false. We say that to our surprise it was not true after all. Science is seen as pursuing and discovering truth rather than as decreeing it. Such is the idiom of realism, and it is integral to the semantics of the predicate 'true'.   (Quine 1995b: 67)

Just as our firm scientific conclusions may become dislodged by further research, so any metaphysical speculations about what determines the extensions of our terms may also be dislodged by further research. In all three of the gold-platinum thought experiments discussed in this chapter a crucial factor in our evaluation of our own previous conclusions or speculations is our continuing practice of regarding our PIWs, PJSSs, and PJSEs for the terms in question as both factual and trustworthy.

As we saw in §§3.9–3.10, Quine himself fails to explicate 'true' in a way that captures his insight about its semantics: his indeterminacy thesis, which presupposes the token-and-ex-use model of words, implies that our PIWs, PJSSs, and PJSEs are not factual. But if we reject the token-and-ex-use model of words, and combine the PJSS-based conception of words with a Tarski-style disquotational truth predicate, we thereby adopt a disquotational conception of truth that captures the realist semantics of the predicate 'true'. We are now finally in a position to see, in addition, that the best way to make sense of the phenomenon of learning from others and to solve the puzzles about sameness of extension across time that I discussed in this and the previous two chapters is to adopt both the Tarski–Quine thesis and the PJSS-based conception of words.

9

Applications and Consequences

9.1. Introduction

As I have emphasized from the start of this book, my answers to the pragmatic questions "Do we need a truth predicate?" and "If so, what sort of truth predicate do we need?" are shaped by my assumption that we desire to clarify and facilitate our inquiries by regimenting our sentences so that we can express logical generalizations, such as "Every regimented sentence of the form '$S \vee \sim S$' is true." It seems that to express such generalizations all we need is a Tarski-style disquotational truth predicate defined for sentences of our own regimented language. If we suppose that there is no more to truth than what is needed for expressing logical generalizations, we may then be inclined to adopt the *Tarski–Quine thesis* that *there is no more to truth than what is captured by a Tarski-style disquotational truth predicate defined for one's own sentences.* As normally understood, however, a Tarski-style disquotational truth predicate tells us nothing about how to apply logical generalizations to other speakers' words or to our own words as we used them in the past. But, as I argued in Chapter 3, we can clarify and facilitate our inquiries only if we can express logical generalizations on other speakers' sentences and on our own sentences as we used them in the past. Our desire to clarify and facilitate our inquiries should therefore motivate us to adopt the *intersubjectivity constraint: a Tarski-style disquotational truth predicate defined for one's own regimented sentences is satisfactory only if it is supplemented by an account of why it is epistemically reasonable for one to regard one's practical judgements of sameness of satisfaction as both factual and trustworthy.*

In Chapter 4 I argued (first) that if we presuppose the token-and-ex-use conception of words, we will see no way to explain why it is epistemically reasonable for a person to regard her practical judgements of sameness of satisfaction as both factual and trustworthy without rejecting the Tarski–Quine thesis, but (second) that if we adopt the PJSS-based conception of words, we can see that the Tarski–Quine thesis and the intersubjectivity constraint are compatible. This may appear to leave it open that we can satisfy the intersubjectivity constraint in a way that commits us to rejecting the Tarski–Quine thesis. As I argued in Chapters 5–8, however, this appearance is illusory: the only way to satisfy the intersubjectivity constraint is to embrace both the Tarski–Quine thesis and the PJSS-based conception of words.

My goal in this final chapter is to sketch several additional ways in which adopting the PJSS-based conception of words transforms our understanding of topics that are central to the philosophy of language. I start by explaining how the PJSS-based conception of words accommodates the observations that motivate many philosophers to embrace the causal theory of reference for predicates, and how one can regiment proper names as descriptions without embracing a description theory that is undermined by radical changes in belief. I recommend that we replace the standard understanding of the division of linguistic labour with a deflationary account that rests on our PIWs and PJSSs, and develop notions of minimal competence and minimal self-knowledge that go hand in hand with the PJSS-based conception of words. I also offer a deflationary interpretation of the thought experiments that support anti-individualism, and show that on the interpretation of anti-individualism that I recommend, it does not posit or presuppose that facts about ex-use determine norms for language use. Finally, I explain why our treatment of logical laws as arbiters of disagreement is of a piece with our pursuit of truth.

9.2. A Deflationary Alternative to the Causal Theory of Reference: Predicates

If we adopt the PJSS-based conception of words, we thereby endorse an alternative to the causal-historical theory of reference for predicates. Recall (from §6.3) that Kripke and Putnam developed the causal-historical theory of reference to explain and justify the PIWs, PJSSs, and PJSEs that clash with methodological analyticity, the thesis that there are sentences we cannot reject without changing the subject. The supposition that some sentences are methodologically analytic rests on the description theory of reference for predicates, according to which an object x satisfies a given predicate F as used by speaker A if and only if x satisfies certain descriptive conditions that A associates with F. Kripke and Putnam used historical examples and thought experiments to show that our PIWs, PJSSs, and PJSEs sometimes conflict with methodological analyticity and the description theory of reference for predicates. They tried to develop an alternative theory of reference that explains and justifies our PIWs, PJSSs, and PJSEs. The motivating idea behind their causal-historical theory of extension is that there must be something about the ex-use of a term prior to a discovery that settles its extension. But the gold–platinum thought experiment of Chapter 6 shows that the causal-historical theory of the extensions of our predicates does not fit with our PIWs, PJSSs, and PJSEs, and hence cannot explain or justify them. I propose that instead of trying to explain reference in terms of causal relations between words, speakers, and things, we embrace the PJSS-based conception of words, and thereby incorporate PIWs, PJSSs, and PJSEs into our understanding of words themselves. Unlike the causal-historical theory, the PJSS-based conception of words is constrained by the context principle and hence cannot fail to fit with our PIWs, PJSSs, and PJSEs.

Kripke himself doubted that his remarks about reference could be developed into a theory of necessary and sufficient conditions for a predicate to be satisfied by a given object. He emphasized that "philosophical analyses of some concept like reference, in completely different terms which make no mention of reference, are very apt to fail" (Kripke 1980: 94). His central goal was "to present a better picture without giving a set of necessary and sufficient conditions for reference" (Kripke 1980: 94). We are now in a position to see that any substantive specification of necessary and sufficient conditions for reference will presuppose the token-and-ex-use conception of words and hence violate the context principle. In place of Kripke's vague and general doubts about prospects for substantive theories of reference, we now have a principled and systematic reason for abandoning the search for such theories, given our desire to clarify and facilitate our inquiries by formulating logical generalizations. At the same time, by adopting the context principle we can respect the kinds of PIWs, PJSSs, and PJSEs that Kripke highlighted in his persuasive arguments against description theories of reference and methodological analyticity.

Putnam also observed that our PIWs, PJSSs, and PJSEs conflict with description theories of reference and methodological analyticity. Like Kripke, Putnam tried to offer an alternative theory of reference that fits with our PIWs, PJSSs, and PJSEs. But, as we have seen, the gold–platinum thought experiment of Chapter 6 shows that Putnam's causal-historical theory of reference violates the context principle. Putnam's Twin Earth thought experiment, of which my gold–platinum thought experiment is a variation, describes a Twin Earth on which speakers apply tokens of w-a-t-e-r only to twin water, which has a molecular structure different from the molecular structure of water. This feature of Putnam's thought experiment misleads him into adopting his *contribution of the environment* thesis, according to which facts about the ex-uses of tokens of w-a-t-e-r on the two planets, including facts about causal relations between those word tokens, speakers, and things and kinds of stuff in the environment, determine the extensions of the tokens. If this were correct, however, then his explanation of reference should work for the gold–platinum thought experiment. But it does not, for reasons I explained in detail in Chapter 6. Hence the explanation fails even for Putnam's own original thought experiment.

I recommend that we accept the PIWs, PJSSs, and PJSEs of the members of the two communities in the gold–platinum thought experiment. For the same reasons, I also recommend that we accept the PIWs, PJSSs, and PJSEs of the members of the two communities in Putnam's water–twin-water thought experiment. In both cases we rely on the context principle and the PJSS-based conception of words to extend our Tarski-style disquotational understanding of satisfaction to encompass the predicates in question. The context principle and the PJSS-based conception of words imply that tokens of w-a-t-e-r have different extensions on Earth and on Twin Earth, even in 1650, before analytical chemistry was developed in either planet, despite the fact that, contrary to Putnam's causal-historical theory, the facts about the ex-uses of those tokens do not determine their extensions.

9.3. A Deflationary Alternative to the Causal Theory of Reference: Proper Names

If we adopt the PJSS-based conception of words, we can also offer a satisfying deflationary alternative to the causal theory of reference for proper names. Recall that, following Quine, I recommend that we regiment proper names as definite descriptions. To do so is simply to settle the logical form of the regimented sentences that are to replace ordinary language sentences that contain proper names, not to offer substantive necessary and sufficient conditions for being the referent of a name. Hence the Quinean method of regimenting proper names does not amount to a description theory of reference for proper names in the sense that this is usually associated with Frege and Russell. Still, the method of regimenting proper names cannot by itself accommodate the phenomena that led Kripke and others to embrace the causal theory of reference for proper names. To accommodate the phenomena, the Quinean method of regimenting proper names must be joined with the PJSS-based conception of words.

To see why, we must examine carefully the phenomena that many have taken to undermine the description theory of reference for proper names. Consider, for instance, Kripke's celebrated Schmidt–Gödel thought experiment:

Let's suppose that someone says that Gödel is the man who discovered the incompleteness of arithmetic . . . in the case of Gödel that's practically the only thing many people have heard about him—that he discovered the incompleteness of arithmetic. Does it follow that whoever discovered the incompleteness of arithmetic is the referent of 'Gödel'? . . . *Suppose that Gödel was not in fact the author of the theorem.* A man named 'Schmidt' whose body was found in Vienna under mysterious circumstances many years ago, actually did the work in question. His friend Gödel somehow got hold of the manuscript and it was thereafter attributed to Gödel. On the view in question, then, when our ordinary man uses the name Gödel, he really means to refer to Schmidt, because Schmidt is the unique person satisfying the description, 'the man who discovered the incompleteness of arithmetic'. . . . So, since the man who discovered the incompleteness of arithmetic is in fact Schmidt, we, when we talk about 'Gödel' are in fact always referring to Schmidt. But it seems to me that we are not.   (Kripke 1980: 83–4)

When we read the italicized sentence, we take Kripke to be inviting us to suppose that Gödel was not in fact the author of the theorem. If we regiment this sentence in the way Quine recommends, we take Kripke to be saying that the x such that $x = $ Gödel was not in fact the author of the theorem. All along, though, we take for granted that an object x satisfies '$= $ Gödel' if and only if $x = $ Gödel. To eliminate 'Gödel' as a singular term, we should regiment '= Gödel' as an unstructured predicate, 'Gödels', and accept that an object x satisfies 'Gödels' if and only if x Gödels. We should do the same, also, for 'Schmidt'. As a result of the regimentations, we will introduced two new predicates (I shall call them name predicates), 'Gödels' and 'Schmidts', and suppose that no x both Gödels and Schmidts. When we entertain the stipulations of Kripke's story, we will also accept that *the person who Schmidts* discovered the incompleteness of arithmetic. Hence we reject the theory that *the person who Gödels* is the person who discovered the incompleteness of arithmetic.

The crucial point is that we trust our PJSSs for Kripke's words, and accept his supposition, which is incompatible with the description theory. Hence we must either reinterpret Kripke's words, perhaps so that 'Gödel' is translated by our word 'Schmidt', or agree with Kripke that the description theory is incorrect. Many are likely to agree with Kripke.

According to Hartry Field, Kripke's example tells us nothing substantive about reference. Instead, it highlights the kinds of inferences we draw from utterances that contain proper names. "What Kripke's example . . . shows," according to Field, "is that we should regard [the supposition that Kripke expresses in the passage quoted above] as grounds for inferring 'Gödel did not [discover] the incompleteness theorem' rather than as grounds for inferring 'Gödel was baptized as 'Schmidt' and never called himself 'Gödel'" (Field 1994: 261). Field's suggestion is problematic in several ways. First, it is unclear *why* we should take the supposition that Kripke expresses in the passage quoted above as grounds for inferring 'Gödel did not discover the incompleteness theorem.' A committed description theorist who believes that Gödel is the one who discovered the incompleteness theorem may refuse to infer that 'Gödel did not discover the incompleteness theorem', and insist, instead, either that Kripke's word 'Gödel' should not be translated as 'Gödel', or that Kripke's supposition that Gödel did not discover the incompleteness theorem is contradictory, and should therefore be rejected. Field's deflationary account of reference and truth is compatible with a wide number of inferences; it does not imply that we should accept the inference Field favours, and not the one that the description theorist prefers. Hence Field's suggestion that we regard Kripke's observations about reference as observations about inferential practice does not explain why the description theorist's response to Kripke's thought experiment is unacceptable.

If we adopt the PJSS-based conception of words, however, we can combine a deflationary account of satisfaction for the name predicates 'Gödels' and 'Schmidts' with our PIWs and PJSSs for the words of Kripke's thought experiment. We can resist the description theorist's response by pointing out that it amounts to a rejection of the context principle, and with it of the PJSS-based conception of words. We have independent grounds for adopting the PJSS-based conception of words; the fact that it fits with our judgements about Kripke's thought experiment is another good reason for adopting it. By supplementing Quine's method of paraphrasing proper names as descriptions with the PJSS-based conception of words, we can simultaneously embrace the spirit of Kripke's thought experiments, hence reject robust description theories of proper names, yet also reject Kripke's causal theory of reference for proper names.[1]

9.4. What is Minimal Self-Knowledge?

If we reject the description theory of reference and embrace the PJSS-based conception of words, as I recommend, then the beliefs one associates with one's words do not determine the extensions of one's words. How then can we make sense of minimal self-knowledge—the familiar fact that (in a sense yet to be clarified) every speaker typically knows without empirical investigation what thoughts his utterances express? To begin with, I propose that we adopt the following constraint on the explication of the phrase 'minimal self-knowledge':

(C1) To take a speaker to use words of her language to express thoughts, make claims, raise questions, and so on is also to take her to have minimal self-knowledge of the thoughts she thereby expresses.

For instance, when Al says, "I have arthritis in my thigh," in the situation described in Chapter 5, we take Al to have said that he has arthritis in his thigh. By (C1), to take Al to have said that he has arthritis in his thigh by uttering the sentence 'I have arthritis in my thigh' is also to take Al to have

---

[1] Recall that if Quinean descriptions are prefixed by Burge's @-operator (Burge 2005: 229–30), they can also mirror the behaviour of rigid names in modal contexts. See Chapter 1, note 21.

minimal self-knowledge of the thought that he thereby expresses—the thought that he has arthritis in his thigh.

Unfortunately, however, (C1) conflicts with the tempting and deeply entrenched assumption that

> (C2) A speaker has minimal self-knowledge only if he has accurate beliefs about the truth conditions of his utterances.

For instance, before Al talks to his doctor, he does not realize that his utterance of 'I have arthritis in my thigh' could not be true, and so he does not fully understand the truth conditions of his utterance. If we accept (C2), we will conclude that Al does not know what thought his utterance of 'I have arthritis in my thigh' expresses, and so he does not know without empirical investigation what thought his utterance of 'I have arthritis in my thigh' expresses. But when we conclude for this reason that Al does not know what thought his utterance of 'I have arthritis in my thigh' expresses, we still take Al's utterance of 'I have arthritis in my thigh' to express the thought that Al has arthritis in his thigh. And when we take his utterance of 'I have arthritis in my thigh' in this way, according to (C1), we take Al to know without empirical investigation what thought his utterance of 'I have arthritis in my thigh' expresses. In this way, (C1) and (C2) conflict.

In the next few sections, I will explain how to resolve this conflict in favour of (C1). I will first explain why so many philosophers are attracted to (C2), and explore its consequences in more detail. I will then elucidate linguistic competence and minimal self-knowledge in terms of our PJSSs and explain how the resulting account of minimal self-knowledge differs from accounts that entail (C2).

9.5. Minimal Self-Knowledge as Second Order

Most philosophers who accept (C2) find it so obvious that they are not inclined to provide any explicit argument for it. To evaluate (C2), however, one must first understand the source of its appeal. As I see it, (C2) is the inevitable consequence of an attractive but flawed line of reasoning. The reasoning begins with the harmless observation that

> (1) A speaker has minimal self-knowledge only if he knows without empirical investigation what thoughts his own utterances express.

This apparently follows from the standard characterization of minimal self-knowledge that I presented above. From (1) we can infer

(2) A speaker has minimal self-knowledge only if he knows what thoughts his own utterances express.

It has long been standard in analytical philosophy to assume that

(3) The thought expressed by an utterance is individuated by the truth conditions of the utterance.

This is best seen as a proposal for clarifying the ambiguous word 'thought' and, with it, minimal self-knowledge, which, given (3), can now be described as the familiar fact that every speaker knows the *truth conditions* of his utterances without investigation. Finally, it seems undeniable that

(4) A speaker knows the truth conditions of his utterances only if he has accurate beliefs about the truth conditions of his utterances.

From (3) and (4) we can conclude

(5) A speaker knows what thoughts his utterances express only if he has accurate beliefs about the truth conditions of his utterances.

And from (2) and (5) we can conclude

(C2) A speaker has minimal self-knowledge only if he has accurate beliefs about the truth conditions of his utterances.

To accept this line of reasoning is to accept that minimal self-knowledge is second order, in the sense that sentences that ascribe to a given speaker *A* minimal self-knowledge of the thought expressed by *A*'s utterance of sentence *s* have the form "*A* knows without empirical investigation that *s* is true if and only if *p*," where '*p*' is replaced by a declarative sentence that expresses the thought that *A*'s utterance of *s* expresses.

To avoid triviality, we cannot allow that to have minimal self-knowledge it is enough to master the merely formal schema "*s*' is true if and only if *s*'. Donald Davidson seems dangerously close to trivializing self-knowledge when he writes:

The speaker, after bending whatever knowledge and craft he can to the task of saying what his words mean, cannot improve on the following sort of statement:

"My utterance of 'Wagner died happy' is true if and only if Wagner died happy."
(Davidson 2001a: 13)

For Davidson, however, even if each speaker's epistemic access to this
biconditional is formal, her first-person use of it makes a substantive
second-order claim about the truth conditions of her sentence 'Wagner
died happy' that is *guaranteed* to be true by the principles that govern
interpretation. As we saw in Chapter 5, for Davidson all interpretation,
including our interpretation of a first-person use of this biconditional, is
governed by a principle of charity that guarantees that "nothing could count
as someone regularly misapplying her own words" (Davidson 2001b: 38).
The principle of charity requires that the interpretation of a speaker's beliefs
about how to apply her words fit with the interpretation of her words in
such a way that she is not generally wrong about the truth conditions of
her sentences. Understood in this way, the speaker's biconditional makes
a substantive claim about the truth conditions of her sentence. Moreover,
according to Davidson, substantive claims of this kind are in general
guaranteed to be true by the nature of interpretation, which is governed
by the principle of charity.

Ultimately the reason that we each have minimal self-knowledge, on
this view, is that interpretation is governed by the principle of charity. This
also explains why those who are attempting to interpret us do not know
without empirical investigation what the truth conditions of our utterances
are. Davidson's second-order account of minimal self-knowledge therefore
accords with (C2), but only because it presupposes his principle of charity.

9.6. Basic Self-Knowledge and Containment

It is tempting to think that if we accept (C2), as many philosophers
do, then we can be sure without empirical investigation that a speaker's
beliefs about the truth conditions of his sentences are accurate only if the
accuracy of these beliefs is guaranteed by an a priori principle that governs
interpretation, such as Davidson's principle of charity. But Tyler Burge
has proposed an account of minimal self-knowledge that challenges this
reasoning. Like Davidson's account of minimal self-knowledge, Burge's
account is both second order and compatible with (C2). Unlike Davidson's

account, however, Burge's account does not rely on a principle of charity. Burge focuses on what he calls basic self-knowledge. An example is the belief that I can express by using the sentence 'I think (with this very thought) that writing requires concentration.' Such beliefs are second order, in the sense that they are "about" first-order thoughts. My belief that I think (with this very thought) that writing requires concentration is "about" the first-order thought that writing requires concentration, but it is not metalinguistic. Burge's explanation of why such beliefs are acceptable is structural: "When one knows that one is thinking that p, one is not taking one's thought (or thinking) that p merely as an object. One is thinking that p in the very event of thinking knowledgeably that one is thinking it. It is thought and thought about in the same mental act" (Burge 1988: 654). In other words, "One knows one's thought to be what it is simply by thinking it while exercising second-order, self-ascriptive powers" (Burge 1988: 656). This formulation makes it clear that according to Burge, minimal self-knowledge is second order, but does not depend for its justification on a principle of charity.

One problem with this account is that it presupposes that in general speakers are in a position to think their first-order thoughts self-ascriptively. It offers no explanation or justification of this presupposition. In the present context, this is question-begging, since Burge applies his account of self-knowledge to "explain" how speakers can know what they are thinking even when they express their thoughts by using sentences whose truth conditions they do not completely understand. For instance, according to Burge, Al would be justified in accepting the belief he would express by using the sentence 'I think (with this very thought) that arthritis can occur in one's thigh.' Hence Al knows that he is thinking that arthritis can occur in one's thigh. This routine application of Burge's account of basic self-knowledge violates Davidson's principle of charity.

To reconcile his account with (C2), Burge might say that to have accurate beliefs about the truth conditions of one's utterances, in the sense relevant to self-knowledge, is simply to be able to use one's utterances to express one's second-order knowledge of the first-order thoughts (truth conditions) that they express. In this sense, one can have an accurate belief about the truth conditions of one's utterances while still being quite confused about the conditions under which they are true. For instance, Al has accurate beliefs about the truth conditions of his sentence 'Arthritis can occur in one's thigh' when he affirms his sentence 'I think (with this very thought) that arthritis can occur in one's thigh', which self-ascriptively expresses the first-order thought expressed by the sentence 'Arthritis can occur in one's thigh.'

According to Burge, all that is required for a speaker to have minimal self-knowledge of the thought she expresses by using a given first-order sentence *s* is that she has minimal linguistic competence in the use of the second-order sentence 'I am thinking (with this very thought) that *s*', where her minimal linguistic competence in the use of the second-order sentence includes but does not augment her minimal linguistic competence in the use of *s*. The standard way of thinking of minimal self-knowledge as second-order, characterized by the argument (1)–(5) above, goes beyond this formal requirement; it implies that minimal linguistic competence in the use of a first-order sentence does not guarantee that one can use that sentence to express one's own thought or belief. According to this way of thinking, a speaker who has the kind of linguistic competence in the use of the first-order sentence *s* that is necessary for second-order minimal self-knowledge of the thoughts and beliefs she expresses by using *s* also has minimal linguistic competence in the use of *s*; but it is not in general true that if a speaker has minimal linguistic competence in the use of a different first-order sentence *s*, she thereby also has the kind of linguistic competence in the use of *s* that is necessary for second-order minimal self-knowledge of the thoughts and beliefs she expresses by using *s*. If she does not have the kind of linguistic competence in the use of *s* that is necessary for second-order minimal self-knowledge of the thoughts and beliefs she expresses by using *s*, then she can "use" *s* only in an attenuated, metalinguistic sense. Strictly speaking, she is not (transparently) *using* the sentence to make claims or express her thoughts and beliefs, she is only *going through the motions of using it*, and does not know what thoughts her "uses" of *s* express.

This reasoning suggests that when we ask ourselves whether we have minimal self-knowledge of the thought or belief we express by using a given sentence *s*, we are asking a substantive question that is not settled by our minimal linguistic competence. We may *take* ourselves to be able to use *s* to express our own thoughts and beliefs, when in fact we can at best only describe our "use" of *s* metalinguistically, without knowing what thoughts we express when we utter *s*.

Several contemporary philosophers have described positions of this kind.
For instance, Gareth Evans agrees with Burge that linguistic interpretation
is not constrained by Davidson's principle of charity, but insists, in effect,
that a speaker who has only minimal linguistic competence in the use
of certain words does not have minimal self-knowledge of the thoughts
that she expresses by using those words. Evans relies on the principle that
"if a speaker uses a word with the manifest intention to participate in
such-and-such a practice, in which the word is used with such-and-such
semantic properties, then the word, as used by him, will possess just those
semantic properties" (Evans 1982: 387). Evans also proposes that we "think
of individuating the words of a language not only phonetically but also
by reference to the practices in which they are used. In these terms, the
requirement on a speaker using a proper name is not that he indicate which
object he intends to be (taken to be) referring to, but that he indicate which
name he intends to be (taken to be) using" (Evans 1982: 384). To this
extent, Evans's approach to linguistic interpretation is compatible with our
PJSSs, and with Burge's recommendations about how to interpret other
speakers. It therefore conflicts with Donald Davidson's principle of charity,
for reasons I explained in Chapter 5.

According to Evans, however, further conditions must be met before a
speaker can be credited with entertaining the thoughts that her utterances
express. For any ordinary practice of using a proper name, there is a group of
speakers who have been introduced to the practice by their *acquaintance* with
the person to whom the name refers. For instance, there is a group of speakers who have been introduced to the practice of using the name 'Maurizio
Pollini' by their acquaintance with Maurizio Pollini. Evans calls members of
this group the "producers" of the name-using practice (Evans 1982: 376). In
some name-using practices, there is also a group of speakers who participate
in the practice of using a particular name even though they are not acquainted with the person to whom the name refers. There are many speakers
who participate in the practice of using the name 'Maurizio Pollini' even
though they are not acquainted with Maurizio Pollini. The speakers may be
introduced into the practice in a number of different ways. Perhaps some of
them are told that "Maurizio Pollini is the greatest living concert pianist",
for instance, while others simply hear on the radio, "That performance of
the Chopin Études, Opus 25, was by Maurizio Pollini." Evans calls such
members of the name-using practice "consumers" (Evans 1982: 377).

According to Evans, consumers of the name-using practice have no role in connecting the name with the person to whom it refers. In contrast, "It is the actual patterns of dealings the producers have had with an individual—identified from time to time by the exercise of their recognitional capacities in regard to that individual—which ties the name to the individual" (Evans 1982: 382). In a similar way, he claims, there are producers and consumers of practices of using natural-kind terms: "it is a central feature of the practices associated with terms like 'elm', 'diamond', 'leopard', and like that there exist members—producers—who have . . . an effective capacity to distinguish occasions when they are presented with members of that kind, from occasions when they are presented with members of any other kinds which are represented in any strength in the environment they inhabit" (Evans 1982: 382).

On the basis of this distinction between producers and consumers of practices of using proper names and natural-kind terms, Evans draws a distinction between participating in a practice, and thereby "using" a given name, on the one hand, and entertaining thoughts about the referent of the name, on the other. He insists that "It is a perfectly intelligible possibility, occasionally realized, that someone can use an expression to refer without being himself in a position to understand the reference" (Evans 1982: 398). One can participate in a practice of using a given name, such as 'Maurizio Pollini', without being a producer of that practice, hence, according to Evans, without being able to use that name to entertain thoughts about Maurizio Pollini. According to this view, a speaker with only minimal competence in the use of a proper name 'N.N.' does not *understand* what is said by using that name in sentences, including sentences of the form 'N.N. is F'. To say that he does not understand in this context, according to Evans is to say that "he does not know the truth-conditions of, e.g., 'N.N. is F'" (Evans 1982: 403). Thus Evans believes that in order for the speaker to understand what she says when she uses a sentence of the form 'N.N. is F', she must know the truth conditions of the thought that is expressed in the practice by that sentence. Although Evans does not make this explicit, he is clearly assuming that to know the truth conditions is to have detailed and accurate beliefs about the truth conditions. But a speaker who has only minimal linguistic competence in the use of 'N.N.' is merely a consumer of the 'N.N.'-using practice, and hence does not have detailed and accurate beliefs about the truth conditions of thoughts she expresses by using that sentence. In this sense, such a speaker does not know the truth conditions of those thoughts. In contrast, Evans believes, producers of the 'N.N.'-using practice do have accurate beliefs about the truth conditions of thoughts they express by using sentences in which the name occurs. Hence producers of the 'N.N.'-using practice are able to use the name 'N.N.' to refer to N.N., and consumers of the practice—those who have only minimal competence in the use of 'N.N.'—are not able to use the name 'N.N.' to refer to N.N.

At the same time, however, Evans wants to grant that consumers of the practice are in a position to "use" the name 'N.N.' But what can the speaker "use" the name 'N.N.' *for* if not to refer to N.N.? Evans hints at an answer when he notes that

There is . . . a powerful temptation to argue that, if someone is competent in the *use* of a proper name (and hence able to function as a link in a chain by which information about its referent can be transmitted), then his acquisition of that competence must itself have put him in a position to entertain thoughts about its referent.   (Evans 1982: 403)

According to Evans, a person who counts as minimally competent in the "use" of a word is not thereby able to use it transparently, in the sense of 'transparently' explained in §4.2. Such a person may nevertheless "function as a link in a chain by which information about its referent can be transmitted". But to function as a link in such a chain, the person must "use" the name in some sense, even if she does not *entertain* the thoughts she expresses by using it in that way. Evans does not actually address the question of how to describe the "use" of the name from the speaker's first-person perspective. She will probably take herself to be entertaining the thoughts that she expresses by using it, even if, by Evans's standards, she is not actually able to do this. Such a speaker counts as "using" her words in some sense, according to Evans, even though she does not use them transparently.

Evans is driven to this conclusion by (C2), the assumption that minimal self-knowledge requires second-order knowledge of the truth conditions of the thoughts one's utterances express, together with his observation that ordinary linguistic interpretation is not governed by the principle of charity. Hence Evans concludes that (C2) is incompatible with (C1). Burge's containment account of basic self-knowledge does not address this sort of position, and therefore does not show that (C1) and (C2) are compatible.

9.7. Minimal Self-Knowledge as First Order

I propose that we reject (C2), and embrace (C1). In my view, to have minimal self-knowledge of the thoughts one expresses by using one's words, it is enough to have minimal linguistic competence in the use of those words. Moreover, in my view, *to make PIWs and PJSSs for another speaker's words is to take her to be minimally competent in the use of those words.* Such competence requires more than simply writing or uttering sentences in which the words occur. What more it requires can only be discovered by examining our practices of taking speakers to be using words of English. For instance, we know that we wouldn't take a speaker to be using the English word 'apple' competently if she applies it only to points of light visible in the night sky. This does not mean that we English-speakers have very strict requirements for competence in the use of the word 'apple'. A child who at first refuses to call a green apple an 'apple' might still be taken to be able to use the word 'apple' to express beliefs and desires about *apples* and to believe that the green apple is not an apple, provided that she has some other beliefs about apples, including some true beliefs that she expresses by using the sentence 'That's an apple.' This does not imply that to use a given word, we *must* make some true demonstrative claims by using that word. Minimal competence in the use of some words can be picked up very quickly, just on the basis of what the speaker was told, even if what she was told is false. The requirements for minimal competence in the use of words vary from word to word, and, in some cases, from context to context. Given the context principle, we have no grip on these requirements apart from our PIWs and PJSSs.

Even though there are no strict requirements for minimal competence in the use of most words, to take someone to express a thought by using a given word is also to take him to have some beliefs that he expresses by using that word. Such beliefs do not *determine* the truth conditions of the thoughts he uses that word to express, since the beliefs may be false or misleading; instead, the beliefs are part of the speaker's present *understanding* of those truth conditions.

Our judgements about minimal competence are intimately linked with our judgements about when a speaker has minimal self-knowledge.[2] To credit a speaker of a given natural language with minimal self-knowledge is to take her to be able to use words of her own language to express thoughts, make claims, raise questions, and so on. Any situation in which we are willing to take another's words at face value is thereby also one in which we will credit her with having minimal self-knowledge.[3] Hence, contrary to (C2), a speaker may have minimal self-knowledge of the thoughts she expresses by using her sentences even if her understanding of the truth conditions of the sentences is partial, confused, or incorrect.

According to the account I recommend, minimal self-knowledge is much more widespread than second-order knowledge of what one is thinking. It is as widespread as the everyday use of language to express thoughts, evaluate beliefs, raise questions, and so on, just as (C1) suggests. The kind of self-knowledge embodied in these everyday uses of language is not best viewed as a *disposition* to form justified second-order beliefs about what one is thinking, either.[4] To credit anyone with being able to form or justify such second-order beliefs, we must presuppose that she already has the kind of minimal self-knowledge that goes with linguistic competence.[5]

I conclude that minimal competence and minimal self-knowledge go hand in hand—the same phenomena that lead us to say that Al believes that he has arthritis in his thigh thereby also lead us to say that Al has minimal self-knowledge of what thought his utterance of 'I have arthritis in my thigh' expresses. To note that ordinary speakers have minimal self-knowledge is not to make a substantive theoretical commitment that

---

[2] This does not imply that a speaker cannot use words that have the same *spelling* as words of a public language so idiosyncratically that her words have meanings different from the meanings that the identically spelled words have in the public language. Such uses would be judged incompetent as uses of the identically spelled public-language words, and yet the idiosyncratic speaker may still express thoughts by using her identically spelled words and have minimal self-knowledge of what thoughts she expresses by using them. This happens much less frequently than most individualists believe, however. And when it does happen, there are usually some words of the public language that she uses competently, and that help other speakers to figure out what thoughts the speaker's idiosyncratic utterances express.

[3] For a more thorough presentation of the points in this and the previous paragraph, see Ebbs 1996 and Ebbs 1997, §§100–23. For a parallel point about what it is to know the meanings of one's own *words*, see Putnam 1988: 32.

[4] See McLaughlin and Tye 1998: 286–7 for a brief description (and apparent endorsement) of a dispositional view of self-knowledge.

[5] This is the kernel of truth behind Anthony Brueckner's criticisms of Burge and Davidson in Brueckner 1992, and the metalinguistic criticism of Burge sketched above.

is independent of and stronger than our initial judgement that in the circumstances described in Chapter 5, Al believes that he has arthritis in his thigh; it is simply to acknowledge that in making PIWs and PJSSs for another speaker's words, we thereby also take her to know what she is talking about in a minimal sense that goes with competence.

It is important to see that, according to my proposal, we do not take a speaker to be minimally competent in the use of a word unless we take her to be able to use the word, in the transparent sense of "use" that contrasts with merely mentioning the word. On this account, there's no gap whatever between taking a speaker to be minimally competent in the use of a given word, on the one hand, and taking her to have minimal self-knowledge of the thoughts she expresses by using it, on the other. Against this, one might think that to have minimal self-knowledge of the thoughts one expresses by using certain words, one must know the dictionary definition or conventional meaning of those words. A speaker who has only minimal linguistic competence in the use of those words might not know the dictionary definitions or conventional meanings of those words and hence might have only a minimal understanding of the thoughts she expresses by using those words.[6] One might think that a minimal understanding of the thoughts one expresses by using one's words is not enough for genuinely "entertaining" those thoughts—not enough for having self-knowledge. This would be similar in some respects to Evans's position, yet apparently couched in terms of a first-order account of self-knowledge.

[6] Paul Horwich claims that

as long as [an] individual has acquired the word from the community and has a minimal understanding of it, the communal language meaning may be correctly attributed to him—he means by it what everyone else means. But he *knows* what it means only to the extent that whatever constitutes its meaning in his idiolect resembles whatever constitutes its meaning in the communal language. (Horwich 1998b: 18)

Suppose provisionally that to make practical judgements of sameness of satisfaction for another speaker's words is also to take her words to have the same *meanings* as ours. Then the passage just quoted implies that we take another speaker's words to have the same meanings as our words if we take him to be minimally competent in the use of those words. Horwich distinguishes between this claim and the claim that a speaker knows the dictionary definitions or conventional meanings of those words. Horwich says that "The degree to which an individual understands the word is constituted by the degree of similarity between what it means in his idiolect and what it means in the communal language" (Horwich 1998b: 17–18). My account of minimal self-knowledge is not an account of knowledge of meaning. But Horwich's account might be understood in a way that conflicts with what I am saying about minimal self-knowledge. For it might be thought that to have minimal self-knowledge of the thoughts one expresses by using certain words, one needs more than minimal linguistic competence in the use of those words. This is the objection I try to answer in the text.

But if minimal linguistic competence is understood in the way that I propose, to credit a speaker with minimal linguistic competence in the use of certain words is simply to accept one's PIWs and PJSSs for her utterances, and thereby to take her to be able to use the words transparently. This is then also sufficient for crediting her with minimal self-knowledge of the thoughts her utterances of those words express. The fact that some speakers know more about the consequences of their utterances and the conditions under which they are true is irrelevant to the question whether speakers who are minimally linguistically competent in the use of a given set of words have minimal self-knowledge of which thoughts their utterances of those words express. Even if other kinds of knowledge come in degrees, minimal self-knowledge does not. One can define a more demanding kind of self-knowledge than the kind of minimal self-knowledge that goes with minimal linguistic competence. In the sense of 'minimal self-knowledge' that I aim to explicate, however, a speaker counts as having minimal self-knowledge of the thoughts her utterances of a given set of words express if she is minimally linguistically competent in the use of those words.

One might object that my account is inadequate because it does not capture all of our intuitions about what it means to say that a given speaker has minimal self-knowledge of what thought her utterances express. But this objection rests on a misunderstanding. The phrase 'minimal self-knowledge' contains only ordinary words, yet there is no established ordinary use of it. Although philosophers agree on a few core constraints on explications of the phrase 'minimal self-knowledge', our intuitions about how to understand it are not independent of our theoretical commitments, and hence do not provide independent constraints on its proper explication. Many philosophers are attracted to a substantive, second-order understanding of minimal self-knowledge that is incompatible with (C1). I have proposed, instead, a deflationary account of minimal self-knowledge that is compatible with (C1). In my view, the deflationary account is the more fruitful one because it fits and further illuminates the PJSS-based conception of words.

9.8. Minimal Self-Knowledge as Practical Knowledge

If we view minimal self-knowledge as first order in the way that I recommend, we will see it as an aspect of our practical knowledge of how to use words, hence as a kind of knowledge how, not knowledge that, or propositional knowledge. Jason Stanley and Timothy Williamson argue that ascriptions of knowledge of how to do something are in fact ascriptions of propositional knowledge, and take their conclusion to discredit any view according to which minimal linguistic competence is a form of non-propositional practical knowledge. Focusing on Michael Devitt's view that linguistic competence is a kind of knowledge how, they reason as follows:

competence with the term t at least involves knowing how to use t with a certain meaning, presumably the meaning that actually has. But if competence with a term t involves knowing how to use t with the meaning it actually has, the linguistic competence with the term does ... yield propositional knowledge about the meaning of that term. For, given a term t which has a certain meaning m, x's knowing how to use t with the meaning m amounts, for some contextually relevant way w, to x's knowing that w is a way for x to use t with the meaning m. (Stanley and Williamson 2001: 444)

This reasoning is general and may therefore seem to apply to the account of minimal competence and self-knowledge that I have proposed. To figure out whether it does apply to my account, we must ask whether according to my account there is an interpretation of 'use' under which

(*) given a term t which has a certain meaning m, x's knowing how to use t with the meaning m amounts, for some contextually relevant way w, to x's knowing that w is a way for x to use t with the meaning m

is true. The answer is "no." To see why, recall that to mention a word, such as 'Boston', one must use a name of that word. For instance, one may use the word ''Boston'' to refer to the word 'Boston'. In contrast, I *transparently* use the word 'Boston' when I say, for instance, that Boston is a populous city. But when I take a speaker to use the word 'Boston' in this transparent way, I regard her as linguistically competent in the use of 'Boston'. If we understand "use" as it occurs in (*) in this way, it would be legitimate to characterize a speaker's practical knowledge of how to use the word 'Boston' to refer to Boston, for instance, as her propositional knowledge that using the word 'Boston' to refer to Boston is a way of using the word 'Boston' to refer to Boston. But this characterization is circular: it presupposes what it is supposed to analyse—the knowledge of how to use 'Boston' transparently to refer to Boston. Hence the transparent sense of 'use' cannot be what Williamson and Stanley have in mind. The sense of 'use' that they have in mind must be *ex-use*—the kind of word use that can be described independent of whether or not the individual is competent to use a word transparently. Their arguments therefore presuppose the doubtful thesis that a speaker's practical knowledge of how to use a language can be described exhaustively in terms of language ex-use.

Perhaps some accounts of minimal linguistic self-knowledge, such as Devitt's, presuppose this doubtful thesis, but mine does not. On the contrary, my proposed elucidation of minimal self-knowledge in terms of the PJSS-based conception of words presupposes the context principle, according to which we have no understanding of the same-word relation apart from our PIWs and PJSSs. The thesis that language use can be described in terms of ex-use amounts to a rejection of the context principle and the PJSS-based conception of words. If we adopt the context principle and the PJSS-based conception of words, on the other hand, then to attribute minimal self-knowledge to a speaker is not to attribute to her any substantive metalinguistic knowledge of how to use her words. When an English-speaker states that Boston is a populous city, for instance, she may know that uttering the sentence 'Boston is a populous city' is a way of saying that Boston is a populous city. But to attribute this disquotational metalinguistic knowledge to her, we must make PIWs and PJSSs for her words that *presuppose* that she can transparently use the sentence 'Boston is a populous city.' We therefore cannot regard her knowledge of the disquotational metalinguistic statement as a characterization or explanation of her ability to use the words 'Boston is a populous city' transparently. I conclude that both minimal linguistic competence and the minimal self-knowledge that goes with it are forms of non-propositional practical knowledge.

9.9. The Division of Epistemic Labour

The first-order, practical conception of minimal self-knowledge that I described in the last two sections fits with (C1), the observation that to take a speaker to use words of her language to express thoughts, make claims, raise questions, and so on is also to take her to have minimal self-knowledge of the thoughts she thereby expresses. This observation is integral to our understanding of the phenomenon of learning from others. As I argued in Chapter 5, if we wish to save the phenomenon of learning from others, we must adopt the PJSS-based conception of words. If we now add our new explication of self-knowledge, we can also infer that to regard ourselves or others as having learned that a particular sentence s that we previously uttered is false we must see ourselves as having had minimal self-knowledge of what thought we expressed by uttering s at some time *before* we learned that it is false. Let us now consider how these observations bear on the philosophical thesis that there is a division of linguistic labour.

Let S be a speaker whose transparent uses of a word w are only minimally competent relative to what I will call the w-experts—those who know most about the topic they identify by their transparent uses of w. According to the standard account of the division of linguistic labour, it may be that

(a) S transparently uses word w at t.
(b) The extension of w as used by S at t is determined by facts about how the w-experts in C ex-use w at or before t.

The thought experiments explored in Chapters 6–8 show that for many words, among them the kinds of words that philosophers focus on when they posit a division of linguistic labour, (b) is false. We must adopt the PJSS-based conception of words and reject (b) if we want to preserve and make sense of the ever-present possibility that even the most trusted experts in our linguistic community are wrong about the extensions of our terms. Hence there is no such thing as the division of linguistic labour, as standardly understood. The hypothesis that there is a division of *linguistic* labour is based in a misunderstanding of cases in which we trust or defer to the judgement of another about some topic that we both identify by transparently using the same word. Properly viewed, such cases illustrate what I call the division of *epistemic* labour among speakers who express thoughts about a given topic by transparently using what they take to be tokens of a single PJSS-based word type.

The division of epistemic labour is more general than the phenomenon of learning from others, since there is no guarantee that when we make PIWs and PJSSs for another speaker's words and trust what she tells us, we are learning from her. The division of epistemic labour relies on trust, which doesn't guarantee truth. Why then is it valuable to us? In the midst of our inquiries we trust what others write or say. We are aware that no one's judgement is guaranteed to be true, so we also seek the benefit of criticism and discussion from others who spend time investigating topics we have spent a great deal of time investigating. This is a pragmatic, conditional motivation for participating in the division of labour: given our interests in inquiry, our limited time and resources, we *want* to participate in a practice in which epistemic labour is shared.

Some speakers know more about some topics than others do. Unfortunately, these are not always the speakers who were treated as epistemically authoritative about those topics. Ideally, we would like our division of epistemic labour to reflect differences in what speakers know. Whether or not they reflect such differences, however, when we trust what others say, we thereby regard them as authoritative. The phenomenon of deference of one speaker's usage to another that is typically associated with "the division of linguistic labour" is best viewed not as a device that enables the reference of the term to be "transmitted" from one speaker to another, but as a case in which one speaker *trusts* another's claims about a given topic, thereby showing that she regards the other speaker as more knowledgeable than she is about that topic.

According to my proposed account of self-knowledge, a speaker who participates in the division of epistemic labour has minimal competence, and thereby also minimal self-knowledge of the thoughts she expresses by using sentences in which those terms occur. One might object to this consequence of my account of the division of epistemic labour, reasoning as follows: "You claim that your account of minimal self-knowledge fits with our ordinary attributions of minimal self-knowledge, and that these are elucidated by our judgements about when speakers are minimally competent in the use of words of a shared language. Yet many individuals who know very little about a given topic are able to participate in the division of epistemic labour regarding that topic. They are minimally competent, and hence, according to you, they have minimal self-knowledge. The trouble is that in many of these cases it would be appropriate to say, of such a speaker, when he uses the term that picks out that topic, 'Don't listen to him—he doesn't know what he's talking about!' In short, your account of minimal self-knowledge doesn't fit with what we are inclined to say about ignorant but minimally competent speakers."

I agree that even if a speaker has minimal self-knowledge in the sense I have described, it may be appropriate to say "Don't listen to him—he doesn't know what he's talking about!" But as I understand it, this is an *epistemic* remark that could be paraphrased without loss with the words "Don't trust what he says—he doesn't know anything about that topic!"[7] If the speaker knows very little about cats, for instance, but she carries on as if she knows a great deal about them, we might say "Don't trust what she says about cats—she doesn't know anything about cats!" All of these critical remarks take for granted that the speaker is competent in the use of the relevant terms to make claims; the main thrust of the remark is that we should not trust those claims. The objection goes further and suggests that the remark conflicts with the assumption that she has minimal self-knowledge. But a closer look at such cases dispels this appearance. Suppose we confront the woman who knows very little about cats with a list of her misunderstandings and errors, and we appeal to an authority she does not doubt. Then she may well look back on her previous performances and say something of the form, "I used to think cats are so and so, but now I'm not so sure." In other words, she takes responsibility for what she thought previously, she does not in retrospect question whether she even knew that she was entertaining thoughts about cats, or that she believed that cats were so and so. In this sense she had minimal self-knowledge even if it would have been appropriate to say "She doesn't know what she's talking about." Contrary to the objection, then, this kind of remark typically expresses an *epistemological* criticism of a speaker's thoughts, one that takes for granted that she has minimal self-knowledge of those thoughts, and hence can participate in the division of epistemic labour.

9.10. Judging Minimal Linguistic Competence across Time

My accounts of linguistic competence, minimal self-knowledge, and the division of epistemic labour imply that we cannot accurately judge minimal

---

[7] See Putnam 1975: 248 for a similar observation about the sense in which a person who thinks that the Vietnam war was fought to help the South Vietnamese "doesn't know what he is talking about".

competence and minimal self-knowledge solely from our present epistemic perspective. Consider, for instance, our current standards for regarding someone as minimally competent in the use of the English word 'Earth'. If we encounter someone today who sincerely utters the sentence 'Earth is not round, but flat, and it is not a planet', and this person appears to be minimally competent in the use the words 'flat' and 'planet', we will likely suspend our initial tendency to take the speaker to be minimally competent in the use of our word 'Earth'. In England many centuries ago, however, the sentences 'The Earth is round', or 'The Earth is a planet' were widely rejected. Yet our English word 'Earth' is in fact linked to those past uses by chains of PIWs across time. Trusting these chains, we commit ourselves to PIWs across time for tokens of E-a-r-t-h, as used by English-speakers long ago. We thereby take these English-speakers to have been minimally competent, *relative to the standards of their time*, in the use of our English word 'Earth'. Hence there is a conflict between what the historical chains of judgements entail and what we are now inclined unreflectively to judge about whether English-speakers long ago were competent in the English word 'Earth'.[8]

I propose that we trust our PIWs and PJSSs across time more than we trust our current unreflective evaluations of the competence of speakers who lived long ago. This fits with my earlier observation that we trust our PIWs and PJSSs across time more than we trust our current speculations about what counts as changing the topic and what counts as saying something different about the same topic. Just as PIWs and PJSSs are central to our grasp of the phenomenon of discovery, so they are central to our grasp of minimal competence and minimal self-knowledge of speakers who lived long ago. As the 'Earth' example shows, our current standards for minimal competence and minimal self-knowledge may differ from the judgements of minimal competence and minimal self-knowledge to which we are committed when we trust our PIWs and PJSSs across time.

One might think that when PIWs and PJSSs across time conflict with our current inclination to judge that speakers long ago were not competent in the use of our words, it is just as reasonable to reject the chains of PIWs, and the PJSSs they license, as it is to reject the inclination. There is no neutral perspective from which to evaluate this concern. The force of

---

[8] I owe this example to Erica Neely.

any philosophical recommendation depends on one's goals and interests. Philosophers who do not care to save the phenomena of agreement and disagreement between speakers, both at a time and across time, and of sameness of satisfaction despite radical changes in theory and belief will not be persuaded by the reasons I have offered for trusting our PIWs and PJSSs across time more than our current inclination to judge that speakers long ago were not competent in the use of our words. My claim is conditional: *if* one wants to save the phenomena of agreement and disagreement between speakers, both at a time and across time, and of sameness of satisfaction despite radical changes in theory and belief, *then* one should adopt the PJSS-based conception of words, and explicate minimal competence and minimal self-knowledge in the way that I sketched above.

9.11. Anti-Individualism, Externalism, and Linguistic Communities

In Chapters 6 to 8 I used Twin-Earth thought experiments to show that there is no way to satisfy the intersubjectivity constraint without adopting the PJSS-based conception of words and the context principle. I want now to explain how my conclusions bear on our understanding of Hilary Putnam's original Twin Earth thought experiments. Like the thought experiments I presented in Chapters 6–8, Putnam's Twin Earth thought experiments (in Putnam 1975) highlight our PIWs, PJSSs, and PJSEs. In the first of these we imagine that Oscar, an ordinary English-speaker who is competent in the use of the English word 'water' but does not accept (or reject) the sentence 'Water is H_2O', utters a sentence containing the word 'water', for instance, the sentence 'Water is a liquid at room temperature.'[9] Since Oscar is a competent English-speaker, other English-speakers take his word 'water' to be the same as their word

---

[9] It helps to imagine a context in which Oscar may actually say this. One possibility is that Oscar is explaining to his son that ice is (solid) water, not just that water *turns into* ice when it freezes. In this context, 'Water is a liquid at room temperature' may be the first of two sentences that Oscar utters, the second one being 'But ice is water, too—water that is at or below the freezing point.' This is compatible with our supposition that Oscar does not know that water is H_2O—Oscar may know that ice is water that is at or below the freezing point even if he forgot, or never learned, that water is H_2O.

'water', hence they take him to have said that *water is a liquid at room temperature*. If, in addition, they think his utterance is sincere, they take him to believe this.

In the next step of his thought experiment, Putnam stipulates that there is a planet called Twin Earth which is just like Earth except that wherever there is water on Earth there is twin water, a liquid with an underlying chemical structure that is very different from the chemical structure of water, on Twin Earth. He supposes that on Twin Earth there lives a physical, phenomenological, and behavioural twin of Oscar, whom I'll call Twin Oscar. Twin Oscar is a normal speaker of Twin English, the Twin Earth counterpart of English. When Twin Oscar utters the sentence 'Water is a liquid at room temperature', his fellow Twin English-speakers take his word 'water' to be the same as their word 'water', hence they take him to have said (when translated into English) that *twin water is a liquid at room temperature*. If, in addition, they think his utterance is sincere, they take him to believe this.

Reconstructed in this way, Putnam's first thought experiment establishes that what a person believes and thinks does not supervene on the facts about his linguistic dispositions, internal physical states, or phenomenal experiences that can be described independently of his physical environment and without using any sentences that express PIWs, PJSSs, or PJSEs for his words. This thesis is what I call anti-individualism.[10] We now have a more general route to the same conclusion. For the context principle implies that the semantic values of a person's word tokens do not supervene on facts about how he ex-uses them. Such facts include all facts about his linguistic dispositions, internal physical states, or phenomenal experiences that can be described independently of his physical environment and without using any sentences that express PIWs, PJSSs, or PJSEs for his words. Hence the context principle implies anti-individualism. If we adopt

---

[10] According to the standard disciplinary history of anti-individualism, in Putnam (1975) Putnam established that the *references* of a person's words are not are settled by his linguistic dispositions, internal physical states, or phenomenal experiences, described independently of his social and physical environment. Burge (1979) is credited with making the corresponding case for beliefs and thoughts—the case for the stronger thesis that I am calling anti-individualism. I have reconstructed Putnam's reasoning in a way that supports anti-individualism. Although I do not accept the standard interpretation of Putnam's reasoning in Putnam 1975, my goal here is not to present a historically accurate account of what Putnam actually thought when he wrote Putnam 1975, but to highlight the methodology that in my view explains what is persuasive about Putnam's reasoning, whether or not he was clear about it.

the context principle, as I recommend, we thereby also commit ourselves to anti-individualism.

Putnam also claimed that even in 1750, *before* the scientists on Earth or Twin Earth discovered the chemical properties of water and twin water, respectively, a competent English-speaker who uttered the sentence 'Water is a liquid at room temperature' thereby expressed the thought that water is a liquid at room temperature, while his Twin on Twin Earth expressed the thought (translated into English) that twin water is a liquid at room temperature. This anti-individualistic conclusion is also a consequence of the context principle: it is because we trust our PIWs, PJSSs, and PJSEs across time that we conclude that in both linguistic communities, looking backward from today, the references of the words for water and twin water did not change when the chemical properties of the liquids to which they apply were discovered.[11]

As we have seen, however, Putnam devised his causal-historical theory of reference to explain and justify the PIWs, PJSSs, and PJSEs across time that his thought experiments highlight. In doing so, he embraced *external-ism*—the thesis that what a person believes and thinks supervenes on facts about his linguistic dispositions, internal physical states, phenomenal experiences *together with* all social or physical facts that one can describe without using any sentences that express PIWs, PJSSs, or PJSEs for his words. The facts relevant to externalism are all facts about *language ex-use*, as I defined that notion. Hence externalism implies that what a person believes and thinks supervenes on facts about language ex-use. In Chapters 6 to 8 I argued that to satisfy the intersubjectivity constraint, and make sense of our PIWs, PJSSs, or PJSEs, we must adopt the PJSS-based conception of words, which is governed by the context principle. The context principle implies that what a person believes and thinks does not supervene on facts about *language ex-use*. Hence the context principle is incompatible with externalism.

[11] Many philosophers assume that in the early 1970s Putnam and Kripke accepted this aspect of the Twin Earth thought experiment only because they believed they could explain it by constructing a causal theory of reference. But both Putnam and Kripke were cautious about whether reference could be given a non-circular explanation in causal terms. Moreover, no viable causal theory of reference has yet been constructed, but the force of the thought experiment remains. In my view, the idea that there is what Putnam called a "contribution of the environment" is rooted in our practice of making and trusting PIWs, PJSSs, and PJSEs across time, and does not depend on the existence of a substantive theory of reference that explains this practice. For more discussion of this point, but with different terminology, see Ebbs 1997 and Ebbs 2000.

316 APPLICATIONS AND CONSEQUENCES

Philosophers who embrace externalism sometimes distinguish between two different ways in which facts about ex-use can determine semantic values: (first) such facts can determine semantic values by linking word tokens with *objects and kinds*, and (second) such facts can determine semantic values by linking word tokens with "social norms" for language ex-use. The causal-historical theory of reference applied to the English word 'gold' is usually taken to explain the first way. But there other words, such as 'arthritis', that apparently do not group objects into natural kinds. An externalist is therefore committed to coming up with some other account of what settles the semantic value of such words as 'arthritis'. One prominent proposal (in Burge 1979 and 1986a) is that medical experts set the standards for the ex-use of 'arthritis'—the "social norms" for its ex-use—and thereby settle its semantic value.[12]

All of these proposals presuppose that semantic values supervene on facts about ex-use. But I have argued that semantic values do not supervene on facts about ex-use. If my arguments succeed, then we should reject all varieties of externalism, whether causal-historical or social, and embrace the deflationary version of anti-individualism sketched above. When truth and words are understood in the way that I recommend, our commitment to anti-individualism is of a piece with our pursuit of truth, not independent or additional to it.

9.12. Truth and Logic

The same holds for the laws of logic: when truth and words are understood in the way that I recommend, our willingness to rely on the laws of logic to facilitate and clarify our agreements and disagreements with others is of a piece with our pursuit of truth, not independent or additional to it. This consequence of my account of truth and words is crucial to my goal of reconciling the Tarski–Quine thesis with the intersubjectivity constraint. I motivated the intersubjectivity constraint by elaborating on Gottlob Frege's observation that we regard logical generalizations as arbiters of collaborative

---

[12] Goldberg 2007 presents and defends a similar view. For criticisms of inflationary versions of anti-individualism like Burge's and Goldberg's, see Blackburn 1988 and Mercier 1993. I think the problems that Blackburn and Mercier expose all stem from the fact that externalist views of meaning and reference presuppose the token-and-ex-use model of words.

inquiry. To explain why, I will first briefly review Frege's explanation of why the laws of logic are central to rational inquiry.

Consider the law of excluded middle, formulated as follows:

(L) Every sentence of the form '$S \lor \sim S$' is true.[13]

In what sense is (L) a *law*? Frege distinguishes two senses of the word 'law': "in one sense a law asserts what is; in the other sense it prescribes what ought to be" (Frege 1964: xv). Note first that (L) is a law in the first sense, one that "asserts what is". Moreover, as Quine emphasizes, we are interested in (L) not because of what it tells us about language, but because of what it tells us about the world. We use a truth predicate to express logical generalizations such as (L) not because these generalizations are about language, but because we cannot actually write out all of the sentences of a given logical form. Our affirmation of the law commits us to affirming any and all of those sentences, and is therefore not primarily an assertion about language, but about what is so. This does not distinguish laws of logic from other laws. Any law, including laws of physics and geometry, for instance, asserts what is so. Moreover, as Frege observes,

Any law asserting what is [so], can be conceived as prescribing that one ought to think in conformity with it, and is thus in that sense a law of thought. This holds for laws of geometry and physics no less than for laws of logic.   (Frege 1964: xv)

Although laws that assert what is so needn't and typically don't also assert that we ought to think in conformity with them, if we aim to judge in accordance with what is so, we thereby also aim to judge in accordance with all statements, including all laws, that assert what is so.

What distinguishes the laws of logic from laws of any other science is that they hold for *every* subject: to judge in conformity with how things are in *any* subject one must judge in conformity with the laws of logic. In this sense, the laws of logic "are the most general laws, which prescribe universally the way in which one ought to think if one is to think at all" (Frege 1964: xv). We must qualify this universal conception of logic if we are to avoid the paradoxes that stem from unrestricted applications of a truth predicate. But we can still say, in a Fregean spirit, that the laws of

---

[13] Frege would not have formulated the law of excluded middle by using a truth predicate. (See Chapter 2, n. 13, and Weiner 2005.) But his conception of logical laws as the most general laws can be recast, with appropriate changes, for generalizations that we express by using a truth predicate.

logic differ from other laws in their scope and application: they cut across the subject matters of the special sciences. To reason about any subject at all, one must reason in accordance with the laws of logic.

To express the laws of logic by using a Tarski-style disquotational truth predicate, we need criteria for deciding, for any given logical form, whether a given utterance is an utterance of a sentence of that form. There are well-known *syntactical* rules for deciding whether one's own current utterances of a regimented sentence of one's current language is an utterance of a sentence of a given logical form. These syntactical rules determine whether or not a sentence of our regimented language results from admissible substitutions of regimented sentences or regimented predicates for schematic sentence or term letters, respectively, in a given logical schema. There are no syntactical rules for deciding whether another person's utterance or one of one's own utterances in the past are utterances of a sentence of a given logical form. But the PJSS-based word types that we identify by syntactical criteria in our own current uses of our regimented language are word types that others can use and that we may have used in the past. By combining the syntactical criteria we can directly apply to our own utterances with our PJSS-based conception of words, we can determine whether another person's utterance, or one of one's own utterances in the past, are utterances of a sentence of a given logical form. When combined with the syntactical criteria, the PJSS-based conception of words licenses us to apply logical generalizations such as (L) to other speakers' words and to our own words as we used them in the past

We may summarize these points as follows. According to the account of truth and words that I recommend,

(1) We cannot commit ourselves to judging in accordance with the truth without also committing ourselves to judging in accordance with the laws of logic, conceived as generalizations that cut across all subjects,

(2) The PJSS-based conception of words is integral to our own Tarski-style disquotational definitions of truth, and

(3) The PJSS-based conception of words, together with the intrasubjective syntactical rules for deciding whether one's own current utterances of a regimented sentence of one's current language is an utterance of a sentence of a given logical form, enables us to express

logical generalizations that we can apply both to other speakers'
words and to our own words as we used them in the past.

In short, according to the account of truth and words that I recommend,
our applications of logical generalizations to other speakers' sentences and
to our own sentences as we used them in the past are of a piece with our
pursuit of truth.

References

Alward, P. 2005. "Between the Lines of Age: Reflections on the Metaphysics of Words", *Pacific Philosophical Quarterly* 86: 172–87.

Austin, J. L. 1962. *Sense and Sensibilia*, ed. G. J. Warnock. Oxford: Oxford University Press.

Barwise, J., and Cooper, R. 1981. "Generalized Quantifiers and Natural Language", *Linguistics and Philosophy* 4: 159–219.

_____ and Etchemendy, J. 2002. *Language, Proof, and Logic.* Stanford, Calif.: CSLI Publications.

Bennett, J. 1988. "Quotation", *Noûs* 22/3: 399–418.

Berger, A. 2002. *Terms and Truth: Reference Direct and Anaphoric.* Cambridge, Mass.: MIT Press.

Bezuidenhout, A., and Reimer, M., eds. 2004. *Descriptions and Beyond.* Oxford: Oxford University Press.

Blackburn, T. 1988. "The Elusiveness of Reference", in P. A. French, T. E. Uehling, Jr., and H. K. Wettstein, eds., *Midwest Studies in Philosophy* 12. Minneapolis: University of Minnesota Press, 179–94.

Boghossian, P. 1989. "The Rule-Following Considerations", *Mind* 98: 507–50.

_____ 1990 "The Status of Content", *The Philosophical Review* 99: 157–84.

_____ 2000. "Knowledge of Logic", in P. Boghossian and C. Peacocke, eds., *New Essays on the A Priori.* Oxford: Oxford University Press, 229–55.

_____ 2001. "How Are Objective Reasons Possible?", *Philosophical Studies* 106: 1–40.

Bonjour, L. 1998. *In Defense of Pure Reason.* Cambridge: Cambridge University Press.

Boolos, G. 1975. "On Second-Order Logic", *The Journal of Philosophy* 73: 509–27.

_____ 1984. "To Be is to Be a Value of a Variable (or to Be Some Values of Some Variables)", *Journal of Philosophy* 81/8: 430–49.

_____ Burgess, J., and Jeffery, R. 2002. *Computability and Logic*, 4th edn. Cambridge: Cambridge University Press.

Borg, E. 2004. *Minimal Semantics.* Oxford: Clarendon Press.

Brown, J. 1998. "Natural Kind Terms and Recognitional Capacities", *Mind* 107: 275–303.

_____ 2000. "Against Temporal Externalism", *Analysis* 60/2: 178–88.

Brueckner, A. 1992. "Semantic Answers to Skepticism", *Pacific Philosophical Quarterly* 73: 200–19.

Burge, T. 1979. "Individualism and the Mental", in P. A. French, T. E. Uehling, and H. K. Wettstein, eds., *Midwest Studies in Philosophy* 4. Minneapolis: University of Minnesota Press, 73–122.

———1986a. "Intellectual Norms and Foundations of Mind", *The Journal of Philosophy* 83: 697–720.

———1986b. "On Davidson's 'Saying That'", in E. Lepore, ed., *Truth and Interpretation: Perspectives on the Philosophy of Donald Davidson*. Oxford: Blackwell.

———1988. "Individualism and Self-Knowledge", *The Journal of Philosophy*, 649–63.

———1993. "Content Preservation", *The Philosophical Review* 102: 457–88.

———2005. *Truth, Thought, Reason: Essays on Frege*. Oxford: Clarendon Press.

Campbell, J. 2002. *Reference and Consciousness*. Oxford: Clarendon Press.

Cappelen, H. 1999. "Intentions in Words", *Noûs* 33/1: 92–102.

Carnap, R. 1942. *Introduction to Semantics* [*Studies in Semantics*, vol. i] Cambridge, Mass.: Harvard University Press.

———1956. *Meaning and Necessity*, 2nd edn. Chicago: University of Chicago Press.

———1990. "Quine on Analyticity", in R. Creath, ed., *Dear Carnap, Dear Van*. Berkeley and Los Angeles: University of California Press.

Cartwright, R. 1994. "Speaking of Everything", *Noûs* 28: 1–20.

Chalmers, D. 1996. *The Conscious Mind*. Oxford: Oxford University Press.

Chihara, C. 1979. "The Semanic Paradoxes: A Diagnostic Investigation", *The Philosophical Review* 88/4: 590–618.

Coady, C. A. J. 1992. *Testimony*. Oxford: Clarendon Press.

Crosland, M. 1962. *Historical Studies in the Language of Chemistry*. London: Heinemann Educational Books Ltd.

David, M. 1994. *Correspondence and Disquotation*. Oxford: Oxford University Press.

Davidson, D. 1984. *Inquiries into Truth and Interpretation*. Oxford: Clarendon Press.

———1986. "A Nice Derangement of Epitaphs", in E. LePore, ed., *Truth and Interpretation* (Oxford: Blackwell).

———1990. "The Structure and Content of Truth", *Journal of Philosophy* 87/6: 279–328.

———1992. "The Second Person", in P. A. French, T. E. Uehling, Jr., and H. K. Wettstein, eds., *Midwest Studies in Philosophy*, 18. Notre Dame: University of Notre Dame Press, 255–67.

———1994a. "What is Quine's View of Truth?", in D. Davidson, *Truth, Language, and History*, Oxford: Clarendon Press, 2005, pp. 81–5. First published in *Inquiry*, 37 (1994), 437–40.

Davidson, D. 1994b. "Radical Interpretation Interpreted", *Philosophical Perspectives* 8: 121–8.

———1996. "The Folly of Trying to Define Truth", in D. Davidson, *Truth, Language, and History*. Oxford: Clarendon Press, 19–37.

———2001a. "First Person Authority", in *Subjective, Intersubjective, Objective*. Oxford: Oxford University Press, 3–14.

———2001b. "Knowing One's Own Mind", in *Subjective, Intersubjective, Objective*. Oxford: Oxford University Press, 15–38.

Davies, M. 1981. *Meaning, Quantification, Necessity: Themes in Philosophical Logic*. London: Routledge and Kegan Paul.

Dennett, D. 1987. "Evolution, Error, and Intentionality", in D. Dennett, *The Intentional Stance*. Cambridge, Mass.: MIT Press, 287–321.

Devitt, M., and Sterelny, K. 1987. *Language and Reality*. Cambridge, Mass.: MIT Press.

Dilworth, J. 2003. "A Refutation of Goodman's Type-Token Theory of Notation", *Dialectica* 57/3: 330–6.

Donnellan, K. 1983. "Kripke and Putnam on Natural Kind Terms", in C. Ginet and S. Shoemaker, ed., *Knowledge and Mind*. Oxford: Oxford University Press, 84–104.

Dummett, M. 1978a. "The Justification of Deduction", in M. Dummett, *Truth and Other Enigmas*. Cambridge: Mass.: Harvard University Press, 290–318.

———1978b. "The Social Character of Meaning", in *Truth and Other Enigmas*. Cambridge, Mass.: Harvard University Press, 420–40.

———1978c. "The Significance of Quine's Indeterminacy Thesis", in *Truth and Other Enigmas*. Cambridge, Mass.: Harvard University Press, 375–419.

———1981. *Frege: Philosophy of Language*, 2nd edn. Cambridge, Mass.: Harvard University Press.

———1991. *The Logical Basis of Metaphysics*. Cambridge, Mass.: Harvard University Press.

———1993a: "What is a Theory of Meaning? (II)" repr. in *The Seas of Language*. Oxford: Oxford University Press, 34–93.

———1993b. "What do I Know when I Know a Language?" repr. in *The Seas of Language*. Oxford: Oxford University Press, 94–105.

Ebbs, G. 1996. "Can We Take Our Words at Face Value?", *Philosophy and Phenomenological Research* 56/3: 499–530.

———1997. *Rule-Following and Realism*. Cambridge, Mass.: Harvard University Press.

———2000. "The Very Idea of Sameness of Extension across Time", *American Philosophical Quarterly* 37/3: 245–68.

＿＿2001. "Vagueness, Sharp Boundaries, and Supervenience Conditions", *Synthese* 127: 303–23.

＿＿2002a. "Learning from Others", *Noûs* 36/4: 525–49.

＿＿2002b. "Truth and Trans-Theoretical Terms", in J. Conant and U. Zeglen, eds., *Hilary Putnam: Pragmatism and Realism*. London: Routledge, 167–85.

＿＿2003. "Denotation and Discovery", in F. Schmitt, ed., *Socializing Metaphysics: The Nature of Social Reality*. Totowa, NJ: Rowman and Littlefield, 247–68.

Eklund, M. 1996. "On How Logic Became First-Order", *Nordic Journal of Philosophical Logic*, 1/2: 147–67.

Evans, G. 1982. *Varieties of Reference*. Oxford: Clarendon Press.

＿＿1985. "Pronouns, Quantifiers, and Relative Clauses (I)", repr. in G. Evans, *Collected Papers*. Oxford: Clarendon Press.

＿＿and McDowell, J., eds. 1976. *Truth and Meaning*. Oxford: Clarendon Press.

Evnine, S. 1991. *Donald Davidson*. Stanford, Calif.: Stanford University Press, 1991.

Field, H. 1973. "Theory Change and Indeterminacy of Reference", *The Journal of Philosophy* 70: 462–81.

＿＿1974. "Quine and the Correspondence Theory", *The Philosophical Review* 83: 200–28.

＿＿1992. "Critical Notice: Paul Horwich's Truth", *Philosophy of Science*, 59: 321–30.

＿＿1994. "Deflationist Views of Meaning and Content". *Mind* 103: 249–84.

Fine, K. 1975. "Vagueness, Truth and Logic", *Synthese* 30: 265–300.

Fodor, J. 1983. *Modularity of Mind*. Cambridge, Mass.: MIT Press.

Forbes, G. 1986. "Truth, Correspondence and Redundancy", in G. Macdonald and C. Wright (eds.), *Fact, Science and Morality: Essays on A. J. Ayer's Language, Truth and Logic*. Oxford: Blackwell, 27–54.

Frege, G. 1964. Introduction to *The Basic Laws of Arithmetic*, trans. and ed. M. Furth. Los Angeles: University of California Press, 1964. First published in German in 1893.

＿＿1978. *The Foundations of Arithmetic*, 2nd rev. edn. German text with English translation by J. L. Austin. Oxford: Blackwell. First published in German in 1884.

Fricker, E. 1995. "Telling and Trusting: Reductionism and Anti-reductionism in the Epistemology of Testimony", *Mind* 104: 393–411.

Geach, P. T. 1962. *Reference and Generality*. Ithaca, NY: Cornell University Press.

Glanzberg, M. 2005. "Minimalism, Deflationism, and Paradoxes", in J. C. Beall and B. Armour-Garb, eds., *Deflationism and Paradox*. Oxford: Oxford University Press, 107–32.

Glanzberg, M. 2006. "Quantifiers", in E. Lepore and B. Smith, eds., *The Oxford Handbook of Philosophy of Language*. Oxford: Clarendon Press, 794–821.

Goldberg, S. 2007. *Anti-Individualism*. Cambridge: Cambridge University Press.

Goldman, A. 1970. *A Theory of Human Action*. Princeton: Princeton University Press.

Goodman, N. 1966. *Structure of Appearance*, 2nd edn. New York: Bobbs-Merrill.

––––– 1972. "Seven Strictures on Similarity", in N. Goodman, *Problems and Projects*. Indianapolis: Bobbs-Merrill Company, Inc., 437–46.

––––– 1976. *Languages of Art*. Indianapolis: Hackett.

––––– 1983. *Fact, Fiction, and Forecast*, 4th edn. Cambridge, Mass.: Harvard University Press.

Grandy, R. 1973. "Reference, Meaning, and Belief", *The Journal of Philosophy* 70: 439–52.

Grice, H. P. 1957. "Meaning", *The Philosophical Review* 66: 377–88.

Hacking, I. 1985. "Rules, Scepticism, Proof, and Wittgenstein", in I. Hacking, ed., *Exercises in Analysis*. Cambridge: Cambridge University Press, 113–24.

Halbach, V. 1999. "Disquotation and Infinite Conjunction", *Mind* 108/429: 1–22.

Hansford, S. H. 1968. *Chinese Carved Jades*. London: Faber and Faber.

Heck, R. G., Jr., 2004. "Truth and Disquotation", *Synthese* 142: 317–52.

Heim, I., and Kratzer, A. 1998. *Semantics in Generative Grammar*. Oxford: Blackwell.

Hilbert, D., and Ackerman, W. 1950. *Principles of Mathematical Logic*, 2nd edn. New York: Chelsea Publishing Co.

––––– and Bernays, P. 1939. *Grundlagen der Mathematick*, vol. ii. Berlin: Springer Verlag.

––––– and Cohn-Vossen, S. 1956. *Geometry and Imagination*, trans. P. Nemenyi. New York: Chelsea Publishing Co.

Hill, C. 2002. *Thought and World: An Austere Portrayal of Truth, Reference, and Semantic Correspondence*. Cambridge: Cambridge University Press.

Horwich, P. 1995. "Meaning, Use, and Truth", *Mind* 104: 355–68.

––––– 1998a: *Truth*, 2nd edn. Oxford: Clarendon Press.

––––– 1998b: *Meaning*. Oxford: Clarendon Press.

Hugly, P., and Sayward, C. 1981. "Expressions and Tokens", *Analysis* 4/1: 181–7.

Jackman, H. 1999. "We Live Forward But Understand Backwards: Linguistic Practices and Future Behavior", *Pacific Philosophical Quarterly* 80: 157–77.

Jackson, F. 1998a. *From Metaphysics to Ethics: A Defense of Conceptual Analysis*. Oxford: Oxford University Press.

––––– 1998b. "Reference and Description Revisited", *Noûs-Supplement: Philosophical Perspectives* 12: 201–18.

Kaplan, D. 1989a: "Demonstratives: An Essay on the Semantics, Logic, Metaphysics, and Epistemology of Demonstratives and Other Indexicals", in J. Almog, J. Perry, and H. Wettstein, eds., *Themes from Kaplan*. Oxford: Oxford University Press, 481–566.

—— 1989b. "Afterthoughts", in J. Almog, J. Perry, and H. Wettstein, eds., *Themes from Kaplan*. Oxford: Oxford University Press, 565–614.

—— 1990. "Words", *Proceedings of the Aristotelian Society*, suppl. vol. 64: 93–119.

Katz, J. 1998. *Realistic Rationalism*. Cambridge, Mass.: MIT Press.

Kitcher, P. 1982. "Genes", *British Journal for the Philosophy of Science* 33: 337–59.

—— 1993. *The Advancement of Science*. Oxford: Oxford University Press.

Kleene, S. C. 1953. *Introduction to Metamathematics*. Amsterdam and New York: Van Nostrand Reinhold.

Kraut, R. 1993. "Robust Deflationism", *The Philosophical Review* 102: 247–63.

Kripke, S. 1975. "Outline of a Theory of Truth", *Journal of Philosophy* 72: 690–716.

—— 1976. "Is There a Problem about Substitutional Quantification?", in G. Evans and J. McDowell, eds., *Truth and Meaning: Essays in Semantics*. Oxford: Clarendon Press, 325–419.

—— 1979. "A Puzzle about Belief", in A. Margalit, ed., *Meaning and Use*. Dordrecht: D. Reidel, 239–83.

—— 1980. *Naming and Necessity*. Cambridge, Mass.: Harvard University Press.

—— 1982. *Wittgenstein on Rules and Private Language*. Oxford: Blackwell.

Künne, W. 2003. *Conceptions of Truth*. Oxford: Oxford University Press.

Lance, M., and O'Leary-Hawthorne, J. 1997. *The Grammar of Meaning: Normativity and Semantic Discourse*. Cambridge: Cambridge University Press.

Larson, R., and Segal, G. 1995. *Knowledge of Meaning*. Cambridge, Mass.: MIT Press.

Lasersohn, P. 2005. "Context Dependence, Disagreement, and Predicates of Personal Taste", *Linguistics and Philosophy* 28: 643–86.

Leeds, S. 1978. "Theories of Reference and Truth", *Erkenntnis* 13: 111–29.

Lepore, E., and Ludwig, K. 2005. *Davidson: Truth, Language, and Reality*. Oxford: Oxford University Press.

—— —— 2007. *Donald Davidson's Truth-Theoretic Semantics*. Oxford: Clarendon Press, 2007.

Lewis, D. 1968. "Counterpart Theory and Quantified Modal Logic", *Journal of Philosophy* 65: 113–26.

—— 1969. *Convention*. Cambridge, Mass.: Harvard University Press.

—— 1974. "Radical Interpretation", *Synthese* 23: 331–44.

Lewis, D. 1980. "Index, Context, and Content", in S. Klanger and S. Öhman, eds., *Philosophy and Grammar*. Dordrecht: Reidel.

Loar, B. 1981. *Mind and Meaning*. Cambridge: Cambridge University Press.

McCarthy, T. 2002. *Radical Interpretation and Indeterminacy*. Oxford: Oxford University Press.

McCulloch, G. 1991. "Making Sense of Words", *Analysis* 51: 73–9.

MacFarlane, J. 2003. "Future Contingents and Relative Truth", *The Philosophical Quarterly* 53: 321–36.

_____ 2005. "Making Sense of Relative Truth", *Proceedings of the Aristotelian Society*, 321–39.

_____ 2008. "Truth in the Garden of Forking Paths", in M. Kölbel and M. García-Carpintero, eds., *Relative Truth*. Oxford: Oxford University Press, 81–102.

McGee, V. 2004. "Tarski's Staggering Existential Assumptions", *Synthese* 142: 371–87.

McGinn, C. 1984. *Wittgenstein on Meaning*. Oxford: Blackwell.

McLaughlin, B., and Tye, M. 1998. "Externalism, Twin Earth, and Self-Knowledge", in C. Wright, B. Smith, and C. Macdonald, eds. *Knowing Our Own Minds*. Oxford: Oxford University Press, 285–320.

Martin, R. L., ed. 1984. *Recent Essays on Truth and the Liar Paradox*. Oxford: Clarendon Press.

Meiland J. 1977. "Concepts of Relative Truth", *Monist* 60/4: 568–82.

Mercier, A. 1993. "Normativism and the Mental: A Problem of Language Individuation", *Philosophical Studies* 72/1: 71–88.

_____ 1999. "On Communication-Based *De Re* Thought, Commitments *De Dicto*, and Word Individuation", in K. Murasugi and R. Stainton, eds., *Philosophy and Linguistics*. Boulder, Colo.: Westview Press, 85–111.

Miller, A., and Wright, C., eds. 2002. *Rule-Following and Meaning*. Chesham: Acumen Press.

Moore, G. 1980. "Beyond First-Order Logic, the Historical Interplay between Logic and Set Theory", in *History and Philosophy of Logic* 1: 95–137.

_____ 1988. "The Emergence of First-Order Logic", in W. Aspray and P. Kitcher, eds., *History and Philosophy of Modern Mathematics*, Minnesota Studies in the Philosophy of Science, 11. Minneapolis: University of Minnesota Press, 95–135.

Neale, S. 1990. *Descriptions*. Cambridge, Mass.: MIT Press.

Parsons, T. 1987. "On the Consistency of the First-Order Portion of Frege's Logical System", *Notre Dame Journal of Formal Logic* 28: 161–8.

Patterson, D. 2002. "Theories of Truth and Convention T". *Philosopher's Imprint* 2/5: 1–16.

Peacocke, C. 1978. "Necessity and Truth Theories", *Journal of Philosophical Logic* 7/4: 473–500.

—— 1998. "Implicit Conceptions, Understanding and Rationality", *Philosophical Issues*, vol. ix: *Concepts*. Ridgeview: Atascadero, 43–88.

—— 2000. "Explaining the A Priori: The Programme of Moderate Rationalism", in P. Boghossian and C. Peacocke, eds., *New Essays on the A Priori*. Oxford: Oxford University Press, 229–55.

Peirce, C. S. 1933. *The Collected Papers of Charles Sanders Peirce*, ed. C. Hartshorne and P. Weiss. Cambridge, Mass.: Harvard University Press.

Putnam, H. 1973. "Explanation and Reference", in H. Putnam, *Mind, Language, and Reality: Philosophical Papers*, vol. ii. Cambridge: Cambridge University Press, 1975, 196–214.

—— 1975. "The Meaning of 'Meaning' ", in Hilary Putnam, *Mind, Language, and Reality: Philosophical Papers*, vol. ii. Cambridge: Cambridge University Press, 215–71.

—— 1983. "On Truth", in L. Cauman, I. Levi, C. Parsons, and R. Schwartz, eds., *How Many Questions? Essays in Honor of Sidney Morgenbesser*. Indianapolis: Hackett Publishing Co.

—— 1988. *Representation and Reality* Cambridge, Mass.: MIT Press.

Quine, W. V. 1940. *Mathematical Logic*. Cambridge, Mass.: Harvard University Press.

—— 1960. *Word and Object*. Cambridge, Mass.: MIT Press.

—— 1961a. "Notes on the Theory of Reference", in W. V. Quine, *From a Logical Point of View*, rev. 2nd edn. Cambridge, Mass.: Harvard University Press, 130–8.

—— 1961b. "Two Dogmas of Empiricism", in W. V. Quine, *From a Logical Point of View*, rev. 2nd edn. Cambridge, Mass.: Harvard University Press, 20–46.

—— 1963. "Carnap and Logical Truth", in P. Schilpp, ed., *The Philosophy of Rudolf Carnap: The Library of Living Philosophers*, vol. xi. La Salle, Ill.: Open Court, 385–406.

—— 1976a. "Truth and Disquotation", in *Ways of Paradox and Other Essays*, rev. and enlarged edn. Cambridge, Mass.: Harvard University Press, 308–21.

—— 1976b. "Truth by Convention" (1935), in W. V. Quine, *The Ways of Paradox*, rev. and enlarged edn. Cambridge, Mass.: Harvard University Press, 77–106.

—— 1981. "What Price Bivalence?", in *Theories and Things*. Cambridge, Mass.: Harvard University Press.

—— 1982. *Methods of Logic*, 4th edn. Cambridge, Mass.: Harvard University Press.

—— 1986. *Philosophy of Logic*, 2nd edn. Cambridge, Mass.: Harvard University Press.

—— 1987. *Quiddities*. Cambridge, Mass.: Harvard University Press.

Quine, W. V. 1992. *Pursuit of Truth*, rev. edn. Cambridge, Mass.: Harvard University Press.

———— 1995a. "Interpretations of Sets of Conditions", in W. V. Quine, *Selected Logic Papers*, enlarged edn. Cambridge, Mass.: Harvard University Press, 205–11.

———— 1995b: *From Stimulus to Science*. Cambridge, Mass.: Harvard University Press.

Rayo, A., and Uzquiano, G., eds., 2006. *Absolute Generality*. Oxford: Clarendon Press.

Rescher, N. 1962. "Plurality-Quantification", *Journal of Symbolic Logic* 27: 373–4.

Resnik, M. 1997. *Mathematics as a Science of Patterns*. Oxford: Clarendon Press.

Rey, G. 1998. "A Naturalistic A Priori", *Philosophical Studies* 92: 25–43.

———— 2006. "The Intentional Inexistence of Language—But Not Cars", in R. Stainton, ed., *Contemporary Debates in Cognitive Science*. Oxford: Blackwell, 237–55.

Richard, M. 2004. "Contextualism and Relativism", *Philosophical Studies* 119: 215–42.

Russell, G. 2008. *Truth in Virtue of Meaning*. Oxford: Oxford University Press.

Schiffer, S. 1996. "Contextualist Solutions to Scepticism", *Proceedings of the Aristotelian Society* 1995/96: 317–33.

Shapiro, S. 1991. *Foundations without Foundationalism: A Case for Second-order Logic*. Oxford: Clarendon Press.

Soames, S. 1984. "What is a Theory of Truth?" *Journal of Philosophy* 81/8: 411–29.

———— 1998. "The Modal Argument: Wide Scope and Rigidified Descriptions", *Noûs* 32: 1–22.

———— 1999. *Understanding Truth*. Oxford: Oxford University Press.

———— 2002. *Beyond Rigidity: The Unfinished Semantic Agenda of Naming and Necessity*. Oxford: Oxford University Press.

Sorenson, R. 2001. *Vagueness and Contradiction*. Oxford: Clarendon Press.

Spivak, M. 1994. *Calculus*, 3rd edn. Houston, Tex.: Publish or Perish, Inc.

Stalnaker, R. 1990. "Narrow Content", in C. Anderson and J. Owens, eds., *Propositional Attitudes*. Chicago: CSLI Lecture Notes.

Stanley, J., and Williamson, T. 2001. "Knowing How", *Journal of Philosophy* 98: 411–44.

Suppes, P. 1957. *Introduction to Logic*. New York: Van Nostrand Reinhold Co.

Tarski, A. 1936. "The Concept of Truth in Formalized Languages", in *Logic, Semantics, Meta-Mathematics: Papers from 1923 to 1938*, trans. J. H. Woodger. 2nd edn. Indianapolis: Hackett, 1983.

———— 1944. "The Semantic Conception of Truth: And the Foundations of Semantics", *Philosophy and Phenomenological Research* 4/3: 341–76.